The Clash of Globalisations

Historical Materialism Book Series

VOLUME 8

SCHOOL OF ORIENTAL AND AFRICAN STUDIES
University of London

Please return this book on or before the last date shown

Long loans and One Week loans may be renewed up to 10 times
Short loans & CDs cannot be renewed
Fines are charged on all overdue items

Online: http://lib.soas.ac.uk/patroninfo
Phone: 020-7898 4197 (answerphone)

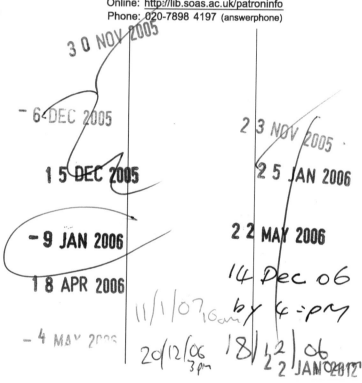

30 NOV 2005

- 6 DEC 2005

1 5 DEC 2005

- 9 JAN 2006

1 8 APR 2006

- 4 MAY 2006

2 3 NOV 2005

2 5 JAN 2006

2 2 MAY 2006

14 Dec 06

11/1/07 10am by 4=pm

20/12/06 3pm   18/12/06

2 2 JAN 2012

The Clash of Globalisations

Neo-Liberalism, the Third Way and Anti-Globalisation

by

Ray Kiely

BRILL

LEIDEN • BOSTON

2005

This book is printed on acid-free paper.

Library of Congress Cataloging-in-Publication Data

Kiely, Ray, 1964–
    The clash of globalisations : neo-liberalism, the third way, and anti-
globalisation/by Ray Kiely.
        p. cm. — (Historical materialism book series, ISSN 1570–1522 ; v. 8)
    Includes bibliographical references and index.
    ISBN 90-04-143 18-1 (alk. paper)
    1. Globalization. 2. Anti-globalization movement. I. Title: Clash of
globalizations. II. Title. III. Historical materialism book series ; 8.

JZ1318.K54 2005
303.408'2–dc22

                                                                    2004065466

ISSN 1570-1522
ISBN 90 04 14318 1

PRINTED IN THE NETHERLANDS

To Emma and Will, with love

Contents

PART TWO

'ANTI-GLOBALISATION'

Acknowledgements

Thanks to Sebastian Budgen, Denis Cattell, Matthew Caygill, Stephen Chan, Alejandro Colas, Paul Gormley, Paul Kennedy, Jim Kincaid, Jens Lerche, Iain Macrury, Alan O'Shea, Ash Sharma, Subir Sinha, Peter Waterman, for support, discussion and inspiration over the course of writing this book, even if some may be unaware of their influence. More generally, thanks to those intellectuals who remain committed to progressive social transformation, and whose work continues to be inspired by this aspiration, rather than the narrow dictates of technocratic, Third-Way academia.

Chapter One
Introduction

From the 1990s onwards, globalisation became *the* key concept, both in academic debate and in mainstream political discourse. In the Western world, it came to be closely associated with the Third-Way political project, which proposed a radical centre ground that transcended statist socialism (in its Stalinist and social-democratic forms) and neo-liberal market fundamentalism. Globalisation was a term commonly used by Bill Clinton and Tony Blair in particular, and, in Britain at least, academic debate and political project embraced, through the work of Anthony Giddens. In the advanced capitalist countries, the idea of a new economy was championed, in which the old boom-bust cycles of industrial capitalism were replaced by ongoing economic growth boosted by the information-led, 'new economy'. At the same time, it was claimed that the developing world could get in on the act too, through the adoption of liberal policies that would attract investment, boost trade, and promote long-term growth. Initially, such investment would be based on the attraction of cheap labour, as this was how the West had developed, and, in the long run, increased investment would promote economic growth, and with this growth higher wages and better living conditions would result.

In terms of the economy then, globalisation was said to refer to an increasingly interdependent world. Information flows transcended nation-states, and knowledge was deemed to be the main source of value in the post-industrial world. In a more favourable climate for investment, capital flows to the developing world would promote growth and reduce poverty. There was thus considerable optimism concerning the global economy, and, indeed, there was a substantial boom in the United States, and a large increase in capital flows to emerging markets in Latin America and East Asia. Some countries and regions did not do so well, such as Japan, much of Western Europe and above all, Eastern Europe and sub-Saharan Africa. But this problem could easily be explained by the champions of globalisation. Clearly, the bad performers had not adapted to the demands of globalisation, and were adopting bad policies. The correct policies involved embracing 'global markets', deregulating labour markets, and leaving the state to play a purely facilitating role, such as provision of education and training for the labour market. The uneven development of the 1990s therefore did nothing to dispel the optimism of the globalisers; indeed, the economic failures reinforced the faith.

Moreover, the hopes for globalisation were not only confined to the economy. The interdependent world was one that reinvigorated cultural experience, so that one could witness distant events within one's own location. Globalisation reinforced a sense of one world, and therefore a sense of responsibility for the needs and rights of distant strangers, and with it the need for a politics that went beyond the narrow confines of state sovereignty. Although Bush Senior's hopes for a New World Order were abandoned after the fiasco of Somalia, humanitarian intervention and ethical foreign policies continued to be promoted. The claim was commonly made that in the post-Cold-War, post-colonial, world, the narrow state interests of the past could be abandoned, and genuine global governance exercised. This optimism was reinforced by the wave of democratisation that swept the former Second and Third Worlds in the 1980s and 1990s, which served to reinforce the idea that there was no sustainable alternative to liberal democracy and free market capitalism. There were still, of course, serious problems, such as global environmental destruction and poverty, but these could be dealt with through concerted action, not least at a global level.

The 1990s was, then, for the advocates of globalisation, a decade of cautious optimism. But the events at Seattle in late 1999 departed from the script. At the World Trade Organisation Millennium Round talks, five days of ongoing mass protest suggested that not everybody was happy with globalisation. A bewildering variety of grievances were aired, including protests against trade liberalisation, global poverty, Third-World debt, the exploitation of cheap labour, the exploitation of animals, environmental destruction, and after 'September 11th' and the US 'war on terror', the growing war drive led by the United States. But these protests did little to dissuade the optimism of the globalisers, as these protests were dismissed as incoherent, lacking in alternatives, anti-globalisation and anti-American. For the globalisers, globalisation was a fact of life and there was no point in trying to resist it. Anti-globalisation thus came to mean the promotion of backward-looking, romantic and unfeasible utopias.

But the description anti-globalisation did beg the question of what exactly was meant by globalisation in the first place. Where had it come from, who was promoting it, in whose interests were they so doing, and what were (and are) its effects? These questions were addressed in part by academics, but they were not necessarily the main focus of debate. Instead, the focus was often on the question of how to measure globalisation, and therefore questioned the extent to which it was a new phenomenon.[1] Of course, politics was not totally ignored. For instance, the extent of capital mobility had implications for state capacity to regulate capital flows.[2] But even questions like these cut across political sympathies, as neo-liberals (and some Marxists) celebrated capital mobility,[3] while most radical writers regretted it.[4] Political questions were therefore treated quite narrowly, particularly within the discipline of sociology, which tended to take globalisation as given. There were important exceptions, such as the radical sociology of Sklair,[5] as well as a great deal of radical geography that specifically attempted to situate globalisation within specific locations.[6] Marxist-inspired international political economy also addressed more explicit political concerns.[7] But, often, the literature failed to

---

[1] Held et al. 1999.
[2] Hirst and Thompson 1996.
[3] Ohmae 1995; Desai 2002; Harris 2003.
[4] Frobel et al. 1980.
[5] Sklair 1991.
[6] Harvey 1989; Cox 1997.
[7] Arrighi 1994; Gowan 1999.

adequately address the questions of origins, power and interests within globalisation. Indeed, this 'lack' was formalised by the development of what Rosenberg calls 'globalisation theory',[8] which is contrasted to theories of globalisation. Globalisation theory makes the claim that globalisation is not something that needs to be explained, but is, in fact, something that does the explaining. Anthony Giddens is regarded as the main exponent of globalisation theory, and his recent works serve as the link between such a theory and the political project of the Third Way. Largely taking not only capitalism, but neo-liberal capitalism for granted, this is a political project that claims to respond to the 'fact' of globalisation, but, in the process, promotes policies that deepen neo-liberal capitalism. This is regarded as being both inevitable – there is no alternative – and desirable.

This books sets out to challenge these arguments, and, in doing so, to contextualise the rise of so-called anti-globalisation movements. In discussing this 'movement of movements', the question of genuine alternatives to neo-liberal globalisation, and indeed, global capitalism, are also addressed. First, however, we need to be clear about what we mean by the term globalisation. In this book, the term is used in two ways. First, it defines a specific period of neo-liberal capitalism, which emerged in the late 1970s and early 1980s. Second, it can be regarded as both an ideology and political project, based on the notion that 'There Is No Alternative' to it. In practice, this amounts to an expansion of neo-liberal policies, even if these are sometimes modified by different forms of state intervention, and involve a wider commitment to notions of community, including a supposed international community. This project attempts to render *contingent* (political, globalising) outcomes as *necessary*, and outside of politics. Specifically, the Third Way is an ideological project that attempts to depoliticise globalisation, while simultaneously adopting policies that expand globalising outcomes. Indeed, Third-Way policies are regarded as a necessary response to the external constraints of globalisation, but these policies are also regarded as desirable in terms of their outcomes. My argument is illustrated through paying particular attention to the question of labour and development, the role of nation-states and international institutions in the international state system, and the uneven development

---

[8] Rosenberg 2000.

of global/international capitalism. The first section of the book focuses on the emergence of both the reality and ideology of globalisation, while the second section focuses on the challenge to both the reality and ideology, and specifically the ways anti-globalisation movements seek to re-politicise the globalisation debate, and in the process, possibly move on towards a broader challenge to capitalism. Chapters 2 to 5 therefore address the questions of agency and power, as well as the history of globalisation, and also consider its social and political effects. These chapters argue that globalisation did not simply arrive from nowhere, but was linked to changes in post-war international capitalism. Chapters 6 to 8 show that anti-globalisation protest and resistance is a response to the changes that have taken place in international capitalism, particularly since the 1970s and especially the 1980s. Seattle was simply a wake-up call to the Western media, as anti-globalisation resistance was commonplace, particularly in the South, since the early 1980s. This could be traced back to anti-IMF protests in the early 1980s through to struggles over land – particularly (though not necessarily most significantly) in Chiapas, Mexico – in the 1990s. In other words, globalisation was related to the neo-liberal restructuring of capitalism in the early 1980s. Neo-liberalism's emergence was a response to the economic crisis of the 1970s, which, in turn, was linked to the end of the post-war Golden Age of capitalism. To understand globalisation then, we need to understand the nature of post-war capitalism, the breakdown of the Golden Age, the neo-liberal response, and the globalisation of the 1990s. And, to understand these, we need a theoretical framework that can both understand capitalism without reducing globalisation to a simple ahistorical manifestation of capitalist development.

Chapters 2 to 5, therefore, situate globalisation in the wider context of international capitalism. Chapter 2 examines the work of two of the most influential globalisation theorists – Anthony Giddens and Manuel Castells. In discussing their work, the issue of whether either of them satisfactorily historicises globalisation is addressed, and this discussion is linked to questions of agency, power and interests. Giddens's work (at least in the 1990s) is largely rejected. Castells's work more thoroughly addresses these issues, but it still tends to fall into the trap of much of the globalisation literature, which is to put forward a technologically-determinist account of social change. This weakness is common in the globalisation literature, but is usually only implicit, as the transition to globalisation is usually taken as given, whereas Castells at least tries to theorise the transition (and in fairness qualifies his determinism in places). The chapter then moves on to suggest that Marx provides a useful starting point, and I go on to examine Marx's account of the origin and development of capitalism, the state, accumulation and uneven development, all of which are crucial to providing a better understanding of contemporary globalisation. This discussion provides the basis for the more concrete examination of contemporary globalisation in Chapters 3–5.

In Chapter 3, I examine the post-war Golden Age of capitalism, examining the nature of post-war US hegemony, the economic boom from the late 1940s to the late 1960s, the crisis of the 1970s, and the neo-liberal restructuring of the 1980s. The last of these is particularly crucial to understanding the globalisation debate, and I focus on restructuring in the United States in the 1980s, and in the debt-ridden developing world. My argument in this chapter is that the rise of neo-liberalism is closely related to the question of US hegemony, and the neo-liberal policies of the 1980s represented a historical defeat for the (limited) social advances of the 1950s and 1960s. In particular, neo-liberalism and revived (but uncertain) US hegemony meant the end of 'labour-friendly' régimes in the First World and 'development-friendly' régimes in the Third (though, of course, 'friendliness' in both cases was limited and unequal).

In contrast to the optimism of pro-globalisation theories, Chapter 4 provides a very different account of globalisation in the 1990s. This was a decade of intensified global inequality, financial instability, low rates of economic growth (at least compared to the Golden Age), marginalisation of certain parts of the world, and an old-fashioned speculative boom in the United States. By the end of the decade, the stock market had crashed in the United States, the emerging markets boom was over in Latin America, Asia's recovery was uneven, and particularly under the new Bush presidency, tensions between states had grown. The optimism of the 1990s was clearly misplaced, and, in this respect, globalisation was a naïve ideology associated with the wishful thinking of the Third Way. Instead, the 1990s can be regarded as an expansion of neo-liberalism in the context of an increasingly dominant financial capital, which itself was linked to questions of state power – and, in particular, the power of the hegemonic US state since 1945. Globalisation was not something that happened 'behind the back' of this wider context, it was derived from it. To be sure, the US state is not in control of globalisation, or global capitalism, and neither is it helpful to reduce all the events in the world to the actions of the US state or its Western allies, as some fundamentalists (of all ideological persuasions) do. But neither was globalisation independent of these power relations.

Chapter 5 reinforces these arguments by examining in more detail the evidence concerning, and explanations for, global inequalities. It challenges the optimism and evidence that suggests an improvement in economic growth, and reduced inequality and poverty in the world economy, and instead reiterates the arguments of previous chapters. In particular, the argument is made that capital has tended to concentrate in certain areas and (relatively) marginalise others, and that therefore the neo-liberal era has intensified uneven and unequal development.[9] This is reinforced by the unstable nature of financial flows (discussed in detail in Chapter 4). Chapter 5 again reiterates the arguments of Chapters 3 and 4 that these flows do not take place 'above' nation states, and that the liberalisation of finance is linked to the project of the US state to maintain hegemony. Once again, this does not mean that the project is without contradictions, or that the US state is completely in control of the process, but *contra* Giddens, it is not one that it outside of these power relations. The chapter concludes by re-asserting my argument that, while globalisation can in part be seen as a novel form of capitalism, at least compared to the post-war era, it is also a political project. It is therefore simultaneously a contested phenomenon, and the ways in which it is contested are the subject of the second half of the book.

The end of Chapter 5 makes the link between contemporary globalisation and anti-globalisation, through an attempted (critical) update of Polanyi's concept of the double movement, in which political movements respond to the development of a market economy that increasingly detaches itself from

---

[9] The recent wave of democratisations in the former Second and Third Worlds – alluded to earlier in the text – is not a major area of concern in this book. Two brief comments should be made at this point, however. First, given increased inequalities – within and between countries – and, indeed, the nature of structural adjustment programmes mean that liberal democracy in this context is weakened and undermined. But, second, having said that, I reject Marxist arguments that seem to argue that (liberal) democratisation occurs *simply* because it is functionally useful to the neo-liberal agenda, as it usually means greater openness to foreign investment. Recognising the ways in which neo-liberalism benefits from and limits democracy, even of a neo-liberal kind, is one thing, arguing that it is simply a neo-liberal sham quite another.

social regulation. This process of detachment can never be completed as markets always rely on collective regulation, but the very process increases social inequality, disorder and injustice. The first movement – market expansion – thus gives way to a second movement – the demand for market-restricting regulation. The rise of anti-globalisation movements constitutes a new double movement, representing anti-neo-liberal globalisation politics, and this issue is taken up in more detail in Chapter 6. The chapter first reviews the critiques made of actually existing globalisation, and then introduces various tendencies within the so-called anti-globalisation movement. These different strands include reactionary anti-globalisers, global reformists, environmentalists, transnational solidarity advocates, autonomists and anarchists, localisers, and revolutionary socialists. The similarities and differences within these perspectives are briefly discussed, and are taken up and elaborated on in Chapters 7 and 8. This is done through a critical discussion of the concept of civil society, and the ways in which this is understood by different movements. The broader implication that these movements may represent a 'new, new Left' is also introduced. Chapter 7 discusses these questions by examining social movements that are primarily nationally – or even locally – based, particularly those in the South. Three case studies – the Zapatistas, the (now defunct) Chipko movement, and the MST in Brazil – are examined in some detail, and some wider implications are addressed. The chapter broadly argues against localist, 'anti-development' interpretations of these (and other) movements, and argues that they do not advocate a straightforward autonomous politics, which is supposedly independent of, or intended to by-pass, nation-states.

Chapter 8 examines the notion of a global civil society 'above' nation-states. It investigates three cases – that of international debt relief campaigns, international labour solidarity, and anti-war campaigns – and focuses on the political dilemmas that arise from these issues. The chapter argues against the view that transnationalising resistance is automatically the most progressive way forward for such movements, but, at the same time, also problematises any straightforward focus on the nation-state. A critical but cosmopolitan anti-imperialism is advocated, based on the aim of transnationalising solidarity without necessarily by-passing nation-states. Finally, Chapter 9 addresses the question of alternatives to actually existing globalisation, and, in doing so, explicitly brings together the two halves of the book. Questions around alternatives to neo-liberalism, agency and wider social and political transformation are addressed in the light of discussion in earlier chapters.

Before moving on to the broader arguments, a few mitigating comments about the book's weaknesses are necessary. First, I refer at times to advanced capitalist countries and the First World on the one hand, and developing countries on the other. Second, I refer to many progressive movements as anti-globalisation. In both cases, this is simply a convenient short-hand. The division between advanced and developing implies no linear approach, as my arguments in Chapters 2 and 9 make clear, and nor does it imply moral superiority, as my arguments in Chapter 8 make clear. Anti-globalisation does not imply anti-all forms of globalisation, as should be clear in Chapters 6 through to 9. Finally, there is the issue of the book's title. It owes something to the notion of Huntington's 'clash of civilisations',[10] but the arguments made in this book are in no way derived from his simplistic analysis. There may however be some parallel between reading his work, less as sober analysis and more as political project designed to become self-fulfilling prophecy, and the political project known as globalisation.

---

[10] Huntington 1996.

PART ONE

ACTUALLY EXISTING GLOBALISATION

Chapter Two
Capitalism, Globalisation and Uneven Development

This chapter outlines the broad theoretical framework
used in the first half of the book, and is concerned
with the relationship between capitalism and
globalisation. In this chapter, more emphasis is placed
on an analysis of *capitalism*, while Chapters 3 and 4
put more emphasis on the analysis of contemporary
globalisation. This separation is strictly one of emphasis
as the two cannot actually be separated, although it
is also crucial that we do not reduce globalisation to
capitalism. However, before presenting an outline
of capitalism, I first establish why it is necessary
to link capitalism and globalisation. I do so by
providing a critique of two influential sociological
accounts of globalisation, associated with the work
of Anthony Giddens and Manuel Castells. Section I
outlines and criticises these approaches, arguing
that Giddens's account of globalisation conflates
agency and outcome, and, as a result, underestimates
the importance of agency, power relations and
historical specificity. Castells's work effectively tries
to incorporate these factors into his analysis, but it
too suffers from considerable inconsistency and
weakness, particularly in terms of its understanding
of social relations.

The second section draws on Marx's work, and
argues that this provides a useful *starting point* for
an understanding of globalisation. However, there

is a need to provide some periodisation of capitalism in order to understand the current period of globalisation. Capitalism has always been globalising, but the term also refers to a specific period of capitalism, that can be traced back to the 1970s. This approach to globalisation provides us with the basis for understanding agency, power relations, and historical specificity, in the globalisation debate. This discussion then sets up the historical account and critique of globalisation in the chapters that follow.

2.1   Globalisation theory: Giddens and Castells

(i) *Giddens*

Globalisation is a term that usefully refers to a specific set of dynamics and concrete processes, which have particular social, economic and political causes.[1] This presupposes the need for a theory of globalisation. On the other hand, Giddens's *The Consequences of Modernity*[2] attempts to construct something different – not a theory of globalisation, but instead something called 'globalisation theory'. He argues that modernity potentially separates people from local frameworks and practices, with the result that every aspect of nature, society and identity becomes available for reflexive choice, and abstractions such as science, rights and markets replace local, traditional norms. This increase in reflexivity therefore simultaneously means a decrease in what is taken as 'given' or 'fixed' in a particular society. The globalisation of high modernity constitutes an intensification of the separation of time and space, and disembedding mechanisms, and increasing reflexivity. Globalisation thus refers to 'the intensification of worldwide social relations which link distant localities in such a way that local happenings are shaped by events occurring many miles away and vice versa.'[3] With the arrival of globalisation, nation-states lose control in the face of global communications, capital flows, new aspirations, and so on. These social changes have enormous consequences, for no individual country can escape its effects, and 'opt out'. This changes the nature of economic policy-making, and undermines state claims to national

---

[1] See, for instance, Harvey 1989.
[2] Giddens 1990.
[3] Giddens 1990, p. 64.

sovereignty. This, in turn, undermines statist conceptions of politics, such as those associated with 'old' social democracy and centralised socialism. For Giddens,[4] these changes mean that there is a need for a distinctive, new radical politics for the global era, which espouses the causes of global governance above nation-states, and life politics of new social movements below them. In the case of global governance, this means among other things, that progressive politics must embrace international institutions that can police global markets and enforce good human-rights practices. In the case of politics 'below' the nation-state, it means the championing of life politics based on reflexive accounts of how we live our lives, reflected in part in the rise of new social movements that embrace different lifestyle choices.[5]

For Giddens, then, globalisation refers to an increase in reflexivity, through a process of 'disembedding' from local places, which, in turn, compresses time and space. What is less clear is precisely how this constitutes a new theoretical framework. Moreover, what is also unclear is precisely how globalisation as a set of processes has arisen, or indeed the power relations that are a constitutive part of globalisation. It is not sufficient to assert that '[m]odernity is inherently globalizing',[6] because it fails to tell us what is distinctive about the current phase of modernity. It may well be true that globalisation entails heightened reflexivity, but it does not tell us how heightened reflexivity came about – at least, not beyond the circular argument that globalisation causes heightened reflexivity. Indeed, many books on globalisation use Giddens's definition cited above as a starting point, and there is little that is problematic in this definition. However, it is a definition ('an intensification of worldwide social relations') that is hardly theoretical. It most certainly is not the basis for a new globalisation theory, and neither is it even a theorisation of a concrete set of social processes that have given rise to globalising outcomes. It is a description, and moreover, it is one that tells us little, if anything, about the character of these social relations, the agents of global transformation, or the (unequal and uneven) outcomes of these globalising processes. Justin Rosenberg[7] is therefore right to argue that while there is nothing necessarily wrong with a theory of

---

[4] Giddens 1994, 2001.
[5] Giddens 1991.
[6] Giddens 1990, p. 63.
[7] Rosenberg 2000, p. 2.

globalisation, *contra* Giddens, this must 'fall back on some more basic social theory which could explain why the phenomena denoted by the term have become such a distinctive and salient feature of the contemporary world'. In his enthusiastic embrace of current processes of social and political change, Giddens loses sight of the forces that have promoted these changes, and he therefore simultaneously fails to examine either the power relations or the unequal consequences of these changes.[8] The result is a conflation of outcome and social agency, with the effect that globalisation is taken as given, and 'outcome' blurs the boundaries of inevitability and desirability. The odd passing reference to new communications technologies or increased capital flows[9] is not sufficient to pass the test of accounting for agency in the globalisation debate. In downplaying agency, globalisation therefore becomes reified in Giddens's account – it is an inevitability that is not open to challenge (or such challenges that do occur are regarded as being fundamentalist). As Rosenberg argues, 'the further Giddens proceeds with the application of time-space distantiation as an alternative theory, the more this has the effect of emptying the world of recognizably social causes'.[10] It is a short step from this account to a politics of the Third-Way, as we will see in Chapters 4 and 5.

These points can be further illustrated through an examination of perhaps the most comprehensive treatment of globalisation to date. Held et al.'s *Global Transformations*[11] is a thorough, and rigorous account of globalisation that examines both theoretical approaches to globalisation, as well as its concrete empirical manifestations. However, its treatment of theoretical approaches is less than convincing. Held and his colleagues divide the debate into three

---

[8] In fairness to Giddens, this is not true of his earlier work – see for instance, Giddens 1987. But his work since 1990 certainly loses sight of classical notions of agency and power. There are probably two reasons for this neglect. First, such is his enthusiasm for the global condition as heightened reflexivity, (traditional, or simple modern) power as domination is regarded as having eroded as a consequence of disembedding global flows. But this ignores the way in which some people have the capacity to influence these flows far more than others – the fact that they do not have absolute power to do so is neither relevant nor novel (see further the argument in the text). Second, the collapse of communism has undermined radical socialist or communist alternatives. This may or may not be true (see Chapter 9), but this does not mean that the Marxist critique of capitalism becomes irrelevant, still less that capitalism's contradictions have been transcended.

[9] Giddens 1990, pp. 76–80.

[10] Rosenberg 2000, p. 89.

[11] Held et al. 1999.

camps – the hyper-globalisers, the sceptics, and the transformationalists. The first two camps focus on quantitative measures of globalisation, such as capital flows, and trade/GDP ratios. The former argues that there has been enormous change while the latter argues that change has been exaggerated and is not historically unprecedented. Held et al. attempt to move beyond this debate by supporting the transformationalist thesis. This approach argues that the debate between the hyper-globalisers and the sceptics focuses too narrowly on quantitative measures of the extent of globalisation, when, instead, we should see globalisation in terms of qualitative change. This approach argues that 'at the dawn of a new millennium, globalization is a central driving force behind the rapid social, political and economic changes that are reshaping modern societies and world order'. They go on to suggest that 'contemporary processes of globalization are historically unprecedented such that governments and societies across the globe are having to adjust to a world in which there is no longer a clear distinction between international and domestic, external and internal affairs'.[12] The direction of these processes of globalisation is uncertain and contradictory. Certainly, the world has in some respects become increasingly globalised, at least compared to the period from 1945 to 1973, but this 'globalisation' has not led to anything like global convergence. Instead, there have been new sources of power and inequality, and the relative marginalisation of some parts of the world, as some are more firmly entrenched in the circuits of global power while others are simply left out. However, no one single state has absolute power as the nature of (unequal) interdependence compels all states to adapt to a globalising world.

There is, undoubtedly, something useful in the transformationalist account, particularly its tendency to define globalisation in terms of a set of processes, rather than an end-state (which is implicit in the hyper-globalisation versus sceptic debate). The direction of globalisation is in many respects uncertain and contingent, and it is also true that globalisation is a process in which there is no overall control. However, much the same point could be made about capitalism – Marx's theory of alienation was based on the notion that neither workers nor capitalists were in control, but also that capitalists had far more power in this anarchic system than workers. This is an

---

[12] Held et al. 1999, p. 7.

important point because the argument made by transformationalists that power is fluid,[13] and that no one is in absolute control, is correct, but hardly novel. Similarly, the transformationalists' attempt to transcend the sceptics versus hyperglobalisers debate is unconvincing. To assert that the transformationalist view based on qualitative change moves us beyond the focus on quantitative change begs the question – for a marked qualitative change presupposes that quantitative change is so great that qualitative change has occurred.[14]

But the main problem with this account is more fundamental. The quotation above refers to globalisation as a 'central driving force' behind rapid changes in the world order. But is globalisation a driving force at all? Is it actually a concept that attempts only to capture some important changes in the contemporary world, but does not say how these have come about? In other words, is globalisation a concept concerned with a series of broadly related *outcomes* or *processes*, but which actually has little to say about *agencies that lead these outcomes and processes*?

Giddens's approach closely parallels these problems. For him, globalisation is an established fact, and attempts to opt out of it are based on fundamentalist and reactionary politics. Less clear is the status of globalisation in his account: is it (i) a new theory used to explain important social changes; (ii) a concept used to understand and clarify a number of important social changes? This is not a semantic point. If globalisation is a theory used to explain the world, then it must explain the mechanisms that account for the change from pre-globalisation to actual globalisation. However, if it is a concept used to aid understanding of a concrete set of processes, then we need to look at other factors that determine processes of globalisation. Put another way, is globalisation determining (the first definition) or determined (the second definition)? If it is the former, as Giddens appears to argue, then the political

---

[13] Held and McGrew 2002, p. 7.

[14] Interestingly, in more recent work, Held and his colleagues have slightly amended their three-fold divide in the globalisation debate. Instead, we have a divide between those that see globalisation as a myth and those who see it as a reality (Held and McGrew 2002, 2003). However, there are still massive divisions within the two camps, and still the question of agency is downplayed. This point is all the more true of Giddens's 1999 survey of globalisation, which divides the debate into radicals (who believe – like Giddens himself – that strong globalisation is an established fact), and sceptics (who dispute this claim).

implications are that political alternatives can only take place within globalisation. But, if this is true, then it is surely more important to talk about the nature of those alternatives than it is to assert the significance of globalisation. An example should illustrate this point. One of the major claims made in favour of globalisation is that, in the last fifty years, global poverty has fallen to lower levels than it did in the previous 500, and that child death rates in the developing world have halved and malnutrition has declined by a third.[15] But it is not at all clear that 'globalisation' can take the credit for this development. To argue that 'globalisation' is responsible for poverty decline since the early 1950s is meaningless. What is it precisely about globalisation that has led to poverty reduction? Who or what are the agents of globalisation and poverty reduction? In other words, the concept of globalisation is developed at such a high level of abstraction in this account as to tell us little. More useful would be accounts that examined the role of the state, aid agencies, and international markets, and how these have changed over time. Most empirically grounded political economists would argue that the last fifty years can at least be divided into two eras, the first (1950s to 1970s) where the state played a leading role in the promotion of development, and the second (the 1980s and 1990s) where states continued to play an important role, but where markets were deemed to play the leading role. This debate is examined in later chapters so need not detain us here. But what should be clear is that it makes little sense to explain two very different policy eras in terms of an over-generalised term such as globalisation.

Giddens's definition of globalisation thus attempts to tell us a great deal about the contemporary world, but, in fact, tells us very little. In one sense, it tries to do too much, arguing that almost all change in the world is a product of globalisation. But, in another sense, it tells us so little because it is theorised at such a high level of abstraction and generalisation. Contrary to Giddens's argument, globalisation should not be regarded as a 'big theory' that can explain current events in the world. Rather, it refers to certain *outcomes* within the current world order, which are determined by other factors. This implies that processes of globalisation are the product of particular social and political agents, and that there are conflicts among these agents. This, in turn, implies

---

[15] UNDP 1997.

that these processes of globalisation are intimately connected to relationships of power and domination.

These comments are not meant as an outright rejection of Giddens's sociology or politics, still less the work of David Held.[16] But it is an argument that Giddens's account is simply too abstract to provide the basis for critical reflection on specific, concrete aspects of the globalisation debate. However, perhaps Giddens's theory can be saved, if we 'fill the gaps', and therefore concretise Giddens's suggestive account with a more grounded approach. It may be then, that globalisation does represent an increase in reflexivity and time-space compression, but we still have to address the question: how does this concretely operate? If we are to fill the gaps in Giddens's work, the question that needs to be asked then is 'what accounts for the specific and distinctive features of "late" or "high" modernity at the end of the twentieth [century]?'[17] In attempting to answer this question, I turn to the work of Manuel Castells.

(ii) *Castells*

In his three-volume work *The Information Society*,[18] Castells attempts to ground the notion of time-space compression within the context of the rise of what he calls the network society. Contemporary society is based on two defining characteristics. First, the continued existence of the capitalist mode of production, based on the generalisation of commodity production, the employment of wage-labour, and the accumulation of capital. Second, the recent growth of an informational mode of development, which has its origins in capitalist restructuring and (autonomous) technological change. It is this new development that provides the basis for the reorganisation of social practices in time and space. Informational networks lead to a culture of 'real virtuality' based on electronic media, particularly information technology and the internet. For Castells, then, 'the enhancement of telecommunications has created the material infrastructure for the formation of a global economy, in a movement similar to that which lay behind the construction of the railways and the formation of national markets during the nineteenth century'.[19]

---

[16] See Chapter 8.
[17] Bromley 1999, p. 9.
[18] Castells 1996, 1997, 1998.
[19] Castells 1993, p. 20.

The implications of this development and expansion of information technology are enormous. The network society is an information-based society and therefore a globalised society. Information flows and the power relations around these flows change the social relations of industrial capitalism. Global information and communications technologies expand and therefore undermine place. Moreover, as a consequence of the instantaneous nature of information flows, social interaction takes place in real time on a global scale. Time and space are therefore compressed, with the result that many of the institutions of industrial capitalism (Giddens's 'simple modernity') are undermined. Central to the organisation of the network society are those informational labourers who create and disseminate information flows. Informational labour both creates and adapts most easily to rapid social change. This labour is both highly educated and flexible, as it can adapt easily to new situations and learn how to learn in a rapidly changing world. In contrast, generic labour is inflexible and also potentially subject to automation by the designs of informational labour. It is therefore relative powerless, and marginalised from the network society, with the consequence that the class solidarities of industrial capitalism are undermined.

These differentials provide the basis for a new social divide in the network society, based on those that are included in the space of flows and those that are excluded from them. Networks 'constitute the new social morphology of our societies. . . . [T]his networking logic induces a social determination at a higher level than that of the specific social interests expressed through the networks: the power of flows takes precedence over the flows of power'.[20] This social dynamic of inclusion/exclusion has implications not only for inequality, but also for resistance. Many new social movements resist through an attachment to the space of places, with the result that many such movements are defensive and backward-looking – or, in Giddens's terms, fundamentalist. Castells does express some hope for the politics of feminist and green movements, and, in particular, their capacity to pursue a project of emancipatory politics within the logic of the network society,[21] but, overall, there is a feeling of pessimism in his work, at least for those excluded from the network society. This is actually an important contrast with Giddens, who regards globalisation

---

[20] Castells 1996, p. 469.
[21] Castells 1997.

as at least potentially inclusive,[22] while Castells[23] argues that the form of globalisation is intrinsically hierarchical, as social exclusion is internal to the dynamic of the network society.

For Castells, the network society is based on a mixture of the continuity of the capitalist mode of production and the discontinuity of the informational mode of development. However, it is the latter which is highlighted at the expense of the former, and, despite recent qualifications in response to criticism,[24] this remains the case. The result is that there is an implicit and sometimes explicit technological determinism in the analysis.[25] Thus, in focusing on the centrality of information and knowledge, Castells naturalises its role and therefore treats it as simply a factor of production rather than as a contested social relation based on private ownership of the means of production. In other words, informational labourers are still subject to control by capital – either through increased surveillance at the workplace (which information technology can actually enhance) or through control of the information generated through patents, copyrights and so on.[26] To his credit, Castells shies away from the superficial analyses of creativity to be found in the work of the likes of Leadbeater,[27] but his excessive focus on informational labour and networks in the 'space of flows' leads him to downplay the power relations *within* such networks. Indeed, given that informational capitalism has encouraged outsourcing to cheap suppliers and a new enclosure of (intellectual) property, the current era displays important signs of continuity with early, nineteenth-century capitalism. Of course, some creative labourers do enjoy considerable bargaining power, but these represent a small minority of service workers. Castells's argument that there is 'a common trend toward the increase of the relative weight of the most clearly informational occupations (managers, professionals and technicians) as well as the overall "white collar" occupations',[28] tends to lump together all service workers as somehow part of the network society. But most white-collar work is not necessarily IT-based, and, even if

---

[22] See Chapters 4 and 5.
[23] Castells 1998; also Hoogvelt 2001.
[24] Castells 2000.
[25] For example, Castells 1996, p. 66.
[26] May 2001, pp. 72–3; Perelman 2002.
[27] Leadbeater 1999.
[28] Castells 1996, p. 218.

it is, most is unskilled and badly paid, and, indeed, many service jobs are more closely linked to the manufacturing sector. Furthermore, the expansion of service work in part reflects the increased commodification of certain forms of work, such as laundry services, fast-food restaurants and paid child-care facilities that were previously carried out under non-capitalist social relations. At the same time, the highly skilled, well-paid informational labourers that enjoy considerable flexibility without (too much) insecurity make up a small proportion of the work force.[29] Informational networks do not therefore transcend capitalism, either in its manufacturing or informational form.[30]

This point can be extended to his wider political analysis. For instance, Castells[31] claims that the state 'has lost most of its economic power, albeit it still has some regulatory capacity and relative control over its subjects'. This argument is close to Giddens's contention that globalisation has intensified time-space compression and in the process made the nation-state less relevant. But both arguments rest on a dualism between states and markets and are therefore in danger of naturalising and technocratising both of these institutional forms. The globalisation of social interaction, including international trade and production, relies on strictly enforceable rules that are implemented by states. The emergence of international institutions that regulate these transactions do not undermine state sovereignty *per se* (though, of course, some states are weaker than others), and in part reflect the *universalisation* of the nation-state system. States and the international economy are not then external to each other, and contemporary developments should not be characterised as a process in which globalisation escapes the control of nation-states, but, instead, one in which states use their sovereignty to redefine their functions in the international order. This has entailed an increase in 'marketisation', but this is a process which itself is state sanctioned and regulated. The economic roles of nation-states are thus not external to, but a central, constituent part of, 'globalisation'. One clear implication is that politics continues to be based on forms of, access to, and pressures on, nation-state – and it is disingenuous to imply (as do some Third-Way ideologues) that this automatically implies reactionary politics.[32] Castells appears to accept

---

[29] Huws 2003.
[30] See also Chapter 8.
[31] 1997, p. 254.
[32] See Chapters 4 and 8.

this point at times, especially in the second edition of *The Rise of the Network Society*,[33] but this acceptance can only undermine his wider arguments concerning a rigid separation of the space of flows from the space of places. Castells's rigid dichotomy between the space of flows and the space of places reflects an exaggeration of the significance of the information revolution. Above all, ICTs have intensified rather than transcended existing capitalist social practices rather than created entirely novel forms of social activity. Moreover, his attempts to break free from charges of technological determinism in the second edition are not altogether convincing, as demonstrated in his claim that the so-called new economy powered by the IT revolution has transcended the boom-bust cycle of capitalism.[34] Overall, then, Castells's work betrays 'a common conceit among the living . . . which presupposes theirs is a time of singular significance'.[35] It would clearly be a mistake to deny that nothing has changed in recent years. Important technological, social and political changes have occurred. Capitalism's dynamic nature leads to constant change, but more important, the last twenty–thirty years have seen changes which are more significant than those that can be explained as simply the result of the ongoing dynamism of the capitalist mode of production. But what is also true is that it makes little sense to describe or theorise these processes in isolation from capitalism, and therefore in isolation from capitalist social relations.[36]

(iii) *Giddens, Castells and politics*

The weaknesses in Giddens and Castells reflect serious problems with much of the globalisation debate, which has too often conflated two issues: first, the extent to which globalisation is a reality; second, the extent to which globalisation is desirable. This confusion is most clear in Giddens's account, for it accepts globalisation as a reality, and then insists that politics must take place within this framework. But the question that then needs to be asked is, which aspects of globalisation are irreversible? Hay and Watson[37] draw out the general implications of this argument:

---

[33] Castells 2000, pp. 135–47.
[34] Castells 2000, pp. 147–62, see also Chapter 4 below.
[35] Webster 2001, p. 10.
[36] This comment is not meant to imply that all sources of domination are reducible to capitalism. It does, however, remain a key source.
[37] Hay and Watson 1999, p. 422.

Like it or not, to accept the radical stance on globalisation as unquestioningly as Giddens does is to appeal to a set of ideas which have long been taken hostage by a distinctively neo-liberal articulation of systemic economic 'imperatives'. Moreover, so long as this continues to be understood as just 'how things are', the political space for democratising globalising tendencies and once more laying neo-liberal 'common-sense' open to question would appear to be strictly limited.

Put differently, globalisation theory too easily accepts the political parameters established by the victory of neo-liberalism in the 1980s, which argued for the primacy of market forces, free trade, liberalised finance and open competition. It is in this context that the so-called Third-Way can be located, for it can be seen as a political project that attempts to depoliticise decision-making processes, and which therefore leaves the neo-liberal policies of the 1980s largely unchallenged. Both Giddens and Castells are therefore 'inclined to overestimate the power and underestimate the limitations of the processes they identify', and 'prone to neglect the extent to which globalization is a quite specific project'.[38] Chapters 3 and 4 will provide an explanation for the rise of globalisation, both as social reality and political project. In those chapters, I situate the rise in the context of the changing (internal) relationship between states, markets and money, within the wider context of the capitalist mode of production. This is not a question of simply stating that globalisation is reducible to the 'logic of capitalism', which is almost as over-generalised as Giddens's assertion that modernity is inherently globalising. But, if we are to understand contemporary globalisation, we need to be able to relate (but not reduce) it to capitalism.

2.2   Capitalism, the state and uneven development

This section attempts to provide a broad outline of the origins, specificity and development of capitalism. The changing nature of international capitalism, and particularly the changes of the last fifty years, are discussed in Chapters 3 and 4. The remainder of this chapter therefore provides some of the historical and theoretical background to the more specific account of the origins and

---

[38] Scott 1997, p. 8.

development of contemporary globalisation in the following two chapters. This section will examine two principal themes. First, it provides some (brief) discussion of the origins of capitalism and then emphasises its distinctiveness through a discussion of the role of accumulation. In examining accumulation, there is also some discussion of the contradictions of capitalism, and, particularly, the tendency towards over-accumulation. Second, and following on from the discussion of over-accumulation in particular, it stresses the unevenness of global capitalism, a theme taken up throughout the book.

(i) *Capitalism, value and accumulation*

If we are to define its origins we also need to understand what is distinctive about capitalism. This is discussed below, but we need to emphasise immediately that capitalism is *not* simply a system of trading relationships. Exchange-based definitions fail to capture what is distinctive about capitalism as a mode of production. Trading activity through markets, including international markets, has occurred for thousands of years. Capitalism, however, is a far newer phenomenon. Its origins lie in the development of specific social relations in the English countryside from around the sixteenth century. In feudal societies, peasants generally had direct access to the means of production, and surplus labour or surplus products were appropriated through direct coercion by landlords and states. In France, for instance, peasants were generally owner-occupiers, and appropriation took place through political forms of exploitation, such as direct coercion and taxation. In England, on the other hand, land was highly concentrated, with landlords owning enormous amounts. A large proportion of the land was owned not by peasants, but was instead leased by landlords to tenant farmers. Landlords extracted rent less by direct coercion as in France, and more by the success of tenants in selling products in a competitive market-place. A growing number of English tenancies were basically economic in nature, in which rents were fixed not by legal obligation but by market conditions. In other words, there was a market for leases, and so competition in the market for consumers and access to land.[39] Agricultural producers therefore became increasingly market-dependent on access to land, with the result that 'advantage in access to the land itself

---

[39] Brenner 1976.

would go to those who could produce competitively and pay good rents by increasing their own productivity'.[40] The most competitive farmers, therefore, had potential access to more land, while the less competitive faced the danger of losing direct access. Wood[41] usefully contrasts France and England through the use of the concepts of market opportunity and market imperative. In France, rents were fixed, which, in theory at least, provided ample opportunity for the development of petty commodity production. Precisely because rents were fixed, potential entrepreneurs could develop new production methods, increase productivity, and sell their output in the knowledge that this would not be taken away from them in the form of rent. This scenario, like most approaches that attempt to theorise its origins, assumes that capitalism was created by the expansion of market opportunity. However, peasants in France generally did not respond to this opportunity with sustained productivity increases. In England, on the other hand, variable economic rents meant that peasants were *compelled* to do so, otherwise they would not be able to pay their rent and would therefore risk losing their lease.

The (long, slow) process of peasant differentiation, in which some peasants were displaced from the land and became wage-labourers, was reinforced by the emergence of a strong state that facilitated, rather than restricted, this market imperative.[42] In the long run, the English social structure based on landlords leasing to capitalist farmers, who, in turn, increasingly employed wage-labourers, facilitated the movement from agrarian to industrial capitalism. This was due to the increase in productivity that fed a rising non-agricultural population, the emergence of a potential and actual labour force displaced from the land, and the competitive accumulation of capital which eventually gave rise to industrial development.[43] This process was to have enormous implications internationally as well as nationally, and I return to this issue below.

What needs immediate re-emphasis is the distinctiveness of capitalism as a mode of production. Capitalism is not simply a quantitative expansion of trade or market exchange, but is the generalisation of *commodity production*. Trade and exchange occur frequently throughout history, but it is only with

---

[40] Wood 2002, pp. 100–1.
[41] Wood 2002, p. 102.
[42] Marx 1976, Chapter 27; Corrigan and Sayer 1985.
[43] Hobsbawm 1962, p. 47.

capitalism that goods are produced primarily for the market. Prior to capitalism, production was first for direct use and then market exchange took place. With capitalism, the overwhelming majority of goods are produced for a competitive market. In non-capitalist societies, both exploiters and producers have direct access to the means of production and/or reproduction, and so there is no necessity to buy on the market those goods necessary for (re-)production, and therefore no necessity to produce for exchange, to sell competitively in the market-place, or to produce at the socially necessary rate.[44] In other words, production for use implies direct access to land, which means that commodity production is restricted. However, proletarianisation, or the separation of producers from direct access to the means of production, implies *at one and the same time* the generalisation of commodity production, precisely because production for direct use ceases to be possible. It is the development of these distinctive capitalist property relations that lay the basis for enormous social, political and technological change as 'capitalist property relations impose the requirement to specialize, accumulate, and innovate or go out of business'.[45]

Capitalism, then, is about the generalised production of commodities. A commodity has both a use-value, which is the particular use that the commodity has, and a value, which is something that renders that particular commodity 'equivalent' or comparable to the value of all other commodities that enter the market. Money plays this role in that it regulates the exchange of commodities through the payment for particular goods, but it also presupposes the existence of social relations in which commodity production is generalised. For Marx, labour is the source of value. The generalised system of commodity production converts the sum of private, individual labour into social labour through the exchange of commodities in the market-place. Value-creating labour is thus specific to capitalist society, it is the particular historical and social form that (general) labour takes in capitalist society. This labour theory of value[46] is a theory that attempts to deal with the historical specificity of capitalist social relations of production, and, in particular, the separation of

---

[44] Brenner 1986, p. 28.
[45] Brenner 1986, p. 42.
[46] A detailed discussion of the labour theory of value is not possible in this chapter. The brief comments in the text suggest that this theory is perhaps best understood as a value theory of labour (Elson 1979; also Weeks 1981, Chapters 1 and 2; Fine and Saad-Filho 2004, Chapter 2).

labour from the means of production, and thus the commodification of *labour-power*. It is not an argument that labour is the source of all wealth, nor is it an accounting device that supposedly measures the actual exchange-value or price of a commodity. Indeed, individual commodities in capitalist society do not necessarily exchange at their value. The theory then is one that reflects the specific development of capitalist social relations outlined above, and, therefore, only applies to those same relations.

Crucial to Marx's argument is that capitalist relations of production separate labour, the source of value, from the capacity to labour, or labour-power. Labour-power's use-value is to create more value in the production process for the capitalist – it is the source of surplus-value. Surplus-value is extracted from the worker through the difference in the value of the commodities produced by the worker's *labour* from the value of the cost of reproducing that same worker's *labour-power*. The latter cost to the capitalist is the wage, the former gain is the value of the commodity or commodities produced by the worker. The capitalist therefore makes a profit through this difference, provided that the commodities produced are sold in the market-place. Surplus-value is, therefore, produced in the sphere of production. Individual capitalists may derive some surplus-value through exchange, by, for example, selling commodities above their value, but it is impossible for all capitalists to do so, as buyers are also sellers. Similarly, some individual capitalists may benefit from a monopoly position in a specific sector, but competition and investment in that sector will eventually drive profits down. The source of surplus-value lies in the process of production, though it is redistributed through processes of exchange and competition between capitals. Surplus-value is extracted in two ways. First, through an increase in the intensity of work and longer working hours, without a corresponding increase in wages. This extraction of absolute surplus-value arises out of the use of greater amounts of labour without an increase in the wage, the cost of reproducing labour-power. The second way is through an investment in new technology and a resultant increase in labour productivity, which leads to a reduction in the labour time necessary to produce a particular good. The result is a decline in labour costs relative to the value of the commodities produced. Both forms of surplus-value extraction persist to this day. However, absolute surplus-value is far less dynamic as profit arises through lowering wages or lengthening the working day. In all capitalist societies, this process of surplus-value extraction is limited by the fact that workers can only work so many hours, and wages can only fall to a certain level before they reach zero. Moreover, wage cuts and uncompensated increases in work hours are eventually resisted by the workers themselves. This does not mean that absolute surplus-value extraction simply comes to an end, as capital may invest in areas where there is considerable state repression of labour, and / or high unemployment, both of which are conducive to the extraction of absolute surplus-value. But the extraction of absolute surplus-value does not lead to a dynamic capitalism. On the other hand, the extraction of relative surplus-value is the basis for the dynamic accumulation of capital, and it was, in part, for this reason that Marx considered capitalism to be the most progressive mode of production in history. Marx and Engels[47] famously argued that:

> The bourgeoisie cannot exist without constantly revolutionising the instruments of production, and thereby the relations of production, and with them the whole relations of society. . . . Constant revolutionising of production, uninterrupted disturbance of all social conditions, everlasting uncertainty and agitation distinguish the bourgeois epoch from all earlier ones. All fixed, fast frozen relations, with their train of ancient and venerable prejudices and opinions, are swept away, all new formed ones become antiquated before they can ossify. All that is solid melts into air, all that is holy is profaned, and man is at last compelled to face with sober senses his real conditions of life and his relations with his kind.

This quotation from Marx and Engels's *Manifesto of the Communist Party* was aimed at understanding the dynamic movement from agrarian to industrial production in nineteenth-century Britain, but it also captures something of the globalising processes that lie at the heart of the contemporary globalisation debate. There is discussion of the notion that the world is increasingly interconnected, that the intensity and velocity of these interconnections is increasing, and that therefore distinct localities are increasingly 'disembedded' – the very things that Giddens describes in his account of globalisation. There is also some notion (and too much optimism) that a genuine global consciousness is developing as a result. But what is also apparent from the first sentence, and which is different from Giddens's account, is a recognition

---

[47] Marx and Engels 1977, pp. 36–7.

of agency, which is related to the notion of competition between capitals. Marx and Engels[48] go on:

> The need of a constantly expanding market for its products chases the bourgeoisie over the whole surface of the globe. It must nestle everywhere, settle everywhere, establish connexions everywhere. . . . The bourgeoisie has through its exploitation of the world market given a cosmopolitan character to production and consumption in every country. . . . The bourgeoisie, by the rapid improvement of all instruments of production, by the immensely facilitated means of communication, draws all, even the most barbarian, nations into civilisation. . . . It compels all nations, on pain of extinction, to adopt the bourgeois mode of production; it compels them to introduce what it calls civilisation into their midst, i.e. to become bourgeois themselves. In one word, it creates a world after its own image.

Thus, for Marx, globalisation is ultimately a product of the dynamism of the capitalist mode of production, which itself is a product of historically specific relations of production. These relations are based on the separation of labour from direct access to the means of production – that is, through the removal of producers from land (see above). This ongoing process was particularly common in England in the seventeenth and nineteenth centuries, and continues (in various forms) throughout the world to this day. With this removal, labourers are forced to find paid employment in order to be able to buy commodities, which enable them to feed and clothe themselves and their families. At the same time, the removal of the producers from the land simultaneously generalises production for the market, or what is called commodity production. When labour has direct access to land, it consumes goods produced on that land (and sells surplus). When labour ceases to have access to land, it consumes goods that are bought through the market mechanism. Displacement of labour from the land – or the commodification of labour-power – simultaneously generalises commodity production. Market societies do not arise spontaneously, they are the product of political and social processes.[49] At the same time, this generalisation of commodity production leads to competition between units of production, as each unit attempts to

---

[48] Marx and Engels 1977, pp. 37–8.
[49] Polanyi 1957.

sell its goods at the most competitive rate in the market-place. If goods are too expensive, then a particular production unit will go bankrupt. Potentially uncompetitive producers can lower costs by cutting wages or increasing the intensity of work, that is they can increase the extraction of absolute surplus-value, but this process eventually comes up against physical limits – wages can only be cut so far, and people can only work so hard. So, an alternative strategy is for capital to invest in new technology, which increases labour productivity – that is, they can extract relative surplus-value. This investment in new technology is however a never ending process, as specific capitals always face the danger of being undercut by innovative competitors. States may protect specific capitals from competition, but, ultimately, capital accumulation is an ongoing, dynamic and never-ending process. This accumulation is uneven and unequal, potentially uncontrollable, and certainly prone to crisis. But what is relevant to our discussion here is that it is a process that is not confined to national borders, and, indeed, never has been. In the quotations above, Marx was clearly wrong in his belief that the global expansion of capitalism would lead to similar processes of capitalist development throughout the globe, and, instead, there emerged an unequal international division of labour. But he was clearly correct that the dynamism of capitalism paved the way not only for nineteenth-century industrialisation, but also twentieth-century (as well as earlier forms of) globalisation.

However, at the same time, the 'freeing' of labour from the land also led to a further separation. In feudal society, the regulation of peasant labour that had access to land was the task of 'the state', or the various sovereign bodies that preceded the rise of capitalist states. There was no economy or civil society separate from the state, because the 'state' effectively was the economy. Peasants worked the land to feed themselves, but 'states' also ensured that landlords received a rent in the form of goods, labour or money-rent. With the emergence of capitalism, the state did not directly regulate the relationship between employer (capitalist) and employee (worker), as this was a purely 'economic' matter. The modern state – based on the creation of a separate political sphere – is thus also (partly) the product of capitalist social relations. The separate economic sphere – the market – is thus no longer directly regulated by the political sphere. Indeed, the very separation of these spheres is accomplished by the rise of capitalist social relations, and these social relations are not necessarily 'contained' by national states.[50] On the other hand, while it may be true that global capitalism does not necessarily require *national* states,[51] the fact remains that such states have historically been crucial to process of capital accumulation, both within and beyond nations. We therefore have a potentially global market existing side-by-side with national states, which themselves may be hierarchically structured within the international state system. It is also important to note that states do not exist in isolation, but as part of an international system of nation-states, and this has implications for international processes of capital accumulation. In particular, and most relevant for our purposes, some states may play hegemonic roles in the international order, and it may be that, rather than undermining nation-states, contemporary globalisation has been actively promoted by some nation-states, as we will see in the next chapter. At certain periods, then, hegemonic states have come to play a leading role in leading and facilitating international or even global capital accumulation, and the hegemonic role of the US state is an important part of the story of the current era of globalisation. Nation-states[52] are inextricably linked to capitalism because their reproduction ultimately depends on the international accumulation process based on the extraction of surplus-value. They serve a number of functions for capital, most notably the protection of private property rights (which ensures the private appropriation of surplus-value) and provision of public goods. In practice, however, states that limit their functions to such a minimalist role are likely to face enormous problems, as states rely on the sustained accumulation of capital for legitimacy and material resources. Capitalist states have, therefore, historically played a crucial role in promoting capital

---

[50] Lacher 2003.

[51] Lacher 2002.

[52] A full consideration of the question of the relationship between nation-states and capitalism lies outside the scope of this work, but see in particular Wood 1991, Lacher 2000 and Teschke 2003. These path-breaking works all suggest that the *nation*-state system pre-dates capitalist modernity, and can be traced back to the pre-capitalist period of absolutism. This system was transformed in the nineteenth century through the development of capitalism within these nation-states, and therefore the growing institutional separation of an 'economic' market and 'political' state. However, continued territorialisation within nation-states – and indeed the universalisation of the nation-state – has also had implications for the shaping of capitalism, as we will see in Chapters 3 and 4.

accumulation, through, for instance, expansionary economic policies, subsidies and provision of infrastructure. Moreover, nation-states in the international capitalist order have promoted the interests of its 'national capitals' within the international state system. It is for these reasons that we can talk of a capitalist state, rather than just a state in capitalist society. On the other hand, states are also sites of conflict in which important concessions can be won by exploited and oppressed groups, and tensions can arise between the internationalising tendencies of capital and the territorial specificity of the nation-state, and so the precise relationship between state and capital is, in some respects, a contingent one. It is therefore mistaken to conceptualise globalisation in terms of capital 'outgrowing' the state, or to rigidly dichotomise a past of national sovereignty and a present of global 'de-territorialised', placeless flows. Rather, we should recognise the fact that the nation-state is a central agency in the promotion of contemporary globalisation. These points have enormous political implications, and are discussed further in Chapters 7–9.

For the moment, we need to return to the question of the accumulation of capital. The process of capital accumulation gives capitalism its distinctively dynamic character, at least in relation to previous modes of production. However, this accumulation process is not only dynamic, but is also prone to crisis. There is a tendency in capitalism towards over-accumulation, in which a labour surplus exists side by side with a capital surplus. Concretely, this means that high rates of unemployment coincide with a surplus of commodities that cannot be sold profitably, idle productive capacity and surpluses of money capital that cannot find outlets for productive and profitable investment.[53] The precise form that such crises take varies, but there is always a tendency towards over-accumulation, and this is ultimately a product of the specific nature of capitalist social relations. In particular, it is a product of the fact that production is ultimately determined by the need to make a profit. The source of this profit is the expansion of surplus-value, and relative surplus-value is extracted by reducing the cost of means of production and labour-power. Each individual capitalist expands their surplus-value, by increasing the amount of commodities produced and economising on costs (labour and means of production). But, at the same time, this surplus-value must be realised through the commodities being sold in the market-place.

---

[53] Harvey 1999, Chapters 6 and 7.

There is thus a tendency to expand production regardless of the limits of the market, and this is because each individual capitalist is compelled to innovate in a competitive environment, which means that they must innovate or face the risk of bankruptcy. On the other hand, the most successful capitalist will, at least for a time, achieve profits above the average rate through a (temporary) monopoly in a particular sector. Accumulation is, therefore, an ongoing process, but the success of capitalists in opening up new markets (and achieving surplus profits) intensifies the tendency towards the over-accumulation of capital. This process is dynamic because the process of expansion without regard for the limits of the market in one branch of production simultaneously expands the market in other branches of production. The tendency towards over-accumulation therefore first manifests itself as uneven development of the various branches of production. However, this dynamism can also become a limit, as goods pile up, machinery lies idle, prices fall, and credit dries up. Such crises manifest themselves through the limited availability of money, which means that customers cannot buy goods, or capitalists cannot invest to renew accumulation. The availability of credit can avert crises by financing new investment and sustaining capitalists through difficult periods. But this eventually exacerbates the problem, as credit expansion means over-accumulation, and the uneven development of capital – which, in turn, fuels the continued expansion of credit. As the tendency towards over-accumulation persists, outlets for profitable investment decline alongside ever expanding credit, which in turn diverts money into speculative financial ventures. At some point, the tendency towards over-accumulation will become a generalised crisis, in which a glut of unsold goods exists alongside a mass of worthless debt and an increase in unemployment.

This cycle of over-accumulation and crisis is broadly accepted by most economists, and it dominated debates over the causes of the world recessions of 1974–5 and 1980–2. For some orthodox economists, these crises were caused by an over-expansion of credit and, so, appropriate monetary policy – and particularly controls on the money supply – was regarded as the solution. This monetarist approach was (briefly) dominant in the 1980s, though the extent to which it was actually put into practice was limited. However, the accompanying emphasis on the need to promote market expansion and (selectively) roll back the state, as well prioritising the control of inflation over full employment, continues to dominate economic policy throughout the world, and is central to the discourse of globalisation. On the other hand, in the 1970s, Keynesians argued that the crisis was caused by insufficient demand, and that, therefore, the state should act as a 'collective capitalist', stimulating demand so that productive activity can be renewed. This approach may have worked in the post-war era, but, by the 1970s, when easy access to credit and inflation existed alongside unemployment, it was less convincing. However, the monetarist approach that promoted a tightening of credit only served to exacerbate the recession, as high interest rates stifled productive investment and led to unsustainable debts in the early 1980s. Both of the mainstream approaches thus only deal with surface manifestations of crisis, which are ultimately linked to the anarchic and uneven accumulation of capital. These issues are addressed in detail in Chapter 3, which examines the post-war boom, the crisis of the 1970s, and the rise of neo-liberalism and the globalisation discourse in the 1980s and 1990s.

(ii) *Global uneven development*

As we have seen, the competitive process of capital accumulation does not lead to equilibrium, but, instead, leads to uneven development. This uneven development can take place not only within, but also between different nation-states. However (and contrary to his arguments concerning competition), Marx was sometimes optimistic that the expansion of capitalism would promote a dynamic process of development throughout the globe. He argued that capitalism is progressive compared to previous modes of production in history, as it led to an unprecedented expansion of the productive forces, and it was this argument that led Marx to sometimes support colonialism. Thus, Marx and Engels contrasted the modernising influence of Western capitalism with backward India, which 'has no history at all'. They went on to argue that 'England has to fulfil a double mission in India: one destructive, the other regenerating – the annihilation of old Asiatic society, and the laying of the material foundations of Western society in Asia'. Marx also gave his (critical) support to free trade for similar reasons.[54]

Colonialism may have been exploitative but it was also deemed necessary, in that it laid the foundations for the capitalist development of 'backward' societies. Capitalism's tendency to develop the productive forces was contrasted

---

[54] Marx and Engels 1974, pp. 80–2; Marx 1977, p. 270.

with the stagnation of pre-capitalist, 'non-historic' societies. Capitalism acted as a 'bridge' to a communist future as the development of the productive forces provides the potential for everybody to live off of the social surplus product – rather than just a ruling class minority. In the words of Cohen, '[s]o much technique and inanimate power are now available that arduous labour, and the resulting control by some men over the lives of others lose their function, and a new integration of man and nature in a new communism becomes possible'.[55] But this possibility could only be realised by the simultaneous development of the proletariat, the 'really revolutionary class'[56] that, united in the process of production, has the power to overthrow the ruling capitalist class.

This approach to Marxism is sometimes described as linear or evolutionary Marxism, as it proposes a theory of history in which all 'societies' (nation-states) pass through similar stages of development based on the gradual development of the productive forces. Marx argued that colonialism was progressive because he, at times, believed that it would lead to an increase in capital investment in the colonies, which would include the development of capitalist social relations, competition between capitals, and therefore sustained capital accumulation based on the extraction of relative surplus-value. The linear Marxism associated with this theory is therefore optimistic about the prospects for global convergence. In the current era of globalisation, this argument has acquired a new significance among (ex-)Marxists who have revived the concept of cosmopolitan capital,[57] first used by Marx and Engels in *The Communist Manifesto*, and cited above. In the 1970s, Bill Warren[58] argued that:

> If the extension of capitalism into non-capitalist areas of the world created an international system of inequality and exploitation called imperialism, it simultaneously created the conditions for the destruction of this system by the spread of capitalist social relations and productive forces throughout the non-capitalist world.

---

[55] Cohen 1978, p. 24.
[56] Marx 1977, p. 229.
[57] Kitching 2001; Desai 2002; N. Harris 2003.
[58] Warren 1973, p. 41.

Expanding on this argument, and applying this argument more explicitly to the era of globalisation, Meghnad Desai[59] contends that globalisation represents progress for the contemporary developing world. Countries that have not received significant amounts of investment 'need to integrate into the global order or they will be left even further behind. The third world needs capitalism because capitalism alone will lead to its growth. No other plausible, feasible alternative has been found'. Warren's position was optimistic, but it still saw the development of capitalist social relations as fundamental to the development of the productive forces. In the work of Desai and others, the focus is less on social relations and more on the technical question of integrating into the world economy through trade and investment liberalisation. Kitching explicitly links the end of imperialism with a new era of globalisation based on the mobility of capital:

> as capitalism passes from its imperialist phase to its globalization phase, it begins to *take revenge* (economic revenge) on that subgroup of the world's workers whose living standards have been artificially raised and sustained by a combination of national economic protection and imperial domination. In particular, the free movement of productive capital, which is a hallmark of the globalization phase, allows the poor workers of the world to play their economic ace card (the low cost of their labor's production and reproduction). It does so by eliminating the capital stock advantage that enabled the richer workers of the world to compensate – in global competition for the higher cost of their labor.[60]

Given that this position is optimistic about the prospects for global convergence between countries, Kitching's argument is quite close to orthodox, neo-liberal theories of international trade. Interpretations of Ricardo's theory of comparative advantage suggest that competition increases the efficiency of production and thereby lowers prices and raises world output. Each country should therefore specialise in producing those goods (or services) that it can make most cheaply – that is, those goods in which it has a comparative advantage. This theory was further developed by Eli Heckscher and Bertil Ohlin in the 1930s.[61] They argued that equilibrium in exchange is based on differences in factor

---

[59] Desai 2000, p. 44.
[60] Kitching 2001, p. 267.
[61] Ohlin 1933.

endowments throughout the world, and that specialisation in production would tend to equalise differences in prices between trading countries. A particular country (A) may have an initial comparative advantage in, say, both cloth and corn, and produce both more cheaply than Country B. However, if Country A produces cloth more cheaply than it produces corn, it should specialise in the former, because it could then produce more cloth which it can exchange for Country B's corn. In this way, world production of both cloth and corn is stimulated and both countries benefit from the trading relationship. The Heckscher-Ohlin model develops this standard argument further, and argues that if corn is labour-intensive relative to cloth, and if labour is relatively abundant in Country B, then that country will specialise in corn production. As production continues, there is a tendency for factor prices (including wages) to be equalised; this is because, as Country B specialises in corn production, its production pattern becomes more labour-intensive, thus reducing labour abundance and increasing productivity and wages. Meanwhile, in Country A, as cloth production increases, labour will become less scarce, and productivity and wages will fall. In the long run, there is a tendency towards equilibrium in international trade.

This can be further illustrated by introducing money into the analysis. Country A produces cloth at a cost of 40 units and corn at a cost of 45, while B produces cloth at 60 units and corn at 50. Initially, A produces both commodities more cheaply and the products are exported to B. A thus has a trade surplus and B a deficit. Clearly, this situation cannot continue indefinitely, but orthodox theory argues that equilibrium can be automatically restored, so long as free trade operates. In a situation of floating exchange rates, devaluation of B's currency will occur as demand for that currency falls. The result will be that its imports (A's exports) will become more expensive, and its exports (A's imports) will become cheaper. Exchange rates will therefore settle at a point where B's competitiveness is restored. Alternatively, in a system of fixed exchange rates, where, for example, currency values are fixed against the price of gold, gold will flow out of B and therefore lead to an expansion of A's and contraction of B's money supply. This will lead to rising prices in A and lower prices in B, so that, once again, equilibrium is restored.[62]

---

[62] See Shaikh 1979.

It was Ricardo[63] who first formulated the theory of comparative advantage, but he also pointed out that such a 'win-win' situation had to satisfy certain conditions. Most crucially, he argued that for free trade to be mutually beneficial, the factors of production (land, labour and capital) must be immobile and countries must have equal capacities to produce goods.[64] This, in turn, rested on the assumptions of balanced trade, perfect competition and full employment. For orthodox trade theory and Kitching, Desai and others, these conditions are not necessary for free trade to be mutually beneficial, and they particularly argue that the mobility of capital favours increased trade and investment for developing countries.

However, if we return to the examples of cloth and corn, and Countries A and B above, there is an alternative scenario. First, in a system of floating exchange rates, the devaluation of B's currency may not lead to an automatic correction based on cheaper exports and more expensive imports. Resources may be slow to move out of cloth and into corn (and vice versa in Country A). This problem may be exacerbated by workers winning higher wages to compensate for higher import prices, or by employers or landlords taking higher profits through the higher prices for their products. There is, thus, some question about the ease and speed with which capital can move from one sector to another, and questions concerning the distribution of income and profits between different social groups. Moreover, it is far from clear that a fall in the money supply will have the desired effect of restoring equilibrium. Instead, as money supply falls, interest rates will increase. This may have the effect of attracting money from Country A, but there is no guarantee that this will be used for productive purposes so that the balance of trade deficit can be reduced. Indeed, high interest rates will discourage investment in production and divert money into unproductive, financial speculation. In this way, uneven development continues through the unequal development of productive structures between A and B. This can continue for some time, as the trade surplus Country (A) diverts money to the trade deficit Country (B), and so assures balance of payments requirements are met, but it is unclear how long this can go on if the trade deficit becomes unsustainable.[65]

---

[63] Ricardo 1981.

[64] Of course, there would be some exceptions due to climate and access to particular minerals, but the basic point is that the theory assumed that all countries had more or less equal structures of production.

[65] See Shaikh 1979–80. One potential way of sustaining this mechanism is to ensure

This scenario can be further illustrated through the example of labour costs. Orthodox theory assumes that, provided the correct (market-friendly) policies are adopted, capital will leave areas where labour costs are high, and move to areas where costs are low. This is the basic argument made by Kitching, cited above. But, as we have seen, the source of profit for capital may not be the absolute costs of labour, or the extraction of absolute surplus-value, but relative costs, or the extraction of relative surplus-value. Thus, to return to the example above, Country A's absolute advantage in both commodities may persist because capitalists in that country may successfully re-invest their capital in new technology, which allows for both higher rates of productivity *and* higher wages to co-exist. A trade surplus will not restore equilibrium, as sustained capital accumulation in Country A will lead to ongoing expansion there, while there is relatively lower expansion in B. This may eventually come up against certain limits, and particularly A's selling of goods to B will be limited, but the key point is that it is perfectly possible for A to enjoy sustained competitive advantages over B. This will be further intensified as high rates of accumulation in A will further expand the market there, and thus further undermine the competitive position of B (though this will be relative and not absolute – see below). Capital – and therefore suppliers, markets, infrastructure, skills and credit – will tend to concentrate in A, and, to a relative extent, by-pass B.

In this view then, just as competition between capitals *within* nations leads to uneven development based on the search for surplus profit and over-accumulation (see above), so too does it occur *between* countries (and sectors across countries). Free trade does not lead to automatic adjustment based on the equilibrium of perfect competition, but, instead, leads to uneven development based on the competitive accumulation of capital, and the unequal competition that occurs as a result. Anwar Shaikh effectively summarises this alternative view:

> It is only by raising both the level and the growth rate of productivity that a country can, in the long run, prosper in international trade. . . . [This] will not happen by itself, through the magic of free trade. On the contrary,

that your domestic currency is also the dominant international currency, without any attachments to a separate measure such as gold. As we will see in the chapters that follow, this is precisely what has occurred since the early 1970s in the case of the US dollar. However, even in this case, there remain questions about the long term sustainability of its trade deficit. See especially Chapter 4.

precisely because free trade reflects the uneven development of nations, by itself it tends to reproduce and even deepen the very inequality on which it was founded. It follows that success in the free market requires extensive and intensive social, political, and infrastructural support.[66]

Thus, rather than the equilibrium of perfect competition, Shaikh rightly argues that uneven development is a central feature of the world capitalist economy. Contrary to both Kitching's hopes and the claims of Hecksher and Ohlin, capital does not automatically move from areas of abundance to areas of scarcity, but actually tends to be attracted to existing areas of accumulation. This is not an absolute law, but the tendencies towards concentration are so great that they undermine any notion of equilibrium through automatic, market-based adjustment. This concentration of capital is a product of the competitive accumulation of capital. The introduction of new technology 'will usually contain an element of monopoly rent, [and so] it is not surprising that scarce factors of production like capital and skilled labour will, contrary to the expectations of orthodox economists, tend to be drawn towards areas where they are already abundant'.[67] Ricardo's provisos concerning the mutual benefits of free trade do not hold, and balanced trade, perfect competition and full employment do not exist. Therefore, countries do not have equal capacities to compete in the world economy, either through resource endowments or absolute costs, and so the unqualified case for free trade is undermined.

This does not mean that the world economy is structured into a timeless core-periphery divide, as underdevelopment theory contended in the 1960s. Neither does it mean that capital absolutely concentrates in some regions and totally marginalises others. Capital does flow to new spaces of accumulation in various forms, such as aid, direct foreign investment, portfolio investment and loans. However, as we will see in the chapters that follow, these flows do not lead to a new equilibrium, but, instead, alongside existing agglomeration tendencies, lead to new manifestations of uneven development, albeit in the context of the dynamic accumulation of capital.[68] Thus, to take one example, contrary to a lot of globalisation rhetoric, the world economy is not a level

---

[66] Shaikh 1996, p. 76.
[67] Toye 1985, p. 10.
[68] Weeks 2001.

playing field in which 'development' automatically takes place though policies of liberalisation. Indeed, in the world economy, the competition between capitals is mediated by relations between nation-states, which, historically, has provided some potential for alleviating the effects of uneven development and unequal competition.[69] Moreover, in a boom period, where there is a high rate of capital accumulation, the worst effects of uneven development can be mitigated in the context of high growth rates and cheap access to credit. For example, in the period from the 1940s to the early 1980s, there were both high rates of economic growth and considerable scope for state intervention to offset competition in the form of cheap imports. The globalisation era has seen a change in both rates of growth, which (with some exceptions) have generally been much slower, and in the forms of state intervention, which have become more 'market-friendly'.

Marx was himself acutely aware of the unequal nature of the interdependent world, arguing for example that New-World slavery made an important contribution to the industrial revolution in Britain. He also explicitly argued that his account of the transition to capitalism in England was not an account of a universal law of history, but was *expressly* restricted to *the countries of Western Europe*.[70] Similarly, he also became increasingly aware that colonialism was not leading to the replication of the English model, as it was not developing capitalist relations of production or promoting widespread capital investment. He criticised the 'bleeding process' whereby the British extracted resources from India for the benefit of the British ruling class, and talked about 'English vandalism' in India, 'which pushed the indigenous people not forward but backward'.[71] Clearly, Marx's more critical view of colonialism was more accurate than his apology for colonialism as the promoter of capitalism, because colonialism in general did not promote sustained capital accumulation through the extraction of relative surplus-value. Instead, capital investment into the colonies was limited, and forced labour based on the extraction of absolute surplus-value was promoted, alongside the reinforcement of peasant labour.[72]

---

[69] Lacher 2000; Chang 2002.
[70] Marx 1984, p. 124.
[71] Cited in Larrain 1989, p. 49.
[72] Emmanuel 1974; Phillips 1987.

Perhaps most important, Marx argued that capitalism was not only a national phenomenon, but that it was global from the start. International capitalism was not only associated with dynamic centres of accumulation, but was also based on a hierarchically structured international division of labour, in which some regions were in a subordinate position compared to others. He argued that 'the veiled slavery of the wage earners in Europe need the unqualified slavery of the New World as its pedestal', and that 'commerce in countries which export principally raw produce increased the misery of the masses'.[73] These comments reflect the ambiguous relationship between capitalism and colonialism.[74] Colonies were integrated into capitalist international division of labour, but *intentional* or planned development hindered capitalist (immanent) development. In the 'advanced' capitalist countries, intentional development such as poor laws and (limited) public health provision was a response to contradictions of immanent development, whereas in the colonies, intentional development pre-empted these contradictions by holding back capitalist development, through for example the reinforcing of peasant production and restrictions placed on 'free' labour.[75] Marx's earlier support for free trade was also qualified, and he argued that protection for industrialists was progressive compared to protection for merchants. In the same speech, he also stated that '[i]f the free traders cannot understand how one nation can grow rich at the expense of another, we need not wonder, since these same gentlemen also refuse to understand how within one country one class can enrich itself at the expense of another'.[76]

It was this analysis – or a one-sided interpretation of it – that later came to be associated with Marxist 'anti-imperialism', at least from the 1928 Congress of the Third International, which first proposed a strategy of alliances against stagnant imperialist capitalism, through to underdevelopment and dependency theories in the post-war period. The Comintern under Stalin argued that imperialism was a reactionary force that had ceased to develop the productive forces in the colonies and semi-colonies, and so Communists should support popular alliances against foreign capital. In the post-war period, and from the 1960s in particular, some radicals argued that the world was divided into

---

[73] Marx 1976, p. 925; Marx and Engels 1974, p. 298.
[74] Phillips 1987.
[75] Cowen and Shenton 1996.
[76] Marx 1984, pp. 269–70.

the developed world and the underdeveloped world, and the former had developed precisely because it had underdeveloped the latter.[77] These theories were undermined by the rise of the East-Asian newly industrialising countries in particular, along with the poor economic and social record of those countries that attempted to 'delink' from the world economy. They also failed to spell out the mechanisms by which underdevelopment supposedly took place, proposing a vague and ahistorical concept of surplus extraction. But if such a surplus was extracted through trade and investment, and this was the reason for the enrichment of the developed world, then the evidence suggested that this was not a very effective strategy, as trade and investment increasingly concentrated in the 'advanced' countries. Indeed, the fact that most trade and production takes place in these established areas, suggests that the uneven development of capital accumulation outlined above, has led to a relative marginalisation of other regions. The poverty of much of the world is in part a product of relative marginalisation by capital, not surplus extraction.[78]

This debate over global uneven development is central to the arguments that follow. It has a resonance way beyond the narrow debates associated with the Marxist tradition, as we shall see. However, within Marxist thought, it has too often suffered from an ahistorical approach to the understanding of capitalism. The evolutionism of linear Marxism has too often given way to the functionalism of underdevelopment theory, whereby particular regions are assumed to take their place in a never-ending hierarchy of the international division of labour. In this account, historical processes of uneven development are replaced by the static concept of underdevelopment, in which all changes that have taken place in the global order over the last two hundred years are reduced to an ahistorical logic of capitalism.[79] Certainly, international capitalism

---

[77] Frank 1969, p. 240.

[78] See Kiely 1995, Chapters 3 and 5. Surplus extraction may, of course, take place through a redistribution of surplus-value. This, for example, may occur through the use of a national currency as the international currency, which allows the country that issues the currency to import goods higher than the value of the currency which pays for such goods (see footnote 8). Indeed, this practice is a feature of the current era of globalisation, in which the dollar plays this role (see Chapters 3 and 4). The argument in the text, however, is that the division of the world into developed and underdeveloped countries cannot be explained through a timeless process of surplus extraction.

[79] Indeed, as we shall see in Chapter 8, while many Marxist 'anti-imperialist' accept the broad thrust of the critique of the economic analysis of underdevelopment theory, they often remain tied to a political analysis in which 'anti-imperialism' becomes

has been characterised by a hierarchical international division of labour, but the particular form that this has taken has changed over time.

Instead of this ahistorical account, we need to *'historicize theory* and problematize globalization as a relation immanent in capitalism, but with quite distinct material (social, political, and environmental) relations across time and time-space'.[80] In so doing, we can better understand that capitalism was globalising from the start, but also the ways in which contemporary globalisation – the main concern of this book – is both distinctive from, and similar to, earlier periods of global capitalism. Our main concern in the chapters that follow is to examine the ways in which globalisation since the 1970s arose out of the crisis of post-war international capitalism. This is reflected in the breakdown of the post-war Bretton Woods system, the 'decline' of US hegemony, and the rise of neo-liberalism and related expansion of the 'free market' and dominance of financial capital.

2.3 Conclusion

This chapter has made five arguments about capitalism and five arguments about globalisation. First, capitalism is the most dynamic mode of production in history. Second, its dynamism is rooted in the competitive accumulation of capital through the extraction of relative surplus-value (which presupposes the emergence of capitalist social relations). Third, this dynamic process is prone to crises of over-accumulation. Fourth, capitalist dynamism leads to the incorporation of more and more parts of the world into its orbit. However, this process is uneven and takes a variety of unequal forms. This undermines optimistic 'developmental' accounts based on the notion of diffusion through cosmopolitan capital, but also pessimistic 'underdevelopment' based accounts of a timeless core-periphery global divide. Fifth, although there is no *necessary* relationship between *national* states and capitalist social relations, the nation-state has been, and remains the dominant form of organising and expanding

---

support for all social and political forces in the developing world against the might of the United States and its allies. In these accounts, the US and/or the West, is often seen as so omnipotent that it is always pulling the strings, so that agency in the developing world is reduced to Western interests, except in situations of overt conflict such as war – when former US allies are miraculously turned into objective anti-imperialists.

[80] McMichael 2001, p. 202.

these relations. From the start, territorially fluid capitalist social relations have been mediated by nation states.

How then, do these points relate to the question of contemporary globalisation. First, it is neither a free-floating (Giddens) nor a purely technologically driven phenomenon (Castells). Second, the precise relationship between nation-states and 'global' capitalist social relations has varied over time. For instance, the crisis of the 1870s paved the way for intensified inter-imperialist rivalries, war and revolution, while the 1930s crisis led to a reversal of the internationalisation of capital. Third, the current era (1971/3 to the present) has seen intensified (and uneven) capitalist globalisation, based, as we will see, on liberalisation of trade, investment and finance. Fourth, these very different tendencies and outcomes cannot therefore be solely explained by the logic of capitalism. We therefore need to look at how specific (and connected but not reducible) *processes and strategies of globalisation* relate to wider social and political structures, and vice versa. In so doing, we are in a better position to understand that these processes have not simply 'come from nowhere' as Giddens claims, and that they are a product of particular agents, embedded in particular places, and based on particular power relations (and therefore relations of conflict). Fifth, and finally, contemporary globalisation must therefore be understood as a specific period within capitalism, but which, to some extent, also has its own distinctive characteristics. These broad points are concretised in the rest of the book, with Chapters 3 to 5 focusing on actually existing globalisation, and Chapters 6 to 9 on the question of political alternatives.

Chapter Three

From Bretton Woods to Neo-Liberal Globalisation

In the last chapter, we argued for an approach that understood contemporary globalisation in terms of a specific relationship to capitalism, but also in such a way that it was not reducible to capitalism. This chapter undertakes this task by identifying the origins of globalisation in the post-war period, and, in particular, the international agreement at Bretton Woods in 1944. The chapter outlines the development of international capitalism from 1944 to significant changes that occurred from the early 1970s through to the 1980s, which ultimately produced the current era of globalisation. These shifts included intensified competition between the leading capitalist states and 'declining' US hegemony, the growing internationalisation of capital, changes in the international monetary system which included the collapse of dollar-gold convertibility and fixed exchange rates, the move to monetarism in the US and UK, and the debt crisis. Together, these changes reflected the emergence of a new era of neo-liberal capitalism in the 1980s.

This chapter documents the shift from the neo-Keynesian, 'Fordist' capitalism from 1947 to the late 1960s and early 1970s, to the neo-liberal era. The opening section examines the Bretton Woods agreement, US hegemony, and the post-war boom. The second section examines the tensions in this system and the breakdown of Bretton Woods and the economic boom, and documents the movement towards neo-liberalism in the 1970s. Section Three then examines neo-liberalism in the 1980s, focusing on US economic policy from the late 1970s onwards, and the 1980s debt crisis (and the relationship between the two).

3.1 The Golden Age: post-war capitalism, 1947 to 1973

(i) *US hegemony and the Bretton Woods agreement*

Eager to avoid the competitive austerity of the 1930s, which included currency devaluations to enhance market share in a context of declining world trade, the capitalist world agreed on the need for a rules-based system after the Second World War. The settlement at Bretton Woods in 1944 was based on an uneasy compromise between neo-classical and Keynesian theory. The first question that needed to be addressed concerned that of what was to be the international currency that would facilitate international trade (which had collapsed in the depression of the 1930s). The British representative, John Maynard Keynes argued for an international currency, the bancor, which could be used to automatically redistribute finance from surplus to deficit countries, thereby insuring that countries would have the buying power to participate in trade on a sustained basis. Keynes envisaged this occurring through an international clearing union, which would act as a kind of international collective capitalist, over and above the wishes of specific capitalist states, transferring savings from surplus to deficit countries, and thereby maintaining effective demand in the world economy. All countries would have an interest in maintaining this system – deficit countries would avoid having to deflate their own economies to restore balance of payments equilibrium, while surplus countries would be provided with a means of using resources, which would otherwise stand idle, and it would guarantee them expanding markets in the deficit countries.

Keynes's ideas were, however, rejected, above all by the United States' government. Instead, the dollar became the international means of payment, in a system in which the prices of national currencies were fixed against the price of the dollar, and the dollar was priced at $35 for an ounce of gold. In 1944, this appeared to be a reasonable solution because the US was by far the most powerful economy in the world, and the rest of the world faced a shortage of foreign exchange. In 1945, the US controlled 70 per cent of the world's financial assets and was as overwhelmingly dominant in terms of productive assets too. For orthodox neo-classical theory, higher wages and costs in the US should have led to an automatic adjustment in which capital left the US and flowed to lower-cost areas, but, in fact, US reserves increased in the immediate post-war era, and the US ran balance of trade surpluses until 1971.[1] This situation was potentially disastrous from the viewpoint of the system as a whole. From the US's point of view, its industries (or some of them) faced potential surplus capacity if they could not find foreign markets, thus threatening full employment if overseas buyers for US products could not be found. This was a particularly acute problem in the immediate post-war period, as the economies of scale generated by technological change and work re-organisation meant that the most advanced industries – such as automobiles – needed continued, expanding demand.[2] There was also the political threat of communism, which was immediately apparent in much of Europe and Japan during and immediately after the war, and became even more of an issue from 1949, following the Chinese Revolution. For the US, the threat of communism was intensified by economic instability, which in turn was caused by a shortage of internationally acceptable money in the capitalist world – in other words, there was a world-wide shortage of dollars. The dollar was therefore effectively used to stimulate the recovery of the capitalist world, as the US ran balance of payments deficits, initially through US Marshall Aid to Europe, and later through very high rates of military spending in Korea (the 1950s) and Vietnam (the 1960s), and increasing rates of direct foreign investment. In this way, a potential liquidity shortage was averted and, between 1950 and 1958, the foreign exchange component of world reserves increased by nearly $7 billion.[3] This expansion enabled some countries to buy US goods on favourable terms, including capital as well as consumer goods. While this was clearly a system which benefited some of the US's potential competitors, there was also some benefit to the US, as it could run

---

[1] These surpluses declined over time, but the reasons had little or nothing to do with orthodox theory as the exposition in the main text makes clear.
[2] Schwartz 2000, p. 180.
[3] Glyn et al. 1990, pp. 69–70.

balance of payments deficits on its overseas accounts without having to deflate its economy – an issue that was also crucial to the system's collapse.

Under this post-war order then, international trade increased through the dollar-gold exchange system. Short-term balance of payments problems were regulated by the International Monetary Fund (IMF), while the free movement of capital (especially financial capital) was strictly regulated by national governments. There was a long-term commitment to free trade in goods and services, reflected in various rounds of selective tariff reduction through meetings of the General Agreement on Tariffs and Trade, but some room for manoeuvre was granted to states so that they could protect themselves from potentially unequal competition (essentially from the United States). Ultimate backing for this system was provided by the military power of the United States, which spent enormous amounts of money and had large military bases overseas. This presence was justified by the need to protect the 'free world' from the supposed threat of communist expansion. In short, the post-war system did not conform to the expectations of neo-classical orthodoxy, and the move towards a system of growing international trade was consciously managed, above all by the United States, which ran balance of payments deficits and dominated the capitalist world in terms of military power.

(ii) *The post-war boom*

The system worked quite effectively for a period of time. This was the so-called Golden Age of capitalism, where the advanced capitalist countries enjoyed high rates of growth in output and consumption, almost full employment, and welfare rights (although these did vary and convergence was far from absolute). The boom was facilitated by high rates of labour productivity, based on a strict division of labour and the utilisation of technology that was mechanised to an unprecedented extent.[4] A virtuous circle therefore emerged in which high rates of profit facilitated high rates of capital accumulation, which in turn led to unprecedented economic growth, high productivity, high wages and expanding demand. Annual growth rates from 1950–73 averaged 2.2 per cent (USA), 2.5 per cent (UK), 4.1 per cent (France), 5 per cent (Germany) and a massive 8.4 per cent for Japan.[5]

---

[4] Armstrong et al. 1990, Chapter 8.
[5] Glyn et al. 1990, p. 47.

This period from around 1947 to 1973 has been described as the era of 'high Fordism'.[6] These unprecedented rates of economic growth were facilitated by the extension of mass production systems to more and more sectors in the economies of the 'advanced' countries, paid for initially by the US balance of payments deficits that were consistently run from 1952. The Fordist system was based on highly capital-intensive machinery, rigid divisions of labour within the workplace, and massive production runs on specific products. This system involved high initial start-up costs, but unit costs declined with the development of large-scale production batches. The Fordist system also promoted the development of mass consumption of relatively standardised products. In practice, this system was unevenly implemented, and many sectors did not develop Fordist techniques. However, it was sufficiently generalised, particularly in the leading economic sectors such as car production, electronics, and light engineering, for it to have a wider impact.[7] High rates of accumulation in these sectors were reinforced by the availability of low-cost primary products, particularly oil, which became the major raw material fuelling the post-war boom. From 1940 to 1974, the proportion of oil in the world's energy supply increased from 21 per cent to over 67 per cent. Before the oil price rises of 1973–4, prices were very low, with crude prices as low as $1.8 a barrel for much of the post-war era.[8]

The development of Fordist techniques was not simply a victory for capital, but also reflected the balance of class forces after the end of the War. For the post-war era also led not only to mass consumption, but also to the development of neo-Keynesian policies that maintained demand and therefore full employment, and the development of welfare states throughout the advanced capitalist world. These developments were acceptable to capital so long as high rates of profit, accumulation and investment were maintained. Indeed, such arrangements even functioned effectively for capital in that

---

[6] Harvey 1989, Chapter 8.

[7] Marxists such as Clarke 1992, 1994, who reject any periodisation of capitalism, overestimate the extent to which general features of capitalism can be used as explanations irrespective of time and place. Certainly the Fordist (and post-Fordist) characterisations can lead to rigid separations of particular periods, but, if used carefully, can lead to sensitivity to the specific nature of periods within capitalism. Clarke, on the other hand, appears content to read off specificities from general features of capitalist accumulation, even though his own work implies the need for more historically specific analyses (see, especially, Clarke 1988).

[8] Itoh 1990, pp. 33–4.

demand for the products in the consumer goods sectors remained high. Once again, this did not mean that the mass production-mass consumption relationship was generalised. Poverty levels remained high, and, within the labour market, there was significant differentiation. In particular, the expansion of labour forces due to rural-urban migration, increased female participation, and international migration provided a crucial source of cheap labour for capital, but also opened up a divide between a relatively privileged core labour force, and those in less privileged positions in the labour market. But the boom was still important in opening up gains for these more privileged sections of organised labour, while, at the same time, their representative organisations (trade unions, and particularly trade-union leaders) generally agreed to accept managerial controls within, and a de-politicisation of demands beyond, the workplace. Labour therefore accepted – or in some cases was forced to accept through repression – a continued subordinate position in society, but also won concessions for the most privileged and organised sectors in the forms of high wages, more consumer goods, promotion prospects and increased social protection.[9] Zolberg[10] characterises this post-war order of governance in the advanced countries as one based on 'labor-friendly regimes', in which the post-war boom rested on an unequal social compromise between capital, labour and the state, which worked effectively so long as profitability and capital accumulation were maintained.

In the developing world, too, there were also high rates of growth. From 1950–75, income per person in the developing world grew by an average of 3 per cent a year, including high rates of 3.4 per cent a year for the 1960s, which was higher than growth rates for the advanced countries in their years of take-off.[11] These rates of growth led to considerable optimism about the potential for development, including in the poorest parts of the developing world.[12] And, in some respects, the post-war order did provide a favourable context for development to take place. For instance, although there was a long-term commitment to free trade in the international order, GATT agreements allowed for some flexibility in terms of trade restrictions. These often worked against the interests of primary producers in the developing world, and there

---

[9] Panitch 1981; Burawoy 1983.
[10] Zolberg 1995.
[11] Glyn et al. 1990, pp. 41–2.
[12] Leys 1996, pp. 107–09.

were complaints that the rich countries were using the GATT in a discriminatory fashion. But, at the same time, in the 1950s and 1960s, many developing countries industrialised behind protective tariffs, and these economic gains were often accompanied by important social gains (which also varied in important respects), such as in health and education. This was particularly true in East Asia, which combined export promotion and import substitution policies, so that (selected) domestic industries were allowed to develop at home, protected from cheap imports from abroad. The most successful exporters were then granted ongoing protection and access to key imports by the state.[13] By the 1970s and 1980s, the first-tier newly industrialising countries (South Korea, Taiwan, Hong Kong, Singapore) had become major exporters, mainly to the richer countries. In the 1970s, for example, South Korea's export growth rates averaged 37 per cent a year.[14] Although the East-Asian miracle was later interpreted as one that was a product of neo-liberal, market-friendly policies,[15] and then later re-interpreted again once financial crises broke out in the region, it should be clear that these were economic miracles in which the developmental state was central. Moreover, while the developmental successes in this region only became apparent in the 1970s and especially the 1980s, these successes originated in state policies carried out from the 1960s. These policies allowed the state to direct capital investment through credit allocation, state planning, capital controls and some public-sector investment.[16] Capital was therefore in some respects heavily regulated by the state, and indeed successful capitalist development rested on such regulation of individual capitalists, as well as authoritarian controls over labour.

In some respects, then, the post-war order can also be characterised as one in which a 'development-friendly' régime existed.[17] The United States supported national liberation for the colonies, so long as such movements were not too radical, and promoted 'development' for the ex-colonies. In the words of President Truman in 1949:

> We must embark on a bold new program for making the benefits of our
> scientific advances and industrial progress available for the improvement

---

[13] Amsden 1989; Wade 1990; Kiely 1998, Chapters 7 and 8.
[14] Kiely 1998, p. 97.
[15] World Bank 1993.
[16] Wade 1990.
[17] Silver and Slater 1999, pp. 208–11.

and growth of underdeveloped countries. The old imperialism – exploitation for foreign profit – has no place in our plans. What we envisage is a program of development based on the concepts of democratic fair dealing. Greater production is the key to prosperity and peace. And the key to greater production is a wider and vigorous application of modern scientific and technical knowledge.[18]

In practice, and despite the concrete advances that were made in the post-war period, much of Truman's statement was either rhetoric or a concrete attempt to de-politicise the issue of what later came to be known as the North-South divide. There was no Marshall Plan for the developing world, aid was often tied to strategic and commercial interests, and development was to be carried out through attracting capital investment, albeit with some state protection. In the context of underdeveloped infrastructures, skills and technology, this effectively meant that cheap and controlled labour was the major attraction for investment.[19] Similarly, at the international level, there was a commitment to multilateralism through the GATT and the UN, but, in practice, this was restricted by discrimination and veto powers, as well as unequal voting power at the IMF and World Bank. It is certainly true that some economic and social advances were made in this period in the developing world, but these were uneven and unequal and, with a few exceptions, never remotely amounted to anything like a 'catch-up' to developed country status. For many, development remained a largely unfulfilled promise. Nevertheless, both the promise of development and the limited but real social advances that were made were generally sufficient to contain revolutionary challenges in much of the developing world in the 1950s and early 1960s (though there were, of course, some key exceptions). However, social and political unrest increased throughout the 1960s and 1970s, with the spread of revolution and the call for a new international economic order, which would restructure North-South relations. These events compounded the challenges to US hegemony.

[18] Cited in Silver and Slater 1999, p. 208.
[19] Kiely 1996, Chapter 3.

3.2 The end of the Golden Age and the rise of neo-liberalism

(i) *The breakdown of Bretton Woods*

As a system of regulating international trade and monetary payments, the Bretton Woods system had its contradictions. The key problem was that the dollar was not only an international currency, it was the US's national currency too. Therefore, its value relative to other currencies ultimately depended on the competitiveness of the United States economy. If it was seriously weakened, its gold reserves would erode, and it would therefore have to devalue. In other words, the dollar would no longer be as 'good as gold'. On the other hand, in 1944 onwards, the supply of international currency to the rest of the world depended on the US transferring dollars abroad – that is, it depended on the US running a balance of payments deficit. This contradiction was a consequence of the fact that the dollar was not only the international means of payment, but was the domestic currency for the United States. The US's decision to run ongoing balance of payments deficits had the effect of undermining its value; as Pillay states, 'instead of providing a mechanism of monetary discipline designed to sustain the purchasing power of the dollar and hence its stability, US policies soon converted this mechanism into its opposite: into an ever ballooning international credit cycle having its source in the American credit economy, and the accelerating deficits in the US balance of payments'.[20] The dollar shortage of the 1940s had become a problem of too many dollars by the late 1960s.

The problem of the dollar shortage was not inevitable, provided that the US maintained its lead in production over any competitors. However, its share of total manufacturing goods in the world market declined from 28 per cent in 1957 to 16 per cent in 1970,[21] and this undermined the international demand for dollars. Moreover, the growth of productivity in the US economy slowed down more quickly, as the absorption of new technologies became exhausted more quickly than in Germany and Japan. This then, was the basic problem faced by the United States. It resolved the problem of dollar shortage by providing international credit from the 1940s, thus allowing the restoration

---

[20] Pillay 1983, p. 25.
[21] Itoh 1990, p. 48.

of international trade through payments in dollars. But this policy was at the long-term cost of undermining its own productive capacity and competitiveness. By the mid-1960s, the US had a constant trade deficit with its two main competitors, Japan and Germany.[22] This problem manifested itself in terms of money, as the US's competitors in Western Europe and Japan no longer needed as many dollars to buy US goods, so dollars stockpiled in European banks. The Eurocurrency market developed from the 1950s and it was basically a market in externally held currencies – mainly dollars. These deposits fell outside the control of normal domestic banking regulations, and so banks that used Eurodollars could lend more cheaply, pay higher interest rates and still make more profits. These Eurodollars reflected the US's erosion in competitiveness, as such dollars would have returned to the US as payment for goods, had it been able to sell more goods to its competitors.[23] In the early 1960s, some attempts were made to impose controls on the export of capital from the United States, but these were far from comprehensive, and the US government recognised that the Eurodollar market was in many respects a welcome development as well as a source of concern in terms of maintaining the value of the dollar. In particular, these markets facilitated the overseas expansion of US capital. This included the expansion of US banks that took advantage of the lack of controls over these dollars, a policy that was tolerated or even encouraged by the US state.[24] It also included the expansion of US transnational companies that set up production sites in Europe, in order to take advantage of market access and higher productivity, and which found the Eurodollar markets a cheap source of finance. This investment further encouraged the development of Fordism in Europe, and led to the intensification of the internationalisation of capital flows, which increased further with the rise of European and Japanese foreign investment. Although TNCs had existed before the Second World War, they had mainly invested in primary products, but, from the 1950s onwards, an increasing proportion of TNC investment was in manufacturing, and it tended to be from advanced capitalist countries to other advanced capitalist countries, although a few richer 'Third-World' countries gained some substantial share of total DFI. The overwhelming tendency, however, was for capital to concentrate in richer

---

[22] Brenner 1998, p. 119.
[23] Schwartz 2000, pp. 204–5.
[24] Helleiner 1994a, Chapter 4.

countries.[25] These processes of internationalisation – of both production and finance – were thus cautiously welcomed by the US state, not least because, in terms of finance, they reinforced the role of the dollar as the main international currency, even though there were serious questions over the dollar's value.

The problem of the value of the dollar was intensified by the US's continued – and growing – military commitments overseas, especially in Vietnam. This escalated the American deficit, so that it was 'importing more and more real resources in exchange for paper tokens whose backing was becoming increasingly devalued, but which the rest of the world was forced to accept by the terms of the Bretton Woods agreement'.[26] The US's trade balance of $10 billion in 1947 and $6.6 billion in 1964, declined to $0.6 billion by 1968. The balance of payments was in constant deficit from 1950, but soared from -$2.5 billion in 1968 to -$19.8 billion in 1971. In that same year, the US ran a trade as well as payments deficit for the first time.[27] Europe was holding more and more dollars, the value of which was being increasingly undermined, and which, in effect, was in exchange for their own output; whereas US consumption could be sustained by the printing of more dollars, but at the cost of further undermining the US's competitive position. The result of this dollar glut was an increase in inflation, enhanced by the fact that productivity increases were slowing down.

It should be clear, then, that while the US dollar deficit was essential to the post-war economic recovery, it was at the long-term cost of undermining the competitive strength of the US economy. There was a basic contradiction between the dollar as the national currency of the US, and the dollar as the international currency. Its value relative to other currencies rested on the viability of the US economy, for if this became so weakened that it could not compete, or if the US government adopted inflationary policies, which increased its balance of payments deficit, its foreign exchange reserves would disappear and it would have to devalue. The basic problem then was that the supply of US dollars to the rest of the world depended on the US deficit, but the stability of the dollar depended on the US economy returning to surplus.

---

[25] See Chapter 5.
[26] Brett 1983, p. 165.
[27] Brett 1983, p. 173.

These problems cut across a number of competing interests. From the viewpoint of the US, the deficit guaranteed military supremacy, but also reflected a decline in US productive power located in the 'home economy', while, at the same time, guaranteeing expanded consumption without normal balance of payments constraints (because of the role of the dollar). From the viewpoint of the European powers, their surpluses meant that their foreign exchange reserves were constantly expanding, but these of course were mostly held in dollars. Devaluation would wipe out the value of some of these savings, but if the US deficit continued, there was the problem of growing inflation – existing side by side with slower rates of economic growth due to falling profit rates and declining productivity increases. In either case, the problem manifested itself as a dollar glut in which excess dollars in the international economy were increasingly worthless.

The struggle between these competing interests culminated in the breakdown of key parts of the Bretton Woods agreement in the period 1971–3. The 1944 agreement was based on four key principles:

(i) the US dollar was to be the main international currency and its value was convertible to gold at a fixed price;

(ii) exchange rates were fixed in the rest of the system, though there was some limited room for managed change in exceptional circumstances;

(iii) open monetary and trading relationships;

(iv) the IMF was to play a key regulatory role in supervising this system and providing short-term balance of payments finance to countries in difficulty.[28]

The first of these was effectively ended by the Nixon administration's decision to abandon gold convertibility and allow the dollar to float downwards in 1971. Whether or not this decision reflected weakness or a new source of strength for the US is a contentious point,[29] but its effects were clear. The US could now continue to sustain a deficit and devalue while still sustaining high levels of imports and consumption. In effect, the size of the transfer of real resources from the surplus countries to the US increased. This had the benefit of expanding the market for output, and left the US to pay for military defence of the existing order, but at the cost of a dollar standard system 'in

---

[28] Brett 1983, p. 173.
[29] See Chapter 4.

which there were no effective limits on the ability of the centre country to debase the value of the tokens in pursuit of its own military and economic objectives'.[30] The end of dollar-gold convertibility was followed by a number of planned devaluations between 1971–3, which in turn led to an abandonment of the system of fixed exchange rates and its replacement by a 'managed floating' system from 1973.

There was considerable optimism concerning this shift to a system of floating exchange rates. Clearly, the fixed rate system did not reflect the real economic power of different states and their currencies and so had to be changed. In accord with orthodox equilibrium trade theories, the hope was that adjustments would be made to the value of currencies, so that an automatic fall in the exchange rate would lead to an automatic increase in the competitiveness of exports, thus restoring trade balances. But, as we saw in Chapter 2, more likely than automatic adjustment is a time lag where labour moves slowly from uncompetitive to competitive industries, and where interest rates increase as the money supply falls. This may have the effect of encouraging speculative flows of money into a country, a phenomenon that increased enormously with the gradual dismantling of capital controls in the 1970s, and which led to an increase in the value of the currency without stimulating productive investment. In other words, the movement away from the fixed exchange rates and capital control system of Bretton Woods, to a new system of floating rates and freer capital movement changed the context of domestic economic policy. In the case of the former, the domestic and the international were reconciled by policies that maintained the value of a domestic currency relative to gold or dollars, and promoted sufficient expansion to maintain full employment, at least in the 'advanced' capitalist countries. Thus, interest rates could be directly used to slow or increase investment and consumption. However, with the development of the Eurodollar market, followed by the end of fixed exchange rates, the context in which state monetary policy operated was increasingly internationalised. Policies designed to maintain growth and employment could now put pressure on the exchange rate and foreign-exchange reserves, as financial speculators would sell local currency in favour of safer foreign currencies. The fall in reserves would have a deflationary effect on the economy. Mainstream economic theory suggests

---

[30] Brett 1983, p. 177.

that a fall in the exchange rate presents no problem as equilibrium can be restored through the increase in competitiveness that will occur through a lower value currency and therefore cheaper exports. However, as we saw in Chapter 2, a more likely scenario is a discrepancy between trade and payments, as high interest rates encourage the movement of (speculative) capital back into a country and therefore currency appreciation, but at the cost of expensive exports and cheap imports – that is, a declining position in terms of trade. Helleiner effectively captures these changes when he states that

> [w]here Bretton Woods sacrificed financial freedom in the interests of preserving exchange rate stability and a liberal trading order, a mirror image emerged in the 1970s and 1980s as stable money and liberal trade were increasingly sacrificed to the goal of financial freedom.[31]

I return to this theme below.

The final two characteristics of the 1944 agreement remained in place, but, even in these cases, some important changes had occurred. First, the commitment to open monetary and trading relationships was reflected in ongoing GATT agreements and the creation of the World Trade Organisation in 1995, but such commitment has been limited by strong disagreement between countries and – not unrelated to such disputes – a highly selective pro-free-trade agenda. The fourth factor – the role of the IMF – remains in place, and in fact has become more significant since 1982. To understand how this occurred we need to examine the causes and consequences of the 1982 debt crisis. This is examined in Section 3 below, along with the question of the response of the US state to declining economic hegemony. But, first, we need to see how the question of US decline related to the end of the post-war boom and the crisis of the 1970s.

(ii) *The end of the post-war boom*

The crises of trade and finance broadly reflected a crisis of production, as uneven development led to the undermining of US productive output and therefore international demand for the dollar. These problems were exacerbated by the end of the boom and the movement towards recession in the mid-1970s. As we have seen, high rates of accumulation in the 1950s and 1960s

---

[31] Helleiner 1994b, p. 173.

were the result of a virtuous circle of high profits, investment rates, productivity, state spending and demand, ultimately facilitated by the international role of the dollar. However, by the 1970s, the circle had turned from virtuous to vicious, as lower profits, investment rates, productivity, combined with slower demand and pressures on state spending, to produce a crisis of high inflation and high unemployment,[32] alongside a wider context of a dollar overhang and intensified competition between the major producers.

This move to recession can be linked to the exhaustion of Fordist systems of production. Once the mechanised systems of production had been introduced to those sectors that could be reorganised on Fordist lines, productivity rates were bound to slow down. Increased productivity could then only occur through the reorganisation of mechanised assembly lines, the intensification of management pressure on labour and the speeding up of already established work practices. Attempts to intensify productivity also gave rise to resistance by labour, which was confident in the face of more or less full employment. The result was a gap between wage and productivity growth, which further fuelled inflation. Government attempts to spend their way out of recession – made easier by the end of fixed exchange rates and exacerbated by the US policy of continued expansion – did not work in this less favourable context, and it simply served to intensify inflationary pressures. These problems were exacerbated further by the oil price increases in 1973–4, which finally tipped the advanced capitalist countries into a major recession in 1974–5. There was a substantial slow down in growth rates for the years 1973–80, compared to 1960–73: for the US, the latter averaged 4 per cent a year, while the former slowed down to 2.1 per cent; for the UK, the averaged slowed from 0.9 per cent; in Germany, the decline was from 4.4 per cent to 2.2 per cent; and, in Japan, growth slowed from a 9.6 per cent annual average to 3.7 per cent.[33] Unemployment rates increased from annual averages (1968–73) of 4.6 per (US), 1.2 per cent (Japan), 0.8 per cent (West Germany), 2.4 per cent (UK) to (1974–9) 6.7 per cent (US), 1.9 per cent (Japan), 3.5 per cent (West Germany), and 4.2 per cent (UK).[34] Inflation also increased over the same period, with an OECD annual average increasing from 2.9 per cent (1960–8), to 5.6 per

---

[32] Glyn et al. 1990, pp. 88–92.
[33] Coates 2000, p. 5.
[34] Green and Sutcliffe 1987, p. 315.

cent (1968–73), to 10 per cent (1973–9).[35] Growth slowed down in the developing world, too, though some of the richer developing countries borrowed heavily from banks in an attempt to maintain growth rates.

By the 1970s, the (advanced, capitalist) world looked a very different place from the 1950s and 1960s. The key features of the boom years – US hegemony through world dominance of production, high rates of growth and consumption, full employment – were a thing of the past. Indeed, given the relatively short period of the Golden Age of 'national capitalisms', and the very particular circumstances after the war, it could be the case that the era from 1947–73 were the *exceptional years*, and the era from 1973 to the present is more of a return to business as usual, albeit still with some novel features that distinguish it from previous eras of capitalist development.

3.3   Neo-liberalism in the 1980s

By the end of the 1970s, it was clear that the old neo-Keynesian policies that had helped to promote the post-war boom were now part of the problem. In particular, they exacerbated the problem of inflation in a context of slower productivity growth, falling profits, floating exchange rates and high state spending. These domestic problems were intensified by the growing importance of financial capital, and in particular the expanding Eurodollar and petrodollar markets, and the move to floating exchange rates from 1971–3, all of which served to increase financial speculation, which, in turn, reflected the global over-accumulation of capital.

It was in this context that the dominance of neo-liberalism was re-established in the 1980s. This involved the promotion of the dominance of the free market and sound money, and it was argued that together these two principles could lift the world out of recession by reducing inflation, and thus sending the right signals to investors in a properly competitive environment. In practice, neo-liberal policies meant the adoption of fiscal austerity (except in the United States after 1982), rolling back the state, privatisation, de-regulation and trade liberalisation. This involved the dismantling of the advances made by organised labour in the advanced capitalist countries, and therefore the end of labour-friendly régimes. Unemployment increased enormously, and welfare-state

---

[35]   Green and Sutcliffe 1987, p. 307.

provision often failed to keep up with public need, especially (among First-World countries) in Britain and the United States. There were some experiments with neo-liberal policies in the 1970s, particularly in Chile after 1973. In Britain from 1976, under a Labour government that borrowed money from the IMF, subject to austere conditions, there was also some movement towards a monetarist agenda. It was also in Britain under Margaret Thatcher from 1979, that neo-liberal policies were most dogmatically embraced, with disastrous consequences for public services alongside a boom for the financial sector. But more relevant to our discussion of globalisation were two other, closely related developments: first, the shifts in US policy from the late 1970s, which relate to wider questions of US state hegemony and the role of international finance; and, second, the emergence of the debt crisis and neo-liberalism in the developing world.

(i) *US hegemony and economic policy*

As we saw above, the US government's decision to abandon the gold-dollar exchange standard and fixed exchange rates potentially gave the US enormous financial power. In particular, it eliminated the need for the US to control its own balance of payments as the dollar remained the main source of international means of payments, and so (theoretically) unlimited amounts of dollars could be released into international circulation. The depreciation of the dollar in the 1970s increased the US's export competitiveness, without having an adverse effect on imports due to the absence of normal external constraints (as well as the US's lesser dependence on imports than its main competitors, including oil).

However, the United States continued to face constraints, albeit in new forms. The uncertainties of floating exchange rates encouraged a further movement away from production and into finance, as companies had to hedge against the risks associated with sudden shifts in the value of currencies. Attempts to regulate the growing Eurodollar market (now strengthened by 'petrodollars' deposited in banks by oil exporters after 1973–4) led to the movement of money into offshore money markets. Financial deregulation was in turn encouraged by the US's loose monetary policies, which further added to the enormous growth of Eurodollars. By the late 1970s, it was clear that the expansionary policies of the Nixon, Ford and Carter presidencies could no longer hold. From the mid- to late 1970s, the US ran record trade and current account deficits. At this point, Saudi Arabia began to sell dollar reserves and leading European countries made plans for developing a new currency, which could potentially become an alternative to the dollar. It was clear that there was a real threat of a crisis of confidence in the dollar, and, therefore, the international system that relied largely on this currency as a means of payment was under threat.

From 1979 onwards under Carter, and especially after the 1980 election of Reagan, there was a shift in policy in the United States. Any imposition of capital controls was rejected, and, instead, a new policy of controlling inflation was introduced. This was mainly implemented through increases in interest rates, which had the effect of squeezing domestic demand, at least in the early period of the Reagan years. It also had the effect of undermining the US as a market for developing countries' exports, and increasing debt payment obligations in the developing world.

However, this tight monetary policy of controlling inflation and sustaining the dollar through high interest rates was accompanied by a growing 'military Keynesianism', in which demand was sustained by running massive budget deficits. These deficits occurred because the Reagan government massively increased military spending in the context of a renewed Cold War with the Soviet Union,[36] while at the same time promoting a policy of reducing taxation. The wealthy in particular enjoyed enormous tax breaks, which had the effect of redistributing income from poor to rich.[37] Both trade and budget deficits were, instead, financed by attracting capital from overseas, including from the Eurodollar markets and from capital starved Latin America, and this capital was attracted by high rates of interest. The high dollar therefore had the effect of keeping domestic prices low, which helped to keep inflation rates low. Thus, the US went from being the largest creditor nation in the 1950s to the largest debtor and foreign capital recipient by the 1980s. These policies also had the side effect of lifting some other countries out of recession, as they stimulated demand for other countries' products. From 1980–5, external demand generated as much as one-third of Japan's and three quarters of West Germany's GDP. In the case of Japan, this linkage was even more direct as around one-third of its total exports went to the United States.[38] Indeed, the

---

[36] Halliday 1983.
[37] Davis 1985, p. 48.
[38] Schwartz 2000, pp. 212, 216.

relationship went deeper than this, as Japan was a major source of funding of the US deficits, and so effectively Japanese financiers provided the credit needed by the US government that continued to subsidise the continued growth of Japanese exports.[39] These policies restored one feature of the post-war order – the hegemonic position of the United States. But, in all other respects, they amounted to a massive break from the post-war order. As Arrighi points out:

> Not only did the US government stop feeding the system with liquidity; more importantly, it started to compete aggressively for capital worldwide – through record high interest rates, tax breaks, increasing freedom of action for capitalist producers and speculators and, as the benefits of the new policies materialized, an appreciating dollar – provoking the massive re-routing of capital flows towards the United States . . .[40]

However, the restoration of US hegemony was not without its contradictions. After a severe recession from 1980–2, Reagan's policies promoted a consumer-led boom[41] alongside a wave of company takeovers in which companies with low share values were bought up, costs, above all of labour were slashed, and therefore unemployment soared and real wages fell. Internationally, the effect of these policies – and in particular the high-value dollar – was to undermine US manufacturing competitiveness. The trade deficit had increased from $25 billion in 1980 to $122 billion by 1985.[42] With another threat of a dollar freefall, a controlled devaluation was agreed through the Plaza Accord in 1985. This paved the way for the recovery of manufacturing, as the devalued dollar made US exports more competitive in the world economy, which was further reinforced by stagnant real wages. However, the recovery was relatively short-lived as the US and the world fell back into recession by the early 1990s. This recession left many US manufacturers in a potentially vulnerable position, which had borrowed heavily to finance mergers and acquisitions, rather than

---

[39] Brenner 1998, p. 184.
[40] Arrighi 2003, p. 66.
[41] The Thatcherite 'boom' in Britain in the late 1980s was similarly consumer-led. While the Thatcher government rejected deficit spending, its deregulation of finance had the effect of making borrowing much easier (which was ironic, given the government's supposed commitment to a policy of controlling the money supply), which boosted consumer spending.
[42] Schaeffer 1997, p. 47.

investment in new plant and equipment. A potential catastrophe was averted by an effective Federal Reserve bailout, which led to substantial interest-rate cuts from 1989–93,[43] which helped to pave the way for the boom in the 1990s, an issue addressed in the next chapter.

By 1991, the US's budget deficit stood at $74 billion and the trade deficit at $4 trillion. The world's main creditor in the 1950s and 1960s had, by the 1980s and 1990s, become the world's largest debtor.[44] Over the same period, the world had moved from one based on state directed capitalist expansion, to one in which the neo-liberal idea of the domination of markets, particularly financial markets, held sway. This was reflected in structural adjustment policies in the indebted developing world (see below), and from 1989 in the former Communist world, to privatisation policies throughout the 'advanced' capitalist countries. The commitment to neo-liberalism was inconsistent – Reagan's government ran enormous budget deficits, for example – but this meant, in effect, that the US acted as a market of last resort to a world economy that was experiencing far lower rates of economic growth than in the 1950s and 1960s. Nevertheless, the adoption of selected neo-liberal policies meant that states had deregulated capital, which, theoretically at least, meant that capital was no longer tied to particular nation-states, and had the freedom to move around the globe.[45] From the 1970s and especially the 1980s and 1990s, more and more countries removed controls on the movement of financial capital and adopted more open policies to investment by productive capital. In the 1990s, this movement of deregulation was extended further, and it was in this decade that the globalisation debate really took off.

From the 1970s, then, the United States dealt with relative economic decline by using the international role of the dollar to try to reinforce its hegemony. In the 1970s, Nixon and Carter pursued expansionary policies and allowed a relatively weak dollar to decline in value, policies which were designed to increase production at home and exports abroad. But the policy led to inflation and to specific threats to the dollar's international role, and so a new tighter monetary policy was introduced by Carter in 1979, and intensified by the Reagan administration in 1980. Reagan's policies of tax cuts for the rich

---

[43] Brenner 2002, p. 68.
[44] Arrighi 1994, pp. 316–17.
[45] Whether or not capital can ever free itself of states is another issue, addressed throughout the book. For more detail on capital flows, see Chapter 5.

alongside massive increases in military spending led to unprecedented increases in the budget and trade deficits. These deficits were financed by attracting capital into the US economy. In the Reagan era, particularly in the early years, the main instrument for attracting these flows was a policy of high interest rates. This policy had devastating international consequences.

(ii) *The 1982 debt crisis: causes and consequences*

By the early 1970s, a number of factors had undermined the post-war boom. These included declining productivity and falling profit rates, the (relative) decline of the United States and the dollar, the rise of (economic) competitors in Europe and Japan, increasing inflation, and social unrest throughout the world but especially in South-East Asia. In 1973–4 a further factor intensified these problems – the price of oil quadrupled as a result of the cut in oil supplies by OPEC countries in response to the 1973 Arab-Israeli war. The significance of these price rises has often been exaggerated for two reasons. First, it ignores the massive (though short-term) increase in the price of grain as the Soviet Union bought masses of US supplies when its own harvests failed and when Cold-War relations between the US and USSR thawed for a brief period. Second, and more important for our purposes, there was probably only around a 20 per cent increase in Eurobank deposits from OPEC throughout the 1970s.[46]

Nevertheless, combined with the wider long-term trajectory outlined above, the price rises were significant. The immediate result was that oil exporters needed to find an outlet for their windfall profits, and oil importers now faced potentially devastating import bills. The oil-exporting countries deposited their windfalls in European banks (or European affiliates of US banks) and these petrodollars added to the already expanding Eurodollar market – the main source of which was the US balance of payments deficit, as we have seen. Banks then loaned these dollars to a small number of countries, mainly located in Eastern Europe and especially Latin America (plus a few larger countries throughout the 'Third World'). Between 1973 and 1982, the total gross outstanding debt of Latin America and the Caribbean grew at an annual rate of 25 per cent, which was almost twice the rate of growth of export

---

[46] Corbridge 1993, p. 30.

earnings and about four times the rate of growth of GNP.[47] Thus, in the 1970s, private bank lending became the major means by which some 'developing countries' gained access to capital, as opposed to official channels such as the IMF and World Bank, as was the case in the 1950s and 1960s.

Banks loaned money at low rates of interest and, in a competitive and unregulated climate, often committed enormous sums to particular Latin-American states – by 1982, the nine largest US banks had committed over twice their combined capital basis to a handful of developing countries. Competition encouraged a 'herd mentality' in which a market leader loaned money and a number of banks quickly followed – a common characteristic of global finance over the last twenty years, as will become clear. The banks presumably calculated that such debts, or at least the interest, would be guaranteed as most of the debtors were Western-friendly military governments, and the citizens of these countries would have to make sacrifices in order to guarantee repayment. As Walter Wriston, Chair of Citibank said in 1976, '[a] country does not go bankrupt'.[48] Banks also made one important decision concerning such debts, which was that much of the interest was set at a floating rate. Government debtors were not too concerned about this policy for much of the 1970s, when interest rates were low and repayment periods (known as maturities) were generally long-term. Moreover, such loans did not have conditions that were often attached in the case of aid. However, from the late 1970s interest rates increased rapidly and repayment periods generally became shorter.

The rise in interest rates in both the United States and among European banks[49] was part of a new strategy aimed at controlling inflation in the 'advanced' capitalist countries (see above). The London Interbank Offered Rate (LIBOR), which was used to set the basic rate of interest for loans to developing countries, increased from 9.2 per cent in 1978 to 16.63 per cent in 1981.[50] The effect of this increase on developing country debtors was devastating, adding perhaps a further $41 billion to their debt (based on average interest rates from 1961–80). Moreover, high interest rates in the US attracted capital

---

[47] Kuczynski 1988, p. 36.
[48] Schaeffer 1997, p. 87.
[49] The interest rate for Eurodollars was set by the London Interbank Offered Rate, or LIBOR.
[50] Corbridge 1993, p. 38.

from all over the world, including from high-debt and low-savings developing countries that needed this capital to help pay back debts. During the height of Mexico's debt crisis in 1982, a Mexican newspaper published the names of 537 Mexicans, each of whom had deposited over a million dollars in Western banks.[51] This combination of high interest rates and capital exports from the indebted countries constituted a reversal of historic proportions. As Arrighi states:

> From then on, it would no longer be First World bankers begging Third World states to borrow their overabundant capital; it would be Third World states begging First World bankers to grant them the credit needed to stay afloat in an increasingly integrated, competitive, and shrinking world market.[52]

These problems were exacerbated by the general decline in commodity prices for many of the products of developing countries. There was a dramatic fall in average commodity prices of one-third from 1980–2,[53] which further reduced the capacity of developing countries to meet their interest payments, a tendency which continued throughout the 1980s. This inability to pay was also partly a product of the new strategy of controlling inflation in the First World, which meant that there was a decline in demand for developing country products. It was also caused by the development of substitute supplies and/or alternative products, such as new sources of oil, energy conservation, and sugar beet rather than sugar cane. But it was also a product of the fact that an increase in world supply of some goods – oil, copper and coffee, among others – in the context of slowing demand, had the effect of lowering the world price for such goods.

In 1982, Mexico was the first country to officially default on its foreign *private* debt, although twenty countries renegotiated their debt payments to *official* bilateral creditors between 1979 and 1983.[54] When non-payment (again, of private debt) threatened to spread to Brazil, there was a real danger that Western banks – who had committed so much capital to Latin America – could fail. This was the start of the (financial) debt crisis. From the viewpoint of Western banks, they faced the prospect that a number of high-debt countries

---

[51] Pastor 1989, pp. 11–12.
[52] Arrighi 1994, p. 323.
[53] Roddick 1988, p. 65.
[54] Corbridge 1993, pp. 40–1.

were in no position to pay back the interest on their loans. What was therefore needed was more money to be loaned to the high-debt countries, but with some guarantee that these countries could meet their debt obligations. However, while it may have been rational from the viewpoint of all the banks to loan more money, in the context of unregulated competition, it made no sense for any one individual bank to carry out this task (as there were no guarantees that all the other banks would follow). Once again, then, we see the problem of uneven development, and how this manifests itself in terms of money through the problem of recycling from deficit to surplus countries. One possible solution was for surplus countries to transfer money to the indebted countries at low or zero rates of interest, a position advocated in the two Brandt reports of the early 1980s.[55]

But this proposal was ignored. This was hardly surprising given that the increasing priorities of Western governments – particularly the United States and Britain – was to reduce inflation and restore rates of profit at home. As regards the developing world, a policy emerged which essentially amounted to a system of policing the debt crisis through granting limited access to new loans provided that they met with the approval of international finance, and particularly the International Monetary Fund. The IMF therefore became a far more active player in the international economy, effectively policing a whole series of economies that faced balance-of-payments difficulties through-out the 1980s. Policing was not, however, just imposed on indebted countries, and the IMF also attempted to ensure that banks continued to lend money to indebted countries, thus ensuring that widespread default could be avoided. This latter policy however met with limited success, and new commercial bank lending to heavily indebted countries fell rapidly in the mid 1980s – from $19 billion in 1983 to $6.7 billion in 1986.[56] Thus, despite the relative lack of power given to the IMF in 1944, reflected mainly in terms of its small amount of financial resources, it became a highly visible institution throughout the developing world, particularly after 1982.[57] It received new (though still quite low) financial resources to help it carry out this task – and, alongside

---

[55] Brandt 1980; 1983.
[56] Corbridge 1993, p. 53.
[57] This is not to deny real conflicts before then, such as in Egypt and Jamaica, but the role of the IMF still underwent a massive change after 1982.

the conditions attached to its loans, this visibility led to massive protests against the institution from the 1980s onwards.[58]

To understand the role played by the IMF in the 1980s debt crisis, and, indeed, that of the World Bank, it is crucial to understand how the debt crisis was viewed by the dominant countries, and the United States in particular. This basically echoed the neo-liberal theories of trade outlined in the previous chapter. Countries that faced severe balance of payments deficits, and therefore faced difficulties in meeting their interest payment obligations, were said to have adopted incorrect policies. What this amounted to was the idea that they were consuming more than they were producing, and importing more than they were exporting. Given that global free markets tend towards equilibrium, or so the argument goes, this must have occurred because of some external mechanism that undermined the efficiency of these economies. What this amounted to was an interpretation of the debt crisis based on the idea that it was the fault of the indebted countries themselves (all of them), rather than a problem caused by the uneven development of the system as a whole. And the basic source of the problem was that there had been too much government intervention in these economies. So, just as inflation and the 1970s recession was caused by 'too much government', so too was the debt crisis of the 1980s. What was therefore needed was a set of policies that would encourage countries to re-adjust their economies, and start to export more than they imported, and produce more than they consumed, therefore enabling them to earn foreign exchange to meet their debt obligations.

Some neo-liberals argued that there was actually no need for an interventionist public institution such as the IMF. Buiter and Srinivasan,[59] for instance, argued that the IMF was, by lending public money, effectively subsidising and protecting the interests of government debtors and Western banks. The result was a 'form of socialism of the rich', in which public money subsidised poor loans and bad debts, which should be left to the disciplinary mechanisms of market forces. Peter Bauer[60] also argued against public money – regarded as a form of debt relief – to bail out bankers and debtors. Other neo-liberals took a more pragmatic stance, particularly when it became clear that

---

[58] See Walton and Seddon 1994; World Development Movement 2001, 2002.
[59] Buiter and Srinivasan 1987, p. 416.
[60] Bauer 1991.

automatic adjustment had potentially devastating consequences for countries that defaulted, not least for the heavily committed Western banks. The US government, in particular, advocated a policy of 'managed neo-liberalism' in which the IMF would play a key role in policing debtor nations, in terms of approving loans made either by the IMF itself or more indirectly the (increasingly diminishing) new loans from banks, subject to certain conditions. This increased role for the IMF did not mean that it suddenly became the institution that Keynes envisaged in 1944. On the contrary, the burden of adjustment was placed solely in the hands of the debtor countries, rather than surplus countries, and this meant that, in practice, enormous policy changes had to be undertaken.

The immediate policy required then was for countries to restore balance-of-payments equilibrium. In this respect, IMF management was a success, as, for instance, Brazil and Mexico quickly moved from current account deficits to small surpluses in just two years (1982–4). But these results were achieved simply by a massive cut in imports. In terms of generating foreign exchange in order to fulfil longer-term obligations, the large debtors faced the problems of falling commodity prices and protectionist measures against some of their goods in the 'advanced' countries. As important, however, was the fact of debt overhang – the debt itself adversely affected the potential for future investment as banks resisted new lending, and therefore potential new sources of productive investment to bad debtors, and some import cuts undermined export growth (as some imports were inputs for export goods), as well as the more obvious costs of debt servicing, which further undermined potential productive investment. From 1985 to 1987, the highly indebted countries transferred $74 billion to creditors – the equivalent of 3.1 per cent of the combined GNP of these countries in that period.[61] These factors undermined the hopes of the Baker Plan for debt management of the 17 biggest debtor countries from 1985–7, which was supposed to be based on growth through adjustment policies underpinned by new financial flows.

The Brady Plan succeeded the Baker Plan in 1988–9, which encouraged banks to enter into voluntary debt agreements with debtor countries. Debt reduction schemes based on secondary market operations were encouraged, which led to a number of debt-equity swaps and to new investment by

---

[61] World Bank 1989, p. xix.

transnational companies and the privatisation of previously state-owned assets. The basis for this system was that a particular bank, say 'Bank A', wanted to get rid of a bad loan to a debtor country. A TNC could invest in the same country knowing that they could win substantial discounts on the initial investment. The TNC would then go through a large bank, which acted as broker. The secondary market would then show that the country's loans were trading at, say, 50 per cent of their real value. 'Bank A' would then receive 50 per cent of its initial loan, paid through the large bank (which received commission) by the TNC. The TNC then received the full amount of the original loan through the country's central bank. In such deals, the broker gained through commission, the TNC through the 50 per cent discount on the investment, and the country through no longer having to pay interest on the loan and the fact that it was now receiving investment. The small bank would make a large loss, but at least with the gain of writing off a bad debt. This plan laid the basis for a positive inflow of capital into Latin America in the early 1990s, and much talk of the leading countries becoming 'emerging markets'. The short-term and volatile nature of much of these flows, and a succession of financial crises, seriously challenges such claims, and I return to these questions in the next chapter.

For the moment, the impact of the 1982 debt crisis and its aftermath needs reinforcing. Some advance in debt management occurred in Latin America, so that average debt-GNP ratios fell from 62 per cent in 1985 to 37 per cent in 1994 (though this has since increased), but, in sub-Saharan Africa, the ratios increased from an average of 76 per cent to 136 per cent over the same period.[62] In the late 1990s, the amount spent on debt servicing exceeded the total amount spent on primary health care and primary education combined.[63] These cold facts illustrate the concrete and brutal manifestation of the effects of global uneven development, which the neo-liberal policies of the IMF and World Bank at best, did little or nothing to alleviate, and at worst, actually intensified. At the same time, it did guarantee repayment to creditors, and it is for this reason that critics argue that the IMF effectively worked as a debt collection agency for international banks.[64] Certainly, from 1982–5, the profits

---

[62] UNDP 1999.
[63] Cypher and Dietz 1997, p. 551.
[64] Bienefeld 1999.

of a number of leading banks soared – for Bankers' Trust, by 66 per cent; for Morgan Guaranty by 61 per cent; and for Chase Manhattan, there was a massive 79 per cent increase.[65]

Historically, the IMF was principally concerned with managing short-term balance of payments deficits, while the World Bank was concerned with longer-term development. From the early 1980s, this division of labour was described as IMF stabilisation and World Bank structural adjustment policies. In practice, however, it was difficult to make a clear contrast between the two, as both institutions were broadly committed to the idea that pro-free market policies were the best way of achieving efficient economic outcomes – the so-called Washington Consensus.[66] This commitment to the 'free market' was, however, highly selective and did not apply to the issue of debt, and both institutions encouraged the nationalisation of private-sector debt, which effectively meant that states, in guaranteeing private-sector debt, protected private agents against the discipline of the 'free market'. This was a clear case of double standards, as the World Bank and IMF preached the virtues of the private sector for indebted economies, but not for their Western creditors. This policy changed to some extent with the introduction of the Brady Plan, and the development of a more market-oriented approach to debt management, but this was limited and could not hide a clear case of double standards.

In terms of the debtors, there was a certain 'family resemblance' between different adjustment policies in different countries. The promotion of market-friendly policies in practice often led to devaluation of a nation's currency (to make exports cheaper), a reduction in state spending (to combat inflation), and wage cuts (to restore private sector 'incentives'/profitability). These policies were closely associated with IMF stabilisation policies, and their (uneven and often quite limited) implementation meant that countries were able to secure new loans from the IMF or (because their creditworthiness improved with IMF 'approval') from other sources. However, the size of the loans was quite small, and the policies themselves had at best mixed results. The effect of devaluation was impossible to predict in advance, and varied according to import dependence and the character of exports. In terms of the former, relatively cheap imports were often needed, as they could be inputs

---

[65] George 1989, p. 39.
[66] Williamson 1989.

for goods, which generated export revenue. In this case, devaluation made things worse as it increased the price of imports. In terms of the latter, some exports did not respond to devaluation because of the low income elasticity of demand for some goods, particularly primary products. In terms of state spending, it was often the case that cutbacks had undesirable social consequences and the IMF assumed that a simple zero sum game existed between the public and private sectors, with investment in the former crowding out investment in the latter. Finally, lower wages had adverse demand effects for those sectors that produced primarily for the domestic market, and failed to secure large amounts of direct foreign investment, at least in the 1980s.[67] World Bank structural adjustment loans from the early 1980s were also associated with 'market-friendly' conditions. These generally included reform of state sending, non-discrimination against exporters, and revision to (state controlled) pricing policy, particularly for agriculture. In one of the most extensive surveys of the effects of adjustment in the 1980s,[68] it was found that such loans had some positive impact on exports and balance of payments, but led to a decline in overall investment, failed to lead to an increase in capital flows or economic growth, and adversely affected the living standards of the poorest.

The basic assumption of IMF and World Bank policies is that indebted countries have chosen economically inefficient policies, which have focused too much on states protecting domestic economies from the opportunities that global market forces can offer. 'Globalisation' in this case thus effectively means countries operating open policies, which allow them to exercise their comparative advantage. This means that countries produce the goods that they can produce most cheaply and efficiently. In practice, this can only be discovered through principles of open competition and therefore trade policies must be liberalised. But competition is far from being free and equal. Extensive non-tariff barriers continue to exist, including subsidies, voluntary export restraints and even import controls. Moreover, even where trade is more liberalised, competition is far from equal. Primary producers face the problem of a low income elasticity of demand for their products, intense competition between a sometimes large number of producers, and therefore a relative

---

[67] Killick 1995.
[68] Mosley et al. 1991.

tendency for prices to fall more quickly than the prices of manufactured goods. Indeed, in some cases, IMF and World Bank policies in the 1980s encouraged falling prices by advising countries producing similar products to increase output, often in the context of falling demand. The advantage of lower labour costs is often more than offset by technological advantages in the 'advanced' countries, which leads to higher productivity and clustering of suppliers in established locations.[69] Together, all these factors undermine the optimism concerning the benefits of adjustment and globalisation. While it may be the case that the debt crisis is over, the development crisis is still with us. The crisis of the 1980s meant the end of 'development-friendly' régimes in the 'Third World', reflected in lower growth rates, social development setbacks, and a substantial loss of state autonomy to international financial institutions.

3.4 Summary

The post-war era was one in which international capitalism was regulated by the international agreement that was signed at Bretton Woods, which itself was ultimately the product of US hegemony. The agreement was one that committed countries in the capitalist world, including the growing number of newly independent nations that emerged from the late 1940s, to a liberal system of free trade. But it was also a system that allowed for considerable leverage in national economic policy-making, including controls on the movement of money capital, as well as some controls on trade and investment. The 1950s and 1960s was generally a period of sustained capital accumulation throughout the world, with high rates of economic growth and considerable social advance, including, in some respects, in the developing world. But, by the late 1960s, it was clear that there were considerable tensions in the system. The US balance of payments deficits that had financed the boom were now undermining US hegemony, and, by 1971, it was running trade as well as payments deficits. The value of the dollar was increasingly under threat, and there was increasing speculation against it from the late 1960s. This occurred in the context of a slowdown in capital accumulation, heightened social and political unrest, and (with the emergence of the Eurodollar market) increased

---

[69] See Chapter 2.

effective deregulation in international financial markets. The US responded to threatened hegemonic decline by effectively devaluing the dollar and simultaneously using the international role of the dollar (agreed at Bretton Woods, but now without a dollar-gold link), in an attempt to increase domestic production and improve competitiveness and export performance abroad. The result was inflation and a potential threat to the international role of the dollar. By the late 1970s, there was a shift towards anti-inflationary policies through high interest rates, which led to a rapid shift from a world order based on cheap lending and borrowing in the 1970s, to one based on very expensive lending and borrowing in the 1980s. In order to meet their interest payment obligations, indebted countries had to increase their foreign exchange earnings as against their domestic consumption, which often led to severe cutbacks in consumption (and production). In the period from 1979–82, state policy in the 'Third World' shifted from one based on developing domestic productive capacity, accompanied in some cases by some forms of social safety nets, to one based on earning sufficient foreign exchange through increasing exports or decreasing imports (with some countries coping with this new general context more effectively than others).[70] This shift was justified on the neo-liberal grounds that pro-free market policies would lead to substantial trade and investment opportunities based on countries exercising their comparative advantage in the world economy. Similarly, in the 'advanced' countries, there was a gradual shift from policies that, in some respects, favoured labour, such as expansionary state spending and welfare states, to ones that favoured the 'free market' (although, of course, the outcome of this general tendency varied according to particular struggles within each of them). Again, these were justified in terms of a universal interest, so that low inflation benefited consumers and labour-market rigidities and the undermining of union power would ensure that everybody could have a job, rather than the

---

[70] It is this general economic differentiation between developing countries that has led to a renewal of the development 'modelling' of neo-liberalism and the Third Way, which essentially points to one success story as a model for all others to follow. But this approach ignores unequal contexts (the uneven development of the global economy), specific social and political features within countries, and the fact that success stories have not followed neo-liberal policies. Moreover, this approach also has little to say about the issue of the impact of one country cutting imports while another country is told to increase its exports. The issue of models of development is addressed further in Chapters 4 and 5. See also Kiely 1995, Chapter 5.

privileged few pricing others out of work. Neo-liberal ideological justifications ignored the over-accumulation of capital, the uneven development between different countries and capitals, and the increased rate of exploitation of labour by capital. In focusing on money, neo-liberalism and monetarism addressed the symptoms but not the causes of the crisis, and its policies of sound money actually intensified problems by creating unemployment and a shortfall in demand. This led to a massive world recession from 1980–82, which was only overcome by the military Keynesianism of the Reagan administration – which, in part, showed that the monetarist solution of 'sound money' had simply intensified the problem by reducing demand and therefore further undermining accumulation.[71] The continued strength of the US economy from 1982 was, therefore, intimately tied up with the interests of other economies, as the US effectively became the market of last resort. This was important in sustaining other economies – the US's competitors among them, including some developing countries that escaped the worst effects of the debt crisis. But, for most of the developing world, the debt crisis undermined growth and social development, and so they faced capital shortage alongside increased interest payment obligations. For *all* countries, the effect of these shifts in the world economy was to alter the context in which they operated, and the policies which they carried out. But what should by now be clear is that (contrary to Giddens for example), globalisation did not emerge literally 'from nowhere', but was itself a product of a number of specific and contradictory agents and interests. These included political and social resistance to the post-war order, not least in the developing world and Vietnam in particular. But there were also agents and strategies promoting 'globalisation from above', and these were reflected in conflicts between capitals and states, as well as attempts by these same states to co-operate with each other in an increasingly unfavourable environment. In terms of US hegemony, there was a sustained effort to facilitate capital mobility, through the development of the Eurodollar market and direct foreign investment in the 1950s. In the 1970s, US policies further facilitated market expansion, through the removal of the gold-dollar fixed price and

---

[71] There are other issues that undermine monetarism too, which need not detain us here. The quantity theory of money on which the theory rests is briefly discussed in Chapter 2. Interestingly, it is a theory that Milton Freidman now rejects. What also needs some recognition is the fact that the deregulation of money – supported by monetarists such as Thatcher – means that controlling the money supply is an impossible task.

effective devaluations in the early 1970s, and the further growth of the Eurodollar market through the oil price rises of 1973–4. Each of these developments cannot be explained through the spontaneous or autonomous development of markets or new technology. There was significant expansion in the demand for financial services as international production and trade increased, alongside the development of financial markets independent of stringent state regulations, and then, in the 1970s, there was the growth of petrodollars and the movement to floating exchange rates. All these factors boosted the re-emergence of global finance, and this was boosted further by the use of new technologies in the 1980s and 1990s. But, at the same time, these developments were also facilitated by the actions of nation-states, and the US state in particular. Facilitating actions included effective support for the development of the Eurodollar market, the end of fixed exchange rates, and successful pressure on other states to liberalise the movement of capital. Furthermore, in the neo-liberal era of the 1980s, states continued to regulate economies, but the regulation that took place was increasingly carried out in order to further the expansion of markets, rather than to limit them. Such market expansion did not alleviate acute contradictions, and currency instability and the debt crisis were just two manifestations of uneven development in the 1970s and 1980s. However, in the 1990s, a new confidence emerged concerning the capacity of global markets to both end uneven development and alleviate poverty. This is the subject of the next two chapters.

Chapter Four

Globalisation and the Third Way in the 1990s

This chapter examines globalisation in the 1990s. Its concern is with globalisation both as political project and socio-economic reality. It therefore examines the political economy of the global Third Way ('the project') and the expansion of 'free markets' ('the reality'). The 1990s was, in some respects, a period of great optimism, a product of the rhetoric surrounding the new economy in the United States, the emerging markets boom in the developing world, and the continued liberalisation of trade in goods and services. These were linked to the Third Way project, and involved the expansion of 'market forces'. At the same time, however, it was also consistently argued that the new politics constituted a break from the neo-liberal fundamentalism of the 1980s, as the state and other public institutions were to play a more active role in regulating the 'global market-place', and this issue also demands some attention.

The chapter therefore deals with a number of broad themes, which are discussed in six sections. The first two discuss the extent to which the Third Way actually constituted a break from neo-liberalism, and so focus on globalisation as a political *project*. The first section revisits the discussion in Chapter 2, and argues that the Third Way is essentially a political project that seeks to depoliticise important areas of decision-making, and particularly takes much of the neo-liberal project of the 1980s as given. This argument is further developed in Section 2, which discusses the emergence of a Third Way in development in the 1990s, paying particular attention to the World Bank. The next two sections focus on the *reality* of globalisation in the 1990s. Section 3 examines the new economy boom in the United States under President Clinton, while Section 4 analyses the emerging markets boom in parts of the former Third World. These sections contrast the rhetoric around these 'success stories' with the reality of financial instability and increased inequality. Both cases reflect the hegemony of finance in the world economy, and Section 5 addresses this issue in more detail. Returning to themes addressed in the previous chapter, this section examines the rise of global finance since the 1970s, and then links this to the question of US hegemony. Finally, Section 6 develops this theme by examining the expansion of the free-trade agenda and the creation of the World Trade Organisation in 1995. Sections 5 and 6 are therefore concerned with question of the relationship between globalisation and *agency and power relations.*

4.1 The globalisation project 1: globalisation and the Third Way revisited

The Third Way is supposed to represent a new politics for a new era, which transcends the old dogmas of neo-liberal market fundamentalism on the one hand, and highly centralised state socialism on the other.[1] This 'new' approach to politics is said to be appropriate to a global era of informational capitalism. Its origins can be traced back to 1992, when the United States' Democrat Leadership Council applied the term to a 'new era' of politics.[2] A major part of the Third Way argument was that it was impossible to escape from the reality of globalisation. It was an argument that assumed that the globalisation of markets and technology were beyond the realm of politics, and that states could only react to these forces in one particular way. This was because globalisation had literally arrived 'from nowhere',[3] it was a fact of life. Thus, in 1999, Tony Blair stated that:

---

[1] Giddens 1998.
[2] See DLC 1996.
[3] Giddens, see Chapter 2.

We are all internationalists now whether we like it or not. . . . We cannot refuse to participate in global markets if we want to prosper. We cannot ignore new political ideas in global markets if we want to prosper. We cannot turn our backs on conflicts and the violation of human rights in other countries if we still want to be secure.[4] . . . Globalisation has transformed our economies and our working practices. . . . Any government that thinks it can go it alone is wrong. If the markets don't like your policies they will punish you.[5]

This statement could be taken as a criticism of the power of 'the markets', and how (through speculating against certain currencies and/or moving money from countries with low interest rates) they undermine expansionary or redistributive policies. But, in fact, Blair leaves this question out of the equation,[6] and globalisation is regarded as a purely external force, with the implication that because of the unquestioned power of 'the markets', governments must adjust accordingly. Al Gore makes this point explicit:

In this fast moving, fast changing global economy – when the free flow of dollars and data are sources of economic and political strength, and whole new industries are born every day – governments must be lean, nimble, and creative or they will surely be left behind.[7]

Giddens goes further, arguing that globalisation is not only inevitable but also desirable.[8] It therefore represents not only a new context for state policy making, but it 'by and large, has been a success. The problem is how to maximize its positive consequences while limiting its less fortunate effects'. John Lloyd makes a similar claim when he argues that the global market provides the basis for a global society, but that it needs to be shaped to meet social needs, including the reduction of poverty.[9] Globalisation is thus regarded as a fact of life that cannot be changed,[10] but also something that can have

---

[4] The issue of 'humanitarian intervention' is briefly discussed in Chapter 8.

[5] Quoted in Kaldor 2001a, p. 153.

[6] Indeed, he has explicitly ruled out any attempts to implement a Tobin tax on speculation, a position not shared by Anthony Giddens. For a detailed consideration of the inconsistency of the Third Way's politics in relation to globalisation, see Kiely 2002b.

[7] Gore 1999.

[8] Giddens 2000, p. 124.

[9] Lloyd 2001, p. 13.

[10] Fairclough 2000, p. 24.

equitable outcomes. For the Third Way, the only alternatives are either the national isolationism of the Right (and Marxist Left) or the local romanticism of the anarchist Left.[11] This approach to globalisation therefore separates the modernising force of the Third Way from the backward ideologies of (national) industrial capitalism. Globalisation and modernisation are irreversible forces, abstracted from real agents and interests,[12] and, therefore, submission to these forces is regarded as both inevitable and desirable. The new modernising force of globalisation is regarded as purely technical and external to real agents and interests, rather than the source of new (and not so new) inequalities of power.

Therefore, states must adopt the correct policies in order to draw on the opportunities that globalisation presents. There are also risks associated with globalisation, including lack of international co-operation, the rise of terror networks, and failed states that do not embrace the promises of globalisation. But, on the other hand, forward-thinking modernisers can embrace globalisation and therefore experience expansion in growth, income and welfare. In the developed world, states must adopt policies that develop the skills of the workforce, so that they can adapt to the information age, and become part of Castells's 'space of flows'. The most advanced countries can therefore compete with each other through the development of a highly skilled, high-productivity, information-led, new economy. Competition in the context of high productivity and high growth will serve to further stimulate growth. The crucial state policy in this respect is investment in skills and education, so that a flexible, skilled labour market ensures competitiveness in the world economy.[13] Meanwhile, the developing world can benefit too, by opening up their economies to investment and competing on the basis of their low labour costs, which will stimulate investment, trade and economic growth. In the long run, such growth will provide the stimulus for a movement away from a low-wage economy to a developed one based on high productivity and output. The key policy in the developing world is, therefore, state reform to ensure greater openness to trade and investment.

In terms of both world-view and government policy then, the Third Way

---

[11] Hain and Benschop 2001, p. 22.
[12] Rustin 2000.
[13] Giddens 1998, p. 99.

pays little attention to the question of power. As we saw in Chapter 2, Giddens upholds an evolutionary account of social change based on the expansion of individual reflexivity, individual understanding and practices.[14] This reflexivity occurs through the progressive overcoming of embedded boundaries of time and space. Modernity is essentially regarded as the enhancement of the power to transcend time and space, with the result that every aspect of society becomes subject to reflexive choice. Globalisation intensifies the overcoming of the boundaries of time and space, and so individuals have the freedom to develop autonomously and reflexively as individuals. Power containers such as nation-states lose control in the face of global competition, communication, and shared aspirations. This process carries risks as well as opportunities, but those seeking to opt out of globalisation are regarded as fundamentalist. The risks are best dealt with by establishing institutions of global governance, and not by a retreat into local traditionalism.

As I argued in Chapter 2, what is most striking about this perspective is its limited approach to agency, interest and power, and this has implications for government policy and understanding wider political processes. If we take the example of the global economy, it may be true that no individual country can afford to opt out of globalisation, as Giddens claims. Similarly, it is true that no one country or agency controls financial markets.[15] But the fact that no particular agency controls a process does not mean that there has been no agency involved in their creation, or that power relations and interests simply cease to exist. Marx distinguished between individual capitals and capital in general, and recognised that the latter compels the former to act in certain ways, but this did not mean that he denied agency or power in capitalist society. Thus, to take an example from the previous chapter, the re-emergence of financial capital's central role in global capitalism is not a simple consequence of modernity (or indeed capitalism), but was a product of certain concrete events (US relative decline, dollar devaluation and the end of fixed exchange rates, tacit US and British support for the Eurodollar market) which were linked to changing interests and attempts to preserve US power. Giddens's effective characterisation of globalisation as a process without agency leads to an understanding of it as essentially given and, like Third Way politicians,

---

[14] Giddens 1990, p. 38.
[15] Giddens and Hutton 2001, pp. 41–2.

outside of politics. A grand theory thus becomes an abstracted empiricism,[16] in which globalisation is reduced to a 'process without a subject'.[17] Globalisation is simply irreversible change, to which modern political projects must respond. The emphasis on a changing world is central to the discourse of the Third-Way, and the word 'change' is also a favourite among Third Way politicians. But, as Fairclough points out, the word is used in a very specific way, which 'involves abstraction from the diversity of processes going on, no specification of who or what is changing, a backgrounding of the processes of change themselves, and a foregrounding of their effect'.[18] Change, like globalisation, thus becomes a 'catch-all' term used in mainstream politics, and 'a most convenient scapegoat for the imposition of unpopular and unpalatable measures'.[19]

Policies that promote labour-market flexibility and structural adjustment are thus justified on the basis that there is no alternative in the era of global competitiveness. But this argument about inevitability is often then confused with desirability as the strategy of progressive competitiveness is supposed to have desirable outcomes. However, optimistic scenarios in which the developed world competes through high-tech, highly-skilled products and the developing world through low labour costs, ignores the uneven development of the world economy and unequal nature of competition. As we have seen, low labour costs can be out-competed by high productivity elsewhere, and it is also far from clear that the skilled IT sector can absorb even a tiny proportion of the labour force in the developed world.[20] Thus, state policies that deregulate labour markets often facilitate the employment of low wage, unskilled, unprotected and insecure employment in the developed world, while adjustment policies in the developing world that are supposed to increase competitiveness often lead to lower rates of investment, growth and social exclusion. When such results occur, the Third Way response is that there simply is no alternative, and that states must therefore have intervened in ways not conducive to market expansion.

---

[16] My use of the idea of grand theory and abstracted empiricism as mirror images is derived from Mills's (1970) critique of functionalist sociology.
[17] Hay 2001.
[18] Fairclough 2000, p. 26.
[19] Hay 2001, p. 17.
[20] See further, Chapter 5.

The discourse of the global Third Way has, therefore, been used in mainstream politics to technocratise, and depoliticise, social and political processes. The period from the 1940s to the late 1970s and early 1980s was explicitly politicised, in that states in the 'advanced' capitalist countries managed labour and money through the use of government intervention. This took the form of appeals to the national interest, incomes policies, wage restraint, and capital controls. Depoliticisation is also a state strategy, a political and ideological project that attempts to place 'at one remove the political character of decision making', in order to change expectations 'regarding the effectiveness and credibility in policy making'.[21] In practice, then, political tasks are handed over to supposedly neutral decision-making bodies, such as the Bank of England, or international institutions and agreements such as the Exchange Rate Mechanism or the WTO, whose rules are binding on elected governments, and whose existence changes the context in which government policy operates. This context is then presented as an objective, non-political *constraint* on government, but it is, actually, one that is in part the *creation* of government. But, once this constraint is created, it is 'justified' as both inevitable (there is no alternative) and desirable (it will have favourable outcomes). It is thus a short step from recognition that the economy is global in scale to an acceptance of the global economy in its current neo-liberal form.[22] This can be illustrated further by examining the development of a Third Way at the World Bank in the 1990s.

4.2   The globalisation project 2: the Third Way and development

This section examines the way in which neo-liberalism has been modified by development institutions in the 1990s, and, in particular, the World Bank. Although not explicitly linked to the US and British Third Way projects, developments at the Bank closely paralleled these debates, as they focused on state policy and institutional change rather than just 'free markets'. But the one-sided focus on institutions demonstrated the limited extent to which policy changes concretely broke from the neo-liberalism of the 1980s. This section therefore examines the concepts of good governance, market-friendly

---

[21] Burnham 1999, p. 47.
[22] Fairclough 2000, pp. 27–8.

intervention and social capital, and assesses the extent to which these ideas, policies and practices, constitute a move beyond or an extension of neo-liberalism. In so doing, I will also briefly address the notion of a 'Post-Washington Consensus', which has also been associated with the World Bank.

(i) *Good governance*

The concept of good governance was first associated with policy reforms in states in advanced capitalist countries in the 1980s and 1990s. These reforms were basically designed to make state institutions act more like the private sector via a process of deregulation, internal competition and, where appropriate, privatisation. This notion of constructing a better, more accountable state was then applied to the developing world, primarily by the World Bank from the late 1980s. The argument was that structural adjustment policies had at best mixed results, not because the policies were misguided, but because the institutions that carried out the policies were inappropriate. Above all, developing countries, especially in Africa, suffered from a 'crisis of governance'.[23] In practice, good governance meant the accountability of government, a clear legal framework which embraced the rule of law, citizen access to reliable information, and transparent, open government, which included the end of corruption.[24] The Bank does not openly commit itself to democracy as part of the process of embracing good governance, but this has been recommended by most developed country governments, and has (selectively) been made a condition in the dispensing of aid since the end of the Cold War.

The World Bank's interpretation of good governance is that it is a means to an end, in which appropriate institutional structures promote the development of an efficient, 'free-market' economy.[25] Free markets are thus still considered to be the main solution to the problems of slow growth and lack of development. State institutions are regarded as being so powerful however, that they have hindered the adoption of the correct policies. Good governance is thus 'synonymous with sound development management',[26]

---

[23] World Bank 1989, p. 60.
[24] World Bank 1994.
[25] World Bank 1997; 2002.
[26] World Bank 1992, p. 1.

which means 'not just less government but better government – government that concentrates its efforts on less on direct interventions and more on enabling others to be productive'.[27] It entails establishing 'the rules that make markets work efficiently' and that 'correct for market failure'.[28] Thus, in its 1997 World Development Report, the Bank explicitly rejected the increasingly sterile state versus market debate, and called for more attention to be paid to the issue of state effectiveness.[29] However, such 'effectiveness' was defined in terms of developing rules and institutions that would 'allow markets to flourish'.[30] Bad policies are said to include the raising of unexpected taxes on the private sector, the redistribution of economic benefits and restrictions on the operation of markets, including import restrictions.[31] A full critical discussion follows below, but one obvious point needs to be made immediately, which relates to the neo-liberal theory of the state more generally. Neo-liberals argue that the state is, in some sense, the problem, because it has not allowed the 'correct policies' to be implemented. But it is also part of the solution, not only because it will have to implement the correct policies, but also because it must reform itself in order for these policies to be carried out. Thus, the conception of the state in the governance literature is inconsistent, a point I return to below.

(ii) *Market-friendly intervention*

The notion of market-friendly intervention is associated with the World Bank's report *The East Asian Miracle*.[32] This was a response to pressure, particularly from Japan, to account for the rapid and sustained growth in the East-Asian region, where, despite free-market rhetoric, the state had played an active role in successfully promoting economic growth. Subsequent developments in both East Asia (the 1997/8 crisis, discussed above) and the World Bank (the resignation of two senior researchers, Joseph Stiglitz in 1999, and Ravi Kanbur in 2000) have added a new twist to these debates, but the content of the report is still important in that it is another example of the World Bank's 'turn' to an institutional analysis which partially breaks from neo-liberalism.

---

[27] World Bank 1989, p. 5.
[28] World Bank 1992, p. 1.
[29] World Bank 1997, p. 25.
[30] World Bank 1997, p. 1.
[31] World Bank 1997, p. 51.
[32] World Bank 1993.

The basic argument of *The East Asian Miracle* is that there was state intervention in the high growth economies, but that this was still 'market-friendly'. This idea was similar to Berger's[33] earlier notion that the state may simulate a free market, in which states intervene as a second preference, preferring to let markets work, or subject interventions to the discipline of domestic and international markets.[34] In East Asia, market-friendly intervention meant macro-economic stability, selective export-promoting interventions, and efficient, independent institutions. Concretely, this meant high human-capital investment, limited price distortions, openness to foreign technology, and effective and secure financial systems.[35] The last factor in this list was quickly forgotten in the 1997–8 crash, when the Bank largely attributed the crisis to financial repression, an argument discussed and criticised in the previous section. Rather confusingly, on the very same page of the 1993 Report, the Bank also recognised the existence of financial repression and even (correctly) argued that this was a key factor in explaining the rapid growth in the first place. However, the broad argument of the Report was that intervention had occurred, but it was irrelevant or unnecessary.

The general implications of this notion of market-friendly intervention are discussed below. Again, though, some specific points can be briefly made, the most fundamental of which is that it completely fails to capture the reality of state intervention in East Asia. In the first tier East-Asian developers (South Korea and Taiwan, above all, but also Singapore), states intervened by directing credit to favoured industries, providing export subsidies to selected producers, protecting through high tariffs and import controls, through restricting foreign investment, and so on.[36] The notion of market friendliness cannot capture the fact that intervention was so extensive. Had it just been market-friendly, South Korea and Taiwan would still be exercising their comparative advantage in rice exports. Given the productivity gaps that existed between these late developers and earlier developers, it is hardly surprising that intervention was so extensive.

---

[33] Berger 1979, p. 64.
[34] World Bank 1991.
[35] World Bank 1993, p. 88.
[36] Wade 1990; Amsden 1994; Kiely 1998.

(iii) *Social capital*

The use of the concept of social capital is a more recent development at the Bank. Associated with the work of Putnam,[37] the concept refers to the development of networks and associations that exist independently of the state. The Bank appears to have adopted and borrowed this concept in order to support the development of a civil society made up of networks independent of the state.[38] According to the Bank, social capital 'refers to the internal social and cultural coherence of society, the norms and values that govern interactions among people and the institutions in which they are embedded. Social capital is the glue that holds societies together and without which there can be no economic growth or human well-being'.[39] For Grootaert, this all-embracing (and meaningless?) concept of social capital is the 'missing link' in explaining economic development.[40] Higher amounts of social capital lead to higher rates of economic development, as such networks can for example lower transaction costs such as information and trust. Thus, whether it is in North Italy or selected villages in Tanzania,[41] high rates of social capital can promote development. Although the precise nature of developmental social capital is rarely, if ever explained, the World Bank adheres to the view that networks that comprise social capital are conducive to development in that they provide a 'space' for the development of appropriate institutions independent of the state.

Again, the more general implications of this concept are discussed below. More specifically, social capital is an extremely vague idea, which can mean anything from society in general – the discovery of which may be a revelation to neo-liberal fundamentalists, but not to anyone else – to social networks. Even in the more restricted sense of the term, it is far from clear how social capital leads to development, let alone which networks are conducive to, and which hinder, development. Social capital thus fails to stand up to critical

---

[37] Putnam 1993; 2000. See also Bourdieu 1986, but, given the far more radical implications of his work, he hardly figures in World Bank discussion. See also Fine 2001, Chapter 4.

[38] I deliberately repeat the word 'appear' in the text, as it is not altogether clear what is really meant by social capital.

[39] World Bank 1998, foreword.

[40] Grootaert 1997.

[41] Putnam 1993; Narayan and Pritchett 1997.

scrutiny, and – like governance and market-friendly interventionism – its theoretical or empirical rigour is far less important than its ideological role.[42]

(iv) *Assessing the institutional agenda*

There is a common theme running through the World Bank institutional agenda from the late 1980s onwards. The dominant interpretation at the Bank is that institutions and organisational networks must be found that promote the efficiency of 'the market' against the inefficiency of the state. Good governance, civil society and social capital are, therefore, means to an end, which is the promotion of an efficient, market-led economy in which government plays a strictly limited role. Indeed, this approach dominates the much trumpeted poverty alleviation agenda of the Bank as well, which also developed in the 1990s.[43] Poverty is seen as a condition in which people are poor because they lack access to income-earning activities generated by the market.[44] Market access – and therefore markets themselves – need to be expanded, and this is to be carried out through a strategy of deregulating markets.[45] The argument notion that markets themselves may be marginalising is therefore discounted from the outset.

Poverty alleviation through a reduction in the power of markets and money is discounted in this approach, which again betrays the Bank's assumption that market provision is intrinsically better than public provision. This perspective applies equally to narrower issues of economic growth too, and the 1993 Report on East Asia, which grudgingly accepts that states can be economically efficient, still holds on to the assumption that markets are more efficient by arguing that state intervention is either irrelevant or corrected by other, efficient interventions that would have occurred anyway in the absence of government intervention.[46] This argument betrays the ideological belief that because states must be inefficient, when economic 'winners' are picked it is either irrelevant or conforms to market principles. In each case, then, states and markets are rigidly separated and the former is simply regarded as a means for the promotion of the latter.

---

[42] Harriss 2001.
[43] World Bank 1990; 1994.
[44] Indeed, Third Way thinkers such as Giddens apply this argument to the global level. See further, Chapter 5.
[45] World Bank 1994, p. 63.
[46] See Kiely 2002a.

Similarly, the Bank argues that corruption has hindered development and that this can be overcome through a process of privatisation, liberalisation and reform of the state.[47] Corruption occurs because of state regulation, and so the state should be rolled back, while, at the same time, those officials still employed by the state should be paid higher wages in order to lower the incentive to continue corrupt practices. Anti-corruption policies are deemed to be important because corrupt practices hinder development, and much is made of the close correlation between low GDP and high rates of corruption.[48] However, even if we leave aside the difficulties of measuring corruption, such a correlation does not prove a causal connection, and indeed it may be that high corruption rates are simply a reflection of low rates of growth. Moreover, corruption has been and is a common occurrence in the most successful developing countries, such as South Korea and China, which suggests that a malign state/benign market explanation is far too simplistic. Indeed, rolling back the state could encourage further corruption as it may undermine regulatory practices necessary to police corrupt practices. This may be true even when those people that remain employed in the state sector enjoy higher salaries, because the incentive to continue corrupt practices may remain in the face of lack of regulation. Moreover, privatisation may increase corruption as state utilities are sold at cheap prices, and therefore access to these bargains will often involve access to state office.[49] The reasons for widespread corruption are thus far more complex than 'too much government', and reflect the wider processes of state formation in post-colonial Africa.[50] Solutions cannot be reduced to a simplistic set of technocratic policies, based on the promotion of limited government and the expansion of market forces.

The neo-liberal theory of the state is incorrect for three principal reasons. First, the question of separation of state and market is a far from straightforward question. Neo-liberals argue that states should intervene to promote law and order, defence, infrastructure and public goods. However, in practice, such minimal regulation would be questioned by most neo-liberals, who would argue for some regulations over say, labour markets, which clearly entails government intervention. Thus, most 'advanced' countries have some regulation

---

[47] World Bank 1997.
[48] Mauro 1998.
[49] Szeftel 1998; Khan 2002.
[50] See Allen 1995; Mamdani 1996; Szeftel 2000.

of employment conditions. But, if this is the case, then where are the boundaries set? In the nineteenth century, some British industrialists opposed restrictions on the use of child labour, claiming that this would undermine efficiency and amounted to government intervention in the free market. In the late twentieth century, the Conservative Party in Britain opposed minimum-wage legislation on similar grounds. Similarly, the question of how a public good can be defined is far from being an objective or purely technical question. Neo-liberals usually make the argument that street lighting is a classic public good because it is impossible to be consumed by one individual person without others also enjoying the benefits. This argument is close to the nineteenth-century distinction between self-regarding acts which only affect individuals, and other regarding acts, which affect society in general, and where there is a case for government intervention. But this distinction betrays a far-from-objective belief that society is little more than the sum of individual, self-interested actions, which therefore excludes from the outset any notion that efficiency may be met through a commitment to the 'public interest' (and thus assumes that privatisation is inherently efficient). The second, related weakness of neo-liberalism is, therefore, that not only is it impossible to rigidly demarcate a public, state sphere and a private, market, sphere, but that the creation of a market economy is actually a product of state policies. The previous chapter showed that the expansion of a global market-place over the last twenty years is far from natural, and has been put in place by nation-states and international institutions that aim to extend the reach of the market-place. The claim that this policy of globalisation is efficient betrays the belief that markets are inherently more efficient than states, which leads us back to the first problem. The third problem is that neo-liberals assume that states are inefficient because they are made up of self-interested individuals that lack the 'accountability' of the competitive private sector. Such individuals are said to be self-interested for the simple reason that people are inherently self-interested. In the private sector, such self-interest is constrained by the principle of competition, but this is not the case in the state sector. But if this is the case, then it is far from clear that neo-liberals can consistently justify the existence (in their theoretical model) of *any* state. Of course, in practice, they do believe in the need for a state to constrain self-interested behaviour, and argue that its existence rests on a (metaphorical) social contract between state and society. But, if such a social contract exists, then this implies that individuals are more than simply self-interested beings. Similarly, neo-liberals recognise the need for (public) law and order, but, if this is the case, then how can we guarantee that such laws represent something more than the self-interest of legislators? More concretely, in practice, neo-liberals recommend as a second-best option to privatisation, the deregulation of the state. But the question then arises: why should state bureaucrats carry out such deregulation if it is not in their self-interest? Again, the only answer can be that state bureaucrats, like human beings generally, are not simply self-interested and may also have some commitment to the collective interest. But, if this is so, then the neo-liberal blanket case for the efficiency of the market over the state collapses. Put in terms of the crudest neo-liberal approach, if, following Margaret Thatcher, there is no such thing as society, then what obliges us to obey laws?[51]

These points are not made to deny that individuals do behave in self-interested ways. Nor is it to deny that we live in a society in which self-interested behaviour is unjustly rewarded, or, indeed, that many laws and regulations favour the wealthy and powerful. But this is not the same point that neo-liberals (inconsistently) make, which is that society is *reducible* to self-interested individual actions; that is, individuals are *always and everywhere* self-interested. Neo-liberalism thus attempts to universalise motivations that are ultimately rooted in far deeper social and political (capitalist) relations, and which are, therefore, deeply implicated in relations of power. Like the political project of globalisation, neo-liberalism is an ideological project, and not a value-free science of human behaviour.[52]

---

[51] See further Durkheim 1957, Kiely 1995, Chapter 6, and Chang 2002.

[52] The Third Way does not necessarily completely uphold the inconsistent ideas of neo-liberalism. In particular, Third Way thinkers argue that neo-liberalism's embrace of naked self-interest can potentially undermine other life values, including responsibilities to others as well as individual rights (Giddens 1998, pp. 26–7), a point I return to in Chapter 9. Nevertheless, as should be clear from the discussion in Section 1, the Third Way in practice does tend to fetishise markets as being both natural and efficient, and for this reason is committed to their expansion. Giddens may well be correct in his argument that states can be inefficient and that central planning does not constitute a viable alternative, but this does not entitle him to make sweeping statements about the self-adjusting capacity of free markets or the relative transparency (pre-Enron) of US capitalism (see Giddens 2001, pp. 5–6; Giddens and Hutton 2001, pp. 19, 34). Like neo-liberalism, the Third Way does believe in the inherent efficiency of markets, and champions the view that states should simply play an enabling role for efficient global markets.

It should be clear, then, that the policy changes made by the World Bank in the 1990s are still broadly compatible with neo-liberalism. The new institutionalism represents a modification of, but not a substantial break from, neo-liberalism. Institutions and networks are 'measured' in terms of their capacity to reduce the costs of market transactions. They therefore play an enabling role that allows taken for granted 'market forces' to operate more efficiently. Constraints on the exercise of individual self-interest through the market-place are identified, and policies are promoted on the basis of their capacity to overcome such constraints. The so-called Post-Washington Consensus of the 1990s therefore represents only a cosmetic break with the neo-liberal Washington Consensus of the 1980s.[53]

This approach to 'development' thus closely parallels the most important interventionist policy advocated by the Third Way for the technologically advanced countries, namely investment in human resources to ensure a skilled, competitive economy. These minor policy changes – in both the developed and developing world – now need to be compared to the reality of the expansion of neo-liberal globalisation in the 1990s, both in the technologically advanced countries (Section 3) and in the developing world (Section 4).

4.3 The reality of globalisation 1: the new economy in the United States

As I showed above, the Third Way is said to be a new political doctrine for new times. Above all, it is said to be appropriate to the development of a new economy, in which flows of information have become more important than manufacturing. This is associated with the communications revolution, the arrival of a globalised, 'weightless' economy, and a post-socialist world.[54] According to Giddens,

> the essence of the economy has changed. What matters isn't how or where goods are manufactured, but the definition of the 'product' that is bought and sold. It is the idea that sells, not the material that is built into its construction.[55]

---

[53] Fine et al. 2001.
[54] Giddens and Hutton 2001, p. 1. The reference is to both Giddens and Hutton but the claim is made by the former in conversation with the latter, who does not accept this argument.
[55] In Giddens and Hutton 2001, p. 25.

Information and knowledge, not material production, are said to be the driving forces of the new economy, and this is closely related to the development of information technology. This technology is the driving force of the new economy, as it allows information to be rapidly transmitted throughout the globe. This, in turn, allows for the development of flexible networks of globalised informational labour, which create and adapt to change at a rapid pace, as opposed to the rigidity of labour associated with manufacturing. As a result, place and time become less important as information can be moved rapidly and can take place in real time on a global scale. The use of information technology can provide immediate information on the demand for particular goods, ranging from supplies to manufacturers to the amount of goods bought in a particular shop, thus allowing goods to arrive 'just in time' and therefore cutting down on transport and storage costs. Some writers – and not just new-economy apologists[56] – make the claim that this has allowed capitalism to transcend the business cycle by providing information which allows consumption and production to remain balanced, at least for those incorporated into the new economy. These (highly contentious and now discredited)[57] arguments have also been associated with Manuel Castells, even if, in his case, he remains critical of the so-called information society.

But the Third Way, on the other hand, paints a more unambiguously optimistic picture. The new economy represents a new opportunity for the advanced capitalist countries to overcome the boom-bust cycles of the manufacturing era, and maintain a high-wage, high-productivity economy. The developing world can also benefit, by initially competing through low wage costs, which, in the long run, will allow for an upgrading to an advanced economy. Crucially, in both cases, market forces must be embraced, and state regulation must ultimately promote free labour markets and free trade in goods, services and money. The state plays a more active role than the neo-liberal fundamentalism of the 1980s, but essentially it is one that allows the market to operate more efficiently. For these reasons, a Third Way-neo-liberal alliance occurred in the 1990s, in Britain, the US and parts of the developing

---

[56] See Hoogvelt 2001, Chapter 5.
[57] The use of information technology can be useful in terms of predicting demand for some parts, some finished consumer goods, and so on. However, it is hardly sufficient to balance supply and demand. The 1990s was an era of massive overcapacity, financial bubbles and financial crises, and hardly one where technology at last facilitated an equilibrium between supply and demand.

world. President Clinton thus continued with Alan Greenspan as Chair of the US Federal Reserve, and he presided over the new-economy boom, arguing that

> [i]t is safe to say that we are witnessing, this decade in the US, history's most compelling demonstration of the productive capacity of free people's operating in free markets.[58]

From 1992–2000, while its main competitors faced economic downturn, there was a boom in the US economy based on relatively high levels of investment and low inflation and unemployment. In 1999–2000, GDP grew by 5.2 per cent, productivity by 4.1 per cent and investment by 11 per cent.[59] By 1999, inflation was just 2.4 per cent and unemployment 4.2 per cent of the workforce, undermining arguments that too low a rate of unemployment would lead to excessive rates of inflation.[60] Moreover, the Clinton administration also managed to reverse the enormous budget deficit that was inherited from the Reagan-Bush Senior years. GDP grew by an average of 3.7 per cent a year from 1993–9, compared to 2.9 per cent from 1981–92, while unemployment was 4.2 per cent by 1999 and inflation only an average 2.4 per cent for the same year.[61]

Its apologists were quite clear about the reasons for the boom. It was a product, not of tangible assets, but of skills, information, ideas and above all venture capital, which facilitated the funding of high-tech start-up firms, based on a more closely integrated stock market, particularly for Initial Public Offerings (IPOs). In the years from 1998–2000 alone, venture capital investment increased from $14.3 billion to $54.5 billion.[62] The stock-market boom was therefore based in part on the expectations of future profits to be made in the dynamic sectors of the new economy, which will facilitate a surge in productivity growth through the use of information technology. Greenspan, for instance, believed that a virtuous circle would be generated, in which the new economy's potential would lead to more investment, an increase in productivity, expectations of higher profits, higher share prices, increasing paper wealth, more borrowing, high investment and consumption growth, high productivity . . . and so on. Writing in the *Wall Street Journal*, leading economist Rudi Dornbusch argued in 1998 that

---

[58] Greenspan 1999.
[59] Brenner 2002, pp. 244–5.
[60] Pollin 2000, p. 35.
[61] Pollin 2000, pp. 29, 35.
[62] Brenner 2002, p. 244.

[t]he US economy likely will not see a recession for years to come. We don't want one, we don't need one, and as we have the tools to keep the current expansion going, we won't have one. This expansion will last forever.'[63]

Even Castells argued that 'the new economy is/will be predicated on a surge in productivity growth resulting from the ability to use new information technology in powering a knowledge based production system', and that 'the overall trend in valuation seems to respond to a rational expectation of the new sources of economic growth'.[64]

Talk of a new era dominated the 1990s boom. But, as in the 1920s and 1960s, such talk was based on a seriously misplaced optimism, as increased investment was financed by a speculative stock-market boom. A massive gap opened up between expected and actual profits, and an inevitable crash followed. Corporate asset values stood at $15.7 trillion at the peak of the boom in the first quarter of 2000, and then rapidly fell back to $10.5 trillion, representing a 33 per cent collapse in prices.[65] Although there was an increase in real profit rates in the 1990s, the increase in share values bore little relation to these increases, and shares were massively overvalued. Thus, the Dow Jones Index increased from 884 (1982) to 10, 500 in 1999, while the hi-tech NASDAQ Index increased from 189 (1982) to 4, 800 in March 2000.[66] The extent of the overvalued stock markets is best measured by examining the ratio between (stock) prices and real earnings, known as the price/earnings ratio. At their peaks, America Online had a price/earnings ratio of 720, Yahoo of 1,468 and e-bay of 9,751, compared to RCA's peak of 73 in 1929, and Xerox's 123 in 1961, which was regarded at the time as being highly extravagant.[67] The NASDAQ Index as a whole had a price/earnings ratio of 400:1 for the first quarter of 2000.[68] In March 2001, many e-businesses collapsed, having never made any money and the NASDAQ price earnings ratio fell back to 154: 1,[69] still far higher than its average from 1985–2000 of 52, but much lower than the 400: 1 of a year earlier. Thus, it was the high-tech industries, the supposed vanguard of

---

[63] Cited in Henwood 2003, p. 3.
[64] Castells 2000, pp. 161, 152.
[65] Brenner 2002, p. 252.
[66] Perelman 2002, p. 205.
[67] Henwood 1999, p. 128.
[68] Brenner 2002, p. 248.
[69] Brenner 2002, p. 249.

the new economy, that were most affected by the crash, particularly the so-called 'dot.coms'. Thus, to take the most extreme example, a new virtual company called TheGlobe.com had a start-up share price of $9 in 1998, and this quickly soared to $97. Less than two years later, its shares were trading at less than $5, and, by early 2003, this had gone down to $0.075.[70]

A number of factors explain this speculative bubble. Government policy encouraged investors by deregulating finance on the one hand, and supporting creditors when they were in trouble on the other. Thus, Greenspan did express some concern over the 'irrational exuberance' of speculators, but did not impose any stringent controls (such as margin requirements) on them, which encouraged massive borrowing to pay for the boom. Banking laws were liberalised so that commercial and investment banking were no longer separated, which encouraged banks to make loans to companies (commercial banking) and then underwrite clients' stock and bond offerings (investment banking). Bailouts were also granted to investors at the first sign of financial crisis. The main buyers of shares were companies, many of whom indulged in a spending spree of stock buy-backs. From 1994–2000, companies repurchased an average of $121 billion a year of their own stocks,[71] which was designed to further inflate the value of their own shares. This practice was further reinforced by the growing practice of paying company managers an increasing proportion of their salary in company shares (from 22 per cent of chief executive officer salaries in 1979 to 63 per cent from 1995–9),[72] so that any increase in share prices increased the value of their stock options. Share prices were further increased by corporate fraud, most notoriously at Enron and WorldCom, in which company managers, accountants and bankers colluded to inflate profit figures in order to further boost share prices. Ultimately, this boom and bust cycle reflected what Crotty[73] calls the neo-liberal paradox, which is that major players in financial markets demand (and depend on) increasing earnings from productive capital, but, at the same time, the very dominance of finance undermines the capacity of productive capital to deliver such earnings. The 1980s solution of reduced labour costs had limited room for manoeuvre in the 1990s as unemployment decreased, and so more desperate measures such

---

[70] Henwood 2003, p. 189.
[71] Pollin 2003, p. 62.
[72] Crotty 2003, p. 274.
[73] Crotty 2003.

as company fraud was commonly practiced, but the basic contradiction re-asserted itself and stock prices fell rapidly.

The stock-market boom could not continue to outpace real economic performance, and despite new-economy rhetoric, it is clear that the boom years did not constitute an unprecedented expansion in the US economy. The annual average growth rate of 3.7 per cent from 1993–9 compared favourably to the 2.9 per cent of 1981–92, but was not much higher than 1977–80 (3.4 per cent) and lower than the 4.8 per cent of the years 1961–8.[74] Annual average productivity growth of 1.8 per cent from 1993–9 was only slightly higher than the Reagan-Bush Senior years (1.7 per cent) and far lower than the years from 1961–8 (3.4 per cent). The development of a high-tech, high-skilled economy did not come about, and state spending fell in real terms by as much as 24 per cent in the Clinton era,[75] and the growth of highly skilled, highly paid IT workers was small. By 2000, they still constituted only around 2 per cent of the US labour force.[76] In terms of the real investment that did occur, much of it was wasted. For instance, telecommunications companies invested heavily in fibre-optic cables, partly in response to a 'report' that internet traffic was increasing at a rate of 100 per cent every three months. From 1996 to the end of the boom, Wall Street raised $1.3 trillion in telecommunications debt, which led to mergers valued at $1.7 trillion. At the end of the boom, the industry collapsed with $230 billion in bankruptcies and fraud, $2 trillion market value wiped out, and $110 billion in defaults. Telecommunications executives, cashing in their options just in time, cashed $18 billion, while over half a million jobs were cut, and, in early 2003, more than 96 per cent of cable capacity was still not being used.[77]

Moreover, if we examine the economy as a whole, then we see that, contrary to the claims made for a new economy, the boom was actually led by consumption and not investment (though this did increase too). The ratio of consumption to GDP (as opposed to investment/GDP) was historically high in the 1990s – at 67 per cent, five points higher than the boom in the 1960s, which has allowed for lower rates of government spending without generating

---

[74] Pollin 2000, p. 29.
[75] Pollin 2003, pp. 74–5.
[76] Henwood 2003, pp. 71–8.
[77] Prins 2002.

a recession.[78] This period also saw a substantial rise in debt, which increased from 65 per cent of disposable income in the 1960s to 94 per cent by the late 1990s, and was financed by a rise in asset values. It was this rise in debt-financed consumption that fuelled the boom and counteracted the effects of the cut in the budget deficit (reinforced by tax windfalls through the stock market boom). Not surprisingly, from 1997–2000, the trade deficit increased two-and-a-half times.[79] There was a substantial rise in stock-market purchases by foreigners in the 1990s,[80] although the value of such purchases was quickly inflated by rising asset prices. Most new purchases were, however, in US Treasury bonds, which increased from $463 billion in 1994 to $1,053 billion by 1997.[81] The US therefore remained dependent on the import of overseas capital, and by 2003, the trade deficit was close to 5 per cent of GDP,[82] the biggest in US history. The nature of the relationship between the US and the international economy is crucial for an understanding of globalisation in the 1990s, and this issue is taken up in Sections 4 and 5 below.

4.4   The reality of globalisation 2: emerging markets in the 1990s

In the last chapter, we saw how the debt crisis had meant that the developing world was a net exporter of capital in the 1980s. However, although parts of the developing world remained marginalised, the 1990s saw a new wave of optimism associated with the rise of the emerging markets, particularly in East Asia and Latin America. From 1990–4, $524 billion in capital flowed into developing countries, an average of $105 billion a year. This annual average was three times the average in the years (1977–82) that preceded the debt crisis, and twelve times the 1983–9 average.[83] In the early 1990s, after years of net outflows to pay back interest on debt, Latin America once again became a net capital importer. The debt crisis was thus deemed to be over, at least for the richer developing countries that again had access to substantial capital inflows. Rather than bank lending, which had been the main source of capital

---

[78] Pollin 2000, p. 31.
[79] Brenner 2002, p. 205.
[80] Pollin 2003, p. 64.
[81] Gowan 2001c, p. 363.
[82] <www.fxcm.com>.
[83] Henwood 1996, p. 14.

for Latin America and East Asia, the main sources of foreign capital in the 1990s were direct foreign investment,[84] plus portfolio investment in foreign stock and bond markets. For much of the 1990s, such investment was regarded as good for development, as it allowed countries to draw on the global pool of financial savings, which in turn would facilitate investment and economic growth. The main factor that encouraged such flows was the adoption of the market-friendly policies outlined in Section 2 above, and so the new emerging markets became 'models' of liberalisation for the rest of the developing world. However, the emerging markets boom came to be associated with increased financial instability, including in most of Latin America, East Asia, Russia and the United States. The problems can be illustrated through a brief examination of three cases: Mexico in 1994–5, East Asia in 1997–8 and Latin America (especially Argentina) at the turn of the century.

(i) *Mexico*

In this new era of globalising financial markets, Mexico was regarded as the model pupil, and it attracted $4.5 billion in 1990, $15 billion in 1991, $18 billion in 1992, and $32 billion in 1993.[85] Most of this money was not intended for direct investment in the productive sector, but flooded into stocks and bonds to make a profit through speculation. Share prices grew by an average of 50 per cent in 1990, 124 per cent in 1991, 24 per cent in 1992 and 48 per cent in 1993.[86] The attractions for foreign capital were high interest rates and an informal linkage of the dollar to peso. However, this capital inflow was mainly confined to unproductive speculation in real estate, and the stock and bond markets, and not in productive investment. The result was that a high interest rate and an overvalued currency encouraged speculation and consumption, while at the same time choking productive investment and therefore exports, and therefore the current account went into deficit. By 1994, this deficit stood at an unsustainable 8 per cent of GDP which, together with an increase in interest rates in the United States, led to capital export, a crash on the stock market, a run on the peso, and a new debt crisis for Mexico. In December 1994 the peso was devalued by 40 per cent. However, this did not

---

[84] This is discussed in detail in Chapter 5.
[85] Bello et al. 2000, p. 8.
[86] Grabel 1996, p. 1768.

lead to stabilisation but, instead, encouraged a further run on the peso. In January 1995, the Mexican government depleted almost 50 per cent of its foreign exchange reserves trying to protect the peso. These events fuelled the fear that Mexico would default on payments to short-term bond-holders. These bonds, denominated in both pesos (the cete) and dollars (the tesobono) offered high returns to investors. The government had been deficit financing its short-term debt through these bonds, and so could have defaulted as its foreign exchange reserves fell along with the flight of portfolio investment. There was also a fear that this crash could spread to the United States, as individual and institutional investors were left with worthless bonds. Relief came in the form of a $20 billion bailout plus $28 billion of additional loans. In return, Mexico agreed to further privatisation and liberalisation, tighter controls on money (higher interest rates), increased indirect taxation, and a reduction in budget and current account deficits. Most of the bailout funds were used to cover tesobono and other bond obligations.[87] The peso crisis of the mid-1990s was the first emerging markets crisis, and from the viewpoint of developing countries, it showed the risks associated with attracting short-term capital inflows, which can quickly become outflows with devastating effects, and how the high-interest-rate, high-exchange-rate policies that attract such investment undermines longer-term investment potential.

(ii) East Asia

If the Mexican crisis carried some dangers, the East-Asian crash of 1997–8 was potentially catastrophic. East Asia had been deemed a region full of miracle economies that, according to the World Bank, did have interventionist governments, but were still compatible with neo-liberal policies as such intervention was deemed to be 'market-friendly'.[88] Given the degree of state intervention that had occurred, this was a highly questionable interpretation, but it was rapidly abandoned in the context of the financial crisis, and the 'East-Asian model' of market-friendly intervention was re-interpreted as a failure of crony capitalism.

The crisis began in Thailand in July 1997, with speculation against its national currency, the baht. This speculation spread to other currencies, most

---

[87] See Grabel 1996.
[88] See World Bank 1993. For critiques, see Amsden 1994, Kiely 1998.

decisive of which was the Korean won. These attacks then led to an enormous withdrawal of money from the region, led by US mutual funds and banks. The result was that local banks could no longer roll over their dollar debts as new lending dried up, and as local currencies collapsed, so did the size of the debt (which was denominated in dollars). The downward spiral continued as local banks refused further credit to industrial companies, and so bankruptcies spread. This sharp movement from boom to crisis led to a shift in perception in the West, often from the same people who had previously regarded the East-Asian economies as neo-liberal miracles. US Treasury Under-Secretary Larry Summers was hardly alone in explaining the crisis as a product of 'crony capitalism'.[89] Similarly, Tony Blair repeated the neo-liberal mantra that '[t]he lesson of the Asian crisis is that it is better to invest in countries where you have openness, independent central banks, properly functioning financial systems and independent courts, where you do not have to bribe or rely on favours from those in power'.[90]

But this account of the crash is extremely superficial. It ignores the fact that East Asia had previously been regarded as a model of market-friendly intervention and, like the debt crisis of 1982, attempts to explain systemic crisis as a simple problem of bad policy. The roots of the crash go far deeper than this, at least as far back as the Plaza Accord of 1985. This agreement led to a devaluation of the dollar, which was good for East-Asian countries whose currencies were fixed to the value of the dollar. The result was a massive boom in manufacturing exports, which was also facilitated by earlier successful interventionist industrial policies (South Korea), and Japanese relocation of industry to South-East Asia (in part to avoid the loss of competitiveness through the upward valuation of the yen). The policy of fixing local currencies to the dollar was carried out in the late 1980s and was designed to promote exchange rate stability. South-East-Asian countries were particularly open to attracting capital from overseas, and even South Korea, which had been quite restrictive in its approach to foreign capital, began to liberalise in response to international pressure from the US and domestic pressure from the large conglomerates, known as chaebols. This manifested itself through membership of the OECD becoming conditional on liberalisation, and the chaebols,

---

[89] See Chang 2000.
[90] Blair 1999.

threatened by competitive pressures, demanding easier access to the cheap short term loans offered by international financial markets.

The result of this liberalisation was a stupendous movement of money into the booming East-Asian economies. In 1996, Indonesia received $16 billion in foreign capital inflows, South Korea $20 billion, Malaysia $13 billion and Thailand $14 billion. Around half of these inflows were not foreign direct investment, but far more mobile portfolio investment (which entered local stock markets) or foreign commercial loans.[91] This build up of debt appeared not to matter so long as the expansion of manufacturing exports continued, but these slowed down from the mid-1990s, and, in 1995, the dollar was revalued through the international agreement known as the 'reverse Plaza' Accord. At this point, the East-Asian economies could have detached from the dollar to maintain manufacturing export competitiveness, but 'addicted to what appeared to be a never-ending bounty of cheap short-term loans, they balked at this, and their currencies rose with the dollar'.[92] Faced with growing international competition (especially from China), in the context of continued lower rates of global growth (see Chapter 5), returns on the value (though not volume) of exports fell in 1996. South Korea's export growth declined from 31.5 per cent in 1995 to 4.1 per cent in 1996; Thailand's from 24.7 per cent to 0.1 per cent; and Malaysia's from 25.9 per cent to 4 per cent.[93] However, the speculative boom persisted, driven by the appreciation of dollar-tied currencies. But by 1997, faced with declining competitiveness and falling profits, money began to leave the region in enormous amounts and the downward spiral of currency speculation, falling equity prices, higher interest payments and bankruptcies began. In 1997 alone, East Asia saw a $93 billion inflow become a $12 billion outflow, the equivalent of 11 per cent of combined GDP for the five main countries affected – South Korea, Thailand, Philippines, Malaysia and Indonesia.[94] The region entered a severe recession. South Korea's per capita income fell from $11,380 in 1996 to $6,472 in 1998.[95] Unemployment increased from 2.1 per cent in October 1997 to 8.6 per cent in February 1999.[96] In Indonesia, unemployment soared from 4.9 per cent to 13.8 per cent and

---

[91] UNCTAD 1997.
[92] Brenner 2002, p. 159.
[93] UNCTAD 1997, p. 14.
[94] Wade and Venereso 1998, p. 20.
[95] Burkett and Hart-Landsberg 2001, p. 111.
[96] Crotty and Lee 2002, p. 669.

real wages fell by between 40 and 60 per cent.[97] There has been some recovery since the late 1990s, particularly in South Korea, where growth rates increased once again from 1999 onwards, and unemployment started to fall. However, the devastating social effects of the recession have not been fully reversed, and fixed investment rates have not returned to pre-crisis levels, and therefore serious questions remain over the sustainability of the recovery and the nature of IMF policies in the region.[98]

The policies recommended by the IMF were as predictable as they were counter-productive – at least from the point of view of the debtors. Faced with serious debt crises, governments received loans from the IMF – Indonesia received $80 billion, South Korea $58 billion and Thailand $17 billion. As had been the case in the 1980s debt crisis, these loans were subject to conditions. For instance, South Korea was to increase its interest rates, devalue the national currency, cut back on government spending, and further liberalise the economy, a pattern repeated in Indonesia and Thailand. The IMF believed that these policies would restore the confidence of international markets and therefore lead to the movement of capital back into South Korea, and the region as a whole. In fact, in 1998, the recession in South Korea deepened, and the economy contracted by 5.8 per cent and industrial investment fell by 21.2 per cent.[99] These policies led to a partial reversal of IMF policy as the Korean government was allowed to lower interest rates and increase its budget deficit half way through 1998. There was also the suspicion that the policies had more to do with protecting the interests of creditors and opening up the region further to foreign capital, particularly financial interests. Certainly, in post-crisis South Korea, there was a gigantic increase of direct and portfolio foreign investment, which increased from its peak in one year (1997) of $8 billion to $62 billion over the next three years. This increase did not, however, lead to an increase in real fixed investment rates, as the investment was made up of acquisition of existing Korean firms and/or the Korean stock market. The percentage of Korean market capitalisation owned by foreigners increased from 2.7 per cent in 1992, to 12.3 per cent in 1997, to 36.2 per cent in January 2002.[100]

---

[97] World Bank 2000.
[98] Crotty and Lee 2002; Stiglitz 2002.
[99] Chang and Yoo 2000, p. 115.
[100] Crotty and Lee 2002, p. 676.

(iii) *Latin America*

At the turn of the century, financial crisis had spread to Latin America, and by 1999 net capital flows to the region stood at similar levels to 1982, when the debt crisis broke out. In 1982, just less than US $40 billion left the region while in 1999, the figure was actually over $40 billion. By the year 2000, debt service/export earning ratios in Latin-America were close to 1982 debt-crisis levels.[101] In the early years of the twenty-first century, Latin-American per capita growth rates averaged just 0.2 per cent a year. Moreover, even the 'successful' decade of the 1990s needs to be put in context, and annual average per capita growth rates were 1.4 per cent, better than the negative rates for the 1980s (minus 0.3 per cent), but considerably lower than the 1950s, 1960s and 1970s.[102] Clearly, the emerging markets boom was something of an exaggeration, and even this so-called boom is now over. Indeed, in 1999, net flows to *all* regions of the developing world were negative.[103] Brazil and Argentina were particularly adversely affected, and the movement in the eyes of the IMF from neo-liberal models to badly run state-led economies was rapid. Argentina, for example, was the fourth largest recipient of foreign capital investment in the early 1990s, but this fuelled a consumer boom, which papered over the cracks of a rising trade deficit. This deficit reflected the fact that, with a few exceptions, there was no investment boom in the productive economy. Indeed, the decision to fix the value of the peso to the dollar on a one to one basis, supported by the IMF as part of an anti-inflationary strategy, undermined export competitiveness. From early 2000, investor confidence in the Argentine economy collapsed, and capital rapidly left the country, which, in turn, started a downward spiral of falling asset prices, increased capital flight, and increasing deficits. By late 2001, the pressure was so great that there was devaluation and default on the foreign debt, as well as ongoing (and continuing) unrest.

The emerging markets boom in the 1990s arose out of liberalisation measures that encouraged foreign capital inflows. These flows replaced bank lending – which had become far scarcer after the 1982 debt crisis – as the main source of capital inflow, at least for the richer developing countries (poorer countries

---

[101] Weeks 2002, p. 183.
[102] Weisbrot and Rosnick 2003, p. 6.
[103] Sutcliffe 2001, tables 86 and 87.

remained dependent on official flows). The flows included direct foreign investment, which was usually defined as investment that led to a controlling share (a 10 per cent or greater equity share) in a company, or investment in financial markets, which usually meant stock, bond, or derivatives markets. The desirability of these flows is discussed below, but it is clear that these flows did not lead to a new economic miracle in any part of the developing world.[104] This was partly because of the severity of the collapse, but also reflected the fact that direct foreign investment often involved take-overs rather than greenfield investment, and that financial flows often had little impact in the 'real' economy. This was not always the case, and some investment spin-offs occurred, especially in East Asia, but, clearly, the 'emerging market booms' were far from economic miracles.

4.5   Global finance and US hegemony

Rather than reflecting a new era, the new-economy and the emerging-markets booms of the 1990s reflected the hegemony of global financial capital. We therefore need to look a little more at financial markets, and the globalisation of finance in particular, taking up the story from where we left off in the previous chapter. We will then also be in a position to relate finance to wider political questions.

(i) *The globalisation of finance*

Like the earlier 1980s debt crisis, there was considerable debate over the causes of financial crises in the 1990s and early 2000s. Neo-liberals – including the Third Way variant – argued that the system as a whole was efficient and that the problem was that some countries had internal problems, which undermined their capacity to properly integrate into the system. As we saw above, the case for financial liberalisation has been most clearly made by McKinnon and Shaw.[105] The McKinnon-Shaw thesis is basically derived from neo-classical economics and contends that financial liberalisation allows for an increase in savings, and therefore investment and economic growth.

---

[104] The Asian miracles pre-date the 1990s and, in the cases of South Korea and Taiwan, are rooted in industrial policies that go back to the 1950s at least.
[105] McKinnon and Shaw 1973.

Financial markets, like all markets, tend towards equilibrium and so crises must be caused by external mechanisms such as state intervention, which repress financial savings and hence accumulation. Indeed, free financial markets are desirable precisely because they can discipline the inefficiencies of state economic intervention. Financial crises occur not because of the nature of financial markets, but because such markets have not been sufficiently liberalised, as recommended by the IMF in the aftermath of the financial meltdown in East Asia. This position is also endorsed by Tony Blair, who has resisted calls for renewed restrictions on capital, 'because you actually want people to be able to move money very, very quickly'.[106]

More critical accounts linked the crises to the volatile nature of short-term, financial flows. The problem with the argument of cronyism is that there are simply too many countries that fail the test of integration, and that the model countries of one year (Mexico, South Korea, Argentina, Brazil, and so on), become the scapegoats the next. Moreover, it hardly fits the case of East Asia, particularly South Korea, which has had historically high rates of domestic savings, even before liberalisation. Critics of McKinnon-Shaw argue that the expansion of financial markets is not necessarily conducive to increased economic growth and, instead, encourages an increase in speculation, which can make countries vulnerable to crisis.[107] In particular, financial flows exaggerate both upward and downward trends in the 'real economy' and thus can exacerbate boom and bust cycles.[108] This can best be illustrated by examining global financial markets in a little more detail.

In the last twenty to thirty years, we have seen a transition from the post-war era of state restrictions on the national and international activities of financial markets, to a period of renewed financial liberalisation. This period of liberalisation has seen the awesome rise of institutional investors, alongside competition between these investors. Thus, in the United States, the percentage of corporate stock owned by households declined from 90 per cent in the 1950s to 42 per cent by 2000, and annual turnover on the New York Stock Exchange increased from around 20 per cent in 1960 to 70 per cent from 1983–7 (when there was enormous takeover activity of companies with low

---

[106] Quoted in Held 1998, p. 26.
[107] Grabel 1996.
[108] Grabel 2003.

share prices), to 100 per cent at the peak of the new-economy boom in 2000.[109] Moreover, this increase in financial activity has occurred in a period of floating exchange rates, which has carried a number of risks and opportunities, both for financial markets and the economy in general. Chapter 3 charted the transition from the Bretton Woods era to neo-liberalism in the 1980s. In terms of finance, in the Bretton Woods era, the US was the main international creditor, the dollar was the main currency, and exchange rates were fixed against the value of the dollar, which, in turn, was fixed against the value of gold. In addition, there were controls on the movement of capital (except in the US), and conversion to foreign currencies took place through central banks. Post-Bretton Woods, the US became a very great debtor from the 1980s, the dollar remained the major reserve currency, but exchange rates were no longer fixed and the dollar was not linked to the price of gold. Capital controls were also gradually lifted in the 1970s and 1980s, though substantial controls still exist in some countries. It is these changes that help to explain the globalisation of finance.

In the context of floating exchange rates, companies face a great deal of insecurity. If investors buy shares in a foreign company with their national currency, and there is a downward movement in the company's national currency, the value of the investor's shares will fall. This may encourage the investor to sell his or her shares. If this occurs on a sufficiently large scale, and there is widespread selling of a company's shares, then the company's assets value will fall. This may well affect the real performance of the company, as its credit-worthiness also falls, making the company vulnerable to takeover when its share price is low. Moreover, the falling currency can intensify these problems. For example, company debts may be denominated in a foreign currency, and therefore devaluation makes servicing these debts more expensive. Imports – including of capital equipment – may also become more expensive. Faced with all these problems, financial market leaders may begin selling shares in the company, which, in turn, will lead to a wider selling spree as investors follow the herd, and sell their shares. Thus, a company may be subject to a devastating selling spree that has little to do with its actual economic performance. This may occur through speculation in national stock

---

[109] Crotty 2003, p. 274.

markets (though these may be controlled by states), but the potential for instability is increased in an era of floating exchange rates.

A similar principle operates within the foreign-exchange markets themselves. Under the fixed-rate system, companies could only obtain foreign exchange through its national central bank. Companies that earned foreign exchange had to convert these earnings back into the domestic currency through its central bank, and could only obtain further foreign exchange through central-bank approval. However, with the floating system, the buying and selling of foreign exchange became an end in itself. From the 1970s onwards, companies – including those involved in the production of real goods and services – increasingly set up investment funds in order to make profits through speculating in foreign currency markets. An investment fund may buy 500 units of Currency B in its own Currency A, with the expectation that the value of B will increase against A, and so make a large profit. However, these investment funds did not just deal with real-time transactions, but may also involve prices in futures markets. The Currency B money bought by the investment fund is actually unlikely to simply 'wait' to be reconverted three months down the line, and, instead, may be loaned to a Company (C) that wants to do real business in the country of Currency B. The investment fund will, therefore, lend to Company C and make an additional profit by charging a rate of interest on the loan. But this leads to potential uncertainty for C, as its debts are now held in a currency other than its own, and may have to pay back more to service its debts (or imports) if that currency devalues. Businesses thus tend to hold monetary assets in a number of currencies. They also may buy ahead in futures markets particular goods or services that they need, in order to secure or hedge against sudden changes in currency values. Futures markets, then, refer to those markets that are derived from, or secondary to, markets in actual goods and services.

Thus, a company may import a raw material from another country. It does so when its own currency is strong and the raw-material exporter's currency is quite weak. This may be an immediate transaction, and the importing company may have benefited from the relative strength of its own currency. But it may be that the transaction is not immediate, and an order is placed in the raw-materials futures market, so that the real transaction will occur in six months time. This transaction thereby involves a third party, the raw-materials futures dealer, who receives a percentage of the price, and has to pay for the raw material in six months time. In a floating exchange-rate system, this involves risk, as the importer's currency may decline against the exporter's in six months time. This will involve a substantial loss, because the futures dealer has agreed to pay the exporter at the current currency conversion rate, rather than the future one six months down the line. The raw-material futures dealer will, therefore, probably hedge against the risk by doing a deal with a dealer in the currency futures market, and buy currency at the current rate. If the currency falls in six months from its current value, then the raw-material and currency futures dealer will make losses. On the other hand, if the currency's value increases, then both futures dealers make substantial gains, based not on real transactions, but rather derived from the original real transaction.

In other words, derivatives markets are credit markets. But they are also bewilderingly complex, as the transactions derived from the original real transactions are potentially endless. The raw-material futures dealer agrees to pay a certain sum of money, in a certain currency, for a raw material, in six months time. But this certain sum of money can, in the meantime, finance all kinds of derived transactions ('secondary' is too restrictive a term to describe the uses to which the credit may be put). Thus, the currency dealer may use the credit to make a deal with another currency dealer, who in turn then may make her own deal, who will also make a deal, and so on. The result is a massive chain of networks, which are all derived from one real economic transaction – and which, incidentally, also means that estimating the values of the derivates markets is probably an impossible task.

There is thus enormous scope here for dealers to make money from the one basic transaction. But, at the same time, there is similarly enormous potential for a catastrophic collapse if things go wrong, and the initial transaction does not occur, for it will lead to default not only by the original importer, but also somewhere down the line for the futures dealers. In theory, futures dealers are required to not enter into transactions above the value of the assets of the investment fund for whom they are working, so that one default does not lead to a chain of defaults. But, in practice, minimum liquidity levels vary across futures markets and states. Moreover, given the amount of futures transactions any investment group may be involved in at any one time, this is very difficult to regulate, as various financial scandals have made clear.

The breathtaking rise of derivatives markets since the 1980s should thus be seen as a response to the problems of uncertainty in the context of floating exchange rates. But, simultaneously, these same markets provide an opportunity for profitable transactions in the context of this uncertainty. This context of risk and opportunity is also intensified by the existence of government securities markets. Government bonds are essentially issued by governments, who promise to pay the bond-holder a fixed amount of interest over a certain period of time. If there is strong demand for a particular government's bonds, this will have the effect of lowering the rate of interest for those same bonds. Thus, Country A's economy is booming, so investment in Government A's bonds is regarded as being a safe bet. Bonds are initially issued at, say, 100 units, and the government pays out 10 units a year on these bonds. Demand for these bonds is high, so their price rises to 200 units. However, the government does not then pay out 200 units a year, but, rather, continues to pay out 100 units a year. This means that there has effectively been a cut in the real, rather than nominal, interest rate on the government bonds. Thus, interest rates are determined not only by government policy, but by the decisions of buyers and sellers of government bonds.

This brief outline of the globalisation of financial markets has, one hopes, clarified some of the material relating to the booms of the 1990s. In the context of a boom, there is likely to be speculation in favour of buying shares, currencies and government bonds, which further fuels the boom. But, if market leaders believe that expectations on future prices – of shares, currencies and bonds – will not be met, then the buying spree will quickly become a selling spree, as the herd follow the market leaders. The mania of the boom period is thus followed by a panic in which buyers all try to sell their (Mexican, South Korean, Argentinian) shares, currencies and bonds, and so the panic eventually becomes a crash.[110] For 'real' (Mexican, Korean, Argentinian) companies, the effect is devastating. Falling share prices will undermine access to further credit, in the context of a currency that is falling in value against other currencies in which debt obligations may have to be met, and in which interest rates are increasing as a result of falling demand for government bonds (or IMF austerity programmes).

These apparently technical issues are, in fact, highly political ones, which

---

[110] Kindleberger 2000.

are 'linked to questions of what sort of societies we want to live in'.[111] The dominance of finance in the world economy thus reflects the broad changes that have occurred since the collapse of Bretton Woods in the early 1970s. From the 1980s, in particular, shareholder capitalism has increasingly come to dominate the world, with the result that profits and high share prices take precedence over full employment and welfare capitalism. Insofar as 'global markets' have outgrown 'national states', this has occurred because states (some more than others) have themselves allowed this process to occur. Globalisation is not, then, simply something that should be taken as given, but in reality reflects the end of 'labour-friendly' and 'development-friendly' régimes discussed in the previous chapter. It is not simply a question of states responding to the external force of globalisation by designing policies that attract mobile capital, for 'the heightened subordination of labour visible in the era of putative globalisation is not economically determined by capital's supposedly unlimited spatial mobility. Instead, it is a political outcome contingent upon the prior creation of a global neoliberal financial environment, which acts to impede the full circuit of capital'.[112] The political implications in terms of alternatives to neo-liberalism are discussed further in the second half of the book, especially in Chapter 9, but, for the moment, we need to discuss further political questions.

(ii) *Financial interests and US hegemony*

In actuality, then, financial markets are the site of a political contest not only between capital and labour (and arguably financial versus industrial capital),[113] but also in terms of relations between nation-states. Thus, during the 1997 crisis, Asian governments attempted a regional solution through a bailout by the Asian Development Bank that was successfully resisted by the IMF and the US Treasury. Malaysia refused IMF conditionality and moved back to a system of capital controls in August 1997. In this system, the ringgit was removed from international currency trading, and exporters had to sell their foreign exchange to the central bank at a fixed rate. Currency was then sold for approved payments to foreigners (for imports, debt service, and so on).

---

[111] Underhill 1997, p. 317.
[112] Watson 1999, p. 71.
[113] See the discussion in Chapter 9.

The ringgit was thus made convertible on the current account (that is, trade in goods), but not the capital account (that is, trade in money). While IMF Managing Director Michael Camdessus saw this return to post-war controls as 'dangerous and even harmful',[114] the policy was not always condemned by mainstream economists.[115] It was, however, vigorously criticised by the United States government, and, to a lesser extent, Britain. Indeed, the US has pushed for liberalisation of capital accounts to be made a condition of membership of the IMF.[116] There are good reasons why this is the case. As the previous chapter made clear, US hegemony has come to rely increasingly upon financial flows. In a country with low levels of savings, to maintain high levels of consumption and investment, it must borrow from the rest of the world, and it is easier to do this if world financial markets are open and integrated. Wall Street wants to do business with the rest of the world, using foreign savings and exploiting the US's position of being the issuer of the main international reserve currency, the dollar. A system of capital controls constitutes a threat to this system, and, therefore, a threat to US hegemony.

This hegemony is not so much imposed on other states, but, rather, states have actively agreed to US leadership. Disagreements continue and more overt economic[117] power may sometimes be exercised, not least in the wake of the East-Asian financial crisis. But the post-Bretton Woods era has seen an enormous amount of co-operation between capitalist states. This is, in part, *because of* the specific nature of US hegemony, particularly the ways in which it functions as a 'market of last resort', on which other countries have come to depend in an era of slower economic growth, and as supplier of the main international reserve currency, the dollar. The fortunes of its economy therefore have implications beyond US domestic policy.[118] The movement away from the dollar-gold standard to a pure dollar – led international monetary system has allowed the US economy to avoid – to some extent, at least – usual balance of payments constraints, and not worry too much about domestic savings and investment (see above, and last chapter). The result has been high levels of debt, ongoing balance of trade deficits, and a business cycle dependent on

---

[114] Quoted in Wade and Veneroso 1998, p. 22.
[115] Sachs 1998; Krugman 1998.
[116] Gowan 1999, pp. 109–15.
[117] Military power is discussed in Chapter 8.
[118] Albo 2003.

stock-market bubbles. This has been maintained by a high level of dependence on inflows of foreign finance, which, if reversed, could have devastating consequences. If foreign investors lose confidence, then money will leave the United States' economy. While this may not be possible in the case of productive capital, where costs are sunk in established factories, it is far easier in the case of government securities and corporate equities and bonds, and a flight of money capital could easily lead to competitive pressures on the value of the dollar. This would leave the Federal Reserve caught in a double bind.[119] It would have to keep interest rates low to provide liquidity to keep the economy moving and therefore defend the value of US assets, but, at the same time, 'it would, even more, need to raise interest rates so as to attract a continuing inflow of funds from overseas to maintain the dollar, thus making it possible for the US to fund its historically unprecedented current account deficit'.[120] But this begs the question of how high interest rates would have to rise to ease downward pressure on the dollar and maintain foreign capital inflows, and how this can be reconciled with more expansionary policies designed to stimulate growth. These are important questions that have enormous implications, not only for the US economy, but for the world economy as well.

4.6 The WTO and the expansion of free trade

In the same period that saw the deregulation of finance, there was also an acceleration of the movement towards free trade. The General Agreement on Tariffs and Trade (GATT), established in 1947, was committed to free-trade principles in that there was a planned long-term reduction in tariffs on imported goods. Successive rounds of GATT talks established this principle, but there were important exceptions. As well as restrictions on the flow of money, some goods were exempt such as textiles and clothing, and agriculture, as well as services. From the 1970s, and especially in the 1980 and 1990s, attempts were made to (selectively) extend free-trade principles, and there was a proliferation of regional trade agreements, and through the GATT the establishment of the World Trade Organisation in 1995. The WTO has a wider remit than GATT,

---

[119] Brenner 2002, p. 283.
[120] Ibid.

including an expansion into services and intellectual property, as well as promoting freer trade in agriculture and textiles. There is also a more formal Dispute Settlement system, where disputes are settled more quickly and not necessarily on the basis of joint consensus and are subject to economic sanctions if there are trade violations.[121] The WTO is committed to continuing the work of GATT in reducing tariff rates, and extending this principle to areas previously either not covered by GATT agreements or areas in which there were often non-tariff barriers to trade. In the case of the former, this included investment regulations, intellectual property rights and services. The latter mainly related to agriculture and clothing and textiles. Thus, the creation of Trade Related Intellectual Property Rights (TRIPs) expands patent protection for established producers. The time period varies, from seven years for trademark protection (but this is renewable for an indefinite period), industrial design protection for ten to fifteen years and copyright for up to fifty years.[122] The General Agreement on Trade and Services (GATS) is designed to subject the public sector to competition from the private sector. In agriculture there is (supposed) agreement that market access should be enhanced and non-tariff barriers in particular be eliminated and limits placed on domestic support systems such as subsidies. Trade related investment measures, or TRIMs, are designed to liberalise investment régimes so that foreign capital is not discriminated against by national states. Finally, the controversial Multi-Fibre Agreement, which effectively protects 'First World' clothing and textiles producers from some foreign competition, is to be phased out. In short, the WTO is committed to an expansion of free trade to most manufactured goods, services and agriculture, and to subject this expansion to formal rules that are ultimately sanctioned by the institution's dispute settlement system. In most cases, there are important loopholes and 'safeguards', but these are ambiguous and contested, and the general movement is towards further liberalisation and competition.

This tendency has also been accompanied by the introduction and expansion of regional trade agreements, such as the European Union's single market, and the North American Free Trade Agreement and planned Free Trade Area of the Americas. This regionalism does not, however, constitute a challenge

---

[121] Panos Briefing 1999, p. 6.
[122] Dunkley 2000, pp. 269–70.

to global liberalisation. Regional agreements are often little more than a recognition of the pre-existing reality of intra-regional trade, and, even when they are not, they should be seen as part of a process which extends rather than restricts, trade and investment liberalisation. Certainly, such agreements may be selective in their commitment to free movement (for instance, of labour in the case of NAFTA), but this is also true of the WTO. Moreover, while these agreements tend to liberalise trade and investment at a faster pace than the WTO, this process tends to be in addition to, rather than at the expense of, inter-regional trade.[123] Furthermore, regional co-operation is often designed to 'pool resources' and thereby achieve economies of scale and scope, and attract foreign investment through increasing market size.

For its advocates, this movement to free trade is both desirable and inevitable. Free trade most efficiently allocates resources and allows countries to exercise their comparative advantage unhindered from the monopolistic practices of the nation state. Market based efficiency in thus said to replace state-led, protectionist inefficiency of the post-war era. Moreover, the WTO represents the most effective institution for the developing world to find a voice in the international arena, as its rules are equally applicable to all countries, and it is based on one member one vote.[124] In keeping with the Third Way emphasis on the need for global governance,[125] it is argued that the WTO protects weaker countries from an unregulated 'law of the jungle' in which might is right. Clare Short,[126] formerly of the British Department for International Development, has thus argued that the WTO is 'a precious international institution' and that 'those who make blanket criticisms of the WTO are working against, not for, the interests of the poor and the powerless'.

However, a number of arguments can be made that seriously challenge these claims. These relate to WTO procedures, selectivity in advocating free trade, and the theoretical case for free trade. In terms of procedures, although the WTO is formally committed to one member one vote, in practice, a vote has never been taken and delegates from the developing world have constantly expressed dismay at the decision-making processes of the institution. The main accusation in terms of procedure is that decisions are taken by powerful

---

[123] Tussie and Woods 2000.
[124] Desai 2000.
[125] Giddens 2001, pp. 17–18.
[126] Quoted in *The Independent*, 30.11.1999.

countries behind closed doors, through secretive meetings that exclude most delegates from developing countries. Along with unresolved disagreements relating to labour standards, investment and competition policy, agriculture and anti-dumping policy, lack of transparency over procedural mechanisms was a major factor in the collapse of the Seattle Round of WTO talks in late 1999. It is also costly and takes time for a dispute to come before the dispute settlement court, and there is no compensation paid by the loser to cover this period of time, and so these factors work as a disincentive against poorer countries bringing such cases. Moreover, the only response to non-compliance with WTO decisions is retaliation by the aggrieved party, and this is a far more costly process for poorer countries than it is for rich ones.

There is also the wider question of loopholes and safeguards in international agreements. Thus, the GATS agreement explicitly excludes defence, central banking and social security. It also excludes services that are said to be based on the exercise of government authority. However, the agreement also states that if parts of these services are already being delivered commercially, or in competition with the private sector, then they can, in principle, be counted as part of the agreement. Government is still entitled to regulate, but not when this leads to unnecessary barriers to trade. There is thus sufficient ambiguity in GATS regulations to suggest that, other than the three services explicitly excluded, any public service may be privatised. If this is not the case, then why are health and education not explicitly excluded, as are defence and central banking? Similarly, in the case of TRIPs, loopholes to extended patents are provided to poorer countries that need to provide cheap, generic drugs rather than expensive patented imports – for instance, when there is proof of anti-competitive practices or in the case of a national emergency. But, again, such loopholes are open to doubt and may be contested by pharmaceutical companies. The most famous case – South Africa – led to a retreat by drugs companies, but this was due to successful pressure against them and not due to WTO flexibility. There are also some room for industrial subsidies, which have led some prominent critics of free trade to argue that WTO rules are not as bad, or openly pro-free trade, as is sometimes implied.[127] There is some truth to this argument, and there may still be some room for manoeuvre for potential late developers. However, it is also true that the WTO outlaws *specific*

---

[127] Amsden 2000.

subsidies, which means that subsidies based on export performance are technically illegal.[128]

The second issue relates to the double standards involved in free-trade 'negotiations'. For, while the IMF and World Bank have preached the virtues of trade liberalisation to indebted countries undergoing structural adjustment, the 'advanced' capitalist countries continue to apply this medicine inconsistently. In early 2002, the Bush administration in the United States imposed 30 per cent tariff rates on most imported steel products, increased export subsidies to specific industries in 2003, and agriculture continues to be heavily protected and subsidised in the European Union and the United States. This has the effect of depriving developing countries of potentially lucrative markets for their products, and leads to the advanced countries exporting cheap agricultural products, which undermine producers in the developing world. It has been estimated that Latin America loses an estimated $4 billion a year as a result of European Union farm policies.[129] 'Advanced' countries can afford to ignore WTO regulations, even if they are subsequently overturned (as with steel). This is because richer countries will be less affected by the penalties imposed for flouting regulations than poorer ones.

More substantive disagreement again came to the foreground at the 2001 talks at Doha, Qatar. At these talks, developing countries won some concessions over patents related to health, but lost out over the reduction of tariffs on textile imports into the 'advanced' countries, particularly the US. On agriculture, developing countries won a slight concession from the European Union over export subsidies, but this is likely to be a major issue of contention in the next few years. For all the detailed negotiations, the fact remains that developing countries face tariff peaks four times larger than developed countries for their key exports to the developed world. This was a major reason for the revolt of the G21 developing countries at the WTO talks at Cancun in 2003.[130]

The third issue relates to the supposed efficiency of markets forces and free trade. This issue has been addressed in some detail in Chapter 2, and will be examined further in Chapter 5, so I will be relatively brief here. The assumption behind the GATS agreement, like structural adjustment programmes in the

---

[128] Toye 2003, pp. 118–19.
[129] Oxfam 2002, p. 10.
[130] Henderson 2003.

1980s and 1990s, is that the private sector is the most effective service provider. This argument rests on the broader notion criticised in Section 2 above, namely that the private sector is more efficient than the public sector, because it allows for competition between innately self-interested human beings. But the assumption that humans are naturally selfish ignores the ways in which humans co-operate in everyday life, and so ignores 'collective rationalities' such as a commitment to public service.[131] There is also strong evidence that the private sector, and 'public-private partnerships' (PPPs) offer worst public services at higher costs – the main 'service' that they offer is to private shareholders, as they are guaranteed a profit, as losses as well as interest are paid for by taxpayers.[132] In this case the public sector simply serves to guarantee profits to the private sector, regardless of performance. In the case of patents, these actually restrict competition by reinforcing the monopoly power of established technological producers, effectively undermining the development opportunities that existed in the case of nineteenth-century developers.[133] The case made for the extension of patents is most clearly argued for by pharmaceutical companies. They argue that extended patents are necessary to recover research and development expenses, and that, in the long run, the new drugs produced will trickle down to the poor. Companies also point out that many governments in the developing world spend more on defence than they do on healthcare. True, but then many companies spend more on advertising than on R & D, and much research is carried out by the public sector, but the private sector reaps the benefits in terms of profits. States in the developing world may overspend on defence and underspend on health (although it should be stressed that adjustment programmes have not discouraged, and often actively encouraged this practice), but this fact does

---

[131] Indeed, given that neo-liberals do believe in the need for a state (albeit a 'limited' one), then they to are committed to some notion of public service. The problem is that such a commitment undermines the neo-liberal case for blanket privatisation.

[132] On PFI/PPPs see Pollock et al. 2001.

[133] Chang 2002, pp. 54–9; Chang 2003, Chapter 8. There are other issues related to intellectual property rights, a full treatment of which lies outside the scope of this chapter. The main case for such rights is that without them, there would be no incentive to innovate in the first place, as competitors will develop cheap or even costless imitations. But this argument ignores the variety of motives for innovation in the first place, discounting from the outset any notion of the 'public good' and successful R & D in the public sector. Moreover, even in the private sector, rents can still be won in the absence of IPRs because of time-lags in developing imitations, the development of technological know how, and marketing the original product.

not let pharmaceutical companies off the hook. Spending on drugs in the whole of sub-Saharan Africa totals around $1 billion, and these sales are very unequally distributed. This amount is less than the value of sales of Viagra in the Western world. Clearly then, '[p]atent protection will not significantly change the relative profitability of finding cures for diseases afflicting rich and poor countries for the simple reason that poor people lack purchasing power'.[134] It may well be unrealistic to expect drugs companies to act in an altruistic way and concentrate on developing low-cost, low-profit drugs for the global poor. But it is equally naïve to simply wait until the poor can afford the most expensive drugs, as though drug company profits are a simple fact of life, which is outside the realm of politics. Instead, there is a need for far more public-sector investment in the development of cheap, generic drugs.

Finally, in terms of free trade, it should be clear by now that, even if it were ever fully implemented, it would not mean a level playing field in the world economy. As Chapter 2 made clear, the notion that free trade is equally good for all ignores the competitive advantages faced by some countries, regions, and sectors over others. Some parts of the world have more advanced technologies, skills, infrastructures, and markets and this increases the barriers to entry for potential late developers. The WTO undermines the capacity of late developers to protect themselves from the unequal competition that they face from established producers. It therefore undermines the ways in which not only South Korea and Taiwan industrialised, but also earlier developers including Japan, the United States, and even Britain. While some influential neo-liberals recognise that earlier developers employed tariffs in their development, they argue that these tariffs were much lower than those used by developing countries, at least before the widespread implementation of structural adjustment policies after 1982.[135] But this ignores the different protectionist measures used in the nineteenth century, the natural protectionism of slow and expensive transportation, and, above all, the fact that the productivity gap between early and late developers is far greater today than it is in the nineteenth century.[136] It also ignores the relative successes of development in the 1950s to 1970s, compared to relative failures since then, an issue addressed further in the next chapter.

---

[134] Watkins 2001, p. 104.
[135] Little et al. 1970.
[136] Chang 2002, pp. 66–8.

The immediate question that needs to be addressed here then, is why the movement towards free trade? Again, this needs to be put into the historical and social context of the end of the post-war boom discussed in the last chapter. As we saw there, the United States faced relative decline and intensified competition, especially from Japan and Germany. From the 1970s and especially the 1980s, it became committed to a free-trade policy, above all in finance, but also in goods and services. This, of course, was and is selective in terms of implementation, but this is bound to be the case when free trade has been expanded as part of a competitive strategy. Thus, as the US in some ways became more protectionist at home, it urged trade liberalisation through the GATT abroad.[137] This was a strategy designed to undermine competitors in the context of a world economy characterised by slowing growth rates. However, it would be a mistake to reduce the selective tendency towards free trade to US policy alone, and free trade undoubtedly suited other interests too. The movement also reflects the inter-penetration of capital across many states, with the result that capitals and states have increasingly supported free-trade, while at the same time continuing to support protectionism in some sectors. Moreover, it is not only capital originating from the 'North' that has promoted free-trade policies. For instance, the Cairns Group in agriculture, which mainly comprises successful agrarian exporters from the developing world, broadly supports free trade as a way of undermining the preferential treatment given to some countries, as well as further developing its exports in higher-value agrarian products. Similarly, some East-Asian capital has rapidly internationalised and also pressurised home states to liberalise finance in order to gain access to cheap money, as in the (disastrous) case of South Korea.

Recent years have seen an intensification of the movement towards so-called free trade, reflected above all in the formation of the WTO, and the attempts through that body to expand the sectors in which the 'free market' operates. The result has been a further strengthening of capital against labour, a further undermining of the space for development in the poorer countries, and further erosion of public provision in the face of market expansion. Neo-liberal policies thus expanded in the 1990s.

---

[137] Shukla 2002.

4.7 Conclusion: Third Way ideology and the reality of globalisation

This chapter has questioned the claim that the Third Way represents a new politics for a new information society. The basis for such claims are most strongly rooted in the new economy and emerging market booms of the 1990s. But these miracles were short-lived, reflected continued global instability, and above all the dominance of financial capital in the world order. Moreover, rather than ushering in a new era of global flows that equally undermined all nation-states, the dominance of financial capital reflected continued US state hegemony and the resurgence of neo-liberalism in the 1980s. Third Way claims of a new era beyond neo-liberalism should be seen in this light. In the 1990s, across the world there were minor modifications to neo-liberal policies, but ultimately the Third Way – in the developed and developing world – both consolidated and expanded neo-liberal capitalism. The effects of such consolidation and expansion are discussed in detail in the next chapter.

Chapter Five
Globalisation, Inequality and Poverty

This chapter expands on the arguments the last
two chapters, with particular attention paid to the
relationship between globalisation and different forms
of inequality. My initial focus is on the various ways
of 'measuring' globalisation, and, in particular, data
related to trade, investment and finance. This data
is then used to critically examine some of the
arguments for and against globalisation, and to make
a 'balance sheet' of the current globalisation era. This
argument is extended through an examination of the
debate around the relationship between globalisation,
inequality and poverty. Advocates of neo-liberal
globalisation rest much of their case for globalisation
as policy on the argument that there has been a
reduction in global poverty, which itself has been
caused by pro-globalisation policies such as trade
liberalisation. But I will question the evidence, and
argue that any success in terms of economic growth
and poverty reduction is based on policies that are
not 'pro-globalisation'. In relating my analysis back
to the theoretical discussion in Chapter 2, I again
stress the centrality of uneven development, and
suggest some reasons why it has taken a particularly
acute, and unequal form, over the last thirty years.
Finally, I re-examine the relationship between
globalisation and inequality through further
consideration of the questions of the nation-state, US

hegemony and the end of the post-war Golden Age of 'labour-friendly' and 'development-friendly' régimes. This section re-emphasises the reasons why inequality has, in many respects, intensified over the last twenty years, and in so doing, returns to themes addressed in earlier chapters.

5.1 Economic globalisation: trade, investment and finance

This section examines the nature and direction of capital flows, with particular attention paid to the globalisation period of the last ten–twenty years. It focuses on trade, investment and finance.

(i) *International trade*

A standard measure of globalisation is to examine the ratio between exports and GDP, which demonstrates the increased importance of international trade in the global economy. Although this measure is not necessarily the same as globalisation, as it refers to trade between nations, it is still a useful measure in that it demonstrates increased interdependence in the world economy. If we examine the trade/export ratio from 1820 to the early 1990s, it stood at a historic high of 13.5 per cent in 1992, compared to just 7 per cent in 1950, 9 per cent in 1929, and 8.7 per cent in 1913.[1] At first sight then, it appears that there is greater trade interdependence in the world economy. However, two important qualifications need to be made. First, the *share* of trade is concentrated, and much of the developing world has seen a *fall in trade share* in recent years. Thus, in the late 1990s, 75 per cent of world exports were from the 'advanced' capitalist countries and only 25 per cent from the developing world, the latter of which includes East Asia.[2] In 1950, Africa's share of world trade was 5.3 per cent, Latin America's 12.1 per cent and Asia 15.2 per cent; by 1970, the figures were 4.1 per cent for Africa, 5.5 per cent for Latin America and 8.5 per cent for Asia; by 1995, Africa's share had declined to 1.5 per cent, Latin America to 4.4 per cent, while Asia's share in-creased to 21.4 per cent, largely a product of the rise of the first-tier NICs and China, none of which have adopted (at least in boom times) 'market-friendly policies'.[3]

---

[1] Baker et al. 1998, p. 5.
[2] UNCTAD 1999.
[3] UNCTAD 1998, p. 183.

Second, the *rate of change* of growth in international trade has not been unprecedentedly high in the last twenty years, when globalisation has supposed to have rapidly intensified. Thus, from 1950–73, the average annual rate of growth of international trade was 1.7 per cent, while from 1973–92 it was 1.1 per cent.[4] The faster growth in the supposedly closed period from 1950–73 was, of course, from a lower base, and was in part a recovery from the contraction in world trade from 1929–50, but the fact remains that the slower growth in the 1980s and early 1990s hardly establishes a case for a qualitatively new era in international trade.

However, in terms of the kinds of goods traded, there has been a significant change. In 1970, 60.9 per cent of total world trade was in manufacturing goods. By 1994, this had increased to 74.7 per cent. But what is more significant than even this substantial rise is the amount that originated from the developing world. In 1970, 18.5 per cent of the total exports from the developing world were manufactured goods; by 1994, 66.1 per cent of the developing world's exports were manufactured goods.[5] All regions within the developing world have seen an increase in the proportion of their exports that are manufactured, including Africa (from 7 per cent in 1970 to 17.8 per cent in 1994). But it is Latin America and Asia which have seen massive increases – from 10.6 per cent in 1970 to 48.7 per cent (1994) for Latin America, and from 22.4 per cent (1970) to 73.4 per cent in 1994 for Asia.[6]

Once again, however, there is a need to treat this data with some caution. The developing world as a whole has seen a proportionate increase in its share of manufactured exports compared to its total exports, and, indeed, this is a tendency that applies to the poorest regions – though not every country within those regions.[7] But this, of course, is not the same thing as increasing market share in the global economy, and as we saw above, while the amount, and the total value of goods exported from the developing world has increased, the share of this amount and value (measured by proportion of world trade) has decreased – with the exception of East Asia. This can be demonstrated by examining the value of manufacturing imports from the developing world to the 'advanced' capitalist countries as a percentage of the latter's total

---

[4] Baker et al. 1998, p. 6.
[5] Baker et al. 1998, p. 7.
[6] Ibid.
[7] UNCTAD 2002a.

'consumption' of manufactured goods. For the United States in 1995, the figure was 7 per cent, a strong increase from just 2.5 per cent in 1980, but still low; for the European Union, the figure was 4.5 per cent in 1995 (and 2.5 per cent in 1980); and for Japan, the figure was 3.3 per cent in 1995, and 2 per cent in 1980.[8] These figures do show quite substantial increases, but they are from very low bases and they remain very low. Moreover, the category 'developing countries' here includes South Korea from the first-tier East-Asian newly industrialising countries' which (along with China and Mexico) account for a high proportion of developing countries' manufactured exports to the 'First World'.[9] One possible reason for the rhetoric concerning jobs relocating to the Third World is that imports from low-cost areas are high in a few well-known, labour-intensive industries, such as footwear and clothing.[10] But, for manufactured goods as a whole, the proportion is very low. The sharp increase in the import penetration of domestic markets for manufactured goods in the 'advanced' countries has occurred, but is largely a product of competition among these same countries (plus a very few select developing countries). The decline in manufacturing employment in the 'First World' is thus more a product of employment shifts to services (many of which are linked to manufacturing), technological and organisational change, and the end of neo-Keynesian full employment policies, rather than a straightforward expansion in manufactured exports from the developing world.[11]

The last twenty or so years have seen the emergence of historically high GDP/export ratios, and increased export of manufactured goods, including from the developing world. This implies both increased interdependence and intensified competition in the world economy. For neo-liberals, this is a welcome development as it means that countries are exercising their comparative advantage, producing their most cheap and efficient goods, and selling them in the world market.[12] But we have also seen that, while the amount and value

---

[8] UNCTAD 1999.
[9] Sutcliffe 2001, table 74.
[10] UNCTAD 1999.
[11] This occurs in some labour-intensive sectors as I have suggested, but is far from a general trend. Some have argued that technological and organisational changes are inseparable from increased competition in manufacturing (see Kitching 2001, Chapter 6). This may be a factor but as we have seen imports from developing countries are low, and establishing causality in this way. The argument that cheap, developing world imports leads to core country restructuring abstracts from all the other reasons for the crisis from the late 1960s.
[12] See Chapter 2.

of trade has increased, the shares of this amount and value are increasingly concentrated. Clearly then, for neo-liberalism, some countries are not exercising their comparative advantage. This implies that they must be continuing to protect inefficient producers through state intervention, which holds them back from increasing their global market share and, ultimately, hinders the movement towards global convergence. Third-Way advocates are essentially saying the same thing when they make the claim that these countries are 'insufficiently globalised'.[13] The solution for these countries is said to be to promote globalisation through policies such as trade liberalisation and increased openness to foreign investment. However, as should be clear by now, most if not all developing countries have carried out at least some policies along these lines, particularly through structural adjustment policies, but the effect has not been an increased share of world trade for these countries.[14] Moreover, the fact that *a few* countries manage to export into potentially lucrative First-World markets does not mean that *all* countries can do so. In the cases of agricultural goods or low-cost labour-intensive manufacturing goods, where developing countries may have a comparative advantage, there is a strong danger that this will lead to oversupply and a collapse in prices, or protectionism – both of which have occurred in recent years.[15] The issue then is not simply about the *amount* of globalisation, but also its *form*, and it is clear, that 'free markets' promote divergence and unevenness rather than convergence and equilibrium. Indeed, in the current context of slower rates of economic growth combined with higher rates of international competition, trade takes on a more coercive character, as we will see.

(ii) *Foreign investment*

The 1990s saw a stunning increase in the amount of foreign investment in the world. The ratio of foreign direct investment (FDI) to world output has increased from 4.4 per cent in 1960 to 10.1 per cent in 1995, though this latter figure was not substantially higher than the 9 per cent figure in 1913.[16] Nevertheless, there have been substantial increases in recent years – at constant

---

[13] Giddens 2002, p. 73; Dfid 2000.
[14] UNCTAD 2002a, pp. 114–15.
[15] Cline 1982; Rowthorn 2001.
[16] Baker et al. 1998, p. 9.

prices, from $59 billion in 1982 to $1.2 trillion in 2000. This was followed by a great fall, down to $735 billion in the economic slowdown in 2001 and $651 billion for 2002. Leaving aside for the moment the figures for 2001 and 2002, the increase in the amount of FDI is also reflected in the very high figures for the annual average rate of growth of FDI from the mid 1980s – 23.6 per cent (1986–90), 20 per cent (1991–5), and 40.1 per cent (1996–2000). However, the distribution of global DFI inflows is, like international trade, heavily concentrated. Between 1993–8, 'developed countries' received 61.2 per cent of world DFI, developing countries 35.3 per cent, and the former Communist European countries 3.5 per cent.[17] In 2001, developed countries received 68.4 per cent, developing countries 27.9 per cent and the former Communist European countries 3.7 per cent. Thus, while there was high growth in the amount of DFI from the mid 1980s to 2000, the direction of that investment was highly unequal, with developing countries as a whole receiving around one-third. Moreover, this third of DFI going to developing countries was itself highly concentrated, with just 5 countries receiving 62 per cent and 10 receiving 75 per cent of this proportion in 2001. The 49 least developed countries received just 2 per cent of the DFI inflows into developing countries and 0.5 per cent of total world FDI in 2001.[18] Moreover, China is the main recipient of FDI going to developing countries, accounting for as much as nearly 50 per cent of the total, but most of this investment is actually from within the East-Asian region, and therefore does not mean a substantial relocation from the capital-rich West.[19]

DFI figures do not completely capture the reality of capital flows for a number of reasons. First, a distinction has to be made between greenfield investment, which constitutes the setting up of new factories, offices and so on, and DFI which essentially takes over existing facilities. It has been argued that this distinction biases the figures against the real proportion of investment that goes to the developing world, as company mergers and acquisitions across nation-states has the effect of increasing DFI, and most of these mergers take place between companies located within the 'advanced capitalist' countries.[20] There is some truth to this argument, but figures such as those

---

[17] UNCTAD 2002b, pp. 3–5.
[18] UNCTAD 2002b, p. 9.
[19] Sutcliffe and Glyn 1999, p. 119.
[20] Bayoumi 1998.

supplied by UNCTAD do make some attempt to incorporate this practice. Thus, UNCTAD's figures for the year 1999–2000 show that DFI inflows to the developed world constituted 80 per cent of total DFI and the proportion going to developing countries constituted only 17.9 per cent.[21] But UNCTAD also point out that this was an atypical year, one characterised by a high degree of mergers and acquisitions among companies in the 'developed countries'. The fact remains that there is a longer-term concentration of DFI among the 'developed' and a few 'developing' countries. Moreover, DFI to the developing world does not always mean the construction of new sites, and may amount to no more than the takeover of local, recently privatised companies. A great deal of the increase in DFI[22] in Latin America in the 1990s fits into this category as states privatised companies as part of structural adjustment programmes. Brazil, for example was the largest recipient of foreign direct investment in Latin America from 1996–2000, with net inflows of $9.6 billion in 1996, $17.8 billion (1997), $26 billion (1998), $30 billion for 1999 and for 2000 before falling off to $22 billion in 2001. However, around $30 billion of these new inflows were purchases of privatised companies.[23] Moreover, at its peak year of FDI inflows (1999), the rate of fixed capital investment in Brazil was 18.9 per cent of GDP, less than the average of 22.1 per cent in the disastrous 1980s,[24] which reflects in part its dependence on a high interest policy to attract financial capital flows. Given that, post-structural adjustment, there are less assets left to be privatised, rates of increase in DFI may actually slow down in the near future – though this may also depend on further market-expanding liberalisation through the WTO.

DFI figures are also said to underestimate developing-country participation in two further ways. First, the impact of a dollar of DFI in a developing country is greater than the impact of a dollar of DFI in a developed country. Second, DFI figures do not tell us about transnational practices such as subcontracting and licensing agreements between transnational companies (TNC) and local companies. There is some truth to both these arguments. But neither of these arguments is sufficiently strong to establish the case that *from*

---

[21] UNCTAD 2002b, p. 5.
[22] Measured in terms of both absolute amounts and an increasing share of total DFI (from 5 per cent in 1986–90 to 11.6 per cent in 2001 – UNCTAD 2002b, p. 7).
[23] Rocha 2002, pp. 21–2.
[24] Rocha 2002, p. 26.

the perspective of global investment figures, the developing world is as significant as the developed world. In other words, it is a fallacy to argue that these qualifications mean that we can talk about global convergence – be it one based on a levelling up process through the global dispersal of investment (neo-liberalism), or an unambiguous levelling down process through the establishment of a 'global factory', as is argued by some 'anti-globalisation movements'.[25] If there is a 'global factory', it is one in which most of the world's population remain locked out, and a disproportionate amount of this population remain in the developing world. Similarly, if there is a levelling-down process, it is not one based on the wholesale relocation of hyper-mobile capital from 'First' to 'Third' World. The figures cited above on 'First-World' imports of manufactured goods from the developing world remain very telling in this respect.

Moreover, the DFI figures actually *over-estimate* both the proportion of DFI that goes to the developing world, and total investment figures. This is because, firstly, the population of the developing world is much higher than the population of the developed world. If one looks at DFI inflows per capita, then the proportion is actually far more weighted towards the developed world. For the years 1995–9, developed countries received $474 on a per capita basis and, for 2001, the figure was $583; for developing countries as a whole, for 1995–9 the figure was $37 and, for 2001, $41.[26] Secondly, FDI contributes only about 5.2 per cent of total world investment, and the stock of world inward FDI constituted only around 10.1 per cent of world GDP in 1995.[27] Thus FDI makes up a relatively small, though growing, amount of total world investment, and it is highly concentrated in relatively few countries. These figures, and many others cited above, are hardly evidence of a global convergence of DFI in the era of globalisation.

For neo-liberals this lack of convergence must again be explained by too much government intervention by developing countries. But, in 2001 alone, 71 countries made 208 changes to their investment policies, 194 of which were more favourable to DFI. Moreover, 2001 was a far from atypical year, and developing countries have consistently liberalised their investment policies

[25] Discussed further in Chapter 8.
[26] UNCTAD 2002b, p. 265.
[27] Hirst and Thompson 1999, p. 45.

in recent years.[28] Based on 1991–3 FDI figures, Rowthorn has argued that for all developing countries to receive DFI levels similar to those received by Malaysia would require a fifteen-fold increase if measured on a per capita basis, which amounts to 3.5 times the amount that OECD countries receive.[29] Even if measured by FDI as a similar percentage of Malaysia's GDP, DFI would have to be 1.7 times the amount going to OECD countries.[30] It should by now be clear that policies that are supposed to attract increased DFI shares may not do so, and indeed have not done so. This is because there are factors beyond openness to investment that influence the reasons why TNCs invest in specific locations. As I argued in Chapters 2 and 3, competitive advantages that accrue to certain locations include clustering of suppliers, markets, skills, research and development, and so on – advantages which developing countries on the whole, do not have. Moreover, DFI on its own is far from being unambiguously positive, even when one is attempting to simply promote economic growth. For example, developing countries may have advantages in terms of low costs in labour-intensive industries (such as footwear and clothing), but without sufficient regulations, potential advantages such as increased linkages and reasonable work conditions are unlikely to be won. At the very least, there is a need for market-restricting regulation of TNC activity, something that neo-liberalism regards as being irrelevant.

(iii) *Finance*

As the previous two chapters showed, the globalisation of the economy in the last twenty years is closely associated with massive increases in international financial flows. Since the ending of fixed exchange rates, there has been a massive and increasing expansion in lending, and of secondary market trading in stock, bond, foreign exchange, and derivatives markets. Overall daily trading in international financial markets is usually of a value over $1 trillion. Much of this trading is speculation, based on expected and actual movements

---

[28] UNCTAD 2002b, p. 7.
[29] Rowthorn 2001, p. 107.
[30] There are, of course, all kinds of methodological problems with this approach, particularly its assumption of zero-sum increases in DFI in one region at the expense of another. Nevertheless, it remains a useful exercise in showing the fallacy of using selected indicators of one country's economic performance as a rigid model for all other countries (which is not to deny that specific lessons can be learnt).

in exchange rates, share prices and so on. As well as a substantial increase in direct foreign investment, developing countries also saw a substantial increase in flows from international capital markets in the 1990s, particularly in the emerging markets in Latin America and East Asia.[31] This increased from $43.9 billion in 1990 to $299 billion in 1997, falling back to $227 billion in 1998 because of the withdrawal of funds from East Asia. From 1990–7, commercial bank loans increased from $3.2 billion to $60 billion, investment in bonds increased from $1.2 billion to $42.6 billion ($53 billion in 1996), and portfolio investment (in developing-country stock exchanges) increased from $3.7 billion in 1990 to $30 billion in 1997, and $49.2 billion in (pre-Asian crisis) 1996.[32]

Government policies have been a crucial factor in the promotion of these financial flows. Structural adjustment policies included the removal of controls on among other things, interest rates, foreign exchange, bond markets, and equity markets. The management of the post-1997 crisis in East Asia has included policies aimed at further liberalising finance, as Chapter 4 demonstrated. However, portfolio investment to developing countries is still proportionately small – the developing world received 9.7 per cent of total global flows in 1991, 9 per cent in 1994, 6.2 per cent in 1998, and 5.5 per cent in 2000[33] – and is concentrated in the richer developing countries, not least the US where it financed the trade deficit under Clinton and the budget and trade deficits under Bush Junior (and before him Reagan and Bush Senior). Moreover, as I have demonstrated in detail in the last chapter, financial inflows are, at best, a mixed blessing. The argument that they are necessary to facilitate trade and investment ignores the fact that financial markets today are mainly speculative in character. Thus, in the early 1970s, on the eve of the abolition of fixed exchange rates, 90 per cent of foreign exchange trading related to trade and investment in (non-financial) goods and services. In 1997, the annual value of trade in goods and services was equivalent to four days trading on the foreign exchange markets.[34] The effect of this domination of financial capital is that potential funds are diverted away from productive investment and into short-term speculation, which, in turn, can encourage higher interest

---

[31] See Chapter 4.
[32] World Bank 1999, p. 24.
[33] Grabel 2003, p. 327.
[34] Singh 2000, p. 16.

rates (which further discourages productive investment). Thus, in the United States, the proportion of non-financial corporation cashflow paid out in the form of dividends actually declined in the 1950s and 1960s, but, from the mid-1980s to late 1990s, it doubled.[35] Uncertainty is also exacerbated by rapid movements in interest rates and exchange rates, which, as we have seen in our examples of the 1982 debt crisis and 1997 Asian crisis, can have devastating effects for the 'real' economy. The dominance of financial flows has served to severely undermine the progressive nature of capitalism in the neo-liberal era, a point taken up further in Chapter 9.

It should be clear that, if we accept the view that the 1980s and 1990s constitute an era of globalisation, then the evidence on trade, investment and finance do not conform to the expectations of neo-liberalism, including its Third-Way variant. Nevertheless, this has not stopped advocates making specific claims for causal links between globalisation, economic growth and poverty reduction. I now turn to a consideration of these claims.

5.2 Globalisation and growth, poverty and inequality

The data discussed above hardly present 'actually existing globalisation' in a favourable light. However, it has still been argued that globalisation either will lead, or indeed has led, to a reduction in global poverty and inequality.[36] Giddens argues that the main problems of underdevelopment 'don't come from the global economy itself, or from the self-seeking behaviour on the part of the richer nations.[37] They lie mainly in the societies themselves – in authoritarian government, corruption, conflict, over-regulation and the low level of emancipation of women'.[38]

---

[35] Crotty 2003, p. 277.
[36] Giddens 2002; Dfid 2000.
[37] Giddens 2000, p. 129.
[38] While it will become clear that I strongly disagree with this statement, it does not follow that I believe that all of the problems faced by developing societies are the fault of the international economy. Developing societies vary enormously in terms of economic growth and social development records despite similar international constraints. 'Internal' pressure for change remains very important, as the second half of the book will argue. My problem with Giddens's contention is that it assumes that international factors – or globalisation – is far more of an opportunity than it is a constraint, and therefore he ignores the power relations that are intrinsic to globalisation. These critical points apply even more strongly to the World Bank.

His basic contention, then, is that global integration through trade and investment liberalisation will encourage competition and therefore efficiency, which in turn will lead to economic growth, poverty reduction and a narrowing of income inequalities – relative and, in the long term, absolute – between countries. This argument is indistinguishable from those made by the IMF and World Bank. This section examines this argument in some detail. First, it reviews and challenges the evidence that inequality and poverty have been reduced. Second, it examines the relationship between economic growth and poverty reduction. My basic argument is that the evidence that there has been a reduction in poverty and inequality is based on one-sided and questionable data, and that there is as much evidence to suggest that inequality and possibly poverty are actually worsening. Moreover, the argument that economic growth leads to poverty reduction is not as straightforwardly positive as advocates claim, though it is also the case that neither is it unambiguously negative as some critics argue. However, what is true is that the growth record, as well as the poverty and inequality records, is not good in the era of globalisation. I also suggest that low growth and, in some respects, growing inequality, is not conducive to the achievement of social justice, and that equality matters. These points are then taken up in the third section, in which I re-consider the era of globalisation by returning to the question of uneven development.

(i) *Poverty and inequality*

The World Bank has argued that poverty and income inequality have fallen in the last twenty years.[39] In 1980, there were 1.4 billion people living in absolute poverty,[40] and, by 1998, this had fallen to 1.2 billion. The Bank has also argued that, while the number of people living in absolute poverty has remained constant from 1987–98, taking into account population increases, this amounts to a fall from 28 per cent to 24 per cent of the world's population.[41] Although other reports from within the Bank have their own set of figures which often contradict such claims,[42] the general message is upbeat: poverty and inequality

---

[39] World Bank 2002b, p. 30.
[40] This is defined as people living on less than $1 a day. This 'dollar' is adjusted to account for local purchasing power, so it does not mean US dollar but a Purchasing Power Parity (PPP) dollar. This is further discussed in the text.
[41] World Bank 2001, p. 3.
[42] Wade 2002, p. 3.

have fallen, and this is due to greater economic integration (globalisation) in the world economy, which constitutes a 'stepping stone from poverty'.[43]

The Bank uses a measure of extreme poverty based on people living on an income of $1 a day. This is based on Purchasing Power Parity (PPP) exchange rates, which are adjusted to take account of the fact that the cost of living tends to be lower in poorer countries than richer ones. Thus, the PPP dollar is not the same as a US dollar, and more accurately reflects local variations in prices. However, what the generally upbeat assessments of poverty reduction cited above do not tell us is that the Bank has changed its method of counting the poor. The Bank started using the $1 a day extreme poverty line in 1980, and it drew on the Penn World Tables in 1985, which quantified international price comparisons, in order to make its calculations. However, in 1993, a new International Comparisons Project was made, and from 2000/1 this was used as the basic measurement of extreme poverty. Thus, the favourable comparison between 1988 and the late 1990s is based on two different measurements, so there can hardly be a case made for an unambiguously clear decline in the amount of people living in extreme poverty.[44]

This is far from being a pedantic point, especially as international targets for poverty reduction have been set for 2015, and which include halving the number of people living in absolute poverty. The different methods used for counting the poor therefore have an impact on the results, and so it is crucial that ways of measuring the poor are consistent and as reliable as possible. The shift from the 1985 count to the 1993 count had the effect of lowering the poverty line in 77 out of 92 countries for which data were available, and these countries contained 82 per cent of the total population of the 92 countries.[45] Moreover, it is not just a problem of changing methods of counting the poor, as both its new and old methods are highly problematic. Purchasing Power Parity is, in principle, a useful way of measuring poverty between countries, because it takes into account differences in buying power between countries. However, the basket of goods that makes up PPP is not appropriate for measuring poverty. If poverty is to be properly measured, then equivalent purchasing power of *which* commodities is a crucial question. But, in identifying cost-of-living adjustments made across countries, the Bank relies on data

---

[43] Wolf 2001.
[44] Deaton 2001; Wade 2002.
[45] Pogge and Reddy 2002, p. 7.

about all commodities, many of which are not consumed by the poor.[46] The use of general consumption PPPs is quite irrelevant as a measurement of poverty as the poor do not consume cars, air travel, most electrical goods, and so on. This measure is likely to underestimate the poor, as food and shelter – the main consumption goods of the poor – are relatively expensive, when measured as a proportion of the poor's income. Thus, Pogge and Reddy use the example of basic foodstuffs. These may cost around thirty times as much in rupees in India as they do in dollars in the United States. On the other hand, services such as drivers and manicurists cost three times as much in rupees as they do in US dollars. This has the effect of underestimating the price discrepancy between rupees and dollars and therefore PPP dollars, because the cheaper services are counted as part of PPP even though they are generally not consumed by the poor.

Moreover, this distortion is likely to worsen over time, which leads to the Bank making unjustified assertions about long-term trends in the poverty count. This is because the Bank makes periodic adjustments from the base year based on new data on economic growth. However, this has the effect of underestimating poverty as consumption patterns shift over time from higher price food to lower price commodities such as services. The fact that there is a growing *general* shift from higher- to lower-price goods does not tell us anything about what is being consumed by the poor who, given that they are poor, are likely to still be consuming relatively higher priced goods. So, with rising general affluence in both the US and India, there will be a growing general shift in consumption patterns towards services. The effect of this shift is that prices of services will have a greater significance in the second year of comparison than in the first, and so the effect will be to lower the new general-consumption PPP, and thus lower the number of poor in India, even though price ratios for goods consumed by the poor remain unchanged. In this case then, there is a downward bias in measuring poverty due to unwarranted assumptions about general consumption patterns, both constantly and over a period of time. Moreover, much of the 'evidence' for falling poverty is a result of important changes in India and China. However, China declined to participate in either the 1985 or 1993 international price benchmarking exercises, and the PPP exchange rate was calculated from estimates of a few

---

[46] Pogge and Reddy 2002; Reddy and Pogge 2002.

price surveys in big cities together with some adjustment for regional price disparities. India did not participate in the 1993 exercise and its PPP figures are based on the 1985 figures plus a few further surveys after this date.[47]

Finally, the Bank's figures are based on household surveys, which have been associated with some massive discrepancies in counting the poor. Thus, based on household surveys, 16.5 per cent of the population of Mali and 48.5 per cent of Tanzania was poor in 1989; by 1994, the figures were 72.3 per cent for Mali and 19.9 per cent for Tanzania.[48] These wild discrepancies may not be completely representative, but they do point to some of the problems of using surveys, which often change their methods of counting the poor, both from year to year and country to country. UNCTAD thus argues that poverty estimates are best made by utilising data from national accounts rather than household surveys, as these tend to be more standardised, both over time and across countries. Moreover, household surveys tend to under-represent the poor and over-estimate the value of domestic goods produced by the poorest households, so national capital accounts data may be of more value for measuring the poorest countries.[49] Using this method of counting the poor, and based on data for thirty-nine of the poorest least developed countries, UNCTAD estimates that the percentage increase in poverty has increased from 48 per cent (1965–9) to over 50 per cent (1995–9) for the $1 international poverty line.[50] This means an increase in the number of people in the 39 countries living on less than a dollar a day has increased from 125 million to 278.8 million over the same period.[51]

The evidence on inequality is also ambiguous. If market exchange rates are used, then there is little doubt that inequality has increased. Developing-country GNP per capita from 1960–99 remained at approximately 4.5 per cent of 'advanced' countries GNP per capita from 1960–99.[52] This means that there has been little change in the relative gap, but a dazzling increase in the absolute gap. Thus, Wade points out that fast growth in countries with low per capita GNP does not necessarily mean convergence between countries.[53] If a country

---

[47] Reddy and Pogge 2002.
[48] UNCTAD 2002a, p. 51
[49] UNCTAD 2002a, p. 47.
[50] UNCTAD 2002a, p. 56.
[51] UNCTAD 2002a, p. 59.
[52] Wade 2001, pp. 18–27.
[53] Wade and Wolf 2002, p. 16.

has a per capita income of $1,000 a year grows at 6 per cent annually, while a country with a per capita income of $30,000 a year grows at 1 per cent a year, the absolute gap continues to widen for forty years before narrowing. Critics of this approach argue that it should be rejected for three reasons.[54] First, it is the relative and not the absolute gap that is important, as the growing absolute gap is unavoidable in the short-term. Second, market exchange rates are irrelevant due to local cost variations, and so the PPP count is better. Third, related to this point, market exchange-rate measures can lead to wild fluctuations in inequality and poverty figures in a country if that particular country undergoes rapid currency devaluation. These criticisms are important, and blanket condemnations of growing inequality are often based on this method without critical reflection on the problems associated with it. On the other hand, the argument that market exchange rates are *totally* irrelevant for measuring inequality is even more problematic.[55] For advocates of greater global integration to be consistent, they cannot discount market exchange rates as a measure of comparison. This is because market exchange rates should, in part, reflect the fact of an increasingly globalised world, and that therefore some countries' currencies impact enormously on other countries. This may be reflected in the capacity of countries to repay debts, pay for imports, including of capital goods, and pay for adequate representation at world summits and international organisations. If globalisation means anything, then it must mean that countries are not just paying for goods and services in their specific locality (which is reflected in PPP dollars), but are also strongly affected by payment for 'international' goods and services, where market exchange rates are more relevant.

The critics still have a point about the limitations of using market exchange rates, and in some (though not all) respects, PPP comparisons are of greater use. If country measurements are weighted to take account of population, then the evidence suggests that inequality is (in relative terms) falling.[56] The basic reason for this fall is the rapid growth that has occurred in China and India in recent years. But this ignores some of the problems of PPP in general

---

[54] See Wolf in Wade and Wolf 2002; Dollar and Kraay 2001.

[55] Even some of the best analysts of globalisation are too hasty in their dismissal of market exchange rates as a basis for comparison. See for example Sutcliffe 2001.

[56] See World Bank 2002; Dollar and Kraay 2002; Giddens 2002, pp. 72–5; Nolan 2004, Chapter 1.

and China and India in particular cited earlier, as well as the rise in inequality *within* these, and most other countries in recent years.[57] It also ignores the increasing international polarisation between the richest and poorest countries, and global polarisation between people.[58] Moreover, the economic growth in China and India has not led to an unambiguous reduction in international inequality. Their high rates of growth have not led to a decline in the absolute gap between them and the richest countries, and it will take many more years of high growth for this to occur. Where there *is* a reduction in both absolute and relative inequality is in the narrowing gap between China and India and other middle-income states such as Mexico, Brazil, Russia and Argentina. This does not mean that the gap between the richest and poorest countries – and even less so between the richest and poorest people – is narrowing.

The evidence that there has been, either an improvement in, or worsening of, poverty and inequality, is at best ambiguous. What we do know is that world inequality remains highly unequal, with the top 30 per cent of the world's people receiving 85 per cent of the income and the bottom 60 per cent receiving just 6 per cent.[59] Clearly, such inequalities are impossible to justify, and do not conform to optimistic pro-globalisation policy prescriptions or outcomes.[60]

(ii) *Economic growth*

The Bank also argues that not only are poverty and inequality falling, but that this is because of good policies, which have promoted economic growth. Above all, these policies are said to be 'globalisation-friendly' and open to market forces. Thus, '[g]lobalization generally reduces poverty because more integrated economies tend to grow faster and this growth is usually widely diffused'. This is because '[a] reduction in world barriers to trade could accelerate growth, provide stimulus to new forms of productivity-enhancing specialization, and lead to a more rapid pace of job creation and poverty around the world'.[61] The IMF is even clearer:

---

[57] Stewart and Berry 1999; Wade 2002, pp. 17–18; Milanovic 2002.
[58] Milanovic 2002.
[59] Wade 2002, p. 20.
[60] Caney 2001; Pogge 2002.
[61] World Bank 2002a, pp. 1 and xi.

Countries that align themselves with the forces of globalization and embrace the reforms needed to do so, liberalizing markets and pursuing disciplined macroeconomic policies, are likely to put themselves on a path of convergence with advanced economies, following the successful Asian newly industrializing economies (NIEs). These countries may be expected to benefit from trade, gain global market share and be increasingly rewarded with larger private capital flows. Countries that do not adopt such policies are likely to face declining shares of world trade and private capital flows, and to find themselves falling behind in relative terms.[62]

Obviously, if we are to take this quotation seriously, we must leave behind the IMF's interpretation of the Asian boom, which (in the case of the IMF) was quickly jettisoned by that organisation the following year.[63] We must also downplay the claims of convergence and treat the claim for global market share with some caution. Presumably, given the decline in proportionate market shares for most regions of the developing world, this must be explained by the adoption of incorrect policies. This claim is explicitly made by the World Bank in *Globalization, Growth and Poverty: Building an Inclusive World Economy*,[64] which is the latest of numerous attempts to establish a causal relationship between globalisation-friendly policies (including structural adjustment), and economic growth and poverty reduction.[65] Given that world inequality and poverty have probably not been falling (above) as globalisation has increased, there is good reason for immediately questioning this contention, but, again, the Bank attempts to establish a causal relationship for specific, 'more globalised' countries. This differentiation between more and less globalised countries is based on measuring changes in the ratio of trade to GDP between 1977 and 1997. The top third of countries are designated as more globalised, and the bottom two-thirds as less globalised. The more globalised are said to have had faster economic growth and poverty and inequality reduction than the less globalised.

However, measuring *changes* in the trade/GDP ratio is not a very useful way of measuring trade openness. The list of more globalised countries includes China and India, which are actually less open than many of the less

---

[62] IMF 1997, p. 72.
[63] See Section 1 above and Chapter 4.
[64] World Bank 2002b.
[65] See for instance World Bank 1983 and 1994. For critiques see Singer 1988, Mosley et al. 1995 and Kiely 1998.

globalised countries. The most globalised countries tend to be ones that initially had a low trade/GDP ratio in 1977. They may still have lower trade/GDP ratios in 1997 than many of the less globalised countries, as the measurement is not the amount of openness but its rate of increase.[66] This again betrays a statistical bias, as it excludes countries with high but not rising trade/GDP ratios from the category of more globalised. This includes a large number of very poor countries dependent on the export of a few primary commodities, and which have had very low and sometimes negative rates of growth.[67] The effect of excluding such poor, low-growth countries with high but constant trade/GDP ratios from the category of more globalised countries is to underestimate the category of high globalisers with low economic growth.

An exaggeration of the relationship between high growth and growing openness also occurs when one critically examines the evidence for China and India. Contrary to the World Bank's assumption of a causal relationship between trade openness and economic growth, the rapid economic growth of these two countries pre-dates their growing openness. Moreover, despite liberalisation, such as the lifting of some restrictions on foreign capital investment, they remain far from open economies. Like the first-tier East-Asian NICs, capital controls remain strong, subsidies still exist and there are still relatively high tariffs on selected imports. Average tariff rates in India did decline from 91 per cent in the 1980s to 50.5 per cent in the 1990s, while China's declined from 42.4 per cent to 31.2 per cent in the same period.[68] However, it is simply wishful thinking to claim that this reduction was the sole cause of the economic growth, as such rates remain extremely high and do not remotely conform to any recognised policy of trade liberalisation along neo-liberal lines. In the case of India, liberalisation in the 1980s was designed to ensure easier access to the import of technology for manufacturing, rather than to exercise comparative advantage through open competition, and, for this reason, the increased liberalisation in the 1990s remained cautious.[69] In the case of China, the Communist Party leadership is aware that further trade liberalisation is likely to have devastating effects for domestic producers, and therefore intensify already latent social unrest.[70]

---

[66] Rodrik 2001.
[67] UNCTAD 2002a, Part 2, Chapter 3.
[68] Rodrik 2000, table 1.
[69] Athreye 2004.
[70] Nolan 2004, Chapter 1.

Thus, the argument that trade openness automatically leads to economic growth is actually only an assumption. There is a failure to specify the precise relationship between trade and growth, it says nothing about the types of goods being traded, and it ignores the impact of liberalised trade on countries at different stages of development.[71] In 1997–8, the trade/GDP ratio for 39 of the poorest, least developed countries averaged 43 per cent, and for 22 of these 39 countries (based on data availability) – around the same as the world average.[72] In the period from 1980 to 1999, the share of these least developed countries in world exports declined by 47 per cent, to a total of only 0.42 per cent of world exports in the latter year.[73] For the World Bank and IMF to establish a causal connection between global integration and slowing economic growth, it would have to be the case that these countries were employing policies that restricted openness. But this is clearly not the case, and, indeed, least-developed countries have actually gone further than other developing countries in dismantling trade barriers.[74] It is thus not the case that market-restricting policies have led to declining global market shares for most of the least-developed countries. Internal factors such as political instability are important factors in explaining poor economic performance, but what is equally clear is that demand for the products of the least-developed countries is (relatively) limited, and therefore the prices paid for these products is low. This is particularly true for primary-good producers. Based on 1985 PPP dollars and weighted for population, the average income gap between the 20 richest countries and 31 least-developed countries has increased from 11:1 in 1960 to 19:1 in 1999. The income gap for those LDCs that diversified into manufacturing and services increased from 8:1 to 12:1, but for those countries still most dependent on (non-oil) primary commodities, the increase was from 16:1 to 35:1.[75] This differentiation is a product of volatile commodity prices and unsustainable foreign debt payments.[76]

The relationship between global integration and poverty reduction is also far from straightforward. The Bank argues that trade liberalisation will reduce poverty, as it will increase demand for unskilled labour, and increase growth

[71] UNCTAD 2002a, p. 102.
[72] UNCTAD 2002a, p. 103.
[73] UNCTAD 2002a, p. 112.
[74] UNCTAD 2002a, p. 114.
[75] UNCTAD 2002a, p. 122.
[76] UNCTAD 2002a, pp. 148–53.

and therefore government revenue. In fact, tariff reduction deprives developing countries of a major source of revenue, particularly as tariffs are far easier to collect than other taxes in cases where public administration is relatively underdeveloped. In India, for example, in 1990 they provided as much as 25 per cent of government revenue.[77] Moreover, the evidence suggests that trade liberalisation does not have the outcomes that the Bank expects, and that poverty has actually increased among LDCs with the most open trade régimes. However, it has also increased by about the same amount for those with the most closed trade régimes, which undermines any simplistic claims made against trade and for autarchy. Between these two extremes are the moderate liberalisers and the more advanced liberalisers, and, here, the evidence suggests that it is the former that have a better record.[78] No straightforward conclusions can therefore be made, beyond the negative ones that trade liberalisation neither unambiguously causes an increase or a decline in poverty. Based on the UNCTAD data, the incidence of poverty fell in 16 LDCs from 1987–99, and only 4 of these saw a decline in their export/GDP ratio. On the other hand, among LDCs in which export orientation increased, there was no general experience of a reduction in poverty – this occurred in 10 out of the 22 countries from 1987–99.[79] Clearly, then, there are no clear correlations between openness and poverty reduction, let alone causal connections. The same report does establish a link between economic growth and poverty reduction, especially for the poorest countries (though I again stress *not for trade openness and growth*), but, even in this case, substantial qualifications must be made. Economic growth alone does not guarantee that income will trickle down to the poorest, and the last thirty years have seen a general increase in inequality within countries. It may still be necessary, particularly for the poorest countries, where there are limited resources to redistribute. However, this does not mean that, in the absence of sustained growth, nothing can be done,[80] and the social

---

[77] Weisbrot and Baker 2002, p. 17.

[78] UNCTAD 2002a, pp. 115–17, esp. chart 33.

[79] UNCTAD 2002a, p. 119.

[80] The issue of the relationship between growth and the kinds of goods produced – and consumed – is taken up in later chapters. Briefly, I reject blanket anti-growth, anti-consumption positions while also rejecting blanket pro-growth positions. The relationship between growth, social development and progress is more complex than that taken by either of these positions, and is an issue of debate within the 'anti-globalisation' movement. See later chapters, and Sutcliffe 1992; 1995; 1999 and Kiely 1998, especially Chapters 2, 8 and 10.

development record of poor countries varies, and has depended above all on social expenditure priorities and ensuring wide access to the potential benefits.[81] But the most effective strategy remains both the promotion of growth and 'market-restricting' regulation of capital, including some commitment to reducing inequality. Neo-liberalism fails on all counts. Hanmer et al. argue that, in order to meet the 2015 Millennium Targets for reducing poverty, countries with high inequality will need growth rates twice as high as those with low inequality.[82] This argument is based on a survey of comparative economic growth from 1985–90, where countries with 10 per cent economic growth and low inequality saw a fall in poverty of 9 per cent, while those with high inequality and similar growth rates saw a fall of only 3 per cent.

Questioning the benefits of free trade does not imply support for a blanket reversal of trade liberalisation, and still less a policy of autarchy, the latter of which is largely a straw-man utilised by pro-globalisers to caricature the proposals of anti-globalisers.[83] What *is* clear however is that the global economy is not a completely benign force, and that the claims made for pro-globalisation policies do not stand up to critical scrutiny. Arguments that champion free trade and comparative advantage abstract from unequal structures of production and the productivity gap between countries, as well as the current domination of financial capital in the world economy. This is not to say that no progress can be made, but it is to say that much of the progress that has been made, in terms of both economic growth and social development, over the last twenty years, is occurring both more slowly and more unequally than in the Bretton Woods era. All agree that, some exceptions notwithstanding, the general trend over the last twenty years has been towards greater global integration. Comparing this period from 1980 to 2000 with the previous twenty-year period (which includes the particularly unstable 1970s), and based on a comparison of growth rates for five categories of countries (based on per capita income) rates of economic growth have fallen for each set of countries. For the poorest quintile, growth averaged 1.9 per cent a year in 1960–80, but averaged minus 0.5 per cent from 1980–2000; for the next poorest quintile the figures were down from a 2 per cent annual average to 0.75 per cent; for the middle quintile the corresponding figures were 3.5 per cent and

[81] Sen 1999, Chapter 1.
[82] Hanmer et al. 2000, p. 2; see also UNDP 2002, Chapter 1.
[83] See, for instance, Desai 2000.

0.9 per cent; for the second richest, they were 3.4 per cent and 1.1 per cent, and the final grouping saw a decline of 2.5 per cent to 1.75 per cent. Improvements in social development indicators – such as life expectancy, infant mortality, literacy, and so on – continued in most cases, but the *rate of improvement* slowed down in the globalising years.[84] Moreover, country mobility in terms of quintile ranking based on per capita income is highly immobile.[85] Even if relative inequality is narrowing (and this remains debateable), absolute inequality is not. Wolf's claim[86] that this does not matter, so long as absolute poverty and relative inequality are decreasing, is based on a selective embrace of globalisation. For globalisation is supposed to lead to some kind of convergence, be it in terms of country mobility for strong globalisers or a narrowing in gaps based on economic performance, as capital moves from capital abundant to capital scarce areas. Neither of these phenomena has occurred.

Of course, such figures do not take account of the high rate of growth of the two most populous countries, China and India, and it is, at bottom, their growth records that are the reason for all the optimism about growth, poverty and inequality in recent years. But there are good grounds for questioning some of the data for these countries in particular, as well as those that measure poverty and inequality more generally. Even if we give the figures the benefit of the doubt, it is still the case that in absolute terms, the gap between rich and poor is growing. For some writers, this does not matter so long as the number of people living in absolute poverty is declining.[87] But the case for globalisation rests on the notion that it will lead to some kind of convergence between rich and poor, which clearly has not been witnessed. Moreover, we need to question the view that inequality is unimportant. The discussion above suggests that poverty is not unrelated to inequality and that poverty reduction targets are likely to be met in cases of low inequality. But there is a more fundamental point to be made, which is that, without some commitment to equality, both within and between countries, there is no possibility of individuals or countries being able to participate in (global or national) society in a freely chosen way.[88] Any commitment to progressive politics must therefore

---

[84] Weisbrot et al. 2002.
[85] Korzeniewicz and Moran 1997; 2002.
[86] In Wade and Wolf 2002.
[87] Desai 2002; Wolf in Wade and Wolf 2002.
[88] Sen 1992.

include a commitment to social equality. Indeed, the one-sided focus on poverty again shows the close relationship between the neo-liberal legacy and the Third Way, as poverty reduction is reduced to a technocratic process of economic growth (and a misguided one at that), in isolation form global power relations and inequalities.[89] Finally, to return to the question of globalisation, one final point needs to be made, and that is that, if poverty has been reduced in the world (and this is seriously open to doubt), then this is largely because of growth in China and India. The World Bank has tried to argue that these are examples of countries that have followed pro-globalisation policies. But like the East-Asian miracle economies before them, these countries do not embrace unambiguously market-friendly, pro-globalisation policies.[90]

5.3 Globalisation and uneven development: US hegemony and the end of 'labour-friendly' and 'development-friendly' régimes

This section starts by examining the relationship between increased competition, expressed through trade dependence, and slower rates of growth? In addressing this question we need to focus less on trade *per se*, and look more at the changing context in which trade operates, which brings us back to the question of globalisation as a political project. In this regard, globalisation should be seen as the implementation of a new form of disciplinary régime. It is one that spells the end of the post-war settlement based on the construction of labour- and development-friendly régimes,[91] and the construction of a new régime based on establishing competitiveness in the world market. At the same time, as we have seen, the globalisation project does not occur 'above' particular places, and particular nation-states. Indeed, globalisation (and inequality) is not only about the relationship between capital and labour, and First World and Third World, but is equally about competition between capitals and states, and how these in turn have influenced the movement from the Golden Age to the new era. The second part of this section therefore re-examines the question of states and globalisation, and in particular the question of the hegemony of the US state. This section reviews the arguments of the previous two chapters, and, in doing so, briefly discusses some other

---

89 Woods 1999; Nederveen Pieterse 2003.
90 Kiely 1998, Chapters 7 and 8.
91 Zolberg 1995; Silver and Slater 1999; Silver and Arrighi 2000.

theoretical perspectives that suggest that globalisation has ushered in a new era of transnational capitalism and/or Empire, which has gone beyond the nation-state.

(i) *Globalisation, labour and development*

As we have seen, labour-friendly régimes, which predominated in the 'advanced' capitalist countries, were not based on government by and for the working class, and exploitation, hierarchy and repression were maintained. Similarly, development-friendly régimes, based in the former 'Third World', were not based on catching up with the West, and capital flows, economic growth and poverty reduction were limited. But, in both cases, 'friendliness' was more then mere rhetoric. The post-war system based on US hegemony had to deal with the issues of growing class conflict in the core and anti-colonial revolt in the periphery – and therefore the global threat of communism. These two political issues 'were recast as technical problems of macroeconomic adjustment and economic growth and development – problems that could be overcome using scientific and technical knowledge backed by government planning'.[92]

In terms of labour-friendly régimes, social compromise was reflected in government and business acceptance of trade unions, workers rights, state welfare and full employment. On the other hand, organised labour had to accept hierarchical management and work reorganisation, reflected in the extension of Fordist techniques to many sectors of the economy. The expansion of mass production guaranteed increases in productivity and therefore increasing wages, which, in turn, kept demand high and led to mass consumption.[93] This social compromise was exported to all of the advanced capitalist countries, albeit in different local contexts with varying degrees of state intervention and union representation. Nonetheless, while the existence of different market-led capitalisms (US, UK), corporatist capitalisms (Germany, Scandinavia) and state capitalisms (Japan) was real enough, all the post-war models were based on some degree of social compromise.[94]

In the case of development-friendly régimes, the US supported the

---

[92] Silver and Slater 1999, p. 205.
[93] See further, Chapter 3.
[94] Coates 2000.

independence aspirations of anti-colonial movements, while at the same time suppressing those considered to be pro-communist. Pro-development policies were limited, aid was often tied to Cold-War considerations and double standards on trade liberalisation frequently occurred at GATT talks, but developing countries were given some room for manoeuvre in regulating trade and investment. The standard development strategy in the 1950s and 1960s was import-substitution industrialisation, which gave states the power to restrict manufactured imports so that a domestic manufacturing base could be developed. This strategy faced a number of problems, which (as well as a sometimes hostile international environment) included limited domestic markets, and a replacement of trade dependence on consumer goods imports with that of capital goods. However, despite neo-liberal rhetoric, the ISI era was also one of better rates of economic growth and faster improvements in social development than have been the case in the last twenty years.[95]

As we saw in Chapter 3, this post-war settlement collapsed in the early 1970s. The neo-liberalism of the 1980s was designed to curb the related problems of inflation and debt, while globalisation in the 1990s was and remains a political project that accepts most of the assumptions of neo-liberalism concerning the free market, capital mobility and free trade. Globalisation is thus in part a political project designed to replace the technocratic management of post-war demand management and development with the technocratic promotion of 'efficient' global markets, in which supposedly everyone can participate. So, in this way, globalisation represents a serious reversal of the limited gains of the post-war order. This can be seen by returning once more to the question of international trade. In this changed context of the overaccumulation of capital, and consequent slower growth, trade takes on an increasingly coercive, disciplinary, rather than complementary role. The post-war boom – in the First World at least – was characterised by oligopolistic firms, fast growth, high profits and rising wages. As Crotty et al. state, '[f]irms could accumulate capital without excessive concern that national AD [aggregate demand – RK] would fail to grow, that imports would steal their customers, that financiers would take huge chunks of future profits, or that their new capital would be made prematurely obsolete by the outbreak of fierce cost-cutting battles over market share. High rates of investment and

---

[95] Kiely 1998, Chapters 6 and 8; Palma 2003.

productivity growth followed'.[96] The breakdown of this system in the early 1970s led to a very different context, '[w]ith AD now consistently inadequate to generate rapidly growing markets or full capacity utilization and with barriers to international competition breaking down everywhere, firms entered a more Hobbesian world'.[97] The result has been an intensification of already increasing competition between a number of producers, as well as falling demand for the products of the biggest losers. These factors have, in turn, been further reinforced by the hegemony of financial capital, which generates pressures to maintain stock-market values in the context of slower rates of growth, and uncertainties in the context of floating exchange rates. In this context, the so-called free market serves to undermine wage growth for workers in the First World *and* economic growth for developing countries that face increasingly intense and unequal competition. Intensified competition does not mean that trade becomes a zero-sum game, but it does mean that it is far less complementary than it was in the boom period, with the result that inequalities between trading agents intensify. Intensified international competition has been used by states and employers to justify increased flexibility in labour markets, and, as we have seen, is an important component of Third-Way rhetoric. But, as we have also seen, in practice increased flexibility, for First-World workers has not, on the whole, meant increasingly skilled and highly-paid jobs in the IT sector, but has, instead, meant insecure and lower-paid work. Employers have certainly used international competition from cheaper imports, or indeed capital relocation, as a political weapon. Thus, between 1993 and 1995, Kate Bronfenbrenner surveyed a number of firms in the United States and found that 50 per cent of all firms and 65 per cent of manufacturing firms that were targets of union organising campaigns threatened to relocate if workers formed trade unions.[98]

But such threats need to be put into a wider context, and we need to be careful about making simplistic assertions about wage competition between workers in different sets of countries. As we saw earlier in the chapter, productive capital on the whole continues to concentrate in selected parts of the world, and manufacturing imports into the 'advanced' capitalist countries

---

[96] Crotty et al. 1998, p. 128.
[97] Crotty et al. 1998, p. 129.
[98] Bronfenbrenner 2001.

from the developing world remain low. Threats of relocation are not the same as actual relocation, and actual relocation is most likely to take place in labour-intensive sectors. Moreover, though there are some exceptional countries, the fact remains that growing unemployment in the core has coincided with lower, not faster rates of growth in the periphery.[99] Thus globalisation undermines the bargaining position of *both* workers in the advanced countries, *and* the developmental capacity of developing countries. Some critics of globalisation have made very different arguments, along the lines of growing investment in the periphery is at the expense of workers in the core countries, which has enormous implications for building global solidarity movements, as we will see in Chapter 8. In fact, this race to the bottom rhetoric is not so far removed from the Third-Way call to lower costs in the face of hyper-mobile capital movements. This is yet another instance of an approach to globalisation that confuses certain visible effects with underlying causes. As Watson points out, 'just because the "effects" of globalisation are visible does not necessarily mean that globalisation can be used to explain their cause'.[100] The end of full employment in the core countries 'is not the result of direct wage competition from the newly industrialising economies. It is the result of a situation of systemic productive capital shortage', and this in turn is due to the increased domination of financial capital in the world economy.

But this dominance of finance is precisely one of the areas which Third-Way politicians simply take for granted. As a result, faith is placed in the role of the state in upgrading labour skills. The Clinton and Blair administrations both promoted strategies of 'progressive competitiveness', in which capital and labour embark on a social partnership to protect 'their' company and 'their' jobs.[101] Competitiveness is maintained by the development of high-skilled, high-value work, which is more competitive than cheaper labour elsewhere.[102] This is in contrast to the neo-liberal fundamentalist strategy of competitive austerity', which, on its own terms, is self-defeating as 'each country

---

[99] The one regional exception is East Asia. However, its boom started at a time when most countries remained relatively closed to foreign investment. Of course, its exports still penetrated First-World markets, but developing-country exports to the First World as a whole remain low (see Section 1 above). The implications of these arguments are addressed in more detail in the second part of the book.

[100] Watson 1999, p. 71.

[101] See also Chapter 4.

[102] Reich 1983.

reduces domestic demand and adopts an export-oriented strategy of dumping its surplus production, for which there are fewer consumers in its national economy, given the decrease in workers' living standards and productivity gains all going to the capitalists, in the world market'.[103] But the strategy of progressive competitiveness suffers from similarly flawed assumptions; these are 'that mass unemployment is primarily a problem of skills adjustment to technological change rather than one aspect of a crisis of overproduction; it fosters an illusion of a rate of employment growth in high tech sectors sufficient to offset the rate of unemployment growth in other sectors; it either even more unrealistically assumes a rate of growth in world markets massive enough to accommodate all those adopting this strategy, or it blithely ignores the issues associated with exporting unemployment to those who don't succeed at this strategy in conditions of limited demand . . .'.[104] Thus, it can be argued that this strategy is no less nationalist than blanket protectionism because, in the context of free trade and slower growth, it effectively exports unemployment to less competitive areas. It also exaggerates the extent to which participation in a supposedly vibrant labour market will alleviate poverty. But, as we have seen, despite the rhetoric concerning a dynamic hi-tech, 'new economy', the fastest growing sectors in 'advanced' capitalist countries are in the low-wage, service economy.[105] Above all, it is a strategy that does not deal with the current intensification of uneven development and domination of financial capital, which is central to actually existing globalisation. Progressive competitiveness therefore does nothing to overcome the problems that face the contemporary global economy, or workers and developing countries that most suffer the consequences.

Given the movement away from labour-friendly régimes since the late 1970s, it is not surprising that inequalities within countries have generally increased. The restructuring of the global economy, and within national economies, has generally led to a re-distribution of income from poor to rich, which has occurred through declining real wages and welfare provision, as well as enhanced opportunities for the development of a super-rich class of financial entrepreneurs. Despite Third-Way rhetoric, this pattern of growing inequality actually intensified in the 1990s.[106]

---

[103] Albo 1994, p. 147.
[104] Panitch 1994, p. 83.
[105] Henwood 1997; Gordon 1999.
[106] Henwood 2003, Chapter 3.

(ii) *Globalisation and US hegemony*

The above analysis is broadly accepted by a number of radical writers, but it is sometimes argued that the transnational nature of this restructuring means that the agents and outcomes of globalisation can no longer be 'tied' to particular nation-states. Indeed, it could be argued that this analysis was implicit in the emergence of transnational protest movements such as those at Seattle, that questioned the legitimacy of international institutions such as the IMF, World Bank, and WTO, more than they did particular nation states. The political implications of such an analysis are examined in detail in Chapter 8. Here, I first want to outline in more depth – and question – the contentions of approaches that suggest that we now live in a world of transnational capital, which is largely independent of particular nation-states.

The theories that have attempted to account for a transnational capital in this way include the theory of post-imperialism, the theory of transnational capitalism and the theory of Empire.[107] The theories of post-imperialism and of the transnational capitalism contend that 'global corporations function to promote the integration of diverse national interests on a new transnational basis'.[108] The development of a transnational capitalist class therefore transcends the old imperialist division of the world. Conflict and competition exist, but these tend to take place between companies rather than states, and even when the latter exists it coincides with, and in some respects is subordinate to, capitalist co-operation beyond the nation-state.[109] Competition thus primarily reflects splits and divisions within the transnational capitalist class, rather than inter-state conflict.[110] An emerging transnational state is composed of transformed international institutions such as the World Bank, IMF and Bank of International Settlements, as well as newer organisations and summits such as the Group of 7 (8), World Economic Forum and World Trade Organisation.

A not dissimilar theory is associated with the work of Hardt and Negri.[111] They argue that US hegemony has (to some extent at least) been replaced by a deterritorialised apparatus of power, which they call Empire. For Hardt

---

[107] Becker et al. 1987; Sklair 1991, 2001; Hardt and Negri 2000.
[108] Becker and Sklar 1987, p. 6.
[109] Harris 2003, pp. 69, 71.
[110] Robinson 2001/2, p. 507.
[111] Hardt and Negri 2000.

and Negri, '[i]mperialism is over. No nation will be world leader in the way modern European nations were'.[112] Therefore, '[w]hat used to be conflict or competition among several imperialist powers has in important respects been replaced by the idea of a single power that overdetermines them all, structures them in a unitary way and treats them under one common notion of right that is decidedly postcolonial and postimperialist'.[113]

There is much of use in these theoretical approaches. They represent genuinely challenging attempts to theorise current structures and processes of capitalist globalisation, recognising the fact that international capitalism has changed enormously since the days of classical Marxism. Above all, they attempt to reformulate an understanding of international capitalism that accepts the reality of international co-operation and regulation, increased international and global interdependence, and the fact that economic competition does not necessarily mean political and military competition. In other words, they clearly argue that 'imperialism' has changed enormously since the days of Lenin. Nevertheless, in the analysis of transnational capitalism, there is a danger of throwing the baby out with the bathwater, which is most clearly seen in relation to the question of the nation-state and US hegemony.

In terms of the nation-state, the basic problem with these approaches is that they tend to set up a rigid dichotomy between global capital and the transnational state on the one hand, and the nation-state on the other. But this is too black and white, for most of the institutions and summits that supposedly represent a nascent transnational state are actually created and authorised by nation-states.[114] This may involve the sharing of sovereignty – for instance, through the European Union – but these are still promoted by, and allied to, nation-states. The nation-state retains a key economic role in terms of taxation, government spending, managing exchange rates, representation at meetings of international institutions, and so on. Moreover, power within international institutions is hierarchical, and unequally structured through the mechanisms and interests of nation-states, and not (for example) transnational corporations – thus, trade disputes through the World Trade Organisation occur between nation-states. The United States has lost in disputes

---

[112] Hardt and Negri 2000, p. xiv.
[113] Hardt and Negri 2000, p. 9.
[114] Burnham 1997.

through the WTO,[115] but the fact remains that sanctions are implemented (or not, as the case may be) through nation-states. This entrenches hierarchical power, not only of capital against labour, but of some states against others. This is because of the time and cost of bringing trade disputes forward to the WTO's dispute settlement mechanism, and the fact that the only sanction is state-imposed trade sanctions. Clearly, sanctions brought by poor states against the US mean far less to the latter than sanctions by the US against the former.[116] It is therefore too one-sided to argue that competition now takes place solely between transnational capitals, and not between states. This is not the same as the competition between state capitals that concerned Bukharin and Lenin, but it is state competition nonetheless. Thus, as we saw in the last chapter, in 2003, serious trade disputes between the European Union and the United States broke out over US export subsidies and steel tariffs, European protection against imported US genetically modified food, and both within the EU and between the EU and US over protection to agriculture.[117] These are clear examples of states (and regional organisations) protecting 'their' capitals.

These comments also have implications for how we understand US hegemony. Once again, a contrast with the transnational capitalism approach is useful. Jerry Harris argues that the fact that the US is the major recipient of foreign investment in the world today reflects its declining hegemony.[118] In one respect, this is perfectly correct, and the US's transition from the world's major creditor to the world's main debtor over the last twenty years reflects the fragile nature of such hegemony. But Harris misses the other side of the equation, *which is the fact that it is precisely because of this capital inflow that the US manages to maintain its hegemony, at least for the moment.*[119] US hegemony is also, at least in part, based on its continued leadership in a number of key industrial sectors, plus the fact that other states and capitals have 'bought in' to the US-led system, even though competition continues to exist between these same powers, and this is because the consequences of opting out are potentially even more damaging. This point applies to capitals and states in

---

[115] Harris 2003, p. 73.
[116] Toye 2003, p. 113.
[117] Islam 2003.
[118] Harris 2003, pp. 69–70.
[119] Arrighi 1994; 2003.

much of the developing world, as well as Europe and East Asia, even though there is much conflict as well, for instance at the WTO. What should be clear then is that, while older Marxist theories of imperialism are of limited use for understanding the present global order, it is also a mistake to conceptualise the transnationalisation of capital in such a way that the role and continued importance of nation-states in general, and the US state in particular, are neglected.[120]

My arguments about US hegemony and globalisation were developed in detail in Chapters 3 and 4, so they can be briefly summarised at this point. The end of the gold-dollar link and of fixed exchange rates from 1971–3 was part of a strategy designed to recover competitiveness in industrial production. In particular, the US governments of Nixon, Ford and (for a time) Carter pursued expansionary monetary policies and a relatively weak dollar, which were designed to increase production both at home and through cheaper exports abroad. However, the policy led to inflation and potentially undermined the international role of the dollar, and so a new tight monetary policy was adopted in 1979 under Carter, and especially under Ronald Reagan. In the early 1980s, the money supply came under tighter control, there were tax cuts for the wealthy, and increased deregulation of capital investment. From 1982 onwards, there was a big increase in military spending and a marked intensification of Cold-War hostilities. The effect of these policies was a massive increase in the US's trade and budget deficits, and an increase in competition for capital investment to finance these deficits. This involved an increase in interest rates to attract financial capital to the US, which, in turn, led to a huge increase in interest payments for countries that had built up debt in the 1970s. The 1980s, therefore, promoted continued US hegemony through the

---

[120] A full theorisation of US hegemony lies beyond the scope of this work, but see Kiely 2005. For important arguments, see among others Arrighi 1994, 2003; Gowan 1999; Bromley 2003; Panitch and Gindin 2003 and Mann 2003. My own outline has avoided taking sides in the US decline versus strenghtening US hegemony debate. Briefly, my position is that US hegemony remains a reality but, economically at least, is one that is far from secure in the future. Also, non-US capitals and states actually 'buy in' to US hegemony, even if competition also remains a reality. US hegemony is not simply imposed, and neither can all political events be read off from the reality of US hegemony. Moreover, military coercion has very different implications throughout the globe, and it does not automatically secure US economic primacy. On these points, see especially Panitch and Gindin 2003 and Bromley 2003, and the arguments made in the text.

expansion of financial capital. At the same time, the United States has the largest trade deficit in the world, and since the 'election' of Bush, a massively increasing budget deficit. In 2001 and 2002, military spending grew by 6 per cent and 10 per cent a year, which amounted to around 65 per cent and 80 per cent of total increases in Federal government spending in those years.[121] Its military budget figures were already far higher than most of the combined spending of the next twelve or so powers, and at least 26 times greater than that of the seven main 'Axis of Evil' countries. At the same time, since early 2000, the Federal budget deficit has grown from 1.8 per cent of GDP to 2.3 per cent, and is likely to rise enormously. In 2001, the trade deficit was a record $435 billion, and current account deficit $400 billion, and these are likely to increase.[122] These deficits have been financed by foreigners speculating in the stock market, buying real estate, acquiring firms or setting up new sites, and buying US Treasury bonds. Equity purchases fell by 83 per cent from 2000 to 2002 as share prices fell, and so there has been a sustained movement into buying government bonds. In 2001, 97 per cent of the US current account deficit was financed by foreign purchases of these bonds. From 1992–2001, the foreign share of US national debt increased from 17 per cent to 31 per cent.[123] None of this necessarily matters, so long as there is confidence in the US economy and the dollar. But, there remain serious questions over the sustainability of annual deficits of 5 per cent of GDP. While this is more sustainable for the US than for other countries because of the international role of the dollar, ongoing deficits are likely to further erode this role. US hegemony therefore continues to exist, but it is a hegemony that is far from solid. What is clear is that this hegemony rests on the continued dominance of financial capital in the world economy.

5.4 Conclusion: globalisation and the anti-globalisation movement

This chapter has challenged the evidence that globalisation has caused increased economic growth and social advance. The era of globalisation has seen a slowing down in rates of economic growth and social improvement and,

---

[121] Brenner 2003, p. 21.
[122] *Monthly Review* 2003, p. 8.
[123] *Monthly Review* 2002, p. 10.

according to most criteria, an increase in inequality. Absolute poverty may have declined, but the data that suggests that this is the case is not reliable and biased towards showing long-term trends in poverty decreases. Moreover, if there have been reductions in absolute poverty, they have not been because of unambiguously pro-globalisation policies, and instead relied heavily on highly active state intervention.

These inequalities can, in turn, be related to the dominance of neo-liberalism since the late 1970s, which can itself be linked to the slowdown in accumulation and the crisis of US hegemony in the 1970s. The movement towards free markets, liberalised investment and the free movement of money have been at the cost of the limited gains made by labour in the North and 'developmental states' in the South (though, of course, a small minority of people in the South have benefited from neo-liberal policies). Inequalities between states have also intensified, and there is a close connection between neo-liberal globalisation and the attempted restoration of US hegemony. All of these inequalities can, therefore, be linked to the globalisation project.

But it is also clear that as a political project, globalisation is also *contested*. The question of concrete alternatives will be addressed in Chapters 6–9, but we should immediately note the (disputed) fact of this political challenge – the rise of the anti-globalisation movement. This movement came together most visibly at the World Trade Organisation talks at Seattle in late 1999, but various forerunners can be identified. These include protests against structural adjustment from the early 1980s, the expansion of international NGOs, especially those concerned with international debt and the environment, protests against free trade agreements such as NAFTA, the Zapatista rebellion in Chiapas, Mexico in 1994, road protests, dam protests, internet activism and much more. Since Seattle, there have been many more protests at international summits, the development of the World Social Forum and regional social fora, and post-September 11, the growth of a massive anti-war movement.[124]

One possible interpretation of these developments can be found by utilising the work of Karl Polanyi, and in particular his *The Great Transformation*, first published in 1944. He argued that the rise of the 'market system' in the nineteenth century was distinct from the market as one means of allocating

---

[124] There is no real history of such a diverse movement, but see Danaher 1996, Danaher and Bacon 2000, Welton and Wolf 2001 and Klein 2002.

resources. This market system did not arise naturally or spontaneously, but was actually the deliberate creation of the state.[125] A separate market economy was thus the product of historical social struggles such as the enclosure of land. Once a 'separate' economic sphere was created, it tended to dominate all aspects of social life – 'instead of economy being embedded in social relations, social relations are embedded in the economic system'.[126] Profit maximisation became the main goal of economic activity as capital commodified increasing aspects of social life, with destructive consequences. Unsurprisingly, this tendency for capital to penetrate into new areas was resisted in the nineteenth century, and attempts were made to 're-embed' the economy into wider social relations. There was thus what Polanyi called a 'double movement':

> While on the one hand markets spread all over the globe and the amount
> of goods involved grew to unbelievable proportions, on the other hand a
> network of measures and policies was integrated into powerful institutions
> designed to check the action of the market relative to labour, land and
> money.[127]

So, in phase one of the double movement, the market became separated from social control which led to conflict, while, in phase two, society restored some control over the market economy. Such means of control included universal suffrage, the rise of 'mass politics', trade unions and so on. The 1930s saw a challenge to the democratic potential of the double movement, in the shape of Stalinism and fascism, but the post-Second-World-War period constituted a renewal of this second movement. With the breakdown of labour- and development-friendly régimes and the resurgence of international finance and free trade, neo-liberal capitalism can be regarded as the first phase of a new double movement.[128] The protests against structural adjustment policies and the IMF and World Bank, the proposed Multilateral Agreement on Investment, the WTO meeting at Seattle and so on, are clearly part of a protest against the tendency of capital to become disembedded from wider social relations, with devastating social consequences such as increased inequality, financial instability, uneven development and environmental destruction.

---

[125] See also Chapter 2.
[126] Polanyi 1957, p. 57.
[127] Polanyi 1957, p. 76.
[128] Hettne 1995; Harris 2000.

These may constitute the beginning of a second phase of a new double movement.

While there is much utility in talking about a second double movement against contemporary neo-liberalism, there is also a need for some caution, as we should not exaggerate the extent to which economy was re-embedded in society in the post-war period. Indeed, while labour was partially decommodified in the advanced countries through the welfare state, this period also saw an enormous increase in commodification through mass production and consumption – in part facilitated by the development of welfare states. This point relates to interpretations of Polanyi's work – was he against what we now call neo-liberalism or was he anti-capitalist?[129] More broadly, this also relates to the questions of alternatives to neo-liberalism, and possibly capitalism, and the related question of whether the very diversity of the anti-globalisation movement undermines the basis for an alternative political project(s). Part Two of this book takes up these issues in more detail.

---

[129] See Lacher 1999.

PART TWO

'ANTI-GLOBALISATION'

Chapter Six

The Politics of Anti-Globalisation and Alternative Globalisations

This opening chapter of the book's second part has two principal tasks. The first is to summarise the main criticisms of the globalising project associated with neo-liberalism and the Third Way. My first section thus broadly summarises five key criticisms of actually existing globalisation made by the 'anti-globalisation' movement. Three of these were discussed in detail in Part One of the book: first, the claim that globalisation has led to increased exploitation of labour; second, that globalisation has led to an increase in social inequality; third, that it has led to an increase in political inequality. In addition, two additional arguments are considered, and discussed in a little more detail: first, that globalisation has led to cultural homogenisation, and, second, that it has intensified environmental destruction. Section 2 then moves on and outlines seven possible alternatives to neo-liberal globalisation: right-wing anti-globalisation, global reform, localisation, global solidarity through the promotion of global civil society, autonomy and anarchism, environmentalism, and socialism. My concern is mainly to introduce and describe, rather than make a detailed assessment of these approaches. Some brief critical comments are made, but detailed analysis of the issues is taken up in later chapters. But this chapter does have a particular concern beyond a broad introduction to the politics of anti-globalisation, and this relates to the notion that we have gone beyond the old Left-Right political divide. This argument rests on a 'spatial fetishism', which suggests that progressive politics must embrace globalisation. I will, instead, argue that anti-globalisation does not necessarily mean being against all forms of globalisation, and that the alternatives positions outlined in the chapter are not mutually exclusive. This argument will then lead on to my conclusion, which sets up the detailed discussion in Chapters 7 and 8. The argument made is that resistance to globalisation can be theorised in terms of the interaction between local, national and global spaces, but that it is wrong to regard one level or space as intrinsically more progressive than the other. This argument is further illustrated through concrete discussion focusing on local and national resistance (Chapter 7), 'global civil society' (Chapter 8) and the question of alternatives (Chapter 9).

6.1   What is wrong with actually existing globalisation?

This section briefly outlines five arguments related to globalisation. The arguments are that globalisation lead to: (i) intensified exploitation; (ii) an increase in social inequality; (iii) (or at least fails to alleviate) political inequality; (iv) cultural homogenisation; (v) (or intensifies) environmental destruction.

(i) Globalisation and increased exploitation

The case of global exploitation is often associated with the link between the consumption of cheap (and not so cheap) consumer goods in the 'First World' and the exploitation of sweat-shop labour in the developing world. This is often linked to the rise of export-processing zones (EPZs), or free-trade zones, which have become increasingly commonplace over the last twenty-thirty years. An export-processing zone is usually a specified area within a country that specialises in manufacturing exports. Companies are often given incentives to invest in these zones, such as duty-free imports of inputs, tax concessions, controls on the labour force, and export subsidies (though these are due to be phased out as they violate WTO free-trade rules). Estimates of the numbers of EPZs, and the number of people employed within them, vary, as some areas are not always officially designated zones. One estimate in the mid-1990s suggested that there were around 200 zones in the world employing around 2 million people,[1] but this figure excluded employment in the special economic zones in China. Naomi Klein[2] suggests that there are around a thousand zones employing around 27 million people. This figure includes the zones in China, but not all employment in these zones is in the private (foreign or local) sector. Whatever the precise numbers, there has been a significant growth in the use of EPZs in the developing world, particularly (though not exclusively) in East Asia, Latin America and the Caribbean.

The rise of export-processing zones, and the increased visibility of sweatshop labour, have been linked to the argument that the increased global mobility has led to a 'race to the bottom'.[3] The core of this argument – at least in its starkest, most unambiguous form – is that capital is now so mobile that it by-passes nation-states, and thereby invests where capital can most benefit from low costs. Such benefits to capital may be low wages, low rates of taxation, and weak environmental regulation. However, while the promotion of export-processing zones does constitute a new competitive strategy in the context of intensified global competitiveness, there is a tendency in this argument to exaggerate the mobility of capital.[4] It is certainly not the case that the employment of cheap labour in these zones has unambiguously undermined manufacturing employment in the 'advanced countries'. Klein's[5] figures for the employment of Mexican workers in the low-wage, export areas on the Mexican border (the maquiladoras) show, despite the general drift of her argument, that while employment may be growing, at 900,000 it remains a very small proportion of the labour force of the United States, including in manufacturing. The figures cited on manufacturing imports in Chapter 5 also confirm this view. Moreover, there is no straightforward relationship between accepting the argument that such a race exists, and the formulation of a progressive politics. Indeed, the argument that there is a race to the bottom can easily lend itself to a nationalist agenda, often with quite reactionary overtones.[6] These points are discussed further below, and in detail in the Chapter 8.

---

[1] Gereffi and Hempel 1996, p. 22.
[2] Klein 2000, p. 205.
[3] Brecher and Costello 1998, pp. 22–5.
[4] See also Chapter 8.
[5] Klein 2000, p. 205.
[6] Buchanan 1998; Tonelson 2002.

(ii) *Globalisation and social inequality*

This issue was examined in detail in Chapter 5, where I suggested that claims that global inequality and poverty are decreasing are based on highly selective evidence. What should be clear from the first half of the book is that intensified global inequalities are the product of the expansion of the market without redistributive mechanisms, the marginalisation of some regions and peoples from capital flows, the hegemony of finance which enriches the very few at the expense of the many, and the practice of protectionism in cases where the developing world may otherwise enjoy potential advantages.

In terms of inequality *within* countries, this has generally increased as a result of privatised provision of basic services, the end of 'full' employment in the 'First World' and undermining of some employment guarantees in the developing world, the erosion of systems of progressive taxation and their replacement by indirect and regressive taxes, alongside the rise of a super-rich financial sector. These are, of course, general tendencies and some poorer groups in the developing world, including medium and possibly small farmers may have won some important gains.[7] Nevertheless, the dominant tendency within countries has been an intensification of inequality between rich and poor. In terms of inequality *between* countries, insofar as there may have been improvements, these cannot be attributed to policies that could be described as 'pro-globalisation'. Moreover, there is nothing like the convergence between countries that trade liberalisation policies promise, and this is because globalisation (trade and financial liberalisation) has undermined the ability of countries to pursue growth-oriented policies, including the capacity to develop successful domestic production as cheap imports flood into poor countries. In this respect, free-trade policies (including WTO regulations) literally 'kick away the ladder' which developing countries hope to climb.[8] The result has been an *intensification* of uneven development, as capital concentrates in some areas and marginalises others.

---

[7] Engberg-Pedersen 1996.
[8] Chang 2002.

(iii) *Globalisation and political inequality*

The relationship between globalisation and political inequality is a particularly complex one. As we saw in the case of the World Trade Organisation,[9] supporters argue that an increase in global governance is a progressive development as it means that weaker countries are not subject to the law of the jungle, and can get their voice heard, especially in institutions where there is one member one vote. But we also saw that, even if we leave aside the question of representation of poorer *people*, many poorer countries complained that the most important decisions were taken behind their backs. Moreover, a stronger country breaking trade rules and facing sanctions as a consequence was likely to have little meaningful effect on its economy, at least compared with the likely effects of sanctions on a weaker economy.

The problem of inequality between states has become more acute since the 'election' of the Bush administration in 2000. US governments certainly acted in unilateralist ways prior to Bush, and have often combined unilateral and multilateral practices. Thus, at Bretton Woods, the particular functions of the new institutions were not as multilateralist as some would have liked (Keynes for instance), and even the supposedly multilateralist President Clinton by-passed international institutions when it suited him. As we saw in Part One, globalisation itself has not eroded US hegemony, and, in fact, is closely connected to it. The issue of unilateralism – and the nation-state – has, however, become a more pressing concern since the arrival of the Bush Junior administration, and are discussed in relation to war in Chapter 8.

(iv) *Globalisation leads to cultural homogenisation*

This argument is closely linked to older concerns that Western cultural imperialism has undermined local cultures and led to a process of homogenisation. Resistance to processes of Americanisation date back to the 1930s in both Nazi Germany and the Stalinist Soviet Union, and became a major issue in post-war Britain.[10] It became an important issue in the developing world in the Cold-War era, and specifically in the context of US intervention

---

[9] In Chapter 4.
[10] Bennett 1982; Strinati 1992; Slater 1997, pp. 64–74.

and the widespread belief that cultural flows had a propaganda effect, justifying wider intervention through the promotion of the 'American dream'.[11] Now the language is couched in terms of the global destroying the local, but the argument is very similar.[12]

The cultural imperialism thesis correctly points to the inequality in cultural flows, and identifies some real tendencies in the global order, such as the visibility of Western brands and products selling particular lifestyles.[13] However, it also exaggerates the degree of homogenisation, assumes that exposure to such products has predictable effects, and tends to romanticise and patronise the local as both authentic and passive. It also assumes that resistance to such products is intrinsically progressive, when, in fact, privileged groups may appeal to national or local authenticity in order to protect vested interests.[14] Western companies thus often find that the best way to realise profits is not to destroy but to work through the local, as in the case of MTV. It is also hard to assume that American television programmes are sending a uniform, pro-US message to the rest of the world – Bush Senior may have liked *The Waltons*, but he most certainly did not like *The Simpsons*. Similarly, it would be difficult to claim that the popularity of hip-hop music in parts of Africa is reducible to a simplistic cultural imperialism.

These critical comments do not mean that companies are fully committed to the promotion of a multi-cultural order, in which all cultures have an equal voice in a global village. It is likely that companies in the culture industries would prefer to promote a culturally homogenous world, not least because this would make the business of realising profits so much easier. But the important point is that, for all the practices that promote homogenising tendencies, there are counter-tendencies that resist full homogenisation. Companies then respond to these by trying to find new ways to make profits, sometimes successfully and sometimes disastrously. These practices do not imply that consumers are sovereign in the market-place, but neither does it mean that people are completely passive and that cultural homogenisation is inevitable.

---

[11] Dorfman and Mattelart 1975; Hamelink 1983.
[12] Barnet and Cavanagh 2001; Norberg-Hodge 2001.
[13] Klein 2000, Chapters 1–7.
[14] Tomlinson 1991.

However, there is a second sense in which we can talk more critically about culture, which moves us beyond a discussion of particular cultural products. Rather than homogenisation, we should instead refer to processes of cultural standardisation. We may consume different consumer goods throughout the world, or give different meanings to similar goods in different places, but more important is the fact of the spread of consumer culture, commodification, and rationalisation. In this respect, globalisation does mean an increase in cultural standardisation, and this is through the promotion of the notion that the 'good society' is one based on the maximisation of production, economic growth and consumption, regardless of social and environmental consequences. In this way, McDonaldisation is less significant as a specific consumer product (though not irrelevant) and more important in terms of the restructuring of an entire way of life.[15] This critique is associated with Marx's account of the commodity and alienation, and Weber's account of rationalisation. In the twentieth century, such critiques were associated with the Frankfurt school, situationism, critical postmodernism and environmentalism, and post-development theory.[16] In this approach, cultural standardisation represents a sense of loss, a feeling that authenticity has been undermined by the forces of consumer capitalism and instrumental notions of efficiency. This critique does not necessarily lead to progressive politics and, like the cultural imperialism thesis, has led to reactionary nationalist leaders resisting progressive change (such as democratisation) on the grounds of incompatibility with indigenous cultural traditions, that are too often deemed to be uncontested and unchanging. Similarly, the notion of loss can easily lead to the romanticisation of a mythical past based on organic national or local cultures, as well as an over-estimation of the degree to which cultural difference has been eliminated. Related to this view is the patronising belief that now that most people in the First World have won some advances in living standards, such improvements should be denied to the developing world. Moreover, and related to this point, standardisation is not all bad, and, in some cases, it may actually be *socially* useful and efficient.[17] The key question then, is that, if we are to 're-enchant the world', then it must be in such a way that rejects

---

[15] Ritzer 1993.

[16] See, among many others, Adorno and Horkheimer 1979, Marcuse 1964, Debord 1994, Polanyi 1957, Jameson 1991, Gorz 1989, Ritzer 1993, and Escobar 1995.

[17] Kellner 1999.

the hierarchies of old in favour of the egalitarianism of the new. I discuss these points further below, and in Chapter 9.

(v) *Globalisation leads to environmental destruction*

Sociological accounts of globalisation often refer to the rise of a global consciousness,[18] and this is most clearly seen in the case of the environment. Since the 1960s, there has been growing concern over the capacity of human beings to dominate nature, reflected in debates over the use of insecticides in the food chain and the population explosion.[19] But it was from the 1980s onwards that there were more sustained attempts to address the issue of the global environment, reflected in the destruction of forests, depletion of minerals and fisheries, air pollution, and the over-exploitation of fossil fuels. The discovery of the 'hole' in the ozone layer above the Antarctic in 1985 was a major factor in promoting a global environmental consciousness. Fossil-fuel burning and vehicle exhausts were particularly implicated in the increase in carbon dioxide, carbon monoxide and nitrogen oxide emissions. Although these chemicals make up a tiny percentage of the atmosphere, like the human body, small increases were sufficient to lead to far reaching environmental changes, such as increased photochemical smog in high sun areas, acid rain and depletion of ozone in the stratosphere. Moreover, accumulation of gases in the lower atmosphere led to a trapping of heat that would otherwise radiate out into space, causing an increase in temperature at the earth's surface – what is commonly known as global warming. This is a phenomenon that increased throughout the twentieth century, particularly so from the 1980s onwards.

From Montreal in 1987, to Rio de Janeiro in 1992, Kyoto in 1998 and Johannesburg in 2002, a host of international conferences have addressed the issue of managing the global environment, but with limited success. Plans to cut carbon dioxide emissions at Kyoto stalled when developing countries argued that plans for all countries to cut such emissions constituted a form of imperialism. Developed countries had developed without strong environmental considerations, but developing countries were now being disallowed from following a similar process of development. The United

---

[18] Robertson 1992.
[19] Carson 1962; Meadows et al. 1972.

States, the main source of carbon dioxide emissions was also far from supportive, and the Clinton government succeeded in watering down the proposals. The Bush administration, supported by Congress, rejected the agreement outright, and so proposed targets for cuts in emissions exclude the United States, by far the worst national offender.

Anti-globalisation politics has been strongly influenced by green politics, and many activists and thinkers argue that the targets at Kyoto not only do not go far enough, but that this fails to tackle the root cause of the problem. For most ecologists – as opposed to environmental managerialists[20] – sustainable development[21] is not simply a case of finding ways to technocratically manage the environment within the current system. Instead, sustainability refers to a radically different kind of society in which economic growth is at the very least problematised, and sometimes rejected. This position can lead to a suspicious attitude to technology, although often great faith is placed in the principle of alternative or appropriate technologies.[22] This argument is part of a much broader critique of industrial (and post-industrial) society, which is based on the premise that such societies regard growth *per se* as a sign of progress, but this is not actually the case – it has led to all kinds of environmental problems, and is no guarantee of happier, more contented society. This is not an argument against growth, merely one that suggests that there is a tendency in capitalist society to promote capital accumulation and economic growth above all other concerns, at the cost of collective forms of association and provision.[23]

These questions are further addressed in Chapter 9. For the moment, we need to dig deeper into the argument concerning the causes of environmental destruction, particularly as we must link this problem to globalisation. If globalisation is associated with the expansion of 'market society', then we need to address the issue of why such expansion is not conducive to a more sustainable society. This entails a brief re-examination of orthodox economic theory, and how it relates to the environment. For neo-classical economics, if there is environmental destruction this is because we do not sufficiently value the environment, and we express this fact through our purchases in

---

[20] On this distinction, see Dobson 2000.
[21] Brundtland 1987.
[22] Pepper 1996, pp. 91–7.
[23] Hamilton 2004.

the marketplace. The problem with this valuation is that the price of commodities only expresses their individual and not their social costs. The price mechanism therefore fails to take account of what orthodox economists call externalities, where the cost is external to the individual product and consumer. In the case of diminishing resources or pollution, those people that cause the problem are not the only ones affected by it. Orthodox theory's supposed solution to this problem is to make individuals accountable through an extension of the price mechanism. Thus, if a forest is rapidly depleted, the solution is to privatise the forest, and the owner could then charge loggers a fee. The forest owner would have an interest in protecting the forest as his or her source of income would be undermined if all the trees were destroyed.

There is a fundamental problem with this free-market solution however, which is that there is no guarantee that the forest owner will preserve the forest in an environmentally friendly way. If it is more profitable to cut down all the trees and build something else, or lease or sell the land to say, an aluminium smelting company, than the owner may well do so. This will have the effect of intensifying the environmental problem, and will not eliminate the problem of externalities caused by the destruction of the forest. This suggests that the concept of an externality is a misnomer – environmental damage is external to neo-classical theory but is not external to the real world. Rather than search for externalities to the theory, we should search for a theory which does not externalise environmental or other social costs.

There are further problems with orthodox theory too. It is impossible to privatise all goods, as some can only be 'consumed' in a collective way. The reality of public goods is accepted by orthodox theory, but these tend to be limited as far as possible, and the assumption remains that most goods can reflect the self-interested, individualised preferences of consumers. But, as we saw in the discussion of the myth of the free market in Chapter 4, conceptions of public goods and regulation are far from objectively defined. The argument that states should intervene in cases of 'other-regarding acts' and leave alone in the case of 'self-regarding acts' assumes that these can easily be defined outside of specific social circumstances. Privatisation as a means to protect the environment is thus a far from neutral process, and reflects the assumptions of neo-classical economics. Similarly, introducing the pricing mechanism to protect the interests of future generations (sustainable development) is impossible in a market-based system and such generations have no say in current market transactions. Moreover, the market implies unequal buying power, as some have greater income than others. Therefore, some will be in a greater position to afford the higher costs that result from attempts to price in environmental damage. The poor will face greater disadvantage in the market-place, paying for the socialisation of environmental costs even though it is most likely that the rich were responsible for those costs in the first place. This final point is also a problem for approaches that seek to provide some environmental regulation, but still largely within a market-led framework, as green taxes and subsidies lead to higher prices and therefore lead to a higher burden for the poor. For similar reasons, it is unclear that economic growth alone will lead to the adoption of environmentally sustainable technologies, as some critics of environmentalism claim.[24] There is little evidence for such a process occurring in the United States, for example, which emits more carbon dioxide than any other country. The fact remains that, even where cleaner goods are produced, the market will still allow for cheaper but dirtier goods.

Markets and the property rights associated with them do not guarantee anything like adequate environmental controls. Orthodox economics assumes that people are naturally self-interested, and so they can best express their preferences through a competitive market-place, and that therefore ways must be found to ensure that the market can properly regulate the environment. But it is the fact that people live in a competitive market-place that compels them, under many circumstances,[25] to act in self-interested ways, rather than vice versa. Thus, 'by assigning prices to natural resources (including "ecosystem services") such policies legitimise the reduction of human-natural wealth to a means of money making'.[26] In capitalist societies, where commodity production is generalised, competition ensures that the cheapest producers survive and the most expensive do not. Although there is some room for niche producers selling expensive, environmentally sound products, the general tendency is to expand through the lowering of unit costs. Environmentally-conscious

---

[24] Lomberg 2001.
[25] Of course, not all acts are self-interested, even in capitalist society. The point is that altruistic acts work against the logic of the competitive market imperative, while the latter acts as a (social) compulsion to act in a self-interested way.
[26] Burkett 2003, p. 112.

individuals are unlikely to survive in a world of competitive capitalism. Competition ensures the accumulation of capital, which means that the expansion of value, and not the expansion – or preservation – of use-values. Moreover, higher prices for a scarce resource is as likely to increase its depletion as capitalists take advantage of high profit opportunities. Furthermore, the formation of powerful vested interests ensures that attempts to regulate capitalists will continually be met by resistance on their part, sometimes successfully as the case of Kyoto makes clear. The environmental crisis is therefore inseparable from the expansion of global capitalism. This means that issues outlined in the first part of the book, such as questions of global inequality and distribution, poverty, debt and market regulation are central to efforts to overcome the problem.[27]

These five criticisms are central to the anti-globalisation case against 'actually existing globalisation'. What then of the proposed alternatives?

6.2 Alternatives to anti-globalisation

This section outlines some of the broad alternatives to neo-liberal globalisation. With the exception of the first of these, right-wing anti-globalisation, the positions are not mutually exclusive, and some theorists fit into at least two or more categories, as will become clear.

(i) Right-wing anti-globalisation

Many advocates of the globalisation project argue that politics has moved away from a traditional Left-Right divide, and that progressive politics must embrace 'the global'. This is the position taken by advocates of the Third Way, many of whom argue that 'anti-globalisation' involves a political convergence between nationalists of the Right and isolationists of the Left.[28] Hostility to globalisation is an ongoing theme of extreme-right politics, including in the developing world. A whole host of extreme right-wing populist organisations have opposed free-trade agreements, the internationalisation of capital, and international institutions such as the United

---

[27] Sutcliffe 1995.
[28] Lloyd 2001; Hain 2002.

Nations, World Trade Organisation, International Monetary Fund and World Bank.

One of the most prominent populists in the United States, Pat Buchanan, has blamed globalisation for the decline of manufacturing employment, the erosion of national sovereignty, increasing immigration, and the movement towards global socialism represented by institutions such as the IMF and World Bank.[29] Another leading populist, Pat Robertson has warned that a new world order is planned based on the elimination of private property, the end of national government and national sovereignty, the erosion of the Christian tradition, the promotion of a world government, all under 'the domination of Lucifer and his followers'.[30] This appeal to tradition is also a unifying theme among other right-wing challenges to globalisation, including Hindu nationalism in India, Islamic nationalisms in the Middle East and Asia, and resurgent fascism in Europe.[31] Right-wing nationalism therefore appeals to 'the people' and the nation as a defensive response to the uncertainties of globalisation. The national (or local) are, therefore, championed as sites of authentic embeddedness against the disembedding effects of globalisation.[32] Appeals to the people and nation are, however, selective and 'the people' tend not to include various minorities, who in part become scapegoats, regarded as being part of the problem of globalisation.

There is undoubtedly *some* crossover with *some* of the politics of (left-wing) anti-globalisation, and this is why Giddens and Third-Way politicians speak and write of fundamentalist reactions to globalisation. Convergence between Left and Right is most apparent in the case of the localist wing of the anti-globalisation movement (discussed below), which promotes a local-first strategy that can have reactionary overtones. In particular, localisation is sometimes attached to a green politics which regards local communities as sustainable only on the basis of restricted numbers, and humans as simply resource constraints on 'Mother Earth'. This can lead to support for immigration controls and/or population controls, and it has led to notorious statements such as that of a member of the radical US green movement, Earth First!:

---

[29] Buchanan 1998.
[30] Robertson 1991, pp. 37, 71.
[31] Hensman 2001, pp. 216–18.
[32] See the discussion of Polanyi in Chapter 5.

> If radical environmentalists were to invent a disease to bring human
> population back to sanity, it would probably be something like AIDS. . . . [T]he
> possible benefits of this to the environment are staggering.[33]

Another prominent Green campaigner, Edward Goldsmith has argued that
the globally sustainable population is around 3.5 billion.[34] David Korten, a
US anti-globaliser prominent in the Seattle protests, also calls for massive
global population reduction, though, thankfully, he does not suggest how
this might come about.[35] Goldsmith has also called for relatively closed
communities, in which 'a certain number of "foreigners" would be allowed
to settle but . . . they would not, thereby, partake in the running of the
community until such time as the citizens elected them to be of their number'.[36]

Clearly, then, there is some overlap between Left and Right in terms of
anti-globalisation, but it is not as great as it is sometimes made out. It is
not altogether clear that this convergence is a new phenomenon, associated
only with globalisation. There have been areas of 'agreement' between Left
and Right since the rise of modern politics, such as responses to the rise of
commercial popular culture and the role of the state in economic management.
Orwell and Hitler were critics of 'Americanisation', but they hardly shared
the same broad political outlook. Similarly, Franklin Roosevelt believed in a
large amount of state intervention in the US economy, but he was hardly a
right-wing fascist. The similarities between left and right critiques of existing
societies in part reflect the problem that the Left faces in developing a
progressive alternative that avoids the problems of romanticising the past,[37]
while not sufficiently transcending the present,[38] a problem that pervaded
'actually existing socialism' in the twentieth century.

But what is also clear is that the anti-globalisation movement is actively
seeking to separate itself from right-wing anti-globalisation.[39] This involves,
for example, a more explicit commitment to global solidarity rather than
national protectionism in the case of free-trade agreements, debt relief and

---

[33] Quoted in Dobson 2000, p. 52.
[34] Goldsmith 1972, p. 57.
[35] Korten 1995, pp. 34–5.
[36] Goldsmith 1988, p. 203.
[37] Löwy 1987.
[38] Corrigan et al. 1978.
[39] Kessi 2001; Monbiot 2002.

war. It also involves the growth of campaigns in solidarity with oppressed minorities and asylum seekers, and therefore against immigration controls. Indeed, it is in this area that the so-called progressives of the Third Way have moved towards a convergence with right-wing anti-globalisation.[40] Above all, however, the anti-globalisation movement has more explicitly argued for global solidarity, justice and equality, which is a million miles away from the politics of the anti-globalisation Right (and for that matter, neo-liberalism and the Third Way). Indeed, the authoritarian impulses of some in the green movement cited above are by far the exceptions, and most green politics is committed to levels of democracy, equality and participation for all that would be rejected by the anti-globalisation of the Right. For this reason, some have argued that the term anti-globalisation should be rejected in favour of a new term such as the 'global justice movement' or 'alter-globalisation'.[41] Achieving such solidarity may involve some movement towards (selective) 'localisation', but this is not in order to exclude foreigners, but is, instead, part of a wider strategy towards promoting global redistribution. Thus, 'locking capital down' to a specific location is designed, in part, to increase the balance of power between contending social forces, providing a greater chance to redistribute wealth (and possibly more), not only within that particular locality, but beyond it as well.[42] This implies that, *contra* the (globalist) Third Way and (localist) small-scale societies, progressive politics is not guaranteed by the 'space' (global, national, local) in which it operates.

(ii) *Global reform*

Third-Way thinkers and politicians tend to argue that anti-globalisation movements are in favour of opting out of globalisation. But, in fact, even the most committed 'localist' believes in the need for global institutions and global reform (see below). What anti-globalisation thinkers argue is that there needs to be a restructuring of the relationship between 'global', national and local levels. Although not without its critics from within the movement,[43]

---

[40] See for instance Giddens 2002b.
[41] Klein 2001; World Social Forum 2002.
[42] Bond 2001, Chapter 12.
[43] Tevainen 2003.

Walden Bello has characterised this restructuring as being part of a process of 'deglobalisation', which would involve the following: production for the local market; local finance (not foreign investment); less emphasis on growth *per se*; the subjection of the market to social control; and the development of community-based and public-sector initiatives, along with the continued development of the (local) private sector.[44] For 'deglobalising' policies to be implemented, new institutions would be created, and these would reject the monolithic approach of the IMF, World Bank and WTO, and, instead, promote a more open-ended system. Bello argues that, for all its faults, the GATT system from the late 1940s to the 1970s allowed for some 'space' for state-managed capitalist development in the periphery. New institutions would, therefore, promote redistributive policies such as international debt cancellation, an international tax on financial transactions, defence of public services, and controls on capital movements.[45]

In practice, global reform would mean the decommissioning of the Bretton Woods institutions and the WTO, a greater role for, and democratisation of, United Nations institutions, including the UN Economic and Social Council of the General Assembly and the UN Conference on Trade and Development. New institutions would also be created, such as a United Nations International Insolvency Court to negotiate debt settlements, a United Nations International Financial Organisation to regulate international finance, including the regulation of a Tobin tax on international financial transactions, as well the enhancement and creation of regional trade and monetary blocs.[46] More explicit localisers call for a General Agreement on Sustainable Trade, to be administered by a World Localisation Organisation.[47] More immediately, the anti-globalisation movement calls for a reversal of the privatisation of goods and services, the liberalisation of trade, and the expansion of patents. This amounts to a defence of 'the commons' against the threat of commodification. Commonly-owned goods refer not only to commonly-owned land and public goods, but also to the modern commons such as health, water, education, and so on.[48] The WTO,

---

[44] Bello 2002, pp. 114–17.
[45] Brecher et al. 2000, Chapter 6; Bello et al. 2000; Houtart 2001; ATTAC 2003.
[46] IFG 2002, pp. 222–37.
[47] Hines and Lang 2001, p. 292.
[48] IFG 2002, pp. 97–102.

and in particular its GATS and TRIPS agreements, represent a new strategy of 'accumulation by dispossession',[49] in which new sectors of society are privatised. A new global régime would, therefore, explicitly limit the right of private appropriation of the commons.

It is clear, then, that anti-globalisation seeks neither to by-pass, or ignore, the global, but to restructure it. This position is not so far away from that of cosmopolitan democrats such as Held,[50] who also seek to democratise global institutions as well as nation-states.[51] In so doing, the global reformists argue, the economy can be re-embedded back into society via a process of global neo-Keynesianism. This issue is addressed further in Chapter 9.

(iii) *Localisation*

Localisation is clearly, in many respects, an anti-globalisation strategy. Colin Hines argues that (actually existing) globalisation leads to a race to the bottom and cultural homogenisation. The race to the bottom is intensified by the environmental costs of transporting goods from distant places, which orthodox economics regards as an 'externality', and the problem of 'the fallacy of composition', in which the export of a particular good may benefit one individual country, but not if lots of other countries try to export the same good. This is because, as the volume of exports of the commodity increases, so the price falls, which, in turn, undermines the terms on which this particular commodity exchanges for other commodities.

The alternative to these problems is a strategy of localisation. The basic principle of localisation is to discriminate in favour of the local. This will 'increase control of the economy by communities and nations, creating greater social cohesion, reduced poverty and inequality, improved livelihoods, social infrastructure and environmental protection, and with these a marked enhancement of all the all important sense of security'.[52] A key principle is

---

[49] Harvey 2003.
[50] Held 1995.
[51] Held and McGrew's (2002, pp. 112–15) critique of the anti-globalisation movement argues that, in focusing too much on protest, it lacks concrete alternatives and is insufficiently pro-active. They note – with some sympathy – important changes in this regard, which relate to the global reform approach outlined in the text. Held's important work is discussed in the context of war and anti-war politics in Chapter 8.
[52] Hines and Lang 2001, p. 290.

that of subsidiarity, which means that 'all decisions should be made at the lowest level of governing authority competent to deal with them'.[53] This strategy does not mean total delinking from the world economy and the absence of international trade. It does, however, mean that such trade will only occur in cases that promote the reconstruction, rather than destruction, of local economies.[54] The strategy therefore does not entail the creation of totally isolated, autarchic communities, but still the principle of self-sufficiency should be applied wherever possible – it is, therefore, close to the green concept of self-reliance. Some global institutions would be needed in order to preserve local autonomies, or 'promote small scale on a large scale'.[55]

Localisation thus advocates the autonomy of localities from malign global processes. The precise boundaries of such localities are not very well defined, but it appears that they may refer to spaces below and above the nation-state, and to the nation-state itself. This principle applies throughout the globe, to countries of North and South alike. Hines therefore supported President Bush's protection of the US steel industry, while Bello regarded this act as an example of the imperialist double standards operating in the advanced capitalist countries. Local autonomy is seen as a desirable alternative because it maintains diversity and avoids the undesirable consequences of global free trade, namely environmental destruction and a race to the bottom. In contrast, local communities can develop a 'subsistence perspective', which is regarded as 'an ecologically sound, non-exploitative, just, non-patriarchal, self-sustaining society'.[56] For Vandana Shiva, pre-colonial India is supposedly an example of one society that most closely approximates this ideal. Such societies are said to be self-sufficient, and therefore they supposedly guarantee food for the local population – in contrast to cash crop production for export in societies integrated into the global economy.[57] These societies also embrace the eco-feminist principle of respect for Mother Earth, in contrast to industrial capitalism, which attempts to (patriarchally) dominate nature.[58] For the extreme localisers, the problems of globalisation are thus transcended by re-establishing

---

[53] IFG 2002, p. 107.
[54] Hines 2000.
[55] Norberg Hodge 20001, p. 242.
[56] Mies and Shiva 1993, p. 297.
[57] Shiva 1989, p. 113.
[58] Shiva 1989, p. xviii; Mies and Shiva 1993, p. 13.

'community' on a lower scale, an argument which clearly echoes previous populist alternative utopias based on the principle of 'small is beautiful'.[59] Clearly, there is something of a reactionary, romantic anti-capitalism in some pro-localisation accounts, particularly that associated with Shiva, and politics based on the principle of 'local first' can lead to an embrace of right-wing anti-globalisation, as discussed above. I return to these questions in Chapters 7 and 9.

(iv) *Global solidarities*

Anti-globalisation politics are often associated with the rise of a so-called global civil society. 'Globalisation' is said to have promoted a new, radical politics (potentially if not actually) located in global civil society. This is associated with Richard Falk's argument that globalisation from above has led to the development of a counter-hegemonic globalisation from below.[60] In this argument, global civil society is above all located in the development of 'people-centred' transnational social movements and non-governmental organisations (NGOs). Anheier et al. define global civil society as 'the sphere of ideas, values, institutions, organisations, networks, and individuals located *between* the family, the state and the market and operating *beyond* the confines of national societies, polities and economies'.[61] Edwards defines it as 'the arena in which people come together to advance their interests they hold in common, not for profit or political power, but because they care enough about something to take collective action'.[62] Richard Falk argues that global civil society 'refers to the field of action and thought occupied by individual and collective citizen initiatives of a voluntary, non-profit character both within states and transnationally'.[63] Finally, Naidoo and Tandon define it as 'the network of autonomous associations that rights-bearing and responsibility laden citizens voluntarily create to address common problems, advance shared interests and promote collective aspirations'.[64] These definitions are all rather

---

[59] Schumacher 1973; Kitching 1982; Biedeleux 1985.
[60] Falk 2000a.
[61] Anheier et al. 2001, p. 17.
[62] Edwards 2001, p. 2.
[63] Falk 2000a, p. 163.
[64] Naidoo and Tandon 1999, pp. 6–7.

imprecise, but they appear to refer to a 'third sector' independent of state and market, and operating beyond the territorial boundaries of the nation-state. Implicit in much of the literature is a contrast between 'bad' state bureaucracy and market profiteering on the one hand, and 'good' global civil society on the other.

Falk utilises a similar contrast in his analysis of globalisation. Globalisation from above is associated with the growing power of corporate capital vis-à-vis countervailing forces, which is reflected in the dominance of transnational corporations, global finance, and the decline of the 'compassionate state'.[65] However, the changes associated with the transnationalisation of capital – growing global interconnectedness and an increase in the speed of such inter-connectedness – also facilitates the growth of a globalisation from below, which is further reinforced by the decline of state sovereignty. This time-space compression means the rise of ongoing global political campaigns, new media (particularly the internet), greater mobility, and the spread of global norms such as human rights and democracy. This is reflected in the enormous growth of membership of international non-governmental organisations, which grew by 72 per cent from 1990 to 2000,[66] and the growing globalisation of the concerns of such organisations, reflected in part in the growing number of international civil society summits.[67]

A more radical variant of this approach is the view that global civil society is based on forms of organisation that are non-hierarchical in character, which in turn provides the basis for greater solidarity across national borders. Naomi Klein argues that the emergence of this non-hierarchical form of organisation was, in part, facilitated by the internet.[68] The world-wide web allows for the rapid spread of information and allows mobilisation to occur 'with sparse bureaucracy and minimal hierarchy; forced consensus and labored manifestos are fading into the background, replaced instead by a culture of constant, loosely structured and sometimes compulsive information swapping'. For these reasons, it makes no sense to talk of a single movement or alternative; it is a movement of movements, with many alternatives. Although he rejects

---

[65] Falk 2000b, p. 49.
[66] Anheier et al. 2001, pp. 5–6.
[67] Pianta 2001.
[68] Klein 2001, p. 147.

he term global civil society, Michael Hardt still more explicitly links global
olidarity to the network form of organising of the movement.[69] He contrasts
novements that uphold the defence of national sovereignty with movements
that propose an alternative globalisation based on democracy. The former
generally organise and mobilise in classically modern ways – that is, through
political parties, or interest groups, which put pressure on nation-states to
implement reform. The latter is based on a horizontal, network form that
bypasses national institutions and which proposes 'the democratization of
globalizing processes' against the decentred but hierarchical global order.[70]
Hardt and Negri, therefore, most explicitly identify a new global solidarity
movement independent of formal, national politics, which is based on
alternative forms of organising and new global solidarity networks. In this
approach, then, counter-globalisation becomes a bottom-up strategy, based
on democratic, transnational social movements, which by-pass (supposedly)
increasingly irrelevant nation-states. Certainly, there has been a recognisable
growth of global solidarity politics, though it is less clear that genuine solidarity
can easily or spontaneously be achieved. Nor is it the case that the nation-
state is irrelevant in the era of globalisation.

Finally, there is some suspicion – though often also recognition of the need
for – global institutions that guarantee global democracy, as these may
undermine direct democracy. At the most libertarian end of the movement,
there is often a suspicion of working with *any* formal organisations, as this
will lead to the co-opting of movements by the agents and institutions that
promote globalisation from above. This is certainly an important issue, as the
independence of international NGOs in particular, has come under scrutiny.[71]
While such blanket criticisms are too one-sided, they do point to real issues
concerning the political limitations and lack of independence of NGOs.[72]
Concern with the terms on which organisations – more overtly political social
movements as much as NGOs – interact with official institutions leads the
transnational solidarity approach to a dialogue with anarchist and autonomist
approaches.

---

[69] Hardt 2002, pp. 114–18.
[70] Hardt and Negri 2001, p. 102.
[71] Hardt and Negri 2000; Petras and Veltmeyer 2001, Chapter 8.
[72] Thomas 1992; de Waal 1997.

(v) *Autonomists and anarchists*

For many anti-globalisation activists, what is most distinctive about the wide variety of movements is the specific ways in which they carry out their politics. Indeed, some even argue that the mode of organisation within these movements is the same thing as its politics.[73] In contrast to the traditional social-democratic and Leninist Left, the new movements are consciously non-hierarchical and decentralised. Influenced by post-1968 'new social movements', particularly those organised around feminism and environmentalism, direct-action protests in the 1980s and 1990s, and the 'postmodern' rebellion in Chiapas, Mexico in 1994, anti-globalisation politics represent a new form of politics, beyond the outmoded modern ideologies of capitalism and socialism. These new organisations are not committed to the capture of state power, either to carry out social reform or to establish a dictatorship of the proletariat. Instead, there is a commitment to 'anti-power', in which new social relationships are constructed, starting at the level of the movement.[74] The movement is not a means to an end, but is an end in itself. For autonomists, anarchists and others, this new way of carrying out a revolution is taking place in the here and now, in the everyday struggles of people across the globe.

This approach begs many questions concerning the nature of power, resistance and hegemony. Moreover, it is far from clear that contemporary, anti-global social and political movements are as committed to autonomism and anarchism as these approaches make out. I examine these issues in detail in the next chapter.

(vi) *Environmentalists*

Much of the discussion in previous sections relates closely to the question of environmentally-friendly alternatives, so we can be quite brief. Green perspectives above all support the idea of promoting sustainable societies. In such societies:

> (1) the rate of utilization of renewable resources has to be kept down to the rate of their regeneration; (2) the rate of utilization of non-renewable resources

---

[73] Graeber 2002.
[74] Holloway 2002.

cannot exceed the rate at which alternative sustainable resources are developed; and (3) pollution and habitat destruction cannot exceed the 'assimilative capacity of the environment'.[75]

What such a sustainable society would look like in practice is subject to considerable debate, but ecologists tend to see the need for a decentralised society, not dissimilar to the localist perspective outlined above. This may include the division of the world into bioregions, which are defined as 'any part of the earth's surface whose rough boundaries are determined by natural characteristics rather than human dictates'.[76] Other local initiatives include Local Exchange Trading Schemes (LETS), based on multilateral trading using local currencies that facilitate exchange but cannot be accumulated.[77] Like the localist perspective, these decentralised initiatives promote the principle of self-reliance, in which production is localised but trade takes place in cases where local production is impossible. However, like localism this account can lead to local and backward-looking chauvinism. Moreover, as we have seen, decentralisation has its limits and there is still a need for supportive global institutions. One of the most famous (supposed) bioregions, that of Shasta in California,[78] is well-endowed with natural advantages, which is not the case for all localities. The issue then becomes one of the relationship between (as well as within) localities. The principle of subsidiarity is based on the notion that self-determination is achieved by allowing political decisions to be devolved downwards as much as possible. But this begs the question of what if one locality wants to pollute? This is not a purely hypothetical question, as the European Union principle of subsidiarity allowed a Conservative government in Britain to embark on a road-building programme that included the destruction of Twyford Down, an area that ecologists were particular keen to preserve.[79] Of course, this irony does not fully undermine the case for sustainability, and greens recognise that there needs to be a massive change in peoples' attitudes and/or social relations, in order for sustainability to be achieved. What *is* clear is that localism and bioregionalism are not *necessarily* conducive to green politics, or at least such politics cannot be reduced to a

---

[75] Bellamy Foster 1999, p. 132.
[76] Sale 1985, p. 55.
[77] Shorthose 2000.
[78] Tokar 1994.
[79] Pepper 1996, p. 308.

question of scale. As in the case of autonomist and anarchist perspectives, these broader issues cannot be evaded.

(vii) *Socialists*

There is, or has been, a great variety of socialisms and socialist movements that this brief section can hardly begin to discuss. Some of the alternatives discussed above can also be characterised as in some sense socialist, and this issue is discussed in more detail in Chapters 7 and 9. Here, I want to briefly address the broad approach of one socialist tradition, associated with classical Marxism. This tradition argued that globalisation may be an important issue, but the underlying one is resistance to global capitalism. Again, this is not so dissimilar from some of the other views discussed in this chapter. What is distinctive about classical Marxism is the emphasis on agency and the vision of a socialist future. Fundamental to the Marxist argument is the notion that the working class, organised in a vanguard political party, is the main agent of socialism. Moreover, socialism cannot be achieved through piecemeal reforms, but must be introduced by a revolutionary process, in which existing institutions that support capitalism are smashed. Marxists place particular emphasis on seeing capitalism as a totality, arguing that the struggle for reforms within the existing system, while not unimportant, will face resistance from the capitalist class, and will have contradictory effects as they only address only the symptoms and not the underlying causes of exploitation and oppression.[80] The future socialist society will replace capitalist society with a system based on central planning that, in contrast to the poor record of the former 'socialist' countries, will be organised on a democratic basis. Most revolutionary Marxists today suggest that none of the so-called socialist societies were actually socialist, and that it is impossible to have socialism in one country.[81]

This brief outline throws up an enormous number of contentious issues. These include the nature of the working class, the nature of capitalism (and different kinds of *capitalisms*), the question of different forms of oppression, the question of diversity, and the authoritarian dangers of vanguard parties and central planning. Some of these issues are examined in Chapter 9, which

---

[80] Harman 2000.
[81] See Callinicos 2003a.

explicitly deals with the question of alternatives within and beyond capitalism. One issue that does need to be addressed immediately, however, is the question of the organised working class. It is a common theme in current academic literature and political debate that the working class has somehow disappeared. It should be clear from arguments made throughout the first part of this book that I reject this argument. There may have been important changes in some of the characteristics of the working class, such as the growth of services and the relative decline of the manufacturing working class (in some locations), but this is not the main issue. Much of the growth in services is linked to manufacturing and/or involves low-wage, tedious work. The decline in manufacturing employment is smaller than is often made out, and ignores the rise of manufacturing employment in parts of the developing world. Indeed, as we have seen, the years of globalisation have not meant the end of capitalism but, in many ways, a resurgence of the most violent, exploitative forms of capitalism, as labour-friendly régimes have been undermined. It is here that the confusion concerning the death of class can be located, because the death of the working class is linked to the political defeats of the working class over the last twenty years, as reflected, for instance, in the decline in trade-union membership. The (sociological) death of class is therefore confused with the (political) death of post-war, corporatist settlements in the 'advanced' capitalist countries. However, recognising the continued existence of the working class does not necessarily mean acceptance of the politics of revolutionary Marxism, but it does mean that reports of the death of the working class are greatly exaggerated.

6.3 Conclusion: globalisation and spaces of resistance

Globalisation theory tends to argue that globalisation is an established fact, and that, therefore, by definition, anti-globalisation politics must be backward looking. This is the accusation consistently made by Third-Way critics of the anti-globalisation movement. What should be clear from the above discussion, however, is that this accusation does not begin to get to grips with the politics of 'anti-globalisation'.

One potentially fruitful way of discussing contemporary politics is Anheier et al.'s formulation of *'positions in relation to globalisation'*.[82] This has the

---

[82] Anheier et al. 2001, p. 7.

advantage of specifying the concrete and dynamic ways in which globalisation is contested. Four positions are identified: supporters, rejectionists, reformists and alternatives.[83] Supporters include transnational business and their allies, who favour global capitalism and support moves towards free trade and free capital flows. They are also said to support 'just wars' against 'rogue states'. Rejectionists are identified as being a mixture of anti-capitalist social movements, authoritarian states, and nationalist and fundamentalist movements. The Left rejects global capitalism, while both Right and Left support the preservation of national sovereignty. Short of the overthrow of global capitalism (the Left), national protection of markets and capital controls are favoured (both Left and Right). Armed intervention in other countries is rejected except when it is in the national interest (the Right), or is rejected as imperialist intervention by the Left. Reformists are composed of most international NGOs, many working in international institutions and many social movements. These actors support the reform of global capitalism, including specific proposals like a Tobin tax and debt relief. They also favour some kind of international policing and civil-society intervention to enforce human rights. Finally, the 'alternatives' position is composed of grassroots groups and some social movements who want to opt out of globalisation and establish local alternative economies. This may include some intervention in conflicts but not the use of military force.

Given that politics is given a central place in the analysis, this approach appears to be a useful starting point for analysis, but, ultimately, it suffers from the same weaknesses as globalisation theory. First, it still tends to take globalisation for granted, reducing it to an established fact to which different perspectives respond. Indeed, at times, globalisation is theorised in such a way that it appears to be a uniformly progressive, and linear process, and statist politics are too easily dismissed as reactionary.[84] Related to this point, the four-way division tends to be too static, ignoring the ways in which movements may adopt different positions on particular issues. Indeed, this point has been recognised by the writers in later articles.[85] But if this is the case, then the 'positions debate' needs reformulating, and the question moves

---

[83] Anheier et al. 2001, pp. 7–10.
[84] See Kaldor et al. 2003, p. 11.
[85] Glasius 2001; Kaldor et al. 2003.

away from rejection or acceptance of globalisation, or the championing of national or local alternatives. Instead, analysis must focus on the interaction *within and between* local, national and global 'spaces'. It is not a question of the 'global' being intrinsically more progressive than the local or national (*contra* the Third Way and Michael Hardt). But neither is it a question of the local being more progressive than the global (*contra* localisation and some environmentalism). The question is instead 'whose global', or 'whose local'? Championing the global in itself, or the local, betrays a 'spatial fetishism',[86] which ignores the social and political forces that operate within and between each sphere. The argument that we have gone beyond Left and Right as we all embrace globalisation repeats the same error. Older political questions about social relations, the role of states and markets, of supranational institutions, of alternatives based on reform and/or revolution, have not gone away. Still less have they been replaced by a (non-)politics based simply on whether one embraces or rejects globalisation. These issues are addressed in detail in the following chapters. Chapter 7 addresses the issue of space through an examination of local spaces below the nation-state, while Chapter 8 examines global spaces above the nation-state. The former rejects crude localisation and the latter crude globalisation approaches to progressive politics, while Chapter 9 focuses on the question of progressive alternatives – within and between local, national and global levels.

---

[86] Massey 2000.

Chapter Seven
Civil Society 1. National Social Movements and Anti-Globalisation Politics

This chapter and the chapter that follows examine in more detail the politics of anti-globalisation. Both focus on the question of whether anti-globalisation represents a new, distinctive, form of politics. Anti-globalisation politics obviously challenges the claims of neo-liberalism and the Third Way, but equally important is an understanding of the relationship between anti-globalisation and older forms of radical politics. This claim can be examined by focusing on local and national politics in this chapter, and global politics in Chapter 8. Of course, such a separation is, in many respects, a false one, and local, national and global 'levels' are not mutually exclusive. Nevertheless, I make the division primarily for analytical purposes. The key unifying theme for Chapters 7 and 8 is a critical interrogation of the notion of civil society, which is examined primarily at local and national 'levels' in this chapter, and at a global level in Chapter 8. It is argued in both chapters that a critical encounter with the notion of civil society is crucial for an understanding of the politics of anti-globalisation.

However, in both chapters, the arguments are illustrated through some empirical as well as theoretical investigation. In this chapter, I proceed in the following way. First, I examine 'traditional' left approaches to radical politics, and suggest some contrasts with 'new social movements', direct-action politics and contemporary anti-globalisation movements (particularly those in the North). In this section, I suggest that, while analyses of new social movements are in some respects problematic, especially in relation to understanding anti-globalisation movements, there is some utility in contrasting new social movements to traditional left politics. The second section then provides an account of 'social movements' in the developing world, with particular reference to three movements that have inspired anti-globalisation politics: the Zapatistas in Mexico, the MST (Landless Workers Movement) in Brazil, and the Chipko movement in India. The third section then critically reflects on the notion of social movements as representing a distinctive new politics, through further examination of the case studies and wider discussion. The focus here is on how social movements interact with the nation-state. Of particular concern is the question of whether contemporary social movements are intrinsically anti-state, anti-modern and anti-development, and, if so, whether this constitutes a productive and progressive way forward for such movements.

In other words, the chapter addresses the question of local spaces 'below' the nation-state – or, put differently, civil-society autonomy from states. This is an important issue with wider implications, because it relates closely to some anarchist and autonomist interpretations of social movements in the South, and the apparent lessons to be learnt for campaigns in the North. I treat these claims with some scepticism, and argue that anti-state politics are not necessarily progressive. Moreover, I argue that many of the social movements in the South have more ambiguous politics than is often suggested, especially in relation to internal organisation and the nation-state. Indeed, my central concern in this chapter is to question the notion that progressive social movements in the South unambiguously reject the state in the name of localisation and/or autonomy (or, indeed, globalised resistance), and that this has implications for anarchist-influenced anti-globalisation movements in the North. On the other hand, I also accept the argument that the vanguard politics of Leninist political parties is prone to authoritarian centralisation, and that the anti-globalisation movement is rightly concerned with the issues of diversity and democracy. Anti-globalisation politics is therefore most productive when it forges a path beyond Leninism and autonomism.[1]

---

[1] Autonomism and autonomy are ambiguous terms, and not necessarily the same thing. Autonomy can refer to independence from state structures, which, in turn, can

7.1 Progressive politics: old and new Lefts

The last twenty years or so have seen enormous political defeats for left-wing politics throughout the world. The breakdown of the post-war order in the 1970s undermined the social gains made in the advanced capitalist countries and the project of development in the former Third World.[2] These gains were not, of course, always put into place by left-wing movements. Developmental nationalists were as often on the right of the political spectrum as they were the left. Policies promoting welfare support and economic expansion were often carried out by right-wing political parties in the Western world. Nevertheless, these advances were generally associated with victories for progressive forces. In many cases, they were associated with 'left-wing' political parties that implemented reforms once in office, and even when the Right introduced reforms, this was often seen as a response to pressure from progressive forces such as organised labour or national-liberation movements. The undermining of such gains since the 1970s, and especially the 1980s, is thus rightly seen as a defeat for progressive politics.

These setbacks were a particular problem for 'reformist' social-democratic politics, whose capacity to implement progressive reforms was increasingly constrained by the power of international finance and the threat of capital flight. As I have already argued in Chapter 4, the extent to which this constraint is either novel or outside of political control is an issue of contention, and at least as important is the way that social democracy has repositioned itself in order to respond to the 'new realities' of globalisation. What is clear is that this ideological shift is one that makes Third-Way social democracy at least complicit with, and even at times an extension of, the neo-liberal political project. In its current dominant form, social democracy thus ceases to be an alternative to neo-liberalism.

But the problems of 'traditional' left politics go deeper than this. The collapse of Communism has also served to undermine the appeal of socialism. The record of 'actually existing socialism' is not a good one. Most socialist

refer to modes of organising and/or strategies of localisation. Autonomism refers to a radical Marxist tradition that developed in Italy in the 1960s and especially the 1970s, which emphasises the creative role of labour as the starting point for analysis of capital (see Cleaver 1979). The two terms are linked however, not least in debates within anti-globalisation movements, as the text makes clear. See further, footnote 17.

[2] See Chapter 5.

governments have had poor human-rights records and made limited progress in terms of economic growth and social development. Of course, much the same point could be made about many capitalist countries, particularly in the developing world, but this point does not address the issue of the desirability of socialism, which should, at least, have a better record.[3] Evidently, 'socialist' countries have faced enormous hostility from capitalist countries, as well as the constraints imposed by isolation and lack of development of the productive forces, but these issues alone cannot fully explain the authoritarian record of 'actually existing socialism'. Similarly, it is not sufficient to argue that, because of this isolation in a capitalist world, the 'socialist' countries were not really socialist at all. This argument is true in a sense, although it evades the issue of what has come to be regarded as socialism. But it also demonstrates a more important evasion, for a one-sided use of the 'external constraint' argument tends to lead to apology, conveniently leaving aside the question of what a revolutionary state should do if it remains isolated. Too often, the implication appears to be that an isolated revolution inevitably degenerates into Stalinism. If this is so, then a call for simultaneous worldwide revolution appears as the only feasible, but highly unlikely alternative. Certainly, Leon Trotsky did not believe that isolation *inevitably* meant Stalinism, and it was precisely for this reason that he proposed a set of alternative *domestic* as well as international policies for the isolated Soviet Union in the 1920s.[4] One clear implication of this argument – and one that returns us to the principal question of this chapter – is that there is a need to pay attention to institutional structures and the question of internal democracy, which, in turn, leads us to a consideration of the state and revolution.

Orthodox Marxism since Lenin has conceived of revolution as a violent overthrow of the capitalist state, led by the working class and organised through a vanguard party. In its place, a dictatorship of the proletariat will be established which will pave the way for a transition to socialism and communism. At times, Lenin's conception of this dictatorship was quite libertarian, as he regarded *all* states as class dictatorships.[5] The proletarian

---

[3] In fact, the social development record of both 'socialist' and capitalist countries does vary considerably. On this debate, see Kiely 1998, Chapters 4 and 8.
[4] Trotsky 1975.
[5] Lenin 1977.

dictatorship would be the first genuinely democratic rule by a class, as this class constituted the majority of the population. But, in practice, the Soviet dictatorship was authoritarian almost from the start, as Lenin abolished the Constituent Assembly when the Bolsheviks failed to gain a majority, and the Party became more authoritarian in dealing with opponents – and supporters. Indeed, Lenin was fully aware of this degeneration and was at pains to deal with it before his death in 1924.[6]

The degeneration of the Russian Revolution can partly be explained by the Civil War, which included considerable foreign-power intervention in support of the counter-revolutionary Whites. By the end of that war in 1921, the Bolsheviks/Communists also faced the task of rebuilding the war-damaged economy, and restructuring agriculture and industry. The expected 'world revolution' – or, at least, revolution in Germany – did not occur, though precisely how a war-ravaged Germany would have saved the Russian Revolution is not altogether clear. Clearly, all these factors influenced the setbacks in Russia, and provided the context for the emergence of a new privileged bureaucratic stratum – even a new exploiting, possibly state-capitalist, class.[7] But it is one thing to accept isolation, war, underdevelopment as significant contributory factors, but quite another to argue that this alone explains the forced collectivisation of the peasantry, followed by the purges of the 1930s. The defeat of socialism is one thing, the mass murders committed by Stalin (and after him Mao and Pol Pot) quite another.

Progressive politics were thus seriously undermined by the record of 'actually existing socialism'. But even those vanguard parties that did not win power were often regarded as authoritarian in their practices, whether it was armed guerrilla movements in Latin America and Asia, or small, isolated vanguard 'parties' in the West. Guerrilla movements often had limited support, and they were even further isolated from popular politics by the wave of democratisation that swept the developing world in the 1980s and 1990s. This process was very limited, particularly as it took place in a neo-liberal context in which social gains were undermined, and decision-making power was, in some respects, transferred from 'sovereign' states to the World Bank and IMF. But, for all its limitations, the process did open up new political spaces in

---

[6] Lewin 1974.
[7] Trotsky 1980; Ticktin 1973; Cliff 1974.

'civil society', and the emergence and strengthening of many 'new social movements'. Many movements faced state repression, as well as neo-liberal policies, but democratisation was not simply a sham.

Clearly, the discussion so far points to the need for a broader debate about how these issues relate to the question of the future of socialism, and of radical politics, more generally. This debate forms part of the agenda for this chapter, and is considered in detail in Chapter 9. What needs to be addressed for now is the question of the emergence of a 'new' progressive politics, for it was in this changing context – of post-Stalinism, democratisation, neo-liberalisation (including of social democracy) and the political defeats of labour and nationalist movements – that such a politics was said to emerge. Such a politics was closely related to the questions of the end of 'grand narratives', and the 'rediscovery' of civil society.

The term civil society has a variety of meanings. In the work of Thomas Hobbes, civil society was contrasted to the state of nature.[8] In the latter condition, there was no security and a potential war of individuals unrestrained by an external power. The state was created to provide such security. For Hobbes then, civil society was simply a society in which the state guaranteed that there would be law and order. However, the potential then existed for a state composed of self-interested individuals to expand its power and undermine any individual freedom beyond the state. State power therefore had to be limited. In its classical-liberal usage, associated particularly with Locke,[9] the focus was very much on the term 'civil' and it meant a society based on the rule of law, and the formal separation of the state from other social organisations. In this way, state power was limited by the existence of a separate social sphere, composed of free, autonomous individuals.

For Marx, this separation of political and economic spheres was the outcome of the rise of capitalist society, and it therefore provided the basis for the alienation, anarchy and inequality that arose out of these social relations. Vested interests in 'civil society' meant that this sphere was not one in which freedom existed, but, rather, one in which there was domination by some over others. Above all, there was the wage relation in which the majority were forced to work for the minority of property owners in order to earn a

---

[8] Hobbes 1968.
[9] Locke 1994.

wage to live. Therefore, the independence of civil society presupposed the division of society into those who only had their labour-power to sell, and the owners of the means of production who bought this labour-power – but also dispensed with it if they wished. Moreover, powerful vested interests in civil society could dominate the state. Marx thus regarded civil society as bourgeois society.

Apart from its appearance in the work of Gramsci in the 1930s (discussed below), reference to civil society was quite rare for much of the twentieth century. However, since the 1980s, the term civil society has been revived and, in the process, the debate has moved on from the liberalism versus Marxism debate. In particular, it came to be associated with the emergence of oppositional movements in Eastern Europe and the collapse of official Communism. This led to what Kaldor problematically calls an activist version of civil society, which 'refers to active citizenship, to growing self-organization outside formal political circles, and expanded space in which individual citizens can influence the conditions in which they live both directly through self-organization and through political pressure'.[10] This version of civil society is therefore explicitly normative, calling for a restriction in the power of the state over its citizens, and the need for the rule of law. But, at the same time, it did not simply promote a return to liberalism, as it also called for a radicalisation of democracy, and the extension of participation, autonomy and diversity in society.

The concept also gained currency beyond the former 'socialist' states, and was also associated with neo-liberalism and (alternative) development. In terms of the former, civil society came to be associated with the pro-free-market policies of national governments and international institutions such as the World Bank. With the retreat from 1980s free-market fundamentalism in the 1990s, the search was on for institutional structures that could support the transition to a 'free-market economy'. This included the promotion of third-sector non-governmental organisations (NGOs), which came to provide services that were previously state-run. This policy was actually started in the 1980s, when there was an explosion in the activities of NGOs, but was perhaps formalised and theorised in the 1990s, when the third sector was more explicitly linked to notions of social capital as a new context for, and

---

[10] Kaldor 2003a, p. 8.

agency of, development.[11] This did not necessarily mean that NGOs were unambiguously linked to neo-liberalism, and many NGOs have been critical of government policies in the last twenty years. Some development NGOs have even increasingly involved themselves in transnational advocacy, which has generally included the promotion of policies at international (mainstream and alternative) summits that are critical of dominant neo-liberal agendas. For some writers, international NGOs are therefore part of an emerging global civil society, or a 'globalisation from below', that challenges neo-liberal 'globalisation from above'.

In this way, NGO activity can be linked to the more radical social-movement organisations in the South, such as the Zapatistas, MST and Chipko movements discussed below. Such movements clearly reject neo-liberalism, and some are even said to reject development. The relationship between this anti- or post-development perspective and civil-society theory is ambiguous, as it could be argued that civil society is a specifically Western idea and therefore irrelevant to the needs and aspirations of people in the South. This perspective sees civil society as inherently modernising, and therefore every bit as Eurocentric as the concept of development. On the other hand, there is some overlap with the concerns of civil society theory in that a post-development perspective champions the call for autonomy from states and markets, and is committed to the protection of cultural diversity. Indeed, post-development theory upholds the notions of diversity and autonomy on the grounds that these represent a counter-hegemonic project to the homogenising discourse of development.

Although he applied the concept to the 'advanced' capitalist countries, the idea of civil society as providing the basis for a counter-hegemonic project is closer to Gramsci's use of the term in the 1930s. In his work, civil society was linked to his theory of hegemony, in which he argued that the ruling class ruled not only through state repression, but also through their ability to persuade the subordinate classes that the 'system' was effective and that there was no alternative to it.[12] Gramsci did not argue that such hegemony could easily be achieved or that it was not resisted. His argument was that, because bourgeois rule was in some sense constructed – it implied a hegemonic *project* – this had implications for socialist strategy. In particular, traditional

---

[11] As discussed in Chapter 4.
[12] Gramsci 1971, p. 238.

left notions of an all out confrontation with the state (a war of manoeuvre) was not a viable strategy in countries with strong civil societies, which, in Gramsci's day, meant Western capitalist countries. Instead, there had to first be a war of position, in which movements developed counter-hegemonic projects – an alternative 'common sense' – within the institutions of civil society. For Gramsci, civil society was the arena through which the bourgeoisie ruled, but it was also the arena in which such rule was contested.

It is this sense of civil society as a 'counter-hegemonic' force that most concerns us in this chapter. This argument appears to be similar to Kaldor's 'activist' view of civil society, but, in fact, there is a crucial difference. Gramsci essentially saw civil society as an analytical device, and argued that conflict took place *within* it. Kaldor, on the other hand, regards civil society as a normative principle and therefore an intrinsically progressive force in direct opposition to the state. My rejection of this over-spatialisation of politics is central to the argument that follows. The rest of this section focuses on the ways in which civil society *organisations* have been conceptualised, examining new social-movement theory, post-development theory, direct-action anarchist politics, and autonomist Marxism, and how these interpretations have influenced and been used by anti-globalisation movements and thinkers. These approaches are linked to the view that the nation-state has not only been undermined from above, through globalisation,[13] but also from below, through a more localised politics.

In the Western world, it is often argued that we have moved from a modern industrial society to a late- or post-modern, post-industrial society, in which the main arena of conflict is no longer over material, economic or distributional issues. Instead, conflict is mainly concerned with 'quality of life, equal rights, individual self-realization, participation and human rights'.[14] The focus is thus said to be on 'life politics',[15] in which rationalisation and commodification are resisted by social movements advocating autonomy. Unlike old labour movements, new social movements are 'not oriented toward the conquest of political power . . . but rather toward the control of a field of autonomy or of interdependence vis-à-vis the system'.[16]

---

[13] A view challenged in the next chapter.
[14] Habermas 1987, p. 392.
[15] Giddens 1991, p. 214.
[16] Melucci 1980, p. 220.

There are problems with the way that new social movements have been conceptualised. Above all, dominant perspectives on new social movements tend to rigidly separate 'post-material' life or identity politics from material, distributional or economistic politics. While a distinction between the two may be made, an overly rigid demarcation is deeply problematic. Anti-racist politics, for example, are rarely just about the politics of recognition or difference, and usually involve demands with material implications. Moreover, such demands are often or even usually made on the state, and are not just about organising independently of 'modern institutions'. Similarly, the politics of 'old' labour movements are not simply material or economistic. Strikes are not just about wage demands, and, even when this is the main cause, they involve wider struggles, not least over culturally contested terms such as dignity and fairness. Such struggles also have wider social implications beyond the immediate demands of the workplace. Indeed, one of the most significant global developments in recent years has been the development of trade-union movements that have explicitly made alliances, both with other social movements and trade unions beyond nation-states.

What most concerns us here is the relationship between these perspectives on new social movements and anti-globalisation politics, particularly those associated with the centrality of non-hierarchical direct action. Influenced by nineteenth-century anarchism, and the autonomist Marxism[17] that first developed in Italy in the 1970s, this approach emphasises spontaneous direct action and the creation of 'Temporary Autonomous Zones', which are said to be spaces beyond the control of the state. Such direct-action protest has developed since the 1960s, often independently of traditional left-wing organised protest, and is often characterised by spectacular and carnivalesque

---

[17] See Wright 2002. A full consideration of the tradition of autonomism lies outside the scope of this book. References to autonomy and autonomism in this chapter are not necessarily critiques of that tradition, though I think that some of the problems of direct action politics can be traced back to that tradition. Briefly, the autonomist tradition argues that a critical analysis of capital must start with the active role of labour, and then move to the reactive role of capital (Cleaver 1979). This argument is useful in re-emphasising the active role of labour in 'class struggle', as against traditions of structuralist and orthodox Marxism (Kiely 1995). However, if labour plays the active role in class struggle and capital a merely passive one, then it is unclear where the structures of power lie in capitalist society, and why there should be resistance in the first place. The reification of structures in structuralist Marxism is therefore replaced by the reification of struggle in autonomist Marxism – including the romanticisation of resistance critically discussed in this chapter.

forms of protest. It has included anti-nuclear protest, free festivals, DIY culture, rave culture and road protests.[18] The abiding principle is not to take over the institutions of mainstream society, but to immediately create a new society independent of that mainstream. This perspective focuses on the importance of non-hierarchical modes of organising within the 'movement of movements'.[19] Direct-action groups such as the Ruckus Society, Reclaim the Streets and the Direct Action Network,[20] emphasise the need for decentralisation, flexible organisation and autonomous structures, which are said to be the best guarantee of preserving diversity and promoting anti-hierarchy. Indeed, in classic anarchist fashion, this mode of organising is regarded as being prefigurative of the creation of a newly democratic global society. Thus, Roger Burbach, one of the most influential thinkers in the US 'anti-globalisation' movement, argues that the most distinctive feature of the movement is its postmodern, decentred politics. He argues that the movement is 'postmodern in the sense that it has no clear rationale or logic to its activities while it instinctively recognises that it cannot be effective by working through a "modern" political party, or by taking state power. It functions from below as an almost permanent rebellion, placing continuous demands on all the powers that be'.[21] De Angelis makes the related point that the politics of the movement are inseparable from its organisational forms. These constitute 'new forms of social cooperation beyond the capitalist market'.[22] Clearly influenced by (among others) direct-action environmental protests, feminist politics, new social movements and the Zapatista uprising in Mexico, the focus is on the diversity of struggles that comprise 'anti-globalisation' politics, united by 'One No . . .', but fragmented by 'Many Yeses'. Such fragmentation is regarded as a desirable alternative to the traditional left mode of organisation, based on hierarchical political parties in which many struggles were subordinated to the achievement of the 'correct line'. Political programmes and the struggle for power are therefore treated with suspicion as they involve complicity with modern politics, through being co-opted by established institutions or through the creation of new hierarchies of power.[23]

---

[18] McKay 1996; Kauffman 2002.
[19] Klein 2001.
[20] Jordan 1998; Sellers 2001; Graeber 2002.
[21] Burbach 2001, p. 11.
[22] De Angelis 2001, p. 115.
[23] Holloway 2002.

This 'quasi-anarchist' approach to politics has also influenced interpretations of social movements in the developing world. This is most clear in the case of post-development theory. Strongly influenced by the work of Foucault, Arturo Escobar, post-development theory's most articulate advocate, argues that development is 'not a natural process of knowledge that gradually uncovered problems and dealt with them'. Instead, development is 'a historical construct that provides a space in which poor countries are known, specified, and intervened upon'.[24] Development is thus a discourse, a particular way of viewing/constructing the world, rather than reflecting it.[25] The effect of the development discourse is the 'creation of a space of thought and action, the expansion of which was dictated in advance'.[26] The construction of a 'backward' Third World in need of development does not reflect reality, but is actually constructed by the discourse of development. Thus, '[p]overty on a global scale was a discovery of the post-World War II period. . . . If within market societies the poor were defined as lacking what the rich had in terms of money and material possessions, poor countries came to be similarly defined in relation to the standards of wealth of the more economically advantaged nations'.[27] The Third World thus comes to be represented as 'a child in need of adult (for which read Western) guidance'.[28] Policies based on population control, technological diffusion, poverty alleviation and so on thus constitute the exercise of 'a regime of government over the Third World, a "space for subject peoples" that ensures control over it'.[29]

The alternative is not to try to re-integrate societies, peoples, and economies into global development, because such development is exclusionary by its very nature. Instead, there needs to be the search for alternatives, in which we 'liberate the imaginary' from homogenising and marginalising capitalist modernity.[30] This liberation involves a championing of the authenticity of grassroots movements.[31] In practice, this may involve support for local, vernacular societies,[32] or support for social movements that are said to construct

---

[24] Escobar 1995, pp. 44–5.
[25] Foucault 1980, p. 115.
[26] Escobar 1995, p. 42.
[27] Escobar 1995, pp. 22–3.
[28] Escobar 1995, p. 30.
[29] Escobar 1995, p. 9.
[30] Escobar 1995, p. 230.
[31] Esteva and Prakash 1998.
[32] Rahnema 1997.

autonomous spaces from modern institutions such as markets, states or foreign capital.[33] Such strategies are regarded as a cultural alternative to modernity, and much is made of the resistant practices of subaltern groups to the homogenising thrust of modernity. But, in addition, these strategies are also regarded as being a necessity, which has come about through the exclusionary mechanisms of global development. Indeed, this marginalisation should not be a cause for regret, as it creates the potential for a re-invigoration of autonomous spaces, or a 'new commons' outside of the modern, formal economy.[34]

In contrast to traditional left politics, then, there has emerged a different kind of politics based on grassroots participation, non-hierarchical networks, and direct action. This is undeniable. But what is more contentious is the claim – made by autonomists, anarchists and post-development theorists – that the 'new politics' represents an outright rejection of some of the key features of modern politics, including formal organisation, and some form of engagement with the nation-state. In the case of social movements in the developing world, it is claimed that these champion a politics of autonomy from 'development'. This interpretation has had an undoubtedly strong influence among anti-globalisation activists. I investigate these claims further in Sections 2 and 3.

7.2   Social and political movements in the South

This section briefly examines some of the most famous examples of Southern social movements, focusing, in particular, on some of the campaigns that have inspired anti-globalisation campaigners in the North. I start by looking at three examples – the Zapatistas in Mexico, the MST in Brazil, and the Chipko movement in India. The outline is brief and fairly descriptive, and I return to an analysis of the politics of these movements, along with others, in Section 3.

---

[33] Escobar 1995, pp. 215–17, 222–3; Esteva and Prakash 1998.
[34] Esteva 1992; Escobar 1995, p. 217; Esteva and Prakash 1998; Carmen 1996.

(i) *Mexico – the Zapatistas*

Undoubtedly one of the most inspirational forces to anti-globalisation activists throughout the world is the Zapatista National Liberation Army (EZLN). This previously unknown political organisation hit the headlines in January 1994, when it occupied a number of towns in the Mexican state of Chiapas. Although the occupation quickly ended, the Zapatistas successfully scaled up their activities, appealing to 'global civil society' for support – and as a way of curtailing potentially total elimination by the Mexican army. The continued existence of the Zapatistas, and their success in publicising their cause internationally, primarily through their charismatic spokesperson Subcomandante Marcos, has been an inspiration to many activists. Moreover, this has been reinforced by the novelty and originality of their approach to politics.

Chiapas is one of the most resource rich of the thirty-two Mexican states, but there is also massive inequality and poverty. Indigenous communities did, however, have some access to communal land (known as *ejidos*), following land reforms implemented in the years following the Mexican Revolution of 1910–20. However, the best land remained in the hands of wealthy farmers, plantation owners and cattle ranchers. Although some of this land was broken up into smaller plots from the 1950s, land concentration increased in the 1970s during an economic boom led by cattle ranching, and petroleum. Small farmers were also displaced via a process of dam construction.[35] Some farmers took advantage of the new opportunities and so class differentiation among the peasantry increased. Influenced by Marxism, liberation theology and movements for indigenous rights, resistance movements developed in the late 1960s and early 1970s. The 1980s was a period of widespread land conflict and social rebellion, which was reinforced by the end of the boom and implementation of structural adjustment programmes that cut back on (limited) government support for smallholders. Instead, the government encouraged large-scale export agriculture, in part to meet interest payments on debt, and new export crops such as soybeans, peanuts and tobacco boomed, and liberalised trade, including cheap food imports. In 1992, under President Salinas, Article 27 of the Mexican constitution was reformed, which undermined

---

[35] Burbach 2001, Chapter 8.

state guarantees to protect the land ownership rights of small farmers, including the *ejidos*. This reform was regarded as a victory for larger landowners and the neo-liberal onslaught, reinforced by Mexico's commitment to the North American Free Trade Agreement (NAFTA). It was in this context that the previously little known Zapatista movement said 'enough' (Ya Basta!) and led the occupation of towns in Lacandon, Chiapas, including the main town of San Cristobal de las Casas. This was carried out on 1 January 1994, the day that NAFTA came into force.

The rebellion was quickly 'defeated' by the Mexican army, and the Zapatistas retreated back into the countryside. However, what followed took many people by surprise. The Zapatistas did not retreat in classic guerrilla fashion, operating secretly away from the public eye, but instead embraced an open politics that appealed to 'civil society'. Outsiders were invited into Chiapas to discuss wider struggles against neo-liberalism, starting with discussion with civil-society movements within Mexico in 1994 and then developing with the organisation of the first Intercontinental Meeting for Humanity against Neo-Liberalism in 1996.[36] Through various communiqués, often first posted on the internet, the Zapatistas have constantly appealed to the outside world for support.[37] In part this can be regarded as a tactical device designed to prevent full-scale repression by the Mexican state, the latter fully aware that the struggle of the Zapatistas is closely followed beyond the borders of both Chiapas and Mexico. But it is also indicative of a different approach to politics, which separates the Zapatistas from orthodox left-wing organisations, including both social democrats and Leninists. For the Zapatistas have shown little interest in 'capturing power', either to implement social-democratic reform or to inaugurate a Leninist dictatorship of the proletariat. Instead, the Zapatistas support the democratisation of civil society, so that the world may be changed 'without taking power'.[38] The Zapatistas are thus part of a radical movement of counter-power or anti-power, in which a diversity of movements and struggles resist not only the exploitation and marginalisation of neo-liberalism, but the homogenising thrust of modern political organisation (of which neo-liberalism is but one example).

---

[36] Klein 2002, pp. 218–19.
[37] Castells 1997, p. 79.
[38] Holloway 2002.

(ii) *Brazil: the MST*

The Movimento Rural Sem Terra (MST – Landless Workers' Movement) was formed in 1984. As its name suggests, it is a movement that focuses on social relations and political organisation in the countryside, and particularly organises land occupations. Brazil has probably the highest degree of concentration of land ownership in the world. This concentration goes back to the colonial era, but continued throughout the nineteenth century, as the power of landowners was unchallenged. This remained the case in the 'modernising' era after 1930, when capitalist industrialisation took place alongside the continued power of the agrarian élite. Indeed, in the period from 1930–64, the industrial capitalist class developed in part out of the agrarian élite, thus blocking the potential for an alliance between the industrial bourgeoisie and rural poor.[39] Hopes for reform in the early 1960s were dashed by the military coup carried out in 1964. Opposition to the military régime culminated in the wave of strikes and rural unrest in the late 1970s, and the military were eventually forced out of power in the mid-1980s.

The unrest of the 1970s included land occupations, and out of these, the MST was formed in 1984. The movement has an essentially open membership, and (in principle) equal rights are given to all family members. The MST champions the causes of land reform, but also links these to support for wider social transformation.[40] The focus of the movement is very much on direct action and participation; as its leading figure João Stedile explains, 'the only way to join is to take part in one of the land occupations, to be active on the ground. That's how we get members'.[41] The MST is not formally attached to any political party, but often there are informal links with the Workers' Party and other left parties.

Land occupations have if anything intensified since the end of military rule, as land concentration continues. Indeed, the development of new technologies after 1964 increased peasant differentiation as only richer farmers and landowners could afford them. In the 1980s and 1990s, trade liberalisation increased food imports and land concentration increased in order to promote

---

[39] Kiely 1998, Chapter 6.
[40] Branford and Rocha 2002.
[41] Stedile 2002, p. 84.

agricultural exports such as soya, coffee, oranges and sugar cane. In addition, the development of more new technologies and particularly new integrated packages of genetically modified seeds further increased differentiation, as these were too expensive for smaller farmers. It has been estimated that 18 per cent of farmers and landowners own land that generates around 66 per cent of agricultural income. Within this group, 2 per cent of the total farmers/landowners account for 60 per cent of total agricultural income. This means that 82 per cent of farmers, amounting to around 3.3 million family farms are more or less marginalised. In the short period from 1996–9, as many as 4.2 million people left the countryside in search of (scarce) jobs in the towns.[42] It is in this context that the land occupations take place.

The MST is one of the most famous social movements in the developing world today. Its direct-action politics is a challenge to a new wave of land concentration that has occurred in the neo-liberal era. The movement champions a non-hierarchical, grassroots approach to organisation, and maintains its autonomy from established political parties, including the Workers' Party.

(iii) *India: the Chipko movement*

This section provides a brief outline of an environmental movement in north India, often known as Chipko. In some respects, this is an odd choice as a case study, as the heyday of this movement was in the 1970s – although it was not until the 1980s that the movement came to prominence in the West. In many respects, a focus on protests against dam projects such as that at the Narmada river, or even the newly created Living Democracy Movement[43] in India would have been more relevant – like the Zapatistas and the MST, these have more immediate resonance with anti-globalisation politics. But there are good reasons for an examination of the politics of the Chipko movement, not least for the ways in which these developed from its founding in 1973, through state responses from the late 1970s and early 1980s, and subsequent political developments. Above all, this concerned the creation of a new state, Uttaranchal, formerly a region in the state of Uttar Pradesh that was granted independence in the late 1990s. Not unrelated to these points is the way in which Chipko

---

[42] Branford and Rocha 2002, pp. 182–4.
[43] Switkes and Diaz Pena 2003; Shiva 2003.

has been represented to the outside world, which has basically been one that sees the movement as localist in inspiration. Chipko is therefore included as a case study because there are important lessons to be learnt from a historical consideration of the movement.

The Chipko movement came to prominence in the early 1970s in the Himalayan region of Uttaranchal, which was then part of the Indian state of Uttar Pradesh. The movement arose out of resistance to the destruction of forests in the region, and the way in which the state-managed Forest Department allocated tree-felling contracts to private companies. In particular, it emerged in response to a decision by the Forest Department to provide hundreds of trees to the Symonds corporation, shortly after the department had refused to grant trees to a small, local company called Dasholi Gram Swarajya Sangh (DGSS). Chipko, which means 'stick to', 'adhere', or 'hug', emerged when local people responded by resisting the planned tree-felling by hugging trees. The movement quickly spread and tree-hugging became a widespread tactic of resistance in the region.

The dominant interpretation of Chipko is that it is an environmentally conscious movement protecting a 'way of life more harmoniously adjusted with natural processes'.[44] In this scenario, the movement promotes a strategy of localisation in response to the homogenising influence of industrial development. Shiva develops this argument, and suggests that the Chipko struggle is based on the promotion of authentic Indian values, which include traditional agricultural production, autonomy from states and markets, and harmony within communities, and between communities and nature.[45] Chipko is thus regarded as a movement that rejects development, and embraces eco-feminist principles. In Shiva's work, this is linked to an account of pre-colonial India, which was said to promote the feminine principle, or *prakriti*.

Indian development has certainly been associated with a deplorable environmental crisis, which has seen large-scale deforestation, soil erosion local climate change, loss of local biodiversity, conflict over water and high levels of urban air pollution.[46] Deforestation has had disastrous implications for the livelihoods of female firewood collectors.[47] Post-development and

[44] Guha 1989, p. 196.
[45] Shiva 1989.
[46] Rangan 1996.
[47] Agarwal 1997.

eco-feminist interpretations of Chipko therefore have an instinctive appeal. However, there are strong grounds for questioning this interpretation, particularly regarding the movement in relation to development, including states and markets, and the construction of Indian tradition. Moreover, the movement was eventually marginalised by new mobilisations around the struggle for an independent state. These issues are addressed further in Section 3 below.

7.3 Social movements and the 'new' politics of resistance: an assessment

How then, do the cases discussed above, and indeed other movements throughout the world, 'match up' to the theoretical discussion outlined in Section 1 above? In this section, I question the autonomist and anarchist interpretations discussed in Section 1 above, first by returning to the case studies discussed in Section 2, and then reflecting on more general implications, not least for anti-globalisation movements in the North. However, I also reject the notion of the need to return to traditional left politics, and instead suggest that a participatory politics beyond Leninism and autonomism is potentially more fruitful.

(i) *The Zapatistas*

In many respects, the Zapatistas are closest to the autonomist interpretation of political and social movements outlined above. There is considerable autonomy from the formal political process, and the movement has called for autonomy for the Chiapas region from the political centre. It has also ingeniously mobilised support from civil-society organisations, not least at an international level. Conceding these points, however, does inevitably beg two questions. First, how is autonomy to be achieved? And, second, how viable is the Zapatista 'project'?

The question of autonomy involves consideration of two issues. First, is the fact that establishing autonomy effectively means that, as it is the very institution that could grant autonomy, the Mexican state cannot be by-passed. Indeed, the Zapatistas have made demands along these lines, calling for military withdrawal and autonomy for the region through the implementation of the San Andres Accords. Moreover, the principle of autonomy begs the question of 'autonomy for whom'?[48] Clearly, Chiapas faces a number of unfavourable external problems and state hostility, but this is not the same as accepting the view that *all* of the problems of the region are external ones. There are important 'internal' questions of control of local resources and redistribution that the issue of autonomy tends to evade.

The second question relates to viability. It is clear that the Zapatistas' demands for implementation of the San Andres Accords have been largely ignored by the Mexican state. A heavily watered-down and largely meaningless bill was passed in 2001 supposedly 'implementing' the Accords, but this was little more than rhetoric. The movement is thus, in many respects, marginalised, and its own rhetoric of local autonomy may actually serve to reinforce such marginalisation. The clear implication is that some form of engagement with wider political processes – which, in practice, the Zapatistas have found unavoidable anyway – is necessary. This implies some further commitment to alliance-building and pressure on the Mexican state.

(ii) *The MST*

The MST also, in some respects, challenges traditional left approaches to political organisation. The movement has an open membership, is sensitive to issues of hierarchy, is autonomous from political parties, and promotes direct action through land occupations. But, on the other hand, there are informal links to political parties, particularly the Workers' Party, there is formal political organisation, and direct action is not the only way in which politics is practised. The movement cannot take an approach to organisation that espouses the principle of non-hierarchical networks, as championed, for example, by Michael Hardt,[49] for the simple reason that the movement's size is too vast for such (non-) organisation to be effective. Moreover, while direct action through land occupation is considered to be an immediate necessity for the landless poor, it is also regarded as part of a strategy that puts pressure on local and national states to implement land reform, which, in turn, is part of a wider strategy of social transformation. Such a strategy may not be Leninist, but it most certainly is not one that conforms to autonomist, anarchist

---

[48] Adler Hellman 1999.
[49] Hardt 2002.

or post-developmentalist principles.[50] Interestingly, the movement's leading spokesperson, João Pedro Stedile, is quite critical of the Zapatistas:

> Our relations with the Zapatistas are simply those of solidarity. Their struggle is a just one, but its social base and its method are different to ours. Theirs is, at root, a struggle of indigenous people for autonomy – and if there's a criticism to be made of their experience, it would be that the slowness of their advance is due to their inability to broaden it into a class struggle, a national one.[51]

(iii) Chipko

The representation of Chipko as an unambiguously anti-modern, anti-development, traditionalist movement autonomous from the state is highly problematic. At most, this perspective refers to one tendency in the Chipko movement, associated mainly with Sunderlal Bahuguna.[52] This approach romanticises pre-colonial India, and especially the place of women in that society. For instance, Shiva's celebration of the feminine principle as the basis for a return to pre-colonial Indian values is endorsed by Bahuguna. But this assertion ignores the facts that this notion was part of the élite Brahmin tradition, and not that of the forest-dwelling communities. Indeed, women and lower castes were not even allowed to read such texts.[53] It is also a fallacy to suggest that women in the region unambiguously embrace such values, and women see the forests as a resource for local subsistence. There is protection of forests, but the stealing of wood from protected trees by these same women is a common practice.[54] The lifestyle for many women is not one that they themselves celebrate, but, instead, it is seen as one of hardship. They do not reject development in itself, but demand rather access to a more equitable and socially just form of development, which includes access to other villages (and therefore roads), water, health care and so on.

---

[50] There are populist forces within the MST, which promote small-scale agriculture and petty commodity producers, and disregard the potential for social differentiation in this system. But the main thrust of the movement is to link land struggles to wider social change.

[51] Stedile 2002, pp. 98–9.

[52] Bahuguna 1989.

[53] Sinha et al. 1997, pp. 77–9.

[54] Sinha et al. 1997, pp. 79–80; Mawdsley 1998.

The emergence of the movement for an independent state of Uttaranchal[55] should be seen in this light, for it was based on the demand for greater access to, rather than autonomy from, 'development'. This demand for a separate state can hardly be regarded as an anti-state, anti-development movement. Indeed, Chipko was never simply a revivalist or an anti-state movement. Direct action was only taken once negotiations with the state had broken down, and preservation of forests was linked to, and actually preceded by, campaigns for social justice, including challenges to the caste and gender inequalities of 'traditional' village communities.[56] Rangan argues that it was the very success of the Chipko movement in winning environmental controls (on tree-felling, road construction, and so on) in the early 1980s that led to its decline.[57] This was because such policies served to reinforce the marginalisation of the forest dwellers, and therefore a movement for a pro-developmental state (Uttarakhand/Uttaranchal) emerged in its place. There is some truth to this argument, though it tends to accept at face value the notion that Chipko was an anti-development movement, when it is clear that the movement was far more diverse than this interpretation allows. But, on both counts, the post-development interpretation is severely weakened: on the one hand, post-development approaches led to intensified marginalisation, and, on the other hand, the movement was not simply one that embraced post-development approaches, and supporters often demanded access to a reconstructed development.

(iv) *Wider implications*

These cases, then, demonstrate that there is a need for caution when autonomist, post-development and anarchist claims are made about social movements in the South (and elsewhere). Here, I want to expand on these points by drawing out some more general implications. As should by now be clear, interpretations (or representations) of many social movements in the South have too one-sidedly focused on the questions of autonomy and moving

---

[55] The movement demanded a new, independent state of Uttarakhand. The governing BJP granted indepdenced to the state in 1998, but insisted on the term Uttarranchal, partly as a means of separating the decision from the popular movement for an independent state.

[56] Sinha et al. 1997, p. 84.

[57] Rangan 1998.

beyond development. The result is a tendency to celebrate resistance without a clear analysis of the effectiveness or ambiguities of such resistance, or to celebrate a backward-looking populism that rejects modernity wholesale. In other words, there is a tendency towards a romanticisation of the local and a romanticisation of resistance, and this has undoubtedly had a strong influence on anti-globalisation movements in the North.

The tendency to romanticise the local was discussed in some detail in Chapter 6, and in relation to the Chipko movement above, so I can be quite brief on this point. What does need a little more emphasis is the fact that it is not only the local, but also the past, that tends to be celebrated. We have already seen this with respect to the work of Shiva and some versions of environmentalism. One prominent post-development thinker writes that 'vernacular societies had a much more realistic view of things. Not blinkered by the myth of equality, they believed that the good of the community was better served by those of its members it considered to be the wisest, the most virtuous, and hence the most "authoritative" and experienced persons of the groups – those who commanded everyone's respect and deference'.[58] This appeal to élitist tradition would probably horrify most anti-globalisation campaigners, while the appeal to authoritative persons is not unlike the rhetoric of modern technocrats running many nation-states and international institutions. But it does show the dangers of simplistic appeals to local cultures and traditions, which have always been based on hierarchy, domination and exploitation.[59] Some of the rhetoric endorsed by campaigners, concerning for example pre-industrial Albion England, pre-globalised agrarian communities, and the need to reclaim the commons should be seen in this light. I return to this point in the Conclusion.

In terms of the romanticisation of resistance, there is a reluctance to critically discuss the politics of diverse social movements on the grounds that this would imply 'capture' by the dominant discourses that such movements are said to be resisting.[60] Similarly, the argument that proposing alternatives through political programmes leads to the violence of closure, in which difference is eliminated usefully warns us of the authoritarian dangers of

---

[58] Rahnema 1997, p. 388.
[59] Kiely 1999.
[60] Escobar 1995, pp. 222–3.

rigid blueprints for social change. But an alternative that is so open-ended that *any* closure is avoided is to descend into an escape from, rather than reconstruction of, politics. Politics is in part about decision-making and any decision involves some form of closure, or some form of eliminating difference. Progressive politics is *anti-* any number of hierarchical exclusions, and so it cannot avoid closure. The point is to make decisions based on the 'economy of least violence'.[61] This issue applies not only to future utopias, but also to the politics of the present, for a one-sided emphasis on forms of organisation can also lead to an underestimation of the potential effectiveness of social movements, avoidance of difficult strategic questions based on promoting solidarity, and questionable tactics at international summit protests, such as the violence of the anarchist movement the Black Bloc. Certainly some activists in the anti-globalisation movement appear to believe that direct action is itself *the* politics, rather than one *part* of a wider movement for political change. Thus, one advocate argues that these 'new forms of organization are its ideology'.[62] Naomi Klein has herself pointed to the limitations of direct action. She describes how, in April 2000, a blockade of the streets surrounding the IMF and World Bank headquarters in Washington collapsed as each intersection of the blockade declared autonomy. The effect was that some continued the blockade while others did not, which made it completely ineffective – delegates to the official meetings simply went down a street which was no longer blockaded. For Klein, this was a metaphor for the strengths and weaknesses of the movement, arguing that the activist network around websites and e-mails 'is better at speed and volume than at synthesis'.[63] For the anti-capitalist movement, the challenge to corporate globalisation could easily turn into 'a movement of meeting stalkers, following the trade bureaucrats as if they were the Grateful Dead'.[64] WTO meetings may not last as long as an interminable Grateful Dead jam, but capitalism has outlived Jerry Garcia. For these reasons, Klein has argued increasingly for a politics of engagement alongside one of negation.

These problems are also clear in one of the key works associated with the anti-globalisation movement, Hardt and Negri's *Empire*. This work is, in many

---

[61] Beardsworth 1996; Parfitt 2002.
[62] Graeber 2002, p. 70; for a sympathetic but critical reflection, see McKay 1998.
[63] Klein 2001b, p. 152.
[64] Klein 2001b, p. 152; also Brecher et al. 2000, pp. 86–8.

respects, more relevant to the considerations of the next chapter, not least because the authors call for global resistance and reject localist utopias as backward-looking and romantic. I partly consider their work here because they are guilty of romanticising resistance. In their work, globalisation is said to have put an end to the imperialist era based on the domination of some nation-states by others. For Hardt and Negri, the new era is above all the product of the struggles of the 'multitude'. However, this has not led to the end of domination and hierarchy, but a new system of decentred, deterritorialised power, called Empire.[65] In the current era, it is not only the industrial working class which acts as the main challenge to capitalism. Instead, Hardt and Negri refer to all those who come under the capitalist norms of production and reproduction, 'all those whose labor is exploited by capital',[66] as 'the multitude', the main oppositional force to Empire. Clearly influenced by earlier conceptions of society as a 'social factory',[67] in which more and more aspects of social life come to be subject to the discipline of capital, the multitude represents the radical counterpower to Empire. This concept of the multitude is linked to Negri's earlier work in the tradition of autonomist Marxism. Indeed, Negri's earlier autonomist position is clearly still influential when Hardt and Negri argue that '[t]he power of the proletariat imposes limits on capital and not only determines the crisis but also dictates the terms and nature of the transformation. *The proletariat actually invents the social and productive forms that capital will be forced to adopt in the future'.*[68] They go on to argue that the US proletariat is 'the subjective figure that expressed most fully the desires and needs of international or multinational workers. Against the common wisdom that the US proletariat is weak because of its low party and union representation with respect to Europe and elsewhere, perhaps we should see it as strong for precisely those reasons. Working class power resides not in the representative institutions but in the antagonism and autonomy of the workers themselves'.[69] In keeping with the determining role of labour, much is made of strategies of refusal of the disciplinary régime.

---

[65] See also Chapters 5 and 8.
[66] Hardt and Negri 2000, p. 402.
[67] Negri 1998.
[68] Hardt and Negri 2000, p. 268.
[69] Hardt and Negri 2000, p. 269.

This may include students experimenting with LSD instead of looking for a job, or young women who refuse early marriage.[70] Beyond this, Hardt and Negri have little to say about the concrete politics of resisting Empire, though they do put forward three (vague) demands in the book's final chapter: the right to global citizenship (and, by implication, no immigration controls); the right to a social wage, or guaranteed income for all; and the right to a re-appropriation of the means of production.[71]

What is clear from this brief outline is Hardt and Negri's hostility to all limits on human action, and by implication, to the principle of authority. Thus, political programmes and institutions (such as trade unions, as cited above) constitute a limitation on human action and emancipation. As stated above, formal politics constitutes a form of closure, and, for this reason, engagement with such politics is rejected outright. Much of this argument is strongly influenced by Deleuze and Guattari's *Anti-Oedipus*,[72] which sees liberation as the expansion of human desire. Despite their commitment to post-structuralism, Hardt and Negri implicitly have a theory of human nature, which assumes that, given an expanded realm of freedom, people will act in increasingly co-operative ways. The fact that people have not done so is said to be a result of existing social arrangements. To an extent, this argument applies to all theories that believe that human society is improvable. But Hardt and Negri's[73] approach to human creativity / the multitude and human enslavement/authority, is too one-sided, and the latter is seen as the sole reason for destruction while the former is truly creative. However, *any* society must have some social arrangements that apply authority, and therefore the restriction of *some* desires – just as 'local' self-determination relies on some form of global enabling (but also constraining) institutions. None of this implies support for existing hierarchies, but neither does it mean that better societies will do without all authority. A second related point, and one more relevant to autonomist approaches to 'actually existing globalisation', is that it is similarly one-sided to see all the actions of the 'multitude' as inherently creative, while authority is always destructive. For Hardt and Negri to be consistent with

---

[70] Hardt and Negri 2000, p. 274.
[71] Hardt and Negri 2000, p. 394.
[72] Deleuze and Guattari 1998.
[73] Hardt and Negri 2000, p. 459.

their analysis, the actions of al-Qaeda must be regarded as being inherently creative.[74]

Where this discussion parallels the more immediate concerns of autonomists within the anti-globalisation movement is in the clear romanticisation of resistance, in which all acts are regarded as resistant, effective and progressive. Democracy – in terms of both current resistance and the future organisation of a new society – entails more than individual autonomy, spontaneity and activist counter-summits. Anarchist and autonomist approaches remain important in that they sensitise us to the ongoing problem of democracy, something that the Left in practice has neglected for far too long. On the other hand, a politics which over-emphasises autonomy can easily descend into one that advocates local delinking or, on a personal level, a politics of 'dropping out' rather than changing the system.[75] Certainly, there is a fine line between advocating social transformation and retreating from mainstream society and from politics based on social transformation. Hardt and Negri are at times guilty of stepping over this line: for instance, in their rather uncritical endorsement of the 1960s hippy counter-culture. A similar point can be made regarding resistance based on spectacular protest. The use of such protests through 'Carnivals Against Capitalism', street parties, reclaiming the streets is important, but one potential result of this approach to politics is that resistance through spectacle 'may offer no more than the experience of managed spectatorship'.[76] Similarly, in relation to the debate around global civil society, networking through the internet 'is not a substitute for traditional political activity and participation'.[77] The Net is an important mobilising tool and it does facilitate genuine participatory dialogue among its participants, but cyberspace, or the politics of the spectacle are no substitutes for other forms of political engagement.[78]

Some of these problems become clear when examining the politics of anti-

---

[74] Rustin 2003.
[75] Pietrese 2000, p. 192.
[76] Scott and Street 2001, p. 50.
[77] Smith and Smythe 2001, p. 204.
[78] See also Chapter 8. A similar point applies to theorists who exaggerate the speed of global interconnectedness to the point where meaning ceases to exist (Baudrillard 1983), or where local places are irrelevant in the face of the 'space of flows' (Castells 1989, 1996). Both approaches are in danger of reifying the global and ignoring the social agency involved in constructing – and resisting – (globalised) locations.

globalisation movements in North America. For example, the over-emphasis placed on decentralisation by North-American movements turns the need to be sensitive to diversity into an absolutist position, in which difference can easily become fragmentation, and struggles become ineffective as a result.[79] Dealing with difference is important, but this, in part, must be done through an awareness of similarity, in order for alliances to take place. Moreover, decentralisation can easily lead to a 'back-door' vanguardism, in which the most active members become effective leaders. Of course, this is true of *all* organisation, but denying this problem guarantees that the effective leaders will be unaccountable. It is only through the creation of structures of formal accountability that this problem can be resolved, or at least controlled. Indeed, the contrast between the MST and, say, the Ruckus Society in the US, is instructive. The former has a mass membership and therefore must have formal organisation, spokespeople, and so on. Such organisation is certainly not Leninist, but neither is it simply a non-hierarchical network. In contrast, the Ruckus Society has just four full-time staff and about one hundred or so people at its camps, but is involved in organising protests involving thousands of people. This situation encourages the summit-stalking that Naomi Klein rightly questions, but also encourages unaccountable hierarchy – indeed, John Sellers[80] of the Ruckus Society admits that 'those closest to the centre get more input than people who are further away from it'.

I am, therefore, suggesting that movements cannot evade the question of organisation, both internally, and through interaction with established systems of authority. However, this is not an argument for a return to a Leninist politics, based on a revolutionary vanguard party, where the capitalist state is 'smashed' and replaced by a dictatorship of the proletariat. This view tends to reduce politics to capturing or smashing the (machine-like) state, and the politics of the everyday tends to be downgraded as a result. The autonomist view is potentially more useful, in that it sees the separation of the political sphere (the state) from the economic sphere (civil society) as a historical product, related to the development of capitalist social relations. Progressive political strategy then becomes one based not on 'smashing' or even 'capturing' the state, but instead one of challenging this separation through the radical

---

[79] Harvey 1996, Chapter 12; Ross 2002.
[80] Sellers 2001, p. 75.

democratisation of both spheres. This approach thus broadens the conception of revolution (which is seen as far more than a simple insurrection) so that everyday practices are part of 'the revolutionary process'. However, the autonomist approach tends towards the view that this can – and, crucially, *should* – occur despite the state. But this strategy of by-passing the state may actually reinforce state power. A brief example illustrates the point. The development of Local Exchange Trading Schemes (LETS) in some respects constitutes a challenge to neo-liberalism. As we saw in Chapter 6, these schemes involve trading of services through the use of a locally specific currency, that cannot be used outside of the system, and is subject to strict controls as a mechanism of accumulation (such as time limits on credit and no interest). Such schemes challenge neo-liberalism through the focus on scale (schemes are highly localised), politics (money is embedded in the community), and community (through the promotion of collective values and trading in money scarce areas or in otherwise non-monetised services). But, on the other hand, in encouraging self-help and voluntary initiatives below the state, the schemes 'can sometimes dovetail with liberal goals of scaling back the role of government and delegating social welfare functions to local civil society groups'.[81] At their worst, then, such schemes let governments off the hook and even encourage the further marginalisation of different social groups. In this respect, the schemes are not so far removed from the self-help approach to social capital endorsed by the World Bank.[82] On the other hand, this interpretation seems too harsh, and the schemes are at the very least necessary 'holding operations' in situations of chronic poverty. Moreover, they may also play a more educational role, in helping to promote more a collective consciousness among participants. But this interpretation still demonstrates the limitations as well as strengths of the schemes, and especially the need for scaling up operations beyond pure localities – and above all, engaging with the massive resources at the disposal of nation-states and the 'private sector'. Which, again, brings us back to the question of the state.

The example of the Indian state of Kerala is particularly instructive in this respect. Much has been written about successful social development within this state.[83] Despite low levels of per capita income, Kerala has a very impressive

---

[81] Helleiner 2000, p. 50.
[82] Discussed in Chapter 4.
[83] Dreze and Sen 1989, Chapter 11; Parayil 2000.

record in terms of literacy and educational levels, infant mortality rates, life expectancy and other health-care indicators. The question, then, is why is the local state in Kerala so responsive to the social development needs of its population? This is, in part, a product of high rates of social mobilisation, but, unlike the experience in many developing countries, this has occurred along less factionalist lines in Kerala, and, in particular, there has been considerable organisation along the lines of class and gender.[84] This mobilisation has also undermined entrenched local interests such as former landowners, which, in turn, has facilitated state autonomy from such groups. Of course, the Kerala experience is limited, and there are still high levels of poverty, unemployment and so on.[85] There has also been a growing tendency towards state centralisation, which has eroded participation. Clearly, the Kerala experience is not a 'socialist utopia', but there are two clear positive lessons. First, that progressive change can occur without 'socialist revolution'. Second, and related to the first point, is that, despite all the 'external constraints', Kerala has seen high rates of participation and social development without the brutalities of Stalinist socialism. Indeed, the tendency towards centralisation has been resisted, especially since 1996 with the launching of the People's Campaign for Decentralised Planning, which has attempted to devolve responsibility for about a third of planned government spending to local bodies.[86] This demonstrates a different approach to collective institutions, where '[t]he state does not define public need for people on their behalf. Rather public need is defined through active partipation. . . . [A]ccountability of state action cannot be assumed but *can* be fought for'.[87]

Similarly, though, to date, less extensively, the development of a participatory budget system in Porto Alegre, Brazil has also involved a mobilisation not only beyond, but within the state. In 1988, Olivio Dutra of the Workers' Party was elected mayor, and the concept of the participatory budget was developed, based on 'shifting decisions on how to allocate municipal resources from the City council to popular assemblies'. Such a process has 'politicized budgetary debates, taking them out of the technocratic and legislative sphere, allowing broad public debate about funding priorities and their social and

---

[84] Heller 2001.
[85] Ramanathiyer and MacPherson 2000.
[86] Isaac and Franke 2002.
[87] Wuyts 1992, p. 282.

political implications'.[88] In this system, popular assemblies decide where money should be allocated, and follow up through an assessment of policy implementation. The participatory budget exists alongside institutions of representative democracy, which, in turn, acts as a restraint on the private sector.[89] Dutro's appointment as Minister for Cities in the elected national government may serve as a basis for the extension of the participatory budget principle to other cites and states in Brazil, although the plan faces the unfavourable context of enormous financial constraints and the IMF. One final point concerning Porto Alegre concerns the fact that it hosted the World Social Forums in 2002 and 2003. Given that the organising committees of the WSF were dominated by (unelected, unaccountable) non-governmental organisations, it is ironic that the venue was only available as a result of the success of a democratic state.[90]

This final point is made not to reject NGOs outright, nor to uncritically endorse 'statist' politics. It is made, however, in order to reject simplistic approaches that champion 'civil society' in opposition to the state, or the local in opposition to the national or global.[91] The politics of progressive social movements is not necessarily concerned with 'capturing' or 'smashing' the state, but neither is it about ignoring the state.

7.4 Conclusion: social movements, cultural politics and the commons

The basic alternative offered by progressive anti-globalisation movements is a commitment to the principle of 'reclaiming the commons'. Put differently, it is a rejection of the increased privatisation, commodification and rationalisation of the globe. As the prominent French activist, Jose Bové argues, '[t]he world is not for sale'.[92] This notion of the commons, and even more the claim that they can be reclaimed, can certainly sometimes be associated with a romantic notion of local communities, in which peasantries are said to be at one with nature and inequality and poverty are either idealised or

---

[88] Sader 2002, p. 91.
[89] Wainwright 2003, pp. 42–69.
[90] Sader 2002.
[91] Heller 2001, pp. 134–45, 152.
[92] Bové and Dufour 2001.

ignored. This position is often proposed as part of the localisation strategies critically discussed above.[93] However, the notion of the commons need not be backward-looking, localist and romantic. Perhaps we should instead talk about *democratisation* of the commons, rather than *reclamation*, as it is difficult to conceive of a time when there was a genuinely democratic commons. Seen in this light, the anti-globalisation movement is based less on a sentimental attachment to the past (though such tendencies certainly exist), and more one that is united through 'working against forces whose common thread is what might broadly be described as the privatization of every activity and value into a commodity'.[94] Diverse campaigns are therefore united through their opposition to the global neo-liberal project, and include opposition to the privatisation of health care, education, natural resources, the expansion of private sector influence in schools, local authorities, the patenting of genes, and the commodifying of politics (through close ties to business and media spin). The intensified opposition to WTO agreements concerning intellectual property rights (TRIPS) and privatisation of public services (GATS) should be seen in this light. The opposition to the increased commodification of the world is thus based on a radical commitment to the notion of the commons, or a commitment to public service.

This idea of the commons is a world away from the technocratic reforms of public services carried out by neo-liberal and Third-Way governments across the globe. The rationale for these reforms is to make public-sector workers more 'efficient' through reforms that try to make such workers behave as if they were operating in the private sector. Thus, these reforms betray an obsession with league tables, efficiency targets, and naming and shaming bad performers. The problem with the rationale for much of these reforms is that it assumes that there is no notion of trust between worker and provider, and so also assumes that workers are not motivated by any notion of public service, but, instead, are motivated by self-interest. This can become a self-fulfilling prophecy, as targets and league tables can make workers behave in more self-interested ways, and indeed spend time fulfilling narrow quantitative targets rather than responding to the needs of users. In other words, such neo-liberal inspired reforms may actually undermine the (non-selfish, public interest) values that motivated people in the first place.

---

[93] Goldsmith and Mander 2001, Part 3.
[94] Klein 2001, p. 82.

The call to reclaim the commons resists the neo-liberal approach that reduces human behaviour to the exercise of a one-dimensional self-interest. However, it also challenges equally technocratic approaches that champion the bureaucratic and paternalist state. Instead, it is based on a politics that aims to radicalise conceptions of public service. Therefore, both the top-down bureaucratic strategy of statist approaches is rejected, alongside the self-interest model of neo-liberalism. In their place, participatory democracy is advocated, whereby democracy is extended through a constant process of negotiation between public citizens and – where representation and/or bureaucracy is unavoidable – through the constant monitoring of decision-makers. Anti-globalisation activists argue that, in this way, the public sphere can be made more accountable, less bureaucratic and, at the same time, more genuinely publicly interested. Although there are no models or blueprints, lessons can be learnt from experiences of participation. In the cases of Kerala and Porto Alegre, for instance, public service is not so much defined in top-down fashion by the state, as it is by and through the very process of participation by various groups in society. It is in this sense that we can talk of democratising the commons.

This notion entails nothing less than a cultural revolution – a new way of life. It is a far cry from neo-liberalism and the Third Way, but also from the authoritarian statist socialisms of the twentieth century. However, it is not purely a change in the consciousness of people, but also a change in the exploitative social relations that exist between people. These social relations entail, not only exploitation and inequality, but also the generalisation of commodity production in a competitive market-place, and this competition by necessity turns self-interest into a virtue. This necessity is forced upon dominant as well as dominated social classes. Despite these social relations, people still behave in ways that cannot be reduced to self-interest, even though they live in a society in which selfish motivations are encouraged. For radical change to take place, there has to be a change in social relations as well in popular consciousness. Moreover, such a cultural revolution starts in the here and now, in everyday struggles against privatisation, deregulation and so on. Of course there is a need for such struggles to be linked to other struggles, but this must be done in a way that does not lead to the subordination of one struggle to that of others. Many anti-globalisation activists therefore argue that there is a cultural revolution in the ways in which they 'do politics'. Thus, to return to the Zapatistas, there is 'one no', but 'many yeses'.

This commitment to an absence of hierarchy, and to an advocacy of open-endedness, has confused many critics who argue that there is a need for concrete alternatives. Certainly, the anti-globalisation movement is right to be sensitive to the issues of avoiding hierarchy and rigid future blueprints that often lead to oppression once oppositional forces win power. The future cannot be predicted precisely because the outcome of struggle is open-ended. But, having said that, a politics that is *so open-ended* as to avoid *any* decisions is one that ultimately evades the question of politics. Politics does involve the making of decisions, and a politics that avoids any 'closure' is a politics in which anything goes. A sensitivity to the democratic needs of others is one thing, an absolute open-endedness quite another. Some elements of anti-globalisation politics – particularly those associated with anarchism – are close to endorsing this open-endedness. The result is a politics of evasion or escapism, based either on romantic localisms or a fetishisation of global resistance. In contrast, the most productive debates among local and national social movements and at the World Social Fora are those which have focused on the two broad questions: first, that of progressive politics at local, national and global levels, without reifying or rigidly separating such levels; and, second, those which have attempted to balance the need for broad principles, policies and organisations to carry these out, alongside awareness of the dangers of rigid models and reintroducing hierarchy.

Chapter Eight

Civil Society 2. No Sweat, No Debt, No War: Transnational Social Movements and Global Civil Society

Despite the fact that many contemporary resistance movements are commonly described as 'anti-globalisation', an alternative argument has been made that these movements champion a 'globalisation from below' that resists globalisation from above.[1] This chapter examines the claim that there is a new politics of global solidarity that transcends national politics. It does so by focusing specifically on three global issues that have at the forefront of anti-globalisation politics – anti-debt, anti-sweatshop and anti-war campaigns. The chapter presents some details on these campaigns, but is most concerned with the dilemmas of building transnational solidarity, both around these specific issues, and more generally. Through the three case studies, I will focus on three main questions. First, on what basis can solidarity be constructed, especially given the different material circumstances faced by people across the world? Second, how do movements engage with established institutions of political power – not only nation-states, but also institutions of global governance? Does a progressive anti-war politics involve no compromise

---

[1] Falk 2000a.

with the nation-state or institutions of global governance, while debt-relief campaigns by their very nature involve some 'compromise'? Third, how do questions of solidarity beyond borders relate to questions of political engagement at local and national 'levels'? The case studies therefore examine not only the nature of transnational organisation or 'networking', a concern that features prominently in the burgeoning literature on global social movements, but also the question of how tactical and strategic questions are addressed. These points are addressed in more detail in the chapter's fifth and concluding section, which critically addresses the wider issues of transnational solidarity, global civil society and global governance.[2]

8.1 Transnational capital and global resistance

The concept of global civil society is associated with cosmopolitan perspectives, which are based on the notion of a worldwide political community and universal human rights that transcend the sovereignty of nation-states.[3] This essentially normative ideal is of course far from being a reality, as cosmopolitan theorists accept. Indeed, I argued in Chapter 2 that, contrary to some of Marx's more optimistic beliefs, which hoped for a cosmopolitan capitalism based on the decline of the nation-state and an 'evening up' of capitalist development, the expansion of capitalism had intensified uneven development and universalised the nation-state system. These arguments are relevant to the concerns of this chapter, which focuses on the question of transnational solidarity in the context of the uneven development of global capitalism. In terms of the concept of global civil society, it will become clear through a consideration of the case studies that the cosmopolitan perspective is a progressive aspiration, and this will become most clear when we consider the issues of imperialism and war. At the same time, cosmopolitanism is not necessarily achieved through a simplistic rejection of politics focused on the nation-state, and it is an aspiration that must take into account, rather than ignore, uneven development.

---

[2] The chapter does not explicitly address in any depth some of the theoretical questions around the concepts of civil society and global civil society, though this is implicit in the substantive discussion. For more general theoretical reflection, see the previous and following chapters.

[3] Held 1995.

These issues become clearer if we more explicitly locate them in the context of debates around globalisation. As we saw in Chapters 2 and 5, some accounts of globalisation attempt to argue that it is a process without a centre. In some accounts, this can take the form of an argument that globalisation is simply what we have become, almost as if it was a force of nature. But, as we also saw in Chapter 5, more radical accounts of globalisation attempt to theorise globalisation in terms of the transnationalisation of capital, so that capital is no longer tied to specific nation-states. Associated with such arguments is the notion that US hegemony is in decline, or at least of less relevance in understanding the globalisation of capital. Hence we have theories of post-imperialism, a transnational capitalist class and transnational state, and Hardt and Negri's conception of Empire. On the other hand, some Marxists have argued that, in reality, very little has changed and that globalisation is simply the latest stage in the development of capitalism and imperialism. My argument in the first part of the book was that globalisation does constitute a real change in the nature of capitalism, but that nation-states remain important agents of globalisation and, therefore, sites of struggle.

These debates suggest that there are at least three radical approaches to understanding globalisation, and these have particular implications for understanding political alternatives to it. The first is associated with the strong globalisation thesis, and argues that the nation-state is increasingly irrelevant. Thus, as already seen, Michael Hardt has argued that the main political division at the 2002 World Social Forum was between a politics of globalised, anti-capitalist resistance on the one hand, and a nationalist defence of state sovereignty on the other. In supporting the former, Hardt argues for a position which 'opposes any national solutions and seeks instead a democratic globalization'.[4] This approach sees globalisation as progressive because it erodes the power of mediating institutions such as the nation-state, and therefore creates a 'smooth space' in which the resistance of the multitude takes place. The second position is that very little has changed, nation-states continue to be the main organisers of the world capitalist system, and that, therefore, resistance should continue to focus on nation-states.[5] The third position, and the one taken in this chapter, argues that it is not a case of *either*

---

[4] Hardt 2002, p. 114.
[5] Halperin and Laxer 2003.

globalised resistance *or* resistance that focuses on the nation-state – and, indeed, such a dichotomy was not the main line of division at the 2002 World Social Forum.[6] Of course there are important tactical questions around these issues, but the essential principle is that neither 'the national' nor 'the global' should be prioritised in isolation from these strategic questions. This was clear in the discussion of national social movements in the previous chapter, and it should become clear in terms of the more explicitly transnational questions to which I now turn.

8.2 No debt

As we saw in Chapter 3, the 1980s witnessed a serious debt crisis that, from the viewpoint of the banks, was resolved by the late 1980s and early 1990s. However, the effects of such a crisis lingered on into the 1990s, and were part of a continued development crisis for parts of the developing world. This was less true of the highly indebted Latin American countries of the 1980s, which, in the 1990s, received new capital inflows in the forms of foreign direct and portfolio investment, albeit with far from straightforward developmental consequences.[7] But, in this same period, attention shifted to the poorest countries that had relatively low debts when measured internationally, but whose debt burdens were particularly high when measured as a proportion of their GNP or the value of annual exports.

Social movements, such as the US Debt Crisis Network and some religious organisations, focused on commercial debts in the 1980s. In the early to mid-1990s, the European Network on Debt and Development launched a campaign to reduce the burdens of multilateral debt,[8] which paved the way for international campaigns for debt relief owed to the IMF, World Bank and 'First-World' governments. In 1996, Jubilee 2000 was launched, which explicitly campaigned through the principle of transborder global solidarity, for debt relief mainly focused on the multilateral institutions.[9] Although officially wound up on 31 December 1999, the legacy of Jubilee 2000 continues through

---

[6] Mertes 2002.
[7] See Chapter 4.
[8] EURODAD 1996.
[9] Jubilee 2000 Campaign 1999.

a number of related organisations, including Jubilee Research, Jubilee South and Jubilee Movement International.

In 1996, unsustainable debt burdens were measured as those countries that faced an annual debt service ratio of 25 per cent. This was not considered to be a great success and, after considerable pressure from Jubilee 2000, the ratio was reduced to 15 per cent in 1999.

There remain considerable problems with the implementation of debt relief, however. For countries to qualify, they still a need to undertake reforms recommended by the IMF or World Bank, which usually means wholesale privatisation and trade liberalisation – reforms that have not been conducive to long-term growth and which are likely to intensify the (relative) marginalisation of these countries from the world economy. This is because the absence of some mechanisms of protection for weaker producers leads to unequal import competition from stronger, established overseas producers, and this is hardly likely to be compensated by breaking into lucrative export markets in new sectors. These policies can also have devastating social consequences as the measures introduced often intensify unequal income distribution and reduce state-run social safety nets for the poorest. The policy conditions attached to debt relief are, therefore, part of the problem. Moreover, despite announcements of debt relief amounting to $110 billion, by early 2003 there had only been a commitment to $62 billion of this amount and, in fact, only $29 billion had actually been cancelled – and, of this, $29 billion, around 50 per cent is accounted for by previous bilateral debt cancellation and not by the HIPC initiative. There are also serious questions concerning the World Bank's measurement of sustainable debt and, given proposed debt-relief timetables, the extent to which highly indebted poor countries may achieve these far-from-generous measures and actually become 'sustainable debtors'.[10]

In terms of putting multilateral debt relief on the agenda, and winning some debt-relief concessions, international campaigns led by Jubilee 2000 have undoubtedly been a success. On the other hand, this campaign has faced a number of dilemmas which also have wider political implications. The first problem relates to the question of which countries should take priority in

---

[10] Jubilee 2000 Campaign 2002.

campaigns for debt relief?[11] Related to this point, there is also the wider question of the extent to which anti-debt campaigns should accept structural adjustment programmes as part of the condition for debt relief. This issue has divided more conservative reformers in Northern-based campaigns from more radical approaches championed by campaigns in the South.[12] In terms of debt relief, one of the great ironies is that the World Bank's problem of defining unsustainable debt is also a problem for anti-debt campaigners, who similarly face the question of priorities. This is a particularly difficult question, as most campaigners realise that in the absence of wider reforms, blanket debt cancellation is neither likely nor necessarily desirable (see below). One of the leading thinkers in the Jubilee 2000 campaign, Ann Pettifor has called for the principles of limited liability and bankruptcy to apply to countries (rather than just companies), so that the never ending spiral of ongoing debt, new loans and ongoing repayments can be ended.[13] This is an important idea that certainly rationalises the principle of debt relief, and it is one that even some IMF economists have entertained, only to be dismissed by more influential leading figures within and beyond that institution. However, it does not entirely deal with the problem of defining unsustainable debt and the question of eligibility.

This leads to the second problem, which is often presented as the relationship between single-issue campaigns and wider political perspectives. If debt relief is to be selective, then some will win at the expense of others. However, if debt relief is wholesale, then countries are unlikely to gain access to new sources of loans, at least in the short term. Put differently, is debt the cause of poverty for the poorest countries or merely a symptom? If this is the case, how does the single-issue campaign of debt relief link up to wider issues of international poverty and inequality? And, related to this question, in campaigns for a radical reduction of poverty and inequality, to what extent should there be engagement with existing international institutions? Is this engagement one aimed at reform of existing institutions or their abolition? This question – should we 'fix' or 'nix' the World Bank, WTO and IMF? –

---

[11] Collins et al. 2001.
[12] Bond 2002, pp. 24–5; Grenier 2003, p. 98.
[13] Pettifor 1998, pp. 119–20.

has been one frequently asked by campaigners since the Seattle protests of 1999.[14]

It is probably fair to say that answers would involve some recognition that the questions are posed too simplistically. For instance, contrary to some one-sided criticisms of debt relief,[15] there are plenty of examples of debt cancellation in history that did not have disastrous economic and social consequences.[16] The question of debt as symptom or cause is important, but the answer is that it is both of these. It is true that debt relief alone is not the simple answer that many of its advocates seem to think, but neither is it as irrelevant as critics claim. Perhaps most important, debt relief must be considered as part of a package of policies, which would include new sources of funding such as taxes on financial transactions and increased aid.[17]

Nevertheless, the campaign for debt relief does show the real dilemmas that exist for transnational civil-society campaigns. These relate to the relationship between specific campaigns and the wider totality; the question of solidarity across national borders and unequal material circumstances; and the issue of engagement with state and international institutions. Similar problems confront the issue of international trade-union solidarity and the campaign against sweat-shops.

8.3   International trade unionism and no sweat

This section examines the (limited) growth of international trade-union solidarity, through specific attention to anti-sweatshop campaigns. Again, while there is some focus on the development of specific campaigns, more attention is paid to the dilemmas faced in constructing solidarity. I will not address the question of the wider transformational power of organised labour in this chapter,[18] but some justification for addressing something as supposedly outmoded as organised labour is required.[19] As I briefly suggested in Chapters 5 and 6, arguments that we have witnessed the death of class confuse the

---

[14] George 2000; Bello 2002.
[15] Allen and Weinhold 2000.
[16] Hanlon 2000.
[17] Toussaint and Zacharie 2003.
[18] See Chapter 9.
[19] This claim is made for instance by Castells 1997, pp. 252–4, 354–5.

end of the corporatist consensus and some changes in employment structures with the end of the working class. In fact, measured in terms of absolute numbers, manufacturing employment levels remain high in the 'advanced' capitalist countries. In the case of the United States, the number of workers in industry increased from 20,698,000 in 1950, to 26,092,000 in 1971, to 31,071,000 in 1998. For the advanced countries as a whole, industrial employment stood at 112 million in 1998, which was 25 million more than in 1950. This was a decline from the figure of 119 million in 1971, but it hardly means the end of the industrial worker.[20] Moreover, many service jobs are closely linked to manufacturing and, even when they are not, they are often low-paid and insecure. Contrary to the fantasies of Third-Way apologists, the growth of secure, highly skilled, highly paid, IT-linked work has been slow and is likely to continue to be very slow. According to US Department of Labor Projections,[21] by 2010, IT-linked jobs will represent less than 2.4 per cent of total employment in the US economy, and, by this date, three out of five jobs will still require less than post-secondary school education. It also needs emphasising that not all of this 2.4 per cent fall into the category of highly paid, skilled workers.

There have been political defeats for organised labour over the last thirty years, not least reflected in declining trade-union numbers, but this relates to the question of politics. Moreover, the linkage of the Fordist (white, male) worker and trade unionism ignores the very real changes that have taken place among trade unions in recent years. The rapid decline in trade-union density has largely ceased, and, in some countries, membership is increasing. Even where decline has not been reversed, there has often been a renewal of older collective agreements and/or the development of new roles and forms of organisation. The former include an extension of the number of workers covered by collective agreements, while the latter include the monitoring of corporate practice, and monitoring of discriminatory practices in the workplace. This includes new practices that attempt to include previously marginalised workers, particularly women and migrant labourers.[22] The end of national corporatist practices within 'labour-friendly régimes' has not meant the end

---

[20] Feinstein 1999.
[21] US Department of Labor 2001.
[22] Harrod and O'Brien 2002.

of trade unions, but their ongoing transformation. This is reflected in the development of new radical, trade unions, such as the Italian Comitati di Base (COBAS), and even the partial transformation of existing unions and federations such as the AFL-CIO and International Confederation of Free Trade Unions.[23] This development of wider links to sectors beyond the organised working class – social-movement unionism – has also become a common practice in the developing world.

Part of this transformation is represented by attempts to internationalise trade-union operations. This practice is not new, and international trade-union federations were created after the Second World War. However, these were organised along Cold-War lines and were therefore particularly divisive.[24] Trade unions were largely committed to national organisation, which reflected the different but related national corporatist agreements that existed in the 'advanced' countries in the post-war world.[25] However, the restructuring of capitalism through neo-liberal policies, intensified competition, financial liberalisation, and the internationalisation of capital, have forced trade unions to adapt to new circumstances, and to more explicitly internationalise, and to change the form of that internationalisation. Such a rethink has also occurred as a response to the industrialisation of the 'periphery', parts of which have successfully exported goods into the domestic markets of the 'advanced' countries. Although the extraction of absolute surplus-value from workers is hardly new,[26] it has become more visible as a result of the growth of world-market factories and export-processing zones since the mid-1960s. The debate over these zones, which are predominantly (but not exclusively) located in the 'developing world', has intensified amidst fears that cheap labour is pricing workers out of jobs in the 'advanced' capitalist countries, an issue reinforced by the growth of trade agreements such as NAFTA.[27] More optimistically, 'no sweat' has become a major issue as there is a growing awareness that the rights of workers in one place affects those in another part of the world and brand loyalty means that the practice of companies comes

[23] Munck 2002, Chapter 7.
[24] Thompson 1977.
[25] Coates 2000.
[26] See Chapter 2.
[27] Moody 1997.

under closer scrutiny.[28] Alongside these developments has been the growth of campaigns against sweatshop production, particularly prominent in North-American universities and therefore independent of official trade-union structures.[29] How, then, do these developments relate to issues of cross-border, transnational solidarity? Three positions can be broadly identified, based on universal labour standards, endorsement of free trade and 'new' social unionism and internationalism.

(i) 'Universal' labour standards

In recent years, fearing a loss of jobs for North American workers as capital relocates to low-cost areas, the AFL-CIO has called for labour clauses in international trade agreements. The AFL-CIO's official protest at the WTO talks in Seattle in 1999 was based on this premise, as was the subsequent launch of the Campaign for Global Fairness. This campaign called for strengthened international solidarity between workers,[30] and rightly supports reform of international finance and criticises corporate practices. In this account, there is said to be a very real basis for labour solidarity, as a transnational bourgeoisie exploits a transnational proletariat, irrespective of particular location.[31] The implication is that the transnational proletariat should globalise in response to the globalisation of the transnational bourgeoisie. In practice, this means putting pressure on those international institutions that are said to represent the interests of transnational capital, such as the WTO. In this way, the protests at Seattle in late 1999 were an unambiguously progressive example of the globalisation of working-class resistance.[32]

However, there are good grounds for questioning this view. At Seattle, one motivation for US labour protest was the assumption that US workers would lose their jobs as a result of competition from cheap labour overseas, and for this reason the AFL-CIO opposed China's entry into the World Trade Organisation.[33] Even if we accept the argument concerning job loss for a

---

[28] Moody 1997; Klein 2000, Chapter 14.
[29] Ross 1997; Featherstone 2002; <www.usasnet.org>.
[30] AFL-CIO 2000.
[31] Robinson and Harris 2000, p. 23.
[32] For a critique, see Silver and Arrighi 2000.
[33] AFL-CIO 2000.

moment, it is clear that, in this case, global solidarity does not automatically follow – more likely is a xenophobic reaction in which foreigners are accused of 'stealing our jobs'.[34] Thus, Teamsters' Union President Jimmy Hoffa recently argued that China's entry into the WTO would cost 1 million American jobs as '[t]here's always somebody that will work cheaper. There's always some guy in a loincloth'.[35]

Similarly, in Britain in the 1980s, both the TUC and the Labour Party supported the expansion of quotas for cheap imports from poor countries like Bangladesh. In the US in the 1990s, the Union of Needletrades, Industrial and Textile Employees (UNITE) gave its support to the 'No Sweat' campaign against sweatshop labour. At a No Sweat conference in 1996, one of the leading theorists of the anti-globalisation movement, John Cavanagh[36] argued that American unions recognised 'that their own interests now lie in helping workers elsewhere. As long as sweatshops exist in El Salvador or Indonesia, US firms will use their ability to source production there to bargain down US wages and working conditions to sweatshop levels'. This argument claims to support universal global solidarity. Thus, on the one hand, workers in the First World would benefit from increased global standards, as these would increase the price of exports from the newly industrialising countries; and, on the other hand, workers in these countries would benefit from higher wages and better working conditions, and so employment would increase as a result of increased demand. However, it is more likely that rising costs in the export sectors would undermine profitability and thus reduce investment and growth. In this case then, making a claim for uniform standards would undermine employment in the developing world. For all its claims to be promoting global solidarity, such a strategy ultimately protects 'First-World' workers at the expense of 'Third-World' workers, thus undermining solidarity and – in the absence of wider social change – condemning the latter to even greater levels of poverty. The fact remains that, while high levels of exploitation exist in 'Third-World' sweatshops, these factories are often seen as desirable

---

[34] At conferences where I have challenged the notion of a race to the bottom, some anti-capitalist sympathisers have argued that it does not matter whether or not there is a race to the bottom so long as it mobilises people. The problem is that bad analysis leads to bad politics, and the rhetoric can mobilise people in ways that encourages xenophobia and worse.

[35] Cited Brecher et al. 2000, p. 54.

[36] Cavanagh 1997, p. 40.

places of employment, when the alternatives may be even worse. The claim made by UNITE researcher Elinor Spielberg[37] that young girls in Bangladesh prefer prostitution to factory work is entirely without foundation.

Such tensions are also apparent within the international trade-union movement. The International Confederation of Free Trade Unions (ICFTU)[38] has proposed social clauses in international trade agreements, while its national affiliates in the 'advanced' countries have generally adopted a 'progressive competitiveness' strategy at home (see below). This has led to accusations of protectionism, for similar reasons to those outlined above. Thus, at the Singapore Ministerial Meeting of the World Trade Organisation in 1996, the Third World Network (TWN) coalition of research institutes argued that the WTO was an institution dominated by the interests of Northern-based élites and so inappropriate as a protector of the interests of Southern-based labour. The ICFTU countered – with some representation from 'Third-World' trade unions – that an anti-social clause position played into the hands of corporate interests, who could take advantage of cheap labour or lack of environmental regulations. The debate – which is essentially the same as the one concerning garment workers discussed above – was largely unresolved as 'the ICFTU could not answer the TWN's criticism of the structural inequality of international economic institutions and the TWN could not advocate a concrete policy proposal to improve workers' rights'.[39]

In this case, then, universal labour standards can easily become protectionist as they ignore the fact that such standards would operate in highly differentiated contexts.[40] There is also a danger in this approach that the mobility of capital, rather than capital itself is blamed for the problems of restructuring – in fact, in the US, declining real wages are most marked in precisely those areas where foreign trade is least significant.[41] Protectionist strategies, including social clauses in trade agreements, thus lead to a narrow nationalism and address

---

[37] Spielberg 1997, p. 113. See Kabeer 2000, pp. 282–3.

[38] A full history of the ICFTU lies outside the scope of this paper. Its origins lie in the Cold War and the split from the World Federation of Trade Unions in 1948. With the collapse of Communism, the WFTU's influence has declined even further from an already low point.

[39] O'Brien 2000, p. 549.

[40] Indeed, a major reason for the collapse of the WTO talks at Seattle in 1999 was over Bill Clinton's 'conversion' to labour clauses in trade agreements.

[41] Gordon 1996, p. 191.

the symptoms (capital mobility) of falling standards rather than the causes (capital restructuring). It most certainly does not automatically pave the way for greater global solidarity.[42]

(ii) *Free trade, 'progressive competitiveness' and global civil society*

For these reasons, neo-liberals and others advocate a system of global free trade. The argument is essentially that participation in open world markets is the most fruitful way forward for developing countries, as this will lead to economic growth, and, in the long run, an improvement in living standards – including, presumably, wages and work conditions. This argument has been advocated by, among others, the World Bank, the World Trade Organisation and Sachs and Warner. But it has also been advocated by 'Third-Way' thinkers such as John Lloyd, and has even been given a Marxist gloss by Meghnad Desai.[43] The argument made is that an open economy will benefit the developing world, as capital will move there to take advantage of low labour costs. Similarly, the Third-Way strategy of progressive competitiveness sees capital and labour as embarking on a social partnership to protect 'their' company and 'their' jobs. 'First-World' competitiveness is maintained by the development of high-skilled, high-value work, which is more competitive than cheaper labour elsewhere.[44] However, as we have seen, the global economy – and global 'free trade' – does not tend to equilibrium. Uneven development is the norm, and it is a product of the normal workings of capitalist competition. This is reflected in the concentration of capital in the world, which has been reinforced by the movement toward global free trade. Seen in this light, global free trade itself can be regarded as a form of protectionism, as it favours stronger producers in an unequal competitive environment. It is, therefore, hardly conducive to the promotion of labour solidarity across borders. This is not to deny that there may be selective cases for the opening up of Western markets to foreign competition – such as in clothing and agriculture – but a blanket 'free-trade' approach abstracts from very different, and unequal,

---

[42] Silver 2003, pp. 8–12, 177–9.
[43] See World Bank 1995, WTO 1998, Sachs and Warner 1997, Lloyd 2001, Desai 2000. Detailed critiques can be found in Weeks 2001b and Kiely 2002a.
[44] Mandelson and Liddle 1996, pp. 96–8.

structures of production in the world economy.[45] It is unlikely to favour sustained economic growth and, even if economic growth was to occur, without sustained pressure on capital it is unlikely to trickle down to the workforce. Instead, a vicious cycle of low wages and poor conditions will coincide with high profits in labour-intensive sectors – precisely those sectors in which the developing world does have an advantage in terms of costs. Moreover, in rejecting labour-standards as unnecessarily interventionist, this view closely mirrors that of Victorian factory owners who opposed the abolition of child labour in nineteenth-century Britain. A passing familiarity with the history of nineteenth-century Britain and the 'living standards debate' demonstrates that social advances (or 'trickle down') did not occur simply as a by-product of economic growth, but were actively *fought for* by those who would not otherwise have benefited from such growth.[46] Thus, advocacy of both universal labour standards and universal free trade abstract from global uneven and unequal development, and thus ignore the fact that 'the equal application of abstract rules in unequal situations can lead to unfair outcomes'.[47]

(iii) *Global solidarity through nation-states*

Anti-globalisation movements and their allies in anti-sweatshop campaigns are far from unaware of these difficulties, and there is strong evidence of a move away from the blanket protectionism discussed above. For example, one prominent US activist, David Bacon[48] opposes universal labour rights and blanket bans on child labour products. The clear implication is that solidarity is best constructed not through trade agreements or free trade, but instead through concrete, grassroots support for the expansion of workers' rights. These dilemmas suggest that, for genuine anti-sweatshop alliances to occur there is an obvious need to support independent trade unions in the 'Third World', and for closer direct interaction between trade unionists and wider social movements, both within and between countries.[49] Among

---

[45] Kiely 2002c.
[46] Hobsbawm 1968.
[47] Massey 2000, p. 23.
[48] Bacon 2000.
[49] Moody 1997; Klein 2000, pp. 439–46.

organised labour movements, there *has* been some grassroots solidarity in recent years, such as direct links between American, Canadian and Mexican workers both before and after the establishment of the North-American Free Trade Agreement.[50] These links, although limited and sometimes contradictory, represented a challenge to the broadly national protectionist orientation of corporatist trade unionism. Global, as opposed to regional, links have also been made between workers, such as support for the Liverpool dockers locked out and dismissed from their jobs in 1995, for Australian dockers in 1998, and for imprisoned South Korean workers in 2000, who were eventually released.[51] Links have also been made to wider social movements, a strategy influenced both by 'Third-World' trade unions and dialogue with anti-capitalist organisations.[52] One important outcome of the Singapore debate was that the ICFTU became more critical of the WTO. At the 1999 WTO Symposia on Trade and Development and Trade and Environment, it broadened its agenda to incorporate issues around wider social and environmental clauses, and thus recognised the need to build alliances beyond the immediate interests of organised labour. These grassroots movements are important as they show that some sections of organised labour have moved beyond narrowly based corporatist trade-union concerns, and are prepared to challenge the hierarchy and bureaucracy of official trade unionism.[53] Social movement unionism is therefore concerned with issues around structural adjustment, capital flight, political reform, debt relief, as much as immediate wage demands, for the simple reason that these cannot be easily separated from the practice of sweatshop labour. For example, the Canadian Labor Congress has called for a large increase in aid and supported the Jubilee campaign for widespread debt reduction,[54] a clear recognition that campaigns for progressive global reforms usually have to go beyond single issue campaigns.

Global solidarity has also in part been facilitated by the use of the internet, an organising mechanism used to great effect by wider 'anti-capitalist'

---

[50] Moody 1997, pp. 253–4.
[51] Hodkinson 2000, pp. 9–10.
[52] On 'social-movement unionism' in the South, see Munck 1988 and Moody 1997.
[53] Trade-union presence remains uneven, however. For instance, there was only limited representation of trade unions at the World Social Forum at Porto Alegre, Brazil, in January 2001.
[54] Robinson 2002.

movements.[55] Clearly, the idea of using 'networks from below' in order to challenge the dominant interests in the 'network society' is an appealing one, and it is a major organising device within the anti-globalisation movement.[56] Anti-sweatshop movements have clearly used this forum to promote closer ties of solidarity with workers overseas, particularly in Indonesia.[57] While the net has been important in developing global solidarities, there remains some need for caution. Eric Lee's[58] assertion that the Web *'contributes by its very nature to internationalism and the ideals of global solidarity'* is overstating the case. It ignores the fact that workers globally (as opposed to regionally) are unlikely to make the movement from virtual to real proximity – at least not as often as the 'summit-stalkers' of the wider anti-capitalist movement. Moreover, the claim that the Web is intrinsically democratic downplays hierarchies, such as the predominance of the English language on union websites and unequal access to the net. It also avoids difficult questions around legitimacy and accountability.[59] Moody thus argues that, while important, net solidarity must be supplemented by 'creating a viable grassroots workers' internationalism [which] requires a grassroots workers' movement at each point of the chain. Workers' internationalism cannot operate like financial markets, with their "product" flying through global cyberspace. It is not enough to "stay in touch" through the Internet. There must be something of substance on the ground at each point'.[60] Clearly, then, the net alone cannot create crossborder solidarity and there is a need for appropriate practices within each 'chain' of the network.

This 'something of substance' implies the continued importance of struggles for progressive change within specific nation-states and localities – a position

---

[55] Klein 2001a.
[56] Smith and Smythe 2001; Scott and Street 2001.
[57] <www.usasnet.org>.
[58] Lee 1997, p. 39.
[59] This is a crucial issue for the wider anti-capitalist movement too. This does not mean that the WTO has any greater legitimacy as is sometimes claimed. These claims ignore issues such as loss of legitimacy in liberal democracies, lack of information concerning multilateral institutions, and above all, the fact that global democracy cannot exist in a world of such enormous inequality – and thus, related to this, the issue of whose interests are represented by both states and multilateral institutions. Nevertheless, while the anti-capitalist movement represents a progressive challenge to 'globalisation from above', it still lacks both democratic accountability and organisational effectiveness.
[60] Moody 1997, p. 267.

recently advocated by Naomi Klein in response to the limitations of 'summit stalking'.[61] Such local and national strategies are not, however, constructed in opposition to international or global solidarity – they are not intrinsically protectionist. For instance, the struggle for capital controls should be seen as part of a progressive global strategy, holding down 'unregulated' global capital flows that undermine both the bargaining power of labour, and the development capacity of the 'Third World'. Thus the free movement of capital disciplines 'First-World' labour through the threat of capital flight. In the 'Third World', capital flight is an endemic problem, which lack of controls intensifies, and inflows are often speculative and short-term (see Chapter 4). National capital controls among 'First-World' states need not be excessively nationalist, provided that they are used in part as a vehicle for the promotion of progressive aid and redistribution policies in the developing world. This policy could include trade with sectors where there is evidence of a 'levelling up' process among producers.[62] Thus, in the case of sweatshop workers, trade could be increased if there was evidence of improvements in wages or work conditions. Such a strategy is a long way from the blanket protectionism discussed above, but at the same time does not embrace a rhetorical internationalism. Again, we arrive back at the conclusion to Chapter 6, which is that social struggles do not necessarily embrace one of the local, national or global levels. Progressive trade-union politics that embraces global solidarity is simultaneously local, national and global, even if this means making strategic choices that emphasise one at the expense of others at particular points in time.

8.4   War and the anti-globalisation movement

The increasingly aggressive military and foreign policy stance of the US government and its allies since September 2001 has forced the anti-globalisation movement to more forcefully address the question of the nation-state, both generally and in relation to war. The assumption prior to September 11th was that global capital by-passed the nation-state from above, while the job of global resistance was to by-pass it from below. As we have seen, these

---

[61] Klein 2002.
[62] IFG 2002, pp. 18–20.

arguments under-estimated the ways in which states promoted globalisation.[63] Having said that, while there is clearly a need to recognise the continued importance of the nation-state, particularly the US state, I want to also suggest that it would be wrong to simply adopt an older, 'orthodox-Marxist' position, based on a one-sided anti-imperialism. Indeed, despite the best efforts of orthodox Marxists to welcome the potential development of a new, anti-imperialist politics,[64] I will suggest that this perspective *has failed to understand the distinctive, transnational and cosmopolitan politics of (parts of) the anti-globalisation movement.*

Cosmopolitan arguments espouse principles of respect for the rights of distant others, as part of an aspiration towards a cosmopolitan democracy.[65] Such a democracy is defined by Archibugi and Held as 'a model of political organization in which citizens, wherever they are located in the world, have a voice, input and political representation in international affairs, in parallel with and independently of their own governments'.[66] This model involves the advocacy, under specific circumstances, of interference with the 'sovereignty' of nation-states in order to protect human rights abuses – though, crucially, this would be in the framework of a clear set of rules that do not exist in the current international order.[67] This is in contrast to realist defences of state sovereignty and the Marxist argument that all forms of intervention constitute a form of Western imperialism. Giddens, in my view correctly, argues that the logic of this rejectionism is to do nothing, and 'the results of inaction were displayed in a horrific manner by the mass murders in Rwanda'.[68] He also rightly asserts that in our increasingly interconnected world, there is 'no such thing as non-intervention'.[69] In some interpretations, then, cosmopolitanism lends itself to support for liberal-humanitarian intervention, which may include the use of military force.[70]

To pass the test of humanitarian intervention, there are a number of conditions that must be met, which relate to means, ends and goals of

---

[63] See Rees 2001; Harman 2000; Kiely 2000.
[64] Reza 2003.
[65] Held 2002.
[66] Archibugi and Held 1995, p. 13.
[67] Archibugi 2002.
[68] Giddens 2000, p. 155.
[69] Giddens 2000, p. 156.
[70] Blair 1999; Hain 2002.

intervention. The most prominent advocate of cosmopolitan democracy, David Held, has argued that 'any defensible, justifiable and sustainable response to the 11th September must be consistent with our founding principles and the aspirations of international society for security, law, and the impartial administration of justice'.[71] Another prominent cosmopolitan thinker, Daniele Archibugi criticised the Afghan War on the grounds that 'a criminal act is not enough to justify the unleashing of brute force', and, in criticising the air strikes that inevitably killed innocent civilians, argued that 'what we need is democratic management of global events, not high-tech reprisals'.[72] These critical comments are far removed from the cosmopolitan principles supposedly championed by Tony Blair, and, indeed, there is a remarkable dishonesty about the regret caused by the deaths of civilians in such wars. The basic argument commonly made from 2001–4 by Blair and Bush was that these deaths were unfortunate accidents, and that what distinguishes these deaths from those caused by terrorists or dictators is that the latter deliberately cause deaths while the former see such deaths as unhappy mistakes. But such 'unfortunate accidents' are inevitable, particularly when cluster bombs are used by military forces. Moreover, this argument betrays circular reasoning, which essentially amounts to the 'argument' that 'we' have less cause to regret because we regret the deaths that take place.[73] Runciman thus argues that '[t]oo often, Blair takes restraint as evidence of good intentions, and good intentions as evidence of restraint. This is circular: you can tell we mean well from the fact that we didn't mean to kill those people; you can tell we didn't mean to kill those people from the fact that we mean well'.[74]

Moreover, given the selectivity and double standards involved in interventions, Marxist have generally argued that ideological justifications attempt to hide the real motives for war, which include inter-imperialist rivalries, competition for resources, and the exercise of dominant state power.[75] This theory of 'new imperialism' argues that the classical-Marxist analyses of imperialism associated with Lenin and Bukharin remain an indispensable

---

[71] Held 2001.
[72] Archibugi 2002, p. 37.
[73] In the case of both the Afghan and Iraq wars, there was no official attempt to count the numbers of victims.
[74] Runciman 2003, p. 8.
[75] Callinicos et al. 1994; Rees 2001; Reza 2003.

guide to understanding the current world order, and that, therefore, anti-globalisation politics must embrace an explicit anti-imperialist programme.[76]

There are, however, at least two reasons for questioning this approach. First, the pre-1914 imperialism included many colonies rather than sovereign states, and, second, there is a greater inter-dependence between capitals, particular among the core capitalist countries, as was outlined in Chapter 5. Many sovereign states are in a subordinate position in the international order, but they have their own set of interests, which are not reducible to the imperialism of the big powers. The argument that post-Cold-War conflicts are simply arenas in which imperialist rivalries were played ignores the local dynamics that led to these conflicts in the first place. Similarly, given the amount of co-operation between core states, it is difficult to argue that these wars were 'really' about inter-imperialist competition. What therefore stands out in this new imperialism analysis is the relative silence on the nature of Milosevic's régime, and the role of al-Qaeda in these conflicts – these simply become functional to the ambitions and rivalries of imperialist states. At its worst, this can lead to the crudest anti-imperialist politics. Thus, Chitty advocates 'a positive defence of the Taliban and Osama bin Laden, as the current representatives of Middle Eastern resistance to imperialist power, in their war against the USA and its proxies'.[77] Far less crudely, Harman warns against taking calls for national liberation at face value, as this can be an excuse to maintain oppression. But he then argues that we should distinguish between the nationalism of the oppressor and oppressed, and that 'anti-capitalists in the West cannot simply sit back and say all rulers are equally bad. We have to throw our main efforts into seeking to thwart the imperialist ambitions of the already powerful'.[78] It ignores the right of Kuwaiti self-determination in the face of the small-power imperialism of Iraq in 1991. Moreover, it implies support for weaker régimes against stronger ones – albeit, selectively, as Iraq is supported against the US, but Kuwait is not supported against Iraq. Such a perspective is as guilty of the double standards with which the 'West' is rightly condemned – Saddam Hussein is opposed when he has the support of the United States, but is supported when he is opposed by the United States. This is a purely reactive (and reactionary) anti-imperialism

---

[76] Callinicos 2003b, pp. 12–13; 2003c.
[77] Chitty 2002, p. 19.
[78] Harman 2003, p. 76.

based on the politics of 'my enemy's enemy is my friend'. It is also one that logically follows from the new imperialism thesis, which reduces the actions of 'small powers' to an irrelevance, a theatre in which the big powers play out their rivalries. But this argument effectively endorses a political imperialism that denounces any agency – progressive or reactionary – in the developing world.

This functionalist account of imperialism is generally accompanied by an instrumentalist account of international institutions. Baxter similarly argues that '[t]here is no possibility of creating a neutral force standing above the states of the world while those states are wedded to a system based on economic and military competition with one another'. In dismissing any hope for progress within the UN, he further argues that ruling classes 'don't turn into radical democrats when they walk through the doors of the General Assembly'. In fact, for Baxter, the UN 'was a tool designed by and for US imperialism', even if at times it is an irritation to the US ruling class.[79] Somewhat inconsistently, he then quotes UN resolutions condemning Israeli incursions into occupied Palestine, which clearly cannot be reduced to US imperialism. These have been ignored, which does show that the US has used the will of the UN and discarded it when it suits its interests, but to accept this argument is not the same as accepting the claim that the UN is simply a tool of imperialism, nor, indeed, that the world would be a better place without the UN.

These critical comments are not made to reject the reality of imperialism, US hegemony, or the continued division of the world into a hierarchy of states and capitals. Still less are they made to uncritically endorse liberal imperialism, or neo-liberal or indeed neoconservative cosmopolitanism. Indeed, neo-liberal capitalism under US hegemony is clearly a major cause of inequality, exploitation and oppression in the world order. But this is *not* a world of inter-imperialist rivalries and colonising powers in the sense of return to the pre-1914 era. The most convincing relevant Marxist account of imperialism is Kautsky's theory of ultra-imperialism, which recognises the possibility of co-operation between nation-states even as capitalist economic competition persists. Kautsky failed to adequately theorise the ways in which this co-operation could be led by a dominant state, and paid insufficient attention

---

[79] Baxter 2003, p. 268.

to the reality of uneven development in this ultra-imperialist order. Nevertheless, his theory is more relevant to understanding the current world order than those of either Lenin or Bukharin. What is equally clear is that, since 1945 at least, the US has not acted as a colonial power, but has attempted to secure its hegemony through allied sovereign states. Insofar as this relates to the 'capitalist market', it is based on the recognition that sovereign states represent an important means of regulating capital. US hegemony is thus exercised through state sovereignty, a strategy that carries all sorts of risks as dominant political actors in the developing world may at times challenge 'Americanism' within their own territories. These challenges have at times forced a variety of interventions based on the idea that what is good for the US state is also good for global capital, but which vary according to a number of political projects and policy proposals which cannot be reduced to the 'logic of imperialism'. Interventions have also taken place in contested areas of state formation where primitive accumulation has been particularly violent, factors which can be linked to the uneven development of capitalism and the relative marginalisation of some areas of the globe. Ironically, the neo-liberal agenda has intensified this marginalisation, in contrast to the 'unequal integration' associated with the colonial era. For all these reasons, post-1945 imperialism has been ultra-imperialist and led by the US state at one and the same time. Equally, the record of these military interventions – despite the rhetoric of promoting human rights and freedom – is poor.

Does this then leave us with an irresolvable problem, where we face a choice between the US as an unaccountable hegemon on the one hand and brutal dictatorships like Iraq on the other? More generally, do we face a choice of choosing a façade of global governance but a reality of US imperialism on the one hand, or ignoring human-rights abuses by dictatorships on the other? Genuine cosmopolitan politics is undoubtedly opposed to war. But, if we are to take the principle of global solidarity seriously, anti-war politics is a necessary but not sufficient condition. Shaw argues that '[f]aced with a bad and unnecessary war, it is not enough to be *against* the war. We must be *for* the victims, all of them'.[80] Halliday makes a similar point when he states that 'a focus solely on the workings and misworkings of US policy can too easily be seen as avoiding the issue of politically evaluating what forces within third

---

[80] Shaw 2002, p. 16.

world countries may be doing themselves and of how outside forces can relate to them'.[81] One can point to the *selective* nature of Western government condemnations, but much the same point can be made against Marxist 'anti-imperialists' who selectively condemn human-rights abuses by pro-Western régimes while largely ignoring (or apologising for) those by anti-Western governments.

The principle of global solidarity therefore means continuing, ongoing, solidarity with oppressed people in régimes, irrespective of whether these have the support of Western governments. This principle should not be 'put on hold' when the United States chooses to undertake an unjustified war. Solidarity must be indivisible, linked to oppressed peoples throughout the world, regardless of whether their government is supported or condemned by the United States or other Western powers. This is in contrast to the old anti-imperialist positions taken on Iraq by the Stop the War Coalition in Britain and ANSWER (Act Now to Stop War and End Racism) in the US. The formulation of solidarity with the Iraqi people on the eve of war should have gone beyond just a politics of no war, and included some strategies that undermined Saddam's régime. Some critics of the war in Iraq have suggested that such strategies could have included continued support for UN weapons inspectors, properly targeted sanctions (as opposed to the catastrophic sanctions that were imposed), human-rights inspectors, and – if necessary – safe havens in immediate humanitarian crises.[82] These, of course, also carry the risk of being imperialist and subject to the charge of double standards, and, in an imperfect world, these are very real dilemmas.[83] Having said that, there is a desperate need for the Left to recognise these dilemmas and move beyond political condemnation of *any* form of 'Western' intervention as imperialist.

What is being advocated here then is an 'anti-imperialist cosmopolitanism'. Some social movements within 'global civil society' have adopted such a perspective. This can be traced back to European disarmament movements towards the end of the Cold War,[84] and there are signs of a substantial developments since September 11th. Thus, the Revolutionary Association of

---

[81] Halliday 2002, p. 172. The original source of this quote is from a *Marxism Today* article published in 1991.
[82] Kaldor 2003b.
[83] Kiely 2005, Chapter 3.
[84] Kaldor 2003c, Chapter 5.

the Women of Afghanistan denounced the 2001 war while equally denouncing the attacks on the US, and al-Qaeda and the Taliban.[85] Organisations such as the Labour Party of Pakistan, the Worker Communist Parties of Iraq and Iran, and the Afghan Revolutionary Labour Organisation, among many others, condemned the US-led war, but equally condemned US enemies such as the Taliban, Saddam Hussein and the Iranian régime. This principle of anti-imperialism together with global solidarity has also come to characterise some of the politics of anti-globalisation movements and thinkers. In an article widely distributed within the anti-globalisation movement, George Caffentzis[86] argued that 'the priority of the anti-globalization movement is to offer an anti-war, anti-patriarchal alternative to the deadly politics of the fundamentalists and their globalizing adversaries'. At the World Social Forum II at Porto Alegre in early 2002, a joint statement was made by social movements, which stated that 'we absolutely condemn [the terrorist attacks], as we condemn all other attacks on civilians in other parts of the world'. The statement went on to 'emphasise the need for the democratisation of states and societies . . .', and that we are 'against war and militarism. . . . We choose to privilege negotiation and non-violent conflict resolution. We affirm the right of all the people to ask international mediation, with the participation [of] independent actors from the civil society'.[87]

These debates include the formulation of new positions based on global solidarity. This, in turn, means some dialogue with existing institutions of 'global governance'. The cosmopolitan perspective argues that global governance is contested and that progressives should support further democratisation within this contest. Classical Marxists tend to argue that this

---

[85] RAWA 2001a and 2001b.

[86] Caftentzis 2001.

[87] World Social Forum 2002. Halliday's (2002, p. 87) somewhat patronising dismissal of the protests at Seattle, which he contrasts with the 'hard headed' socialists of the twentieth century, needs to be seen in the light of these quotations. Unfortunately, too many socialists in that century were committed to support for one of the most repressive régimes the world has ever seen – either the Soviet Union or China. There was also support for all kinds of reactionary political forces within the developing world, including from Trotskyists otherwise critical of 'actually existing socialism'. Hard heads need to come to terms with this legacy, which is not as benign as Halliday implies – and is somewhat odd given his own break from crude anti-imperialist politics. Too-easy dismissals of anti-globalisation movements betray a lack of concrete analysis of the debates within the movements.

is too optimistic about the prospects for democratisation as it ignores the structured inequalities that pervade both the system of nation states and global civil society. However, institutions of global governance are highly unequal, often reflect powerful state and capital interests, but they are not *reducible* to the interests of such states and, like nation-states, are open to contestation. Some political and social arrangements – at the level of the nation-state[88] *and* in terms of global governance – are better than others. These, of course, have to be struggled for, but this should be through genuine global solidarity rather than *just* anti-imperialism. Indeed, given that a consistent and critical cosmopolitanism rules out unilateral enforcement, it can be used to *challenge* rather than reinforce imperialist rule. As Bartholomew and Breakspear suggest,

> why not consider developing norms of cosmopolitan law and justice viewed as part of a long term anti-imperialist struggle against American power and domination and in favour of addressing the problems of the UN, multilateralism and human rights, rather than relegating them to the 'dustbin of history' or side-stepping them . . .[89]

8.5 Conclusions: global solidarity, the nation-state and transnational civil society

This chapter has focused on three principal, closely related, questions faced by campaigns closely associated with global justice: the relationship between single-issue campaigns and wider social change; the issue of engagement with existing institutions, both nationally and internationally; and the question of constructing genuinely global solidarity. Issues of debt relief, labour standards and opposition to war are all clearly cosmopolitan issues requiring transnational solutions. Debt relief is related to the question of global poverty; labour standards to the issue of exploitation at work; and war to the issue of the

---

[88] Those crude Marxists that simply assert that global governance is simply capitalist governance neglect the different institutional forms that make up such governance and homogenise capitalism as though only one single form of capitalism can exist in the world economy. In this respect, they mirror the view of Stalinist dogma in the early 1930s, which argued that there were no differences between social democrats and fascists as both supported capitalism.

[89] Bartholomew and Breakspear 2003, p. 136.

hierarchical system of nation-states. But each of these issues then faces dilemmas (of strategy and principle) in terms of the relationship between the state and 'global civil society'. Debt-relief campaigns pressure nation-states, partly because states may be creditors but also because representatives of states dominate international institutions. Labour-solidarity campaigns that attempt to by-pass states through promoting international labour standards can actually have the effect of encouraging reactionary state policies, such as protectionist measures against lower-cost producers. Such campaigns therefore focus attention on local organising, pressurising nation-states to improve local contexts in poorer countries, as well as crossborder solidarity campaigns. Anti-war campaigns, particularly in pro-war 'advanced' capitalist countries, clearly demand a reversal of a policy of going to war against weaker states. But, equally, there are broader issues of solidarity with peoples against dictatorships, and so anti-war politics is slowly moving beyond straightforward anti-imperialism to focus on questions of cosmopolitan solidarity within 'global civil society'.

These broad comments return us once more to the question of spaces of resistance. First, it again needs to be stressed that there is nothing *intrinsically* more progressive about global civil society than say, politics centred on nation-states or localities below nation-states. Global civil society is hierarchical, contested and far-from-democratic, and it is not sufficient to simply appeal to global resistance to ensure progressive politics. There are important strategic questions about how to 'globalise' – thus, some trade unions point to pressures on international institutions such as the WTO, whereas Hardt and Negri prefer to completely by-pass established institutions, but both cases abstract from the uneven development of global capitalism and the unequal local contexts in which labour operates. Simplistic appeals to global labour or the transnational multitude evades these difficult political questions. Moreover, globalisation has not undermined the nation-state, and movements in global civil society are not inherently democratic or progressive. These points lead back to the positions outlined in Section 1, and the argument made by some critics that the main focus for progressive politics remains the nation-state.[90] There is certainly a danger that, in making overly generalised appeals to global civil society to by-pass the nation state, neo-liberal politics can result.

---

[90] Wood 1996; Halperin and Laxer 2003.

For instance, Kaldor[91] seeks to make the claim that multilateral states in the global order are precisely those that are most globalised – as measured by trade, investment, and so on. But this contention reduces globalisation to a policy choice to be made by states, and divides the world into more and less globalised states – an argument close to World Bank interpretations of globalisation criticised in Chapter 5. Indeed, as we have seen, anti-globalisation politics in the 'advanced' capitalist countries initially accepted the mainstream globalisation 'end of the nation-state' thesis and focused its protests on international institutions. It was, therefore, not surprising that Hardt and Negri's work, with its focus on the transnational multitude, had so much resonance within certain sections of the movement.

But, equally, it would be wrong to reject outright transnational solidarity, or the opportunities that exist to extend this principle in practice. As I argued above, there is much utility in mobilising peace movements against war and against dictatorship, in ways which in some (but certainly not all) respects transcend nation-states. But this is not the same thing as making a blanket call for by-passing state power in the name of global resistance. States do promote reactionary politics, but so too do global civil society actors. Opposing state policies around war is a progressive policy, but so too is pressure on nation-states to implement capital controls. Such controls can then help to finance more progressive policies, both national and international. Solidarity does not simply occur in the space of global civil society and outside of specific localities or nation-states.

This final point brings us back to the first two questions addressed in the chapter, and how these relate to the three case studies. Debt-relief campaigns can, in some respects, be seen as a classic example of a single-issue campaign. International debt for the poorer countries is a specific manifestation of the uneven development of the world economy over the last twenty–thirty years, and is not (contrary to anti-debt-relief arguments) simply a product of the individual irresponsibility of nation-states. But it is precisely because it is a symptom of this world economy that debt relief is not, on its own, sufficient. This leads to difficult strategic questions for debt-relief campaigns, such as how to engage with existing institutions of global governance and nation-

---

[91] Kaldor 2003c, p. 138.

states, and support for prioritising debt relief for certain countries. This leads to difficult dilemmas in promoting solidarity, but what is equally clear is that such campaigns are not only addressed to international institutions, but to particular nation-states. While debt relief is a global campaign, it is clearly not one that by-passes nation-states.

'No sweat' and international labour solidarity campaigns also face difficult strategic dilemmas. So-called universal standards ignore the different material circumstances faced by labour throughout the world, and they therefore easily become protectionist. On the other hand, unregulated capital flows tend to concentrate in the 'advanced' countries, and leave workers at the mercy of the worst employment practices when they are 'fortunate' enough to receive investment. Again, the question becomes one of relating specific agendas to wider issues, and of engaging with nation-states and international institutions. A 'global-first' strategy is meaningless, and there is a need to construct 'something of substance' at local and national levels. This something can then be linked to wider 'global' questions. Labour solidarity therefore also needs to deal with the question of particular nation-states. In terms of anti-war politics, the question of 'the totality' is particularly important. It is not sufficient to claim that 'the totality' is reducible to the actions of (Western) imperialist states, though, of course, this remains central, but there is also a need to focus on the nature of dictatorial régimes that should be consistently opposed. The question of global solidarity is therefore only partially addressed by 'anti-imperialist' movements. Thus, while there is a danger of anti-sweat campaigns being too global, and ignoring particular nation-states, the opposite problem arises for anti-war politics, namely focusing exclusively on one's own nation-state at the cost of constructing genuine global solidarity.

These issues in turn lead us back to the concerns around single issues and the wider totality. In practice, Marxists have traditionally attempted to move from single issues to the wider totality through the strategy of transitional demands.[92] These are demands that are made on the existing system, but which may not be achievable within such a system. They are therefore 'stepping stones' to an understanding of the system as a wider totality. It could be argued that, in changing specific parts of 'the system', the totality itself is in

---

[92] Trotsky 1973; Callinicos 2003.

many respects also changed. Nineteenth-century capitalism differs enormously from early twenty-first century capitalism for instance. Similarly, debt relief does not address the issue of global uneven development, but it could potentially free up some resources that could make a difference, no matter how small. Recognising the changing nature of capitalism (surely a major feature of 'the system') does not mean endorsement of capitalism, though it does mean recognising that some capitalisms are better than others.

Similar points can be made regarding engagement with nation-states and international institutions. Transitional demands imply recognition that some accommodation can be met within 'the system', and therefore some institutions at least provide some space for carrying out reforms. This would include debt relief or workers' rights, carried out by states and international institutions. But, if this is true, then a similar case could be made for strategies designed to alleviate or regulate the conduct of war. Transitional demands need to be made at this level too, and this does mean that pressure must be placed on nation-states and international institutions such as the United Nations. If concessions can be won at the level of the nation-state, then they can also be won at the 'level' of global governance. Indeed, this is one reason why global solidarity is so important. Of course such concessions are likely to be imperfect, contradictory, reversible, or even unachievable, but this is precisely why struggles to win and defend them occur. These issues are taken up further in the next chapter.

Chapter Nine

Anti-Globalisation and Progressive Politics: Capitalism, Socialism and Populism in the Twenty-First Century

This chapter more broadly examines the question of progressive politics in the age of globalisation. It examines three questions concerning the future of progressive politics: first, the progressiveness of capitalism; second, the question of alternatives *within* capitalism, and particularly alternatives to neo-liberalism; third, the question of agency and resistance to neo-liberal global capitalism. These issues are related to debates addressed by contemporary anti-globalisation movements, and they expand on themes examined in previous chapters. This chapter is, therefore, divided into three sections that correspond to these issues, and is completed by a fourth section that briefly examines the question of alternatives *to* capitalism. The first section addresses debates concerning the expansion of capitalism in the developing world, and whether this constitutes an advance for progressive politics. If this is the case, as some writers suggest, then the implication is that anti-globalisation politics constitutes nothing more than reactionary populism. My main argument in this section is that, first, neo-liberal expansion is not the same thing as the expansion of capitalism, and that anyway the progressiveness of capitalism cannot be 'measured' outside of the agents that promote and resist capitalist advance. The second section examines the question of alternatives within capitalism, focusing in particular on the prospects for and viability of a new era of 'managed capitalism' in which markets are more tightly controlled. The third section returns to the question of agency in the globalisation debate, focusing again on both those agents that have promoted contemporary 'globalisation from above' and re-examines the social and political forces that could transform 'globalisation from below', and therefore bring about radical and progressive change. This involves some re-examination of the role of the state, the working class, social movements and resistance in a globalised, individualised world. Finally, Section 4 concludes by drawing on the arguments of the previous sections and revisiting once again the question of progressive alternatives to both neo-liberal globalisation and capitalism.

9.1 The progressiveness of capitalism

Anti-globalisation movements are often accused of being both anti-capitalist and anti-economic growth. At their worst, movements are accused of advocating the construction of small-scale societies, which, in the name of a mythical 'community', will effectively share poverty. Anti-globalisation is thus the latest form of populism, and post-development theory represents its current theoretical justification.[1] The discussion in previous chapters showed that this criticism does apply to some localist tendencies within the movement, but not all of them. Moreover, it is far from clear that, in supporting financial hegemony and free trade in isolation from state-directed industrial policy, supporters of 'actually existing globalisation' themselves have the policies to support sustained economic expansion, at least compared to the so-called Golden Age from 1948–71. In this section, however, I want to instead focus on an earlier debate from within the Marxist tradition in development studies, which emphasised the progressive nature of capitalism when compared to previous modes of production. As discussed briefly in Chapter 2, the argument of 'linear Marxists' in the 1970s and 1980s was that capitalism was progressive compared to previous modes of production because it developed the productive

---

[1] Kitching 1982, 2001; Kiely 1998, Chapter 2.

forces, and created a class, the proletariat, that would (in the short term) improve living standards and (in the long term) overthrow capitalism.[2] This argument has become less influential over the last twenty years, as neo-liberal hegemony has undermined the dynamic nature of capitalism, which is reflected in lower growth rates and financial instability. Nevertheless, given the reaction of some on the Left to the rise of the anti-globalisation movement, it remains important.[3] For these 'linear Marxists', anti-globalisation entails either a reactionary withdrawal from global capitalism (what used to be called delinking),[4] or, at best, the development of a 'backward capitalism', which has all the worst features of capitalism (exploitation and poverty) without its progressive features (dynamism, higher living standards).[5] Indeed, some writers argue that there are considerable grounds for optimism in the current era of globalisation. Capitalism's tendency to uneven development was above all caused by the restrictive policies of nation-states, and, so, the increase in flows of capital beyond the control of states can potentially lead to the dispersal of capital throughout the world, and therefore a levelling up for the poorer parts of the world. When they are not romantic, anti-globalisation politics are, despite the intentions of protestors, designed to protect the privileges of comparatively rich workers in the First World.[6] In the era of contemporary globalisation, the transcendence of (state) borders means that capital at last takes on a cosmopolitan character and the less-developed countries reap the benefits of global capital flows and begin to catch up with the West.[7]

It is true that anti-globalisation politics can be both populist and protectionist. We have discussed in previous chapters the examples of localisation and protectionist trade unionism. But it is equally clear that the proponents of a new cosmopolitan capital are hopelessly wide of the mark. First, they tend to rigidly separate market and state in a way criticised throughout this book. But, even if we grant them this separation, the argument does not convince. For, essentially, they suggest that uneven development can now be alleviated because 'the market' will allocate resources in a more equitable and efficient

---

[2] Warren 1980.
[3] Halliday 2000; Kitching 2001.
[4] See Amin 1976. See also his slightly revised position in Amin 1997.
[5] See Lenin 1957. See also Mueller 1980 and Emmanuel 1982.
[6] Desai 2000.
[7] N. Harris 2003.

way than state-directed capitalism. Developing societies will, therefore, be in a position to take advantage of low costs and attract investment in order to compete in the world economy, at least provided that the First World reduces its protectionist policies. However, in the era of globalisation, inequalities have increased, growth has slowed down, and capital has tended to concentrate even further in established areas of accumulation. This is not only because of the role of the state, but because new capital investment tends to be attracted to existing areas of capital accumulation. Insofar as we can talk about 'market forces' in isolation from the state, these too tend towards uneven development based on the concentration of capital. If this is the case, then we also have to recognise that the movement towards free trade (including in financial services) represents, above all, the interests of already powerful capitalists, who tend not to invest in capital-scarce areas. Indeed, seen in this light, the double standards of Western countries ('free trade for them, protectionism for us') is hardly surprising, as the concept of 'the market' abstracts from the social and political relations that underpin market transactions. There are, of course, some examples of ongoing capitalist development in the world order – the current high growth rates in China and India, and in an earlier era, the rise of South Korea, Taiwan, Hong Kong and Singapore. But none of these can be regarded as examples of development led by 'market forces'; like earlier 'developers', the role of the state was central to capitalist development.[8] As a result of adjustment conditionalities and WTO rules, earlier 'spaces' for development are being increasingly undermined in the era of neo-liberal globalisation.[9] The opportunities identified by the theorists of cosmopolitan capital are, in fact, constraints, and thus their approach is indistinguishable from that of the World Bank and suffers from the same weaknesses.

The theory of cosmopolitan capital is essentially a theory that attempts to update Marx's argument that capitalism was a necessary stage for societies to pass through on the way to socialism.[10] Whether or not he equated society and nation-state is an interesting point, and perversely, in this respect, it is the cosmopolitans who appear to be guilty of nation-state fetishism. But what

---

[8] Chang 2002.
[9] Wade 2003b.
[10] See Chapter 2.

is more interesting is the notion that the capitalist development of the productive forces is a necessarily progressive stage before a later transition to communism. This argument repeats the claims made by Bill Warren in the 1970s, and, in many respects, Desai, Kitching and Harris see themselves as updating Warren's work for the contemporary era. Whether Warren's optimism concerning the progressiveness of capitalism could be applied to the neo-liberal era, as opposed to the post-war era of high rates of growth, is questionable, and careful consideration of the empirical record in sub-Saharan Africa by one Warrenite, suggests that it is not.[11] The Warrenite position concerning capitalism's progressive role should not therefore be confused with any notion that neo-liberalism is progressive, or, indeed, conducive to the sustained accumulation of (productive) capital. Warren himself was acutely aware of the failings of some developmental states, but equally aware that successful capitalist development rested on the need for a strong and 'interventionist' state, not least so that capital itself could be disciplined to invest in production rather than divert (and export) into speculative ventures.

Having said that, some further points concerning capitalism's progressive role is necessary, as Warren's position also has its problems, which relate to the question of the productive forces and the need for further economic growth. First, there is some resemblance between Plekhanov's regret that the Russian working class were revolting in 1917 when the 'objective conditions' were not yet ripe for socialism,[12] and the regret that current populist movements have arisen that constitute a threat to the need for further economic growth and 'progress'. Waiting for the 'right' amount of economic growth before making other efforts to alleviate the human condition does reek of old-fashioned historical inevitability, excessive determinism and the revival of Menshevism. Indeed, it needs pointing out that, while economic growth may be an important condition for improving the human condition, it is certainly not sufficient, an obvious point in these 'environmentally-friendly times'. This point is also made not only to advocate a predictable 'economic growth plus safety net and/or redistribution' development strategy (though this is important), but to suggest that, even in conditions of dire poverty, some

---

[11] Sender 1999.
[12] Thus, on his death-bed, Plekhanov asked his friend Leo Deutsch, 'Did we not start the Marxist propaganda too soon, in this backward, semi-Asiatic country?' (cited Löwy 1981, p. 34).

progressive social change is possible – a point accepted by Kitching.[13] Such policies may need 'modern' institutions such as the state to implement them, but without concerted pressure from social movements, these are unlikely to be carried out.

It may be that I have caricatured the arguments of linear Marxists, and that they do indeed recognise the need for pressure from below for progressive social change. For instance, Sender and Smith argue that there is a need for strengthening of progressive class forces, and that, instead of casually blaming foreign capital for a country's problems, there is a need to address more concrete issues of trade-union rights, working conditions, and so on.[14] It should be clear that there is indeed a need for concrete improvements in these areas, and that foreign capital should not be blamed for all the problems a country faces (though this is not to deny the lack of democracy in international institutions or the fact that developing countries are 'unequally integrated' into the world economy). But the focus on trade unionism leads to a further problem, as it is the organised working class that is seen as the progressive class in history, and progressive politics exclusively focuses on their needs. However, progressive politics based solely on expanding trade-union rights seems particularly restrictive in an era when employment in the easier to organise formal sector and trade-union membership have fallen in many countries, or continue to relate to a small minority of the work-force. Indeed, in developing a strategy of social-movement unionism, many trade unions have themselves recognised this fact and have attempted to make alliances with other labouring groups who, presumably for linear Marxists, do not represent 'progress'.[15]

Moreover, even the development of trade unionism is restricted in this approach, above all by the necessity of the construction of a developmental state. The rejection of the neo-liberalism of the theories of cosmopolitan capital is replaced in Warrenism by the placing of great faith in the adoption of a state-directed capitalism as the main agent of 'progress'.[16] Given its dismissal of populist anti-capitalism (including contemporary anti-globalisation movements), it is ironic that this argument is not so far removed from the

---

[13] Kitching 2001, pp. 141–2; see also Sen 1999, Chapter 1.
[14] Sender and Smith 1986. See also Warren 1980.
[15] Waterman 2001.
[16] Sender and Smith 1986, p. 112; Sender 1999, 2002.

global reformism of Walden Bello, which argues that nation-states need some autonomy from pro-free-market institutions in order to promote development. But this approach, at least in the form advocated by linear Marxists, separates the state from wider social relations, and therefore fetishises the state as a purely technical instrument. Bello, on the other hand, does see some role for social movements in making development more 'people-friendly' – for his critics, a classically populist statement, but, given the commitment of the Warrenites to trade unionism, there is presumably some room too in the latters' approach for working-class controls on the developmental state.[17] Nevertheless, the market fetishism of theories of cosmopolitan capital is replaced by the state fetishism of linear Marxism, in which the productive forces are developed by capitalism guided by a developmental state, and in which the 'non-progressive' classes are regarded as fodder in the onward march of 'progress'. Moreover, the focus on the need to strengthen working-class institutions does not comfortably coincide with a linear Marxism that champions the development of a strong state committed above all else to developing the productive forces, for developmental states have tended to justify repression of the former in the name of the primacy of the latter.

Linear Marxists reject the argument that socialism is a possibility in 'backward' societies, and so suggest that (state-directed) capitalism is the best means of developing the productive forces, and therefore a bridge to socialism.[18] But this argument tends to assume that there is a 'normal' form of capitalist development, and that politics is simply about the technical search for repeating that norm. It also exaggerates both the desirability of 'advanced' capitalism and the ways in which it supposedly acts as a bridge to socialism – much (though clearly not all) of the productive forces developed would be inappropriate in a democratic socialist society, as this includes for example the over-production of arms, cars and environmentally harmful products.[19] It is possible to employ a radical critique of exploitation, alienation, rationalisation in capitalist society without then romanticising the poverty of the developing world.[20] Indeed, it is a strangely one-sided Marxist position

---

[17] Bello 2002, p. 117.
[18] Sender and Smith 1990, p. 132.
[19] Sutcliffe 1992, 1999.
[20] This point applies to the critical sociology of Durkheim and especially Weber, as well as to Marx. It could also be applied to cultural critiques of capitalism, such as that associated with the Frankfurt school. See also Sections 3 and 4 below.

that calls for 'more capitalism' in the developing world (a call which again suggests an implicit norm) but seems blind to its downside. This is all the more true in an era in which financial capital is so powerful.[21] Finally, and perhaps most important, it must be stressed that the progressiveness of capitalism is inseparable from acts of resistance to its worst effects. That is, capitalism's progressive nature – its tendency to develop the productive forces – does not inevitably follow from the development of capitalism, but is part of a movement from the extraction of absolute to relative surplus-value, which, in turn is, to some extent, the product of class struggles. The progressiveness of capitalism is therefore not only a product of economic growth *per se*, but of acts of resistance which have particular progressive effects, of which economic growth, with all its contradictions, is one. Reducing capitalism to a model in which politics becomes a search for ahistorical causal factors, reads history backwards and downplays the importance of resistance. We therefore need to distinguish between the progressiveness of capitalism *in the abstract,* and the progressiveness nature of *specific forms of capitalism,* which in turn is linked to the question of resistance. In the next three sections, then, we need to examine the issues of *different capitalisms/alternatives within capitalism, agency and globalisation,* and *socialism/alternatives to capitalism.*

9.2   Alternatives within capitalism

Section 1 argued that debates concerning the progressive nature of capitalism as a mode of production suffered from two weaknesses. First, in the case of cosmopolitan capital, the progressiveness of capitalism was confused with the expansion of neo-liberalism, the latter of which undermined the former. Second, the argument for the progressiveness of capitalism tended towards over-generalisation, and paid insufficient attention to specific forms of capitalism, even when state-directed capitalism was proposed as a progressive alternative to neo-liberalism. This section expands on these criticisms, and focuses on the question of progressive, capitalist alternatives to neo-liberalism.

There are three alleged social-democratic alternatives to neo-liberalism. The first of these, the Third Way, has been discussed in detail in earlier chapters

---

[21] Indeed, one could argue that Warren's work may have had some (though not much) validity in the 'Fordist' era, but is less relevant today.

and so we can be brief. This perspective argues that globalisation is an external force that has changed the context of domestic policy-making, so that it is now imperative that market-friendly policies are adopted by progressive political parties. This involves state intervention to promote skills for labour markets, alongside openness to foreign investment and trade. The argument is that such policies are inevitable, but a leap is then made which assumes that they are also desirable, and that, provided market imperfections are corrected, the expansion of global market transactions is desirable for all. In this respect, the Third Way does not represent a progressive alternative to neo-liberalism, but rather an extension of its principles. Moreover, as we have seen, this has involved a considerable retreat from the uneven and unequal, but still very real, advances of the Golden Age. But this does not quite deal with the question of inevitability, because it may be possible to accept the 'globalisation as constraint' argument without necessarily accepting that such policies will have desirable outcomes. Are we then stuck with a globalisation that does not deliver the goods for all on the one hand, and no hope of progressive (local, national or global) alternatives on the other? We therefore need to examine in more detail the other two social-democratic alternatives: the second alternative to neo-liberalism focuses on the nation-state, and the third focuses on international institutions and 'global reform'.

The 'national alternatives' position essentially argues that alternatives to neo-liberalism remain viable and that, in many respects, they remain a reality. In this account, the state is contrasted with the market, and it is either argued that the latter may still 'select' statist models, or that, in a world of limited capital mobility, the former still has considerable power over the latter.[22] Garrett's position essentially accepts much of the arguments concerning the hyper-mobility of capital,[23] but draws a different conclusion from neo-liberals and Third-Way thinkers, namely that capital may 'select' corporatist models and invest in nations with social-democratic régimes such as Sweden. Hirst and Thompson on the other hand, take a sceptical position in the globalisation debate, arguing that limited capital mobility means that nation-states maintain considerable room for manoeuvre and so can both attract and discipline capital for socially progressive ends. A similar argument is made by Hutton,[24]

---

[22] Garrett 1998; Hirst and Thompson 1999.
[23] These are briefly discussed in Chapter 2.
[24] Hutton 1995, 2002.

who supports the reconstruction of a stakeholder capitalism against the neo-liberal shareholder capitalism that dominates in the United States and Britain. Weiss argues for the relevance of these arguments to the developing world, suggesting that there are lessons to be learnt from the state-guided capitalist development in East Asia, at least prior to the financial crisis of 1997–8.[25] In these arguments then, there is a call for a 'return' to the labour- and development-friendly régimes that characterised the period from 1948–71, with increased social protection for labour in the 'First World', and increased space for development in the former 'Third World'. This would involve a rolling back of the power of 'the market', and therefore increased (but selected) state protection to industries, particularly in the developing world, and to labour markets, particularly in the First World. In both cases, there would also be an increase in controls in financial markets, and, therefore, an expansion in socially useful, productive investment. Indeed, it could be argued that these approaches champion the need for a diversity of capitalist models in the world today (although each would be more socially desirable than neo-liberalism), and that space for these alternative models would be opened up by increased controls on financial capital. The Marxist class struggle between capital and labour is, therefore, replaced by a neo-Keynesian struggle between (reactionary) financial and (progressive) industrial capital.

In practice, this position, which focuses on the nation-state, is not incompatible with the idea that these reforms would be backed up by reform of international institutions, which is essentially the third social-democratic position. This may involve more international agreements to implement taxes on financial speculation, a co-ordinated movement towards international capital controls, agreements that offer more generous protection to producers in developing countries, as well as more basic immediate reforms such as debt relief and increased aid flows with less conditionalities attached. Such measures are frequently advocated by leading thinkers in the anti-globalisation movement.[26]

One of the most interesting detailed set of proposals concerning global reform has come from the prominent British activist, George Monbiot.[27] He

---

[25] Weiss 1998. See also Amsden 1989; Wade 1990.
[26] George 2001; Bello 2002; ATTAC 2003.
[27] Monbiot 2003.

argues for restructuring based on the decommissioning of the World Bank and IMF and the promotion of a new International Clearing Union (ICU), and a system of international trade that would level the playing field between different producers. His proposed ICU represents a return to Keynes, and a more fundamental restructuring of the global economy than that entailed by the introduction of capital controls and the Tobin tax. As we saw in Chapter 3, Keynes envisaged a set of mechanisms that would guarantee long-term trade balances across the globe. Following Keynes, Monbiot argues that there is a need to change the relationship between creditors and debtors, or surplus and deficit countries.[28] In particular, what is needed is an incentive for surplus countries to spend their surplus money in debtor economies. For Keynes, this would occur through an International Clearing Union, and its currency, the bancor. The bancor would be exchangeable with national currencies at fixed rates of exchange. In other words, the bancor could fulfil the function of measuring a country's deficit and surplus. In this system, every country would have an overdraft facility in its bancor account, which would be equivalent to half the average of its trade over the last five years. Deficit countries that went too far into deficit (that is, using more than half its overdraft allowance) would be charged interest, which would increase with the size of the overdraft. They would also be obliged to reduce the value of their currency and prevent capital export. So far, this scenario is not so different from that envisaged by the IMF, which places the burden of trade imbalances firmly on the debtor country. However, Keynes envisaged a system whereby surplus countries (creditors) also had responsibilities. If they had a credit balance of more than half the size of their overdraft facility, they would be charged interest on that account, and would have to increase the value of their currency and allow capital export. If, at the end of a financial year, the credit balance exceeded the value of its permitted overdraft, the surplus would be placed in the ICU's Reserve Fund. The result for the surplus country would be that exports would become more expensive, as currencies appreciated, and imports would cheapen for similar reasons. In this way, credits and debts would clear. The rationale for these proposals is clearly explained by Monbiot:

---

[28] Monbiot 2003, pp. 165–71.

> A Clearing Union releases weak nations from the deficit trap, in which they must seek to produce an ever greater volume of exports in the hope of generating a sustained trade surplus, even while other, more powerful nations are trying to do the same. It ensures that demand for their exports is mobilized when it is most needed, and that nations are obliged to cooperate. Instead of seeking to beggar each other by simultaneously pursuing a trade surplus, those nations in surplus will, if the mechanism works, voluntarily go into deficit, just as the deficit nations need to go into surplus.[29]

In this approach, the burden of adjustment is shared by creditor and debtor, rather than just the latter. The severe conditions on debtors that arise from the current régime are thereby reduced, along with an international game of competitive austerity. Of course, this does not completely deal with the question of uneven development. Rather, it attempts to deal with the question of the *balance* of trade between nations. Crucially, it does not deal with the question of the *conditions* under which nations trade with each other. Monbiot therefore argues that there needs to be important changes in this respect as well. Indeed, these changes must precede the formation of an International Clearing Union as there first needs to be a period of 'catch-up' by the poorer countries. For Monbiot, this can be facilitated by a system of discrimination *in favour of* the poorer countries – as opposed to the current system that discriminates *against* these countries. These include tariff barriers for selected economic sectors, strict conditions on foreign investors, and exemptions from intellectual property rights – the very conditions which allowed for the development of the 'First World'. At the same time, rich nations would be required to end their trade restrictions, particularly those that discriminated against the developing world.

A less radical version of global social democracy is advocated by David Held who, as we have seen, is the leading advocate of cosmopolitan democracy. In terms of a global alternative economic programme, Held advocates the need for a basic income for all, increased social control over companies, investment and the movement of capital.[30] Unlike Monbiot, Held's proposals are intended to go 'with the grain' of capitalism, and include the setting of low rates of interest and the creation of more public institutions to encourage

---

[29] Monbiot 2003, p. 171.
[30] Held 1995, Chapter 11.

investment in marginalised areas, alongside an increase in corporation taxes, democratic control of pension funds and the creation of new worker-led investments.[31] These proposals are explicitly linked to the argument briefly discussed above, namely that there is a diversity of models of capitalism, and that neo-liberalism should be rejected.[32]

These social-democratic, corporatist alternatives to neo-liberal capitalism are important. They all quite correctly reject the crude globalisation thesis associated with the Blair-Clinton Third Way, which suggests that, in the face of capital mobility, there is no alternative, and that states must simply respond to these forces of global mobility. Indeed, globalisation has not led to a clear and unambiguous convergence, certainly in terms of outcomes,[33] but also, to an extent, in terms of policy. For example, comparison of the welfare states of European countries in the 1980s and 1990s shows considerable divergence in terms of spending and payments.[34] Hirst and Thompson's argument concerning the continued power of the nation-state therefore remains relevant. But there are also some awkward questions for social democrats, both for those that focus on the continued resilience of the nation-state, and for those that attempt to construct a cosmopolitan social democracy. The first point is that, while convergence may not have occurred, there are still some important similarities across nation-states. Indeed, statist models have come under increasing pressure in recent years, with recession, unemployment, stagnant wages and/or financial crisis in Japan, Sweden, Germany and East Asia,[35] and the growing neo-liberalisation of state policies in these countries. These changes have not been caused by globalisation *per se*, as if this was some driving force beyond human control, but rather they reflect the restructuring of capitalism along neo-liberal lines. While they are correct to question the notion that globalisation has *caused* significant social, political and economic change, Hirst and Thompson are less convincing in their argument that very little has changed in the era of globalisation.[36] As I outlined in the first section of the book, a lot has changed, and this can be broadly described as a movement

---

[31] Held 1995, pp. 258–66.
[32] Held 1995, p. 249.
[33] See Chapter 5.
[34] Hay 2003.
[35] Coates 2000, pp. 234–44.
[36] Hirst and Thompson 1996, pp. 15–17.

towards neo-liberal globalisation. In fairness, Hirst and Thompson do accept that some changes have occurred, and correctly argue that these are not external to nation-states, but in part carried out by them. They then draw the conclusion that states can reverse processes of (neo-liberal) globalisation and restore a 'distributional coalition' through the construction of a 'social consensus'.[37] This may be a possibility, but it does beg the question of why so many states have carried out neo-liberal policies in the first place – some with more vigour and enthusiasm than others maybe, but there remains a common pattern. One possible explanation is that neo-liberal tendencies are dominant in capitalist societies, at least when they reach a certain stage of development. Corporatist models of capitalism based on close links between state, industry and finance may be subject to enormous pressures, as firms press for independence from banks and states, preferring to choose between a number of financial investors, which offers better rates of return and dispersal of risks as opposed to national savings.[38] This point relates not to the alleged spatial mobility of capital, but to capital's specific functions.[39] As Grahl argues,

> [i]t remains the case that shareholder value is not – or not only – an ideology, but a real consequence of financial globalization. It represents a new balance of forces between proprietors and managers, very much in favour of the former. And it is driven not only by the as yet very limited cross-border market in equities, but also by the global transformation of currency and debt markets in ways which universalize these pressures, even in economies where equity itself is traded predominantly among domestic agents. The visible effect is to reinforce, in the most powerful way, the familiar drive towards more complete and immediate market disciplines in other areas, in labour and output markets. Trade liberalization or labour market 'flexibilization' alone would only sharpen pressure on *some* product markets, some categories of labour and so on. The shareholder-value drive, in contrast, tends to eliminate the notion of a sheltered sector by imposing the same norms of cost, price and profit as prevail elsewhere.[40]

[37] Hirst and Thompson 1996, p. 146.
[38] Grahl 2001; Smith 2003, pp. 16–17.
[39] Watson 1999.
[40] Grahl 2001, pp. 40–1.

Seen in this light, a progressive strategy that seeks to support industrial capital at the expense of financial capital is problematic at best. Indeed, given the rise of significant financial departments within major industrial firms, some might suggest that the strategy is doomed to failure. At the very least, this discussion suggests that a strategy that supports a revived national corporatism against neo-liberal globalisation must provide a better theoretical account of the 'laws of motion' of global capitalism and the role of the nation-state. Thus, Held's argument that public investment should be encouraged to invest in marginalised areas implies that socially useful investment can 'trump' the tendency of capital to invest in already established areas, and therefore alleviate the tendency to promote uneven development. Similarly, the economic proposals put forward in Monbiot's work can be seen as an attempt to alleviate this problem. His proposals represent a call for the renewal of an international Keynesianism, enforced by global institutions committed to the principles of cosmopolitan social democracy. This is not the first time that such calls have been made since the Bretton Woods agreement.

Indeed, some of Monbiot's proposals are not so far removed from the call in the 1970s for a new international economic order (NIEO), and in milder form, the proposals of the Brandt Reports of 1980 and 1983. The NIEO argued for a redistribution of wealth from rich to poor countries through a variety of mechanisms. Above all, it proposed a system of price guarantees for the products exported from the developing world to the 'First' World. These guarantees could take the form of fixed prices, or a price compensation scheme if there were significant falls in international prices for specific commodities. In addition, the NIEO called for more investment in the developing world, but also more national control over this investment. Similarly, there was a call for more aid with less conditionalities. In the Brandt Reports,[41] these arguments were said to be good not only for the poorer countries, but for the richer ones too, as economic growth and poverty reduction in the poorer countries would mean an expanded market for the products of the richer countries. This emphasis on mutuality exists to this day in the rhetoric of most politicians in the richer countries, even though in most cases aid budgets fall well short of UN recommendations and more attention is paid to lifting

---

[41] Brandt 1980, 1983.

countries out of poverty through market-led growth rather than international redistribution alongside growth. But even leaving aside the fact that the NIEO and Brandt have largely been by-passed by a movement towards neo-liberalism, there are further problems with these proposals. It is not only that they have not been carried out, it is also that, *in terms of issues of power rather than justice*, there are good reasons why they have not been implemented. These proposals assume that capital from different countries will simply meet the burden of redistribution in a voluntary and co-operative way. It may indeed be rational from the viewpoint of the system as a whole for redistribution to occur, but each individual capital (or nation-state) is unlikely to voluntarily agree to such an agreement, not least because they fear that other individual capitals and states will not agree.[42] This is a particular problem for the ICU proposal, for, as we have seen, there were good reasons why this was not accepted by the United States at Bretton Woods, which related to the power gained through issuing the hegemonic currency. These advantages included fewer limitations on credit creation than other countries, and the funding of trade deficits without a necessarily significant loss to the value of the dollar. Indeed, this system has helped to preserve US hegemony *and* (due to the US economy acting as a 'market of last resort') avoid a generalised world-wide crash of 1930s proportions in the context of the global over-accumulation of capital. Certainly, winning agreement for the ICU does lead one to ask whether the US state would give up its position as the main issuer of the international currency, and, indeed, whether other states would necessarily want this as well.[43]

Moreover, redistribution between states is not the same as redistribution between peoples, and it could be argued that 'Third-Worldist' proposals like the NIEO represent the interests of dominant classes and élites from within the developing world. There is no guarantee that such a redistribution will benefit the dominated classes and other people in the developing world. This proposal falls into the same trap as the localisation thesis, which assumes that local capital will behave in a more progressive way than foreign capital. Despite his commitment to a 'Third-Worldist' perspective,[44] Monbiot does

---

[42] For a similar argument in relation to the debt crisis, see Chapter 3.
[43] T. Smith 2003, p. 23.
[44] For instance, his work is full of references to 'the people' of the North benefiting from the exploitation of the South. The problem with this argument is that the

attempt to deal with these problems. For instance, he is fully aware of the fact that local capital is as likely to take advantage of cheap labour as foreign capital. He argues that this can be dealt with through the creation of a Fair Trade Organisation, which would enforce certain minimum social and environmental standards. In addition, existing institutions such as the ILO could be strengthened, so that there could for example be proper regulation of transnational companies. There would also have to be full cost accounting for production, including environmental costs. Each country in the world order would be allowed a certain amount of greenhouse gas emissions, and any that fell above an annual quota would have to be paid for by buying a specified amount of another country's quota. One likely effect of this implementation of the principle of 'contraction and convergence' would be an increase in local processing within the developing world, as the costs of such processing would be cheapened as compared with foreign processing. Much of this processing would add value to the goods produced in the developing world.

Monbiot's proposals amount to a radical redistribution of wealth and income, and the encouragement of more socially and environmentally friendly production throughout the globe. But, at the same time, there are enormous questions that he tends to neglect. For instance, who will bring about such a radical restructuring of the world order, and, as important, who is likely to resist such an order? Will market exchange (and the accumulation of money) be properly controlled so that the inequalities generated by capitalism do not return? The proposed institutions may go some way to alleviating this problem, but what if some countries or companies do not play by the rules of the game? These issues, in turn, lead on to a wider question, which is at what point is capitalism so heavily regulated that it ceases to be capitalism, but something else?

In some respects, both the statists and global reformists envisage a return to the Golden Age of capitalism from 1948–71, in which there was sufficient space to allow for labour- and development-friendly régimes. This may entail

---

mechanisms of exploitation are never spelt out, and usually rely on contradictory arguments (see Kiely 1995). This does not mean, of course, that some parts of the world are in a subordinate position in terms of politics, economics and culture, as I have argued throughout this work, but this is a different matter.

a proposed radicalisation of the Bretton Woods era – Monbiot and Held for instance, support a system led by Keynesian ideas alongside some further cosmopolitan reforms. Given the expansion of employment, labour rights, welfare states in the First World, and independence and some economic and social advance in the Third, one can see why there is a nostalgia for the Golden Age. But, at the same time, there was also persistent inequality, the threat of nuclear war, and superpower intervention in the developing world. Perhaps, above all, it needs to be re-emphasised that the current global order emerged out of the ruins of the post-war order, which leads Callinicos to ask the question how would a 'revised version of the post-war economic system avoid the tendency that ultimately destroyed the original?'.[45]

Callinicos is quite right to ask this question, but his proposed answer also requires further consideration, as he suggests that reformist strategies are, ultimately, limited as they only address the symptoms of the contradictions of capitalism, while revolutionary Marxists attack the system as a totality. He therefore argues that the anti-globalisation movement must ultimately become not only anti-capitalist, but revolutionary in the tradition of classical Marxism.[46] This tradition certainly has a point. Like evolutionary Marxists and some arguments associated with neo-liberalism, social democrats tend to abstract from historical specificity, and assert that, as reforms have been won in a specific time and place, these can be extended irrespective of particular conditions. This argument tends towards an evolutionary approach to social change, proposing models that abstract from specific social and historical outcomes. Thus, for instance, the rise of East Asia does show that successful capitalist development remains a possibility, but this does not mean that an East-Asian model of state-guided development can simply be exported to other developing countries. This argument ignores the specific conditions that led to the rise of East Asia in the first place, which included substantial aid in the context of the Cold War, land reforms in the context of struggle for land and Communist insurrection, the development of institutional state structures that disciplined (and repressed) labour and capital, and relatively open access to established markets in the First World.[47] East Asia's rise was

---

[45] Callinicos 2001, p. 397.
[46] Callinicos 2003a, pp. 83–103.
[47] Kiely 1998, Chapters 7 and 8.

not simply the product of a number of prescribed, technocratic reforms that can be used as a blueprint for other nation-states. Instead, its emergence must be located in the context of a turbulent history of civil wars, superpower intervention, peasant struggles, state development and authoritarian repression. A similar point can be made with regard to the Bretton Woods agreement itself, as this emerged after a thirty year period of two World Wars, the rise of Bolshevism and fascism, the great depression, and growing struggles for national liberation. The implementation of the proposals advocated by Held and Monbiot, or, indeed, the national reforms advocated by Hirst and Thompson, presuppose considerable social conflict.

But, on the other hand, the reformist position has its strengths and the revolutionary position its weaknesses. Clearly, some *capitalisms* are more desirable than others, and even if capitalism does have certain 'laws of motion' or 'conditions of existence', the precise form that these take will vary. Thus, as I argued in Chapter 8, debt relief does not end the uneven development of global capitalism, but it can still constitute an important social advance in the context of this uneven development. Tony Smith, a severe critic of cosmopolitan social democracy still accepts that '[r]eforms that only improve matters on the margin can still alleviate human suffering to a profound extent'.[48] This point is indeed correct, but it also suggests that such reforms – given that they can alleviate suffering 'to a profound extent' are not simply 'on the margin'. Indeed, the revolutionary tradition does tend towards a functionalist account of the 'laws of motion' of capitalism, arguing that specific manifestations of inequality, uneven development and over-accumulation are *necessary* requirements of the capitalist mode of production. There are certain 'laws of motion' associated with capitalism (in general), but these laws do not operate entirely independently of social struggles, and therefore manifest themselves in particular ways. For example, famine is undoubtedly the most severe manifestation of inequality in the world today. Evolutionary accounts argue that it is caused by a lack of capitalism, while functionalist accounts argue that it is ultimately caused by 'the logic of capitalism'. But both accounts abstract too easily from specific conditions, and both tend towards explanations and solutions rooted in historical inevitability. For the

---

[48] T. Smith 2003, p. 30.

evolutionists, the problem is caused by lack of capitalism, and the solution is the implementation of policies that will deepen capitalist development, and thus promote catch up to levels where famine is avoided. Evolutionary accounts – be they neo-liberal, Third-Way or social-democratic – tend to repeat the dualist analyses of classic modernisation theory, and assume that catch-up occurs either despite (in dualist terms, in isolation from) the inequalities of the global order, or indeed because that order represents an opportunity for catch-up (or, in dualist terms, because one country has done it, all can do it). The functionalists quite rightly point out that nation-states do not develop in isolation from each other, and development in some regions can coincide with marginalisation elsewhere. But they then tend to go on to make the far stronger point that certain *manifestations* of uneven development are *necessary conditions* of global capitalism. This view of the totality is far too rigid and politically disabling, as it tends towards an argument that laws of motion exist entirely independently of the actions and struggles of human beings, and that these laws manifest themselves in functionally necessary ways.[49] In this way, the inevitable capitalist development proposed by evolutionary theories is replaced by the inevitable capitalist underdevelopment of functionalist Marxism. It is a short step from an analysis of 'the totality' to one in which the view is that (in the absence of total revolution) 'there is no alternative'.[50]

On the other hand, as we saw in Chapter 7, anarchist and autonomist alternatives, which argue that history is *entirely* contingent on struggles is too open-ended. The result is a fetishisation of resistance, and politics tends to be reduced to spontaneous direct action. This ultimately apolitical approach ignores the effectiveness (or otherwise) of different forms of resistance, as well as the fact that resistance in itself may not always be progressive. It also

---

[49] These comments echo debates in the 1970s over the conditions of existence and laws of motion of capitalist society. A rigid structuralism (Hindess and Hirst 1975), in which structures were completely determining, was quickly replaced by an excessive voluntarism, in which constraints all but disappeared from view (Hindess and Hirst 1977). Alternative approaches recognised that structural constraints were historically constituted, and therefore changeable, but were no less real for that (Corrigan and Sayer 1978). Thompson (1977) therefore talked of 'structured processes'. These issues are discussed further in relation to the state and globalisation in Section 3 of this chapter.

[50] Gibson-Graham 1996.

ignores the fact that, while blueprints and models abstract from real processes are dangerous, there remains some need for broad alternative outlines of more progressive societies, and, indeed, for institutions that can guarantee democratic forms of empowerment.

This discussion suggests that the rigid dichotomy between reform and revolution is one that should be rejected. Reforms can be won in capitalist societies, and have been won. On the other hand, they have been won under specific conditions that may (or may not) mean that the generalisation of their implementation is problematic. Moreover, such reforms are far from irreversible. What is being suggested here, then, is a politics of consistent 'follow-through' which, like the autonomists, recognises that forms of struggles are not separable from the vision of better societies, and that struggles themselves will have unpredictable, uncertain outcomes. But, at the same time, there is also the need for a recognition that struggles take place in very unequal contexts, and that some will be more effective than others, and some will involve participation 'in and against'[51] existing institutions of power – which, as I argued in Chapters 7 and 8, may be local, national and international. This focus on struggle and open-endedness has, of course, largely abstracted from the question of agency, both generally and specifically related to globalisation. This is discussed further in the next section.

9.3   Agency, globalisation and anti-globalisation

This section focuses on the question of agency, globalisation and anti-globalisation. It starts by briefly re-examining the question of the state and globalisation, and then moves on to examine the question of agency in relation to anti-globalisation politics.

(i) *The state and globalisation*

This section briefly revisits the arguments outlined in Chapters 2–5. It focuses in particular on the question of the relationship between states and globalisation (and vice versa). This book has rejected accounts of globalisation which suggest that global markets (or other global flows such as communications and media)

---

[51] LEWRG 1980; Wainwright 2003.

have outgrown or even killed off the nation-state.[52] Moreover, it has also argued that, even when the state is said to be alive and well, many accounts still one-sidedly focus on the question of the impact of globalisation on nation-states, as if the line of causality was simply one-way, and that states merely responded to globalisation, and changed their behaviour accordingly.[53] My counter-argument has been that states – and some states more than others – have been agents of globalisation. Having said that, it is not sufficient to reduce globalisation to the actions of nation-states, as if they were the *only* major actors in the international order, as realist theories imply.[54] Indeed, these two contrasting accounts tend to set up a similar rigid dichotomy, in which the 'global' transcends the 'national', and so the former is relevant for the current era, while the latter applied to an earlier, pre-global system of sovereign nation-states. However, as Lacher argues,

> state-centrism was *always* an inadequate basis for conceptualising modern social and international relations. The sovereign state ... was *never* truly a container of society, and modern social relations always included crucial global dimensions.[55]

The alternative approach suggested here, is not to set up a rigid dichotomy between national and global, and suggest that one dominates the other according to particular historical periods. Instead, one needs to recognise the global character of capitalist social relations *from the outset*, and the ways in which these have interacted with the national organisation of the 'purely political state'. Chapter 2 argued that the expansion of commodity production simultaneously meant the expansion of the market and the creation of a separate institutional sphere, which came to be known as 'the economy'. This economic sphere had no *necessary* connection to national territorial spaces. Spaces could never be completely transcended, as production and exchange had to take place somewhere, but the important point is that this was not necessarily nationally specific. On the other hand, the creation of an economic sphere separate from the political sphere – the nation-state – did not mean that the two existed in total isolation from each other, nor, indeed, that one

---

[52] Harris 1994; Ohmae 1995.
[53] Held et al. 1999.
[54] Waltz 1979.
[55] Lacher 2003, pp. 522–3.

could exist without the other. Rather, the point was that, in pre-capitalist societies, surplus was appropriated through political mechanisms, and so the characterisation of institutions as economic or political made no sense. In capitalist societies, surplus appropriation takes place through the market-place, or the dull compulsion of economic relations, rather than access to state revenues.[56] The institutional separation of economics and politics therefore occurs with the development of capitalist social relations. This separation also presupposes a territorial dichotomy between global markets and national states, something that is also true from the beginning of capitalist social relations. The notion that there was a relatively straightforward correlation between globality and nationality (whatever the direction of causation) is problematic, because, in fact, territorial states pre-dated the emergence of capitalist social relations.[57] Nevertheless, with the emergence of such relations, the character of national sovereignty changed, as surplus appropriation occurred through the market.[58] However, the emergence of clearly demarcated economic and political spheres did not mean that 'the logic of global capital' dominated 'the logic of the national state', or that the latter dominated the former. Instead, world market interactions were mediated by state boundaries and these states came to represent their national capitals on the world stage. This representation did not occur because states simply functioned in any simple way for the interests of their capital. Indeed, in terms of carrying out specific policies, there was (and is) considerable autonomy for state managers from specific capitals. But, at the same time, the very existence of the state as a separate institutional sphere reinforces capitalist class relations, and the legitimacy and material resources of the state are linked to success in securing the conditions for sustained accumulation. The functions of securing legitimacy and accumulation can come into conflict, and the fact that the state is also

---

[56] A point well made, ironically, by Giddens 1985, p. 278.
[57] Lacher 2000; Teschke 2003.
[58] Indeed, these points apply to the current period, as the formation of separate economic and political spheres is far from complete, and persists in particularly violent form in parts of the former colonial world. In stating this point, I am not suggesting that the process is a simple linear one, whereby the former colonies simply catch up with the more 'advanced' capitalist societies. Rather, I am suggesting that the process is one riven with conflict and violence, with no inevitable outcome, and it is one that is complicated by the fact of existing global hierarchies in terms of states and capital accumulation. Indeed, for all these reasons, World Bank policies (and cosmopolitan capital analyses) based on the need for a simple package of trade liberalisation and good governance seem hopelessly naïve, a point powerfully made by Brown 2003.

the main site for political conflict only heightens these contradictory tendencies. These problems are further increased by the fact that state actions may disrupt the accumulation of capital, and the fact that sustained capital accumulation will often rely on locations beyond state territory.[59]

This discussion thus suggests that it is a mistake to rigidly demarcate national and global (or indeed economic and political) spheres, and, instead, they need to be conceptualised in terms of the changing internal relations between them. In this way, we have the basis for a better understanding of the relationship between states and contemporary globalisation. Thus, as we saw in Chapter 4, the movement towards neo-liberalism took place in the context of declining US economic hegemony, slower rates of capital accumulation, increased competition between states and capitals, the growing internationalisation of capital and the associated increase in transnational company investment in manufacturing and re-emergence of global financial markets, and increased social and political unrest. The movement towards neo-liberalism can be traced back to the end of fixed exchange rates and dollar-gold convertibility, and the emergence of the Eurodollar and petrodollar market, but the late 1970s and early 1980s was a crucial turning point, as the US imposed policies of tight money and, therefore, high interest rates, and this had devastating consequences for the post-war order. Although they varied in intensity, other advanced capitalist states also adopted increasingly neo-liberal policies. There were some half-hearted calls for capital controls in the 1970s, but the general direction – especially in the 1980s – was for further deregulation of capital controls, not least to try to maintain and advance competitive advantage in a liberalising world, in which foreign direct investment and financial flows were increasingly transcending any straightforward link to national boundaries.[60] In the developing world, the formerly development-friendly régimes faced the prospect of meeting debt obligations through running trade surpluses through cutting imports and thus consumption, and, in the longer run, they faced the prospect of world-market discipline as protectionist policies were gradually eroded.

These general tendencies varied in their intensity, and neo-liberal policies were resisted by labour and other social movements, political parties and

---

[59] Lacher 2000, pp. 206–7.
[60] Panitch and Gindin 2003.

nation-states, with varying degrees of success. For these reasons, there was no straightforward convergence around a set of neo-liberal policies, and therefore proposed alternatives to neo-liberalism within capitalism persisted, and will continue to persist. Nevertheless, there has also been a clearly identifiable tendency based on the adoption of neo-liberal policies, which has, in turn, changed the international 'rules of the game', and the emergence of the Third Way – and its acceptance as these rules as uncontested fact – is perhaps the most visible example of this tendency.[61] Broadly speaking, then, there have been three main moments of neo-liberal restructuring: the 1970s, when neo-liberalism re-emerged in response to economic crisis; the 1980s, when neo-liberal policies were implemented; and the 1990s and early years of the twenty-first century, when neo-liberal policies were consolidated, often by social-democratic parties that now accepted the neo-liberal context as irreversible, and, in many respects, further implemented such policies.[62] The recomposition[63] of the state has therefore been central to the promotion of globalisation, which has further intensified globalising processes (which then have an impact back on nation-states). State sovereignty still exists, and nation-states maintain many key functions, but, at the same time, state capacities to translate this authority and sovereignty into effective control 'are becoming limited by a complex displacement of power upwards, downwards and outwards'.[64] This has meant the erosion of the neo-Keynesian state, be it

[61] Panitch and Leys 2001, Chapters 11 and 12.

[62] Overbeek 1999.

[63] There is an extensive literature on restructuring that has only been touched on in this book. Much of this revolves around the extent to which the advanced capitalist countries have moved from a Fordist to post-Fordist mode of capital accumulation. The latter is said to involve flexible production methods (often using information technology and 'just-in-time' supply methods), flexible labour (drawing on a core of skilled, and a periphery of dispensable unskilled, workers), flexible relations between suppliers and final producers, flexible markets (based on niche consumer products which replace mass markets), and a restructured state that responds to the needs of this new form of capitalism. My own view is that this division between Fordist and post-Fordist capitalism is exaggerated, as it ignores significant continuities such as the ongoing importance of mass production, over-estimates the flexibility of production methods, and tends towards a functionalist theory of the state. On the other hand, it is equally mistaken to deny the changes that have occurred in recent years, and there is a need for periodisation in order to account for these changes – recognition of change does not mean denying that these changes are contested, or that there are specific and local variations in more general tendencies. For a critical survey of these debates, which is explicitly related to the question of development, see Kiely 1998, Chapter 9.

[64] Jessop 2002, p. 212.

labour- or development-friendly, but it has not meant the erosion of the nation-state.

In practice, of course, these processes of state restructuring, neo-liberalism and globalisation are messier, and more contingent and contested than the above outline suggests. In Chapter 2, I argued that a satisfactory approach to globalisation must incorporate an understanding of agency, power and interest. But this does not mean that recognising the existence of power relations in the promotion of globalising tendencies means that there is a straightforward, functional relationship between agency, power, intent and interest. Thus, Gowan's very useful analysis of US statecraft based on the removal of the dollar-gold link, US military intervention, and US hegemony suggests a relatively unambiguous preservation and intensification of US power since 1971.[65] In many ways a diametrically opposed argument to that of Gowan, Robinson argues that globalisation has given rise to a transnational class, and as a result a nascent transnational state has also emerged.[66] This argument tends towards a functionalist theory of the state, in which national state and national capital coincide, and transnationalisation of capital therefore gives rise to a transnational state. Both approaches suffer from the notion that power, interests and actions can simply be read off from each other in a linear process of capitalist development, when, in fact, such restructuring occurs through very specific material and ideological conflicts, discussed further below. As Gowan himself at times recognises, US hegemony post-Bretton Woods has been far from straightforward, and the movement of the dollar against other currencies reflects continued instability and uncertainty alongside successful crisis management and order. But, on the other hand, both Gowan and Robinson have the virtue (whatever the merits of the specific arguments) of recognising the realities of power relations, and the fact that the changes that have occurred in recent years are the outcome of power struggles, which, however contested and uncertain, have also led to very real changes in the global order.[67] Above all, these relate to the increased marketisation of politics, and I now turn to a re-consideration of this issue.

---

[65] Gowan 1999.

[66] Robinson 2000.

[67] Which is why some autonomist perspectives on state restructuring have limited utility (see Bonefeld 1991). Recognition of the contested nature of restructuring is not the same thing as denying the reality of the changes that have occurred, and autonomist

(ii) *Globalisation and post-politics*

The discussion above – and, indeed, throughout most of this book – has focused on the political economy and political sociology of globalisation. I have argued that globalisation does not mean the transcendence, but rather the expansion of, capitalism. However, I have also argued that globalisation is not simply reducible to capitalism, and that there is a need for greater historical specificity in accounting for contemporary globalisation. If this is the case, then an argument could be made that while there may be a link between capitalism and 'globalisation from above', this actually tells us little about agents of resistance, and the question of globalisation from below. Put differently, the erosion of the 'public sphere' has meant not only the increased marketisation of social life, but also the increased erosion of oppositional politics that can challenge these tendencies. This argument usually involves the following claims: first, that we have witnessed the end of class politics; second, that we live in an age of increased individualisation and risk; third, we live in an age in which the commodity, the spectacle or rationalisation have so triumphed that resistance has become localised or meaningless; and, fourth, we live in an age where there has been a retreat from, rather than reconstruction of, politics.

The argument that we have witnessed the end of class politics needs to be treated with caution. If we take this argument to mean that class is no longer an important issue in today's world, then it is clearly absurd. Globalisation has involved the expansion of capitalism, and, in some respects, the intensification of inequality, both internationally and globally. Moreover, as Harman[68] forcefully argues, the size of the manufacturing working class has not fallen massively in most countries, and, globally, it has actually increased, as has routine service work, much of which is linked to manufacturing.[69] But is the continued existence of class inequality, and the expansion of the formal working class, the same thing as the persistence of class *politics*? Too often, the undoubted existence and indeed growth of the working class is taken as sufficient proof that class politics is alive and well. Indeed, the argument that

---

perspectives conflate the two. For a very useful critique, see Bieler and Morton 2003. Giddens, on the other hand, effectively denies the existence of power relations altogether.

[68] Harman 2002.

[69] See also Chapters 5, 6 and 8.

often follows amounts to little more than assertions about the primary role of the working class in the struggle for socialism.[70] The increase in working hours and falling real wages in the 'advanced' capitalist countries certainly point to the continued relevance of class as a source of inequality,[71] but they also demonstrate the political defeats that have been suffered in recent years. Of course, defeats are never final, and can be reversed, but simply asserting the primacy of the working class is not a particularly constructive contribution to that project. Indeed, given the general tendency (in the Western world at least) towards declining trade-union density and strike rates,[72] it reads too much like an article of faith rather than a constructive engagement. In other words, the continued existence of the working class *in itself* tells us little about the question of the working class as a class *for itself*, and assertions about the primary role of the working class do not address this wider question.

This issue is reinforced by wider arguments concerning the decline of the public sphere.[73] The (alleged) end of labour as a collective subject has intensified the emergence of individualised society.[74] A number of sociologists have argued that modernity is the first individualised society. Giddens argues that modernity is a post-traditional order in which, in contrast to feudal societies based on ascribed status, there are no fixed identities, and so we are compelled to choose from a 'pluralisation of lifeworlds'.[75] Although he is sensitive to the notion that this compulsion to choose is a source of anxiety,[76] Giddens has increasingly emphasised that this pluralisation has enhanced opportunities, and is therefore optimistic about the prospects for global capitalism and politics that adapts to these new times. Bauman on the other hand, is far more pessimistic.[77] He addresses the question of politics in the neo-liberal era, and suggests that we have seen an intensification of the individualised (postmodern) society, in which free market, neo-liberal capitalism triumphs over collective values (see further below). In terms of politics, the current era is characterised by an unprecedented shallowness, in which the

---

[70] Wood 1986; Harman 2002.
[71] Basso 2003.
[72] Jeffreys 2000.
[73] Leys 2003; Marquand 2004.
[74] Bauman 2001, Chapter 1; Castells 1997.
[75] Giddens 1991, p. 84.
[76] Giddens 1991, p. 81.
[77] Bauman 1999.

old ideological differences are displaced by personality disputes, spin, and celebrity culture. This does not mean that ideology has ended, but it does mean that there is only one ideology, which is the ruling, neo-liberal ideology of consumer capitalism. Politics committed to genuine collectivism, and the reconstruction of the public sphere, are said to be in crisis.

These points lead us back to the question of the nature of the anti-globalisation movement. Does the rise of this movement mean 'the end of the end of history',[78] or is it simply another meaningless spectacle, another retreat from, rather than reconstruction of, (alternative) politics? Furedi is quite certain that the anti-globalisation movement, like the 'new social movements' before it, does indeed represent a retreat from politics.[79] Anti-globalisation is simply another version of anti-politics. What is interesting about Furedi is that he holds no truck with 'postmodern' thinkers such as Baudrillard, or theorists of late modernity such as Beck. Indeed, he argues that these too are complicit with the retreat from politics.[80] He argues that there has been a retreat from politics – both by élites and non-élites – and that the old ideological conflict between capitalism and anti-capitalism has ended. Instead, we now have a micro-politics based on lifestyles, which actually means an endorsement of anti-politics. There is no longer a sense of the universal, and, instead, there is simply a whole host of fragmented movements, which broadly accept the wider social structure. The anti-globalisation movement, with its massive diversity of issues and no overarching ideology or direction, is just the latest manifestation of a retreat from politics.[81]

While not necessarily rejecting this view outright, Furedi's view does betray a certain nostalgia for the old certainties, the old politics of capitalism versus communism. Indeed, Furedi was a leading figure in a small Leninist party in Britain in the 1970s and 1980s. The problem, however, is that this very nostalgia demonstrates the limitations of his argument. First, it is highly selective nostalgia – a clear division between capitalism and communism has never been at the root of official party politics in most 'advanced' capitalist countries, and the capitalist-communist divide of the Cold War was based

---

[78] Klein 2001.
[79] Furedi 2004.
[80] Furedi 1996, in Schuurman 2001.
[81] Heartfield 2003.

on a Communism that was hardly a desirable alternative to capitalism.[82] Second, Furedi's analysis is itself symptomatic of the anti-politics that he decries, and there is an implicit call for individuals to 'pull themselves together' so that real politics can return from the grave – a strangely anti-sociological and voluntaristic approach to understanding 'anti-politics'.[83] It is almost as if, in the absence of a united working class awaiting leadership from 'the vanguard', there can be no meaningful politics. But it is precisely this simplistic division that is the problem. If certainty – and real politics – mean commitment to class essentialism, vanguardism, rigid models for the future, support for Stalinism, crude Third-Worldist anti-imperialism, then certainty (and real politics) have indeed ended. But good riddance to certainty – Marxism's future must be based on engagement with, and not rejection of, the politics of anti-globalisation.

Having said that, this response does not provide a full response to these criticisms, for anti-globalisation politics does face real dilemmas in terms of reconstructing politics. Above all, there is the question of the 'civil-society' fetishism that I analysed in Chapters 7 and 8. There is a tendency to valorise 'local' or 'global' resistance, and, sometimes, this is seen as taking place either below or above the nation-state. In either case, civil society is conceptualised in such a way that it is regarded as autonomous from the state, and somehow intrinsically democratic.[84] The result is an intensification of the escape from politics. Reconstruction can only take place through transcending such rigid dichotomies of local/national, and civil society and state. As Boggs argues, 'the point is not to embrace some fetishized notion of civil society *against* the state . . . but rather to anticipate a lengthy process of social transformation of both'.[85] Politics that simply focuses on civil society is deeply depoliticising, and, indeed, closely parallels those accounts of social capital that were rejected in Chapter 4.

---

[82] As Furedi himself once usefully demonstrated. See Furedi 1987.

[83] But one that is fully consistent with a vanguardism that regrets the fact that the proletariat have not fulfilled their 'historic task' of joining the party and overthrowing capitalism. This approach is not incompatible with liberal-humanist approaches that believe in progress through reason, and which then throw their hands in the air with dismay at the failure of 'the masses' to embrace reason. For a hugely entertaining analysis along these lines, see Wheen 2004, a sometimes acute analysis of our times, but one marred by precisely this problem.

[84] Colas 2002, 2004.

[85] Boggs 2000, p. 278.

On the other hand, anti-globalisation movements are far from unaware of these problems. As we saw in Chapter 7, 'local' social movements *do* place demands on states and political parties while simultaneously preserving their own independence from such bodies, and the organisations that have more determinedly adopted a 'pure autonomy' approach have had to face difficult strategic questions. Similarly, in Chapter 8 we saw how international campaigns have simultaneously placed demands on nation-states, and the growing international opposition to war has made this a priority. On the other hand, this has also led to important debates concerning questions of solidarity, which do not simply repeat the anti-imperialist politics of old. This is certainly a politics beyond the 'summit stalking' of 1999–2001, and has meant moving beyond pure protest and resistance to formulating alternatives, rather than championing a vacuous, anti-political open-endedness. At the same time, as debates at World Social Forums have made clear,[86] constructing alternatives does not mean proposing rigid models. The failures of socialism in the past can in part be attributable to the imposition of inflexible models that failed to take account of historical specificity.

Questions around the 'primary role' of the working class should be seen in this light. It is not that workers will or will not play their 'historic role', but rather a question of finding ways of transcending the fragmented and divided nature of the working class. This does mean engagement with non-class identities, and politics beyond the workplace. The fact that capital sees labour only as labour does not mean that labour only sees itself as labour. Indeed, given the uncertainties associated with restructuring, it is not surprising that labour has tended to 'draw non-class borders and boundaries as a basis for claims for protection from the maelstrom'.[87] This is not to 'write off' the working class as intrinsically sexist or racist. Such a statement implies that the working class is simply white and masculine, it denies the important occasions when solidarity has been established, and the significant changes that have occurred among trade unions in recent years.[88] It does, however, suggest that there is a need to move beyond simplistic assertions concerning the central role of the organised working class, trade unions, and repetitive calls for general strikes.

---

[86] Fisher and Ponniah 2003.
[87] Silver 2003, p. 22.
[88] Waterman 2002.

Finally, there is the question of spaces of resistance, and the relationship between local, national, international and global. I suggested earlier in this chapter that a simple return to the Bretton Woods system, and especially the system as envisaged by Keynes, is unlikely. But this does not mean that, in the absence of immediate transnational change, local or national based resistance is irrelevant. As Kitson and Michie state, '[t]he real question . . . is not whether it is best to act at the national or international level; it is how best to secure international action. . . . Action at the local, regional, national or bloc level, far from being a utopian alternative to the real international stage, might in reality prove a prerequisite of co-operation'.[89] Local and national actions may have local and national consequences, but they may have international consequences too. To repeat an earlier point, it is not so much the 'space' in which politics occurs, but the social and political implications within and between these 'spaces'.

9.4 Conclusion: alternatives to capitalism?

Arguments in favour of the efficiency of market societies are usually based on two perspectives. The first, neo-classical argument suggests that the market order reflects exchange between rational, calculating individuals who choose to trade in order to maximise their utility. The second argument, most famously associated with Hayek, shares the view of neo-classical theory that the market is the most effective way of allocating resources, but is more concerned with the dynamic effects of markets. In particular, markets are efficient because they promote competition and innovation. Indeed, it is the very uncertainty and unpredictability of markets that gives rise to the dynamism of market societies. Market societies therefore promote dynamism, but also promote order because they allow individuals to pursue their own ends and provide for their needs. Competition is thus central to the main cases made for the dominance of market forces. In neo-classical theory, competition is said to lead to equilibrium, while, in Hayek's work, it leads to dynamism in the context of a society in which no one is in control. There are echoes of these arguments in contemporary cases for globalisation, such as Giddens's emphasis

---

[89] Kitson and Michie 2000, p. 26.

on the efficiency of US capitalism, and in LeGrain's argument that corporations do not rule the world, as they too are subject to competitive forces beyond their control.[90]

This book has argued against both these positions. Competition does not lead to neo-classical equilibrium, and, while it certainly does lead to dynamic competition, this can have socially destructive effects. In particular, the speculative nature of financial markets can exaggerate trends in 'real' economic behaviour and have a disastrous impact as a result. But it is also clear that competition within markets is highly unequal, cannot be separated from the action of states, and is part of a process of capital accumulation that is indeed dynamic, but is also prone to crises of over-accumulation. Related to these points, while it is certainly not a system which any single agent (corporation, state, or entrepreneur) is in total control, and, indeed, it is misplaced to argue that corporations rule the world,[91] it remains true that some have much greater control and power, and therefore some benefit far more than others.

Moreover, market societies tend to dominate more and more aspects of social life, and this has enormous social and political implications – not least of which is neo-liberal suspicion of the collectivist aspirations of democracy.[92] Marx, Weber and Durkheim attempted to theorise the emergence of 'market society' through the concepts of alienation, rationalisation and anomie. Although there are important differences between these three concepts, they are united in their attempt to understand the displaced nature of subjectivity in modern capitalist society. In pre-capitalist societies, identities were relatively fixed, at least compared to those in capitalist societies. The notion of an autonomous individual is literally the creation of capitalist society, and this is both invigorating and frightening. Social divisions continue to exist, but these are ultimately rooted in the 'purely economic' relations of the market, rather than being defined in terms of one's place in a fixed hierarchy. In practice, of course, the nature of sexist and racist ideologies does mean that social divisions are not as purely economic as this distinction implies, and, indeed, this has wider implications, not least for labour. But the rise of specific institutional forms in capitalist society does undermine older, fixed hierarchies. As we saw

---

[90] Giddens and Hutton 2001; LeGrain 2002.
[91] Korten 1995.
[92] Kiely 1995, Chapter 6.

in Chapter 2, globalisation further undermines localised 'traditions', and Giddens, for one, sees this as a progressive development. This may be true, but it is also one that is profoundly contradictory – progressive, on the one hand, but a source of disorder on the other. This is not only because of intensified (relative) inequality and instability associated with capitalism that Giddens takes for granted, but also because rationalised consumer capitalism tends to increasingly dominate more and more aspects of social life.

Thus we arrive back at Polanyi's notion of disembedding, or, more concretely, the global expansion of 'market forces' at the expense of 'the commons' or the 'public sphere'. But as well as focusing on these questions of political economy, it is also clear that this is a phenomenon that goes to the heart of subjective experiences in late consumer capitalism. For we live in an increasingly individualised world dominated by the commodity, in which collective notions of the public sphere are increasingly marginalised. At the same time, in what amounts to another manifestation of the same phenomenon, the notion that 'There Is No Alternative' is increasingly prevalent. But, even in the richer Western world, this is not a world in which individuals necessarily feel secure, and this is precisely because of the tendency to declare 'the market' or 'globalisation' – real sources of anxiety and insecurity – off-limits from political discourse and debate. The result is something approximating the anti-politics discussed above, in which media spin, scandals and political-party hostility hide broad agreement on fundamentals.

Even worse, (formal) politics tends to be reduced to the search for scapegoats for the condition of insecurity, so that, for example, asylum seekers or some 'other' are blamed for the running down of public services, as though the latter was a natural force outside of political decision-making. This is one reason for the selectivity of the Third Way's embrace of globalisation, as 'market forces' are inevitable while free movement of labour is an enforceable decision necessary in a climate of racism, fear and uncertainty. However, this kind of politics only reinforces such an unhealthy climate, as it fails to address the causes of uncertainty and insecurity. Of course, these tendencies are far from novel, but they have probably intensified over the last thirty years, at least compared to the Bretton Woods era. In this same period of neo-liberalism and globalisation, mainstream political parties across the globe have increasingly adopted neo-liberal policies, but these have simultaneously been accompanied by broader social programmes, such as Margaret Thatcher's commitment to family values. The Third Way, particularly in its Anglo-American forms, has embraced notions of community and responsibility as a response to the excessive individualism of neo-liberal fundamentalism.[93] However, this attempt to reconcile 'market forces' and 'community' rests on vague notions of community and social capital, and the burden of responsibility rests on the poor and all those marginalised by processes of globalisation, while, at the same time, rights are expanded for the privileged few. As we have seen, this one-sidedness is essentially a product of the Third Way's complicity with neo-liberal capitalism, and its acceptance of the social and political inequalities that this has engendered.

Radical alternatives, therefore, must endorse a social transformation that above all else extends, expands and transforms the public sphere or 'the commons'. This entails an expansion of social ownership and a fundamental challenge to the power of capital. Part of this challenge must include the de-commodification of human labour-power which, as argued in Chapter 2, is the basis for the generalisation of commodity production. Such de-commodification entails the expansion of the commons in order to guarantee non-market access to the means of social and biological reproduction. But, crucially, a democratic socialist alternative will not be established simply through the establishment of a 'dictatorship of the proletariat' and the abolition of private property. The search for alternatives must avoid inflexible models and blueprints for a pre-determined future. The record of socialism is one in which party-states dominated most aspects of life, from rigid central planning to the destruction of any social interaction or individual rights that was not permitted by the state. These disasters were, in part, a product of revolutionary isolation in technologically backward countries, and the commitment to develop the productive forces in order to catch up with the West, but, equally, they reflected the lack of democracy and tolerance of excessively hierarchical political parties. Future alternatives will involve collective regulation, and the socialisation of property, but it will also mean individual rights, political pluralism, democratic accountability and participation, and socialised markets.[94]

---

[93] Etzioni 1988; Giddens 2002.
[94] On democratic, negotiated planning that focuses on socialising rather than abolishing markets, see Devine 1988; Elson 1988, 1999; and Blackburn 1991.

These very general comments tell us little about how we move from the dominance of neo-liberal, global capitalism, to what amounts to a democratic socialist future. What should be clear from the discussion in this and previous chapters is that the means and the ends of social transformation cannot be separated. The struggles of the present are based on social improvement that undermines the dominance of capital. This involves commitment to a whole host of reforms which, if implemented, are likely to have contradictory effects in capitalist society. These include some of the issues addressed in previous chapters such debt cancellation, capital controls, taxes on financial transactions, as well as issues not explicitly addressed such as basic incomes for all, increased progressive taxation, and massive reduction in military budgets.[95] These reforms may enhance the space for further reforms, but, also, they may be reversed or may have unexpected and socially regressive consequences. But, then, the pressure must be for further reforms – not in any technocratic sense of negotiation, but through the struggles of social movements for a better world. This involves struggles that challenge the dominance of 'the market' and the capitalist state, and so involves the struggle to democratise social relations. This struggle does not simply mean a full-frontal attack on 'the capitalist class' or a simple 'capturing' or 'smashing' of the capitalist state. Capitalism's rule manifests itself in highly mediated ways, and it is difficult, and sometimes impossible, to clearly identify 'the enemy', or the agency of domination. To take one example that has been central in this book, uneven development is not caused by any individual capitalist or corporation, but, rather, reflects the systemic tendency for capital to concentrate in certain areas, and therefore marginalise other places. In this case then, it is not only the *presence* of capitalists that creates the problem; indeed, the bigger problem is the *absence* of an agency that can alleviate or transcend this tendency. What this example suggests is that progressive politics is not simply about identifying 'the enemy', but also involves the construction of new collective alliances, agencies and institutions that challenge and undermine some broad tendencies of a capitalist-dominated order. As suggested earlier in the chapter, this 'reformist' position also involves 'follow-through', in order to ensure that these new agents are not undermined by the resources that are at the disposal of private capital and the state. A consistent challenge therefore does move

---

[95] Callinicos 2003a, pp. 132–9.

on to questions of widening and strengthening these new democratic agencies, and progressively socialising resources. A major task for progressive politics into the twenty-first century is thus to balance a commitment to genuine democracy, pluralism and diversity with concrete, institution-based challenges to neo-liberal, capitalist globalisation.

Chapter Ten
Conclusions

This concluding chapter provides a summary of the main arguments of the book. Two closely related questions are briefly re-addressed: first, what do we mean by globalisation? Second, what changes have occurred in recent years, and what are the implications of these changes for contemporary politics? The first question, therefore, returns to questions related to the different usages of the term globalisation, while the second brings us back to the question of politics, and thus the 'clash of globalisations'. In addressing the first question, globalisation will be examined in terms of *process, project and outcome*. The second question will then draw on this discussion, to re-examine once again the nature of 'anti-globalisation' politics.

10.1 Globalisation as process

Globalisation can be said to relate to the recent intensification of capital and other flows. But as I argued in Chapter 2, merely describing an intensification of such flows does not amount to an explanation for such flows, and still less does it amount to a new theoretical perspective that can be utilised to understand the changing world. In order to understand these changes, we need a historical and social analysis that is sensitive to the question of agency. In Chapter 2, I argued that capitalism was, from the start, a global phenomenon, but that it was simultaneously organised by nation-states – even though the latter actually had their origins in a pre-capitalist international system. At the same time, capitalism is the most dynamic form of society that has existed in human history, and so the precise form of globalisation – and the international state system – has varied over time. Therefore, contemporary globalisation must be situated historically, and cannot be reduced to an ahistorical logic of capitalism. I then situated contemporary globalisation in the context of the post-war international agreement, which was characterised by the hegemony of one state (the US), the Cold War, and in the capitalist world, controls on the movement of capital, especially finance capital, and a longer-term commitment to free trade. This system was effectively a transitional compromise, but it was one that allowed for important (though limited) gains for labour in the 'First' and development in the 'Third' World. But it was also one that gave rise to a number of contradictions, which included the global over-accumulation of capital, social and political unrest, US economic decline, the internationalisation of capital, and intensified economic competition between the 'advanced' countries. These contradictions gave rise to gradual, messy, and resisted processes of state restructuring, led by, but not reducible to the United States. These neo-liberal policies were based on the promotion of 'market forces' and anti-inflationary policies, which were generalised to the indebted world and, after 1989, the former Communist world, and, to some extent, to Europe and Japan. States began to promote competitiveness and export performance (and trade liberalisation) above industrial policy, import substitution, welfare and full employment policies. In the 1990s, social democracy accommodated itself to these policies, above all in Britain, with the promotion of the Third Way. Contemporary globalisation was regarded as an established fact (though the principle did not apply to asylum seekers or economic migrants, or protected economic sectors in the First World), when, in fact, it had its origins in the neo-liberal policies in the 1980s.

10.2 Globalisation as project

Globalisation as a political project is most closely associated with the Third Way. As we have seen, in its current usage, the Third Way refers to a 'new politics' beyond neo-liberal *laissez faire* and state-led socialism, in both its Fabian and Stalinist forms. Although there are some specific differences among Third-Way politicians (and former politicians) such as Blair, Clinton, Cardoso and Jospin, all agree that globalisation has changed the context in which (formal) politics operate. In terms of economic policy, the Third Way represents both a (small) break from, and (large) accommodation to, neo-liberalism. This is in part because globalisation processes are said to be inevitable, and therefore outside of the remit of politics, and also in part because globalisation, if properly managed, is said to lead to new opportunities for a just world order. The Third-Way global project thus essentially attempts to explain globalisation in terms of inevitability (process) and desirability (outcome). But, as we saw above, globalising processes are not inevitable, and though they have certainly changed the context in which politics operate (at least compared to the Bretton Woods era), they are rooted in neo-liberal policies. In this respect, the accommodation to neo-liberalism is immense, particularly by the Blair government in Britain.

But, at the same time, there is some break in terms of economic policy, and this relates to the relationship between states and markets. Neo-liberal fundamentalists of the 1980s argued for limited government so that self-adjusting and efficient market forces could operate. The Third Way accepts the notion that market forces are efficient but challenges the notion that they are entirely self-adjusting. A greater role for the state is therefore envisaged, so that market imperfections can be overcome. In this way, state policy is reduced to technocratic modelling, designed to overcome imperfections in otherwise optimal outcomes. Social exclusion is thus regarded as being a product of insufficient incorporation into a globalising world, and states must therefore play the role of re-incorporating workers excluded from the informational economy, and reincorporating countries excluded from the global economy. In the First World, this means intervention in labour markets, both to promote 'flexibility' and skills in order to attract investment in a high-tech, high productivity economy. At the same time, state reforms in the developing world are needed so that market forces can operate effectively and also attract investment, initially in low cost sectors where these countries have a comparative advantage. These policies are reinforced by free-trade agreements, and above all the World Trade Organisation. But, as we saw in Chapters 4 and 5, this strategy of progressive competitiveness in the context of free trade has not worked. The booms of the 1990s were essentially speculative, and reflected the dominance of financial capital that was re-established through the neo-liberal policies of the 1980s. On the whole, the 1990s and early 2000s have seen low rates of growth, and continued high rates of poverty and inequality. In the 'First' World, the high-wage, high-tech sector accounts for only a small proportion of employment, and in the 'Third' World, there has been limited success in attracting foreign investment and new investment in productive activity. By the turn of the century, the so-called new booms in Latin America had collapsed, giving way to new financial crises. China and India have challenged these trends, and it is their successes that have often been drawn on to support 'globalisation'. More sophisticated pro-globalisation analyses rightly point out that both countries have not adopted those policies of financial liberalisation that are broadly advocated by the US state, the Blair government in Britain and the IMF,[1] and so, in this respect at least, they have not adopted supposedly pro-globalisation policies. But neither have they adopted unambiguous free-trade policies, and, while tariff rates have been reduced, they remain high and part of a wider protectionist package. As we saw in Chapter 5, World Bank attempts to characterise these two countries as 'high globalisers' rests on very selective evidence. Just as China and India are now regarded as the 'miracle economies' of globalisation, so, in the past, East-Asian economies were regarded (and some continue to be regarded, despite the financial crash) as 'miracle economies' of neo-liberalism. But, in both cases, the state has been far too 'interventionist' to fit the supposed model. This should not surprise us, because, rather than seeing labour or nations as insufficiently globalised, the approach taken in this book has been to emphasise that globalisation is intrinsically uneven and unequal. As we noted in Chapter 2, this has been true throughout the history of capitalism, but contemporary globalisation has, in many respects, intensified unevenness and inequality.

The Third-Way global project does not just apply to economic policy. It has also been associated with notions of community and responsibility in the context of a market-driven society.[2] This has included a great deal of reference to the international community, and the notion that such a community should

---

[1] Bhagwati 2004.
[2] See Chapter 9.

combine to defeat authoritarian states and terrorist networks. Clinton and Blair, in particular, stressed the need for humanitarian intervention, and the necessity for such a policy is said to have increased since the terrorist attacks on the US in September 2001. For some writers,[3] the 'election' of the Bush administration and the terrorist attacks spelt the end of the era of globalisation. Bush has taken a far more unilateralist position in international affairs than the Clinton administration, the latter having preached the virtues of multilateral cooperation. This is said to be reinforced by the decision of the Bush administration to by-pass the UN in the run up to the war in Iraq, the imposition of protective tariffs on US steel and agriculture and against Chinese imports, and non-co-operation with a whole host of international institutions and agreements. But this notion of a total break between Clintonite globalisation and Bush US unilateralism is not convincing. Clinton was far from consistently multilateralist, and was quite prepared for example to ignore the UN in launching attacks on Sudan, Iraq and Afghanistan as well as the bombing of Serbia in 1999. On the other hand, it is not clear that the Bush administration is against neo-liberal expansion. What his adminstration does appear to promote is 'neo-liberalism for them', but 'not necessarily for us', and, in this respect, Bush's government is little different from previous presidencies from Reagan onwards. Indeed, given the US's expanding trade deficit and, post-Clinton, a renewed budget deficit, the Bush régime is highly dependent on continued commitment to policies that promote the free movement of capital. Similarly, while the government has shown some hostility to the WTO, this has not been at the cost of a commitment to free trade. Rather, free trade is promoted through bilateral trade agreements – which, indeed, actually hasten trade liberalisation (albeit only for those countries that are part of the agreement). The breakdown of talks at Cancun in 2003 reflected more ongoing economic tensions between different states, not least some in the developing world, rather than a move back towards generalised protectionism. These points do not negate the fact that the Bush régime is more unilateralist than its predecessor, but this does not mean the end of globalisation.[4] Indeed, as we have seen throughout this book, globalisation

---

[3] Gray 2001; Lobe 2003.
[4] Kiely 2005.

has not eroded an international state system based on hierarchies of power. The Bush régime has been more explicit about the interests of the United States than Clinton's government, but the former remains (selectively) committed to the expansion of globalisation.

Moreover, as we saw in Chapter 8, the Bush administration sees no contradiction between the interests of the United States and the interests of the global community; for the neo-conservatives, they are one and the same thing. This is because of the US's manifest destiny to rule the world for the good of all its people. As two prominent neo-conservatives ask, 'what is wrong with dominance, in the service of sound principles and high ideals'.[5] This is not so far removed – in practice at least – from the (supposed) cosmopolitan commitments of Blair's globalisation, when he talks of the need for the 'international community' to protect the rights of individuals. Indeed, there is considerable overlap between the messianism of neo-conservatism and Blairism, to the point where their delusions, half-truths and lies are clear to everybody but themselves and their unquestioning supporters. But the (desirable) commitment to cosmopolitanism begs the question of who speaks for the international community, and what action can be taken to protect such rights. To point to these problems is not to endorse a crude relativism, as some Third-Way advocates imply.[6] Rather, it is Blair's cosmopolitanism that is guilty of relativism, because it essentially endorses the right of one or two powers to determine international action. As I argued in Chapter 8, the laudable commitment to cosmopolitanism is incompatible with the right of one agent to determine what can be universal principles. These comments are not made to endorse crude cultural relativisms or crude anti-imperialist dogmas, but they are made to point out that the interventions supported by Bush and Blair are neither cosmopolitan nor democratic.

10.3   Globalisation as outcome

The above discussion has covered much in terms of an understanding of the outcomes of globalisation. The Third Way sees globalisation as both inevitable

---

[5] Kaplan and Kristol 2003, p. 108.
[6] Lloyd 2001.

and desirable. Globalisation's desirability is supposedly shown through its favourable outcomes, which include higher rates of growth, poverty reduction, and a genuine international community (albeit on US terms, backed by its loyal ally). The reality has been somewhat different – increased inequality in the context of lower growth, the undermining of advances made for labour after 1945 in the First World, and of the small advances made in terms of development in the Third. We also now have an increasingly unstable world, in which the rich few attempt to lock themselves away from the instabilities around them. For its advocates, these problems are said to be caused by insufficient globalisation. But this book has argued that the *form* taken by globalisation has been intrinsically hierarchical, in terms of both capital flows and the system of nation states.

Capitalist society is based on the capital-labour relation in which surplus-value is extracted from workers through the wage relation. This relation promotes the separation of a purely political state and a purely economic market. In reality, the two are not separate, but are two institutional forms of capitalist social relations. How they are internally related varies in different periods of capitalist society, and, as we have seen, the last twenty to thirty years has seen an increase in the rule of markets and money. This rule has not occurred through markets and money simply outgrowing the state, but through state strategies that have allowed the more direct rule of 'the market' (which, of course, has continued to be regulated by the state). This has had enormous implications for formal politics, as 'the market' and 'globalisation' have increasingly come to be regarded as areas beyond human control. As a result, there has been an intensification of tendencies always present throughout capitalism's history, namely the commodification and trivialisation of politics and the public sphere. In this context, social problems are increasingly regarded as being either external to, or resolvable by, 'the market', which is fetishised as a sphere that is either beyond human control or as the only possible method of service delivery. Public action is thus increasingly reduced to spontaneous, short-lived and irrational moments of collective angst, usually involving scape-goating of 'outsiders' who are blamed for insecure situations which they had no part in creating. Such events are usually reinforced by the reaction of politicians, who quickly dispense with their commitment to the rhetoric of globalisation and cosmopolitanism. The result is a further erosion of collective action, the public sphere, and 'anti-politics'. But it could be argued that the rise of anti-globalisation politics have reversed this downward spiral, as a new double movement has emerged to challenge the rule of 'market forces'.

10.4 The clash of globalisations

The rise of anti-globalisation politics can be traced back to the neo-liberal adjustment policies carried out in the developing world in the 1980s. These continued into the 1990s and beyond, and have influenced campaigns focused on debt, war, sweatshops, the environment, land reform, workers' rights and so on. But it is this very fragmentation which has been frustrating to many left theorists and activists, because it reinforces the erosion of meaningful collective action and 'anti-politics'. For such critics, these campaigns do not constitute a new Polanyian double movement, as they are too diverse, fragmented and incoherent to represent a real challenge to the current global order.[7]

My discussion of these issues in Chapters 6 to 9 gave no definitive judgment on these issues, but I suggested a number of themes that go some way to constituting an answer. First, 'old-(new-)left' writers tend to be guilty of over-generalisation, and point to the antics of a few anarchists or labour protectionists in the 'advanced' countries. I stressed in Chapters 6 and 7 that the 'movement' has firm origins in the South. Moreover, old-left critics tend to romanticise the certainties of the older era of left politics, some of which can be usefully rejected. On the other hand, the old Left does point to important weaknesses within *some* anti-globalisation movements. These relate to an uncritical celebration of direct action and (autonomous) resistance, a suspicion of *all* forms of organisation, an absolute open-endedness in terms of alternatives, and a one-sided focus on civil society as an intrinsically progressive sphere, be it above or below the nation-state. These problems are particularly acute among autonomist and anarchist wings of the movement, though it again needs stressing that these are more commonly found in the 'advanced' capitalist countries. Moreover, the weaknesses addressed are increasingly being debated within the movement itself, not least at world, regional, national and local

---

[7] Halliday 2002; Furedi 2004.

social fora.[8] What should be clear is that the so-called anti-globalisation movement, or global justice movement, represents the best opportunity for the reconstruction of left politics in a generation. In a world of rule by capital and an unequal system of nation-states, whose most powerful leaders act in increasingly dangerous ways, and in which opposition has been dominated in recent years by reactionary political forces, such a reconstruction is needed more than ever.

---

[8] Wainwright 2004.

References

Adler Hellman, Judith 1999, 'Real and Virtual Chiapas: Magic Realism and the Left', in *The Socialist Register 2000*, edited by Leo Panitch and Colin Leys, London: Merlin.

Adorno, Theodor and Max Horkheimer 1979 [1944], *Dialectic of Enlightenment*, London: Allen Lane.

AFL-CIO 2000, 'Campaign for Global Fairness': <www.aflcioorg/aboutaflcio/ecouncil>.

Agarwal, Binar 1998, 'Environmental Management, Equity and Ecofeminism: Debating India's Experience', *Journal of Peasant Studies*, 25, 4: 55–95.

Albo, Greg 1994, '"Competitive Austerity" and the Impasse of Capitalist Employment Policy', in *The Socialist Register 1994*, edited by Leo Panitch, London: Merlin Press.

Albo, Greg 2003, 'The Old and New Economics of Imperialism', *The Socialist Register 2004*, edited by Leo Panitch and Colin Leys, London: Merlin.

Allen, Charles 1995, 'Understanding African Politics', *Review of African Political Economy*, 22, 65: 301–20.

Allen, Tim 1992, 'Prospects and Dilemmas for Industrialising Nations', in *Poverty and Development into the Twenty First Century*, edited by Tim Allen and Alan Thomas, Oxford: Oxford University Press.

Allen, Tim and Diana Weinhold 2000, 'Dropping the Debt for the New Millennium: Is It Such a Good Idea?', *Journal of International Development*, 12, 6: 857–75.

Ali, Tariq 2003, 'Recolonizing Iraq', *New Left Review*, II, 21: 5–19.

Amin, Samir 1976, *Unequal Development*, Hassocks: Harvester.

Amin, Samir 1997, *Capitalism in the Age of Globalization*, London: Zed.

Amsden, Alice 1989, *Asia's Next Giant*, Oxford: Oxford University Press.

Amsden, Alice 1994, 'Why Isn't the Whole World Experimenting with the East Asian Model to Develop?', *World Development*, 22: 627–33.

Amsden, Alice 2000, *Industrialization under New WTO Law*, Geneva: UNCTAD.

Anderson, Perry 2002, 'Force and Consent', *New Left Review*, II, 17: 5–30.

Anheier, Helmut, Marlies Glasius and Mary Kaldor (eds.) 2001, *Global Civil Society 2001*, Oxford: Oxford University Press.

Archibugi, Daniele. 2000, 'Cosmopolitical Democracy', *New Left Review*, II, 4: 137–50.

Archibugi, Daniele 2002, 'Demos and Cosmopolis', *New Left Review*, II, 13: 24–38.

Archibugi, Daniele and David Held 1995 'Editors Introduction', in *Cosmopolitan Democracy*, edited by Daniele Archibugi and David Held, Cambridge: Polity.

Arrighi, Giovanni 1994, *The Long Twentieth Century*, London: Verso.

Arrighi, Giovanni 2003, 'The Social and Political Economy of Global Turbulence', *New Left Review*, II, 20: 5–71.

Athreye, S. 2004, 'Trade Policy, Industrialization and Growth in India', in *Making the International*, edited by Simon Bromley, Maureen Mackintosh, Will Brown and Marc Wuyts, London: Pluto.

ATTAC 2003, 'Financial Capital', in *Another World is Possible*, edited by William Fisher and Thomas Ponniah, London: Zed.

Bacon, David 2000, 'Will a Social Clause in Trade Agreements Advance International Solidarity', in *Globalize This!*, edited by Roger Burbach and Kevin Danaher, Monroe: Common Courage.

Bahuguna, Sunderlal 1989, 'Deforestation in Himalaya and the Way to Survival', in *Deforestation, Drought and Desertification*, edited by Nalini Jayal, New Delhi: INTACH.

Baker, Dean, Gerry Epstein and Robert Pollin 1998, 'Introduction', in *Globalization and Progressive Economic Policy*, edited by Dean Baker, Gerry Epstein and Robert Pollin, Cambridge: Cambridge University Press.

Baran, Paul and Paul Sweezy 1966, *Monopoly Capital*, New York: Monthly Review Press.

Barnet, Richard 1996, 'Stateless Corporations: Lords of the Global Economy', in *Corporations are Gonna Get Your Mama*, edited by Kevin Danaher, Maine: Common Courage Press.

Barnet, Richard and John Cavanagh 2001, 'Homogenisation of Global Culture', in *The Case Against the Global Economy*, edited by Edward Goldsmith and Jerry Mander, London: Earthscan.

Bartholomew, Amy and Jennifer Breakspear 2003, 'Human Rights as Swords of Empire', in *The Socialist Register 2004*, edited by Leo Panitch and Colin Leys, London: Merlin.

Basso, Pietro 2003, *Modern Times, Ancient Hours*, London: Verso.

Baudrillard, Jean 1983, *In the Shadow of the Silent Majorities*, New York: Semiotext.

Baudrillard, Jean 1988, *Selected Writings*, Cambridge: Polity.

Bauer, Peter 1991, *The Development Frontier*, Hemel Hempstead: Harvester Wheatsheaf.

Bauman, Zygmunt 1999, *In Search of Politics*, Cambridge: Polity.

Bauman, Zygmunt 2001, *The Individualized Society*, Cambridge: Polity.

Baxter, John 2003, 'United Nations,' in *Anti-Imperialism: A Guide for the Movement*, edited by Farah Reza, London: Bookmarks.

Bayoumi, Tamin 1998, 'Comment', in *Globalization and Progressive Economic Policy*, edited by Dean Baker, Gerry Epstein and Robert Pollin, Cambridge: Cambridge University Press.

Becker, David and Richard Sklar 1987, 'Why Postimperialism?', in *Postimperialism*, edited by David Becker, Jeff Frieden, Sayre Schatz and Richard Sklar, Boulder: Lynne Rienner.

Bellamy Foster, John 1999, *Marx's Ecology*, New York: Monthly Review Press.

Bello, Walden 2001, 'The Global Conjuncture: Characteristics and Challenges', *International Socialism*, 91: 11–19.

Bello, Walden 2002, *Deglobalization*, London: Zed.

Bello, Walden, Nicola Bullard and Kamal Malhotra (eds.) 2000, *Global Finance*, London: Zed.

Bennett, Tony 1982, 'Theories of Media, Theories of Society', in *Culture, Society and Media*, edited by Michael Gurevitch, Tony Bennett, James Curran and Janet Woolacott, London: Methuen.

Berger, Fred 1979, 'Korea's Experience with Export-Led Development', in *Export Promotion Policies*, World Bank, Washington: World Bank.

Bhagwati, Jagdish 2004, *In Defence of Globalization*, Oxford: Oxford University Press.

Bideleux, Robert 1985, *Communism and Development*, London: Methuen.

Bieler, Andreas and Adam David Morton 2003, 'Globalisation, the State and Class Struggle: A 'Critical Economy' Engagement with Open Marxism', *British Journal of Politics and International Relations*, 5, 4: 467–99.

Bienefeld, Manfred 2000, 'Structural Adjustment: Debt Collection Device or Development Policy', *Review*, 23, 4: 533–82.

Bircham, Emma and John Charlton (eds.) 2001, *Anti-Capitalism: A Guide to the Movement*, London: Bookmarks.

Blackburn, Robin 1991, 'Fin de Siecle: Socialism after the Crash', in *After the Fall*, edited by Robin Blackburn, London: Verso.

Blair, Tony 1999, 'Doctrine of the International Community: Speech to the Economic Club of Chicago': <www.fco.gov.uk>.

Blair, Tony 2001, 'Labour Party Conference Speech': <www.politics.guardian.co.uk/labour2001>.

Boggs, Carl 2000, *The End of Politics*, New York: Guilford.

Bond, Patrick 2001, *Against Global Apartheid*, Lansdowne: University of Cape Town Press.

Bonefeld, Werner (ed.) 1991, *Post-Fordism and Social Form*, London: Macmillan.

Bourdieu, Pierre 1986, 'The Forms of Capital', in *Handbook of Theory and Research for the Sociology of Education*, edited by john Richardson, New York: Greenwood.

Bové, José and Francois Dufour 2001, *The World Is not For Sale*, London: Verso.

Brandt, Willy 1980, *North-South: A Programme of Survival*, London: Pan.

Brandt, Willy 1983, *Common Crisis*, London: Pan.

Branford, Sue and Jan Rocha 2002, *Cutting the Wire*, London: Latin America Bureau.

Brecher, Jeremy and Tim Costello 1998, *Global Village or Global Pillage*, Cambridge, MA.: South End Press.

Brecher, Jeremy, Tim Costello and Brendon Smith 2000, *Globalization from Below*, Cambridge, MA.: South End Press.

Brenner, Robert 1976, 'Agrarian Class Structure and Economic Development in Pre-Industrial Europe', *Past and Present*, 70: 30–74.

Brenner, Robert 1986, 'The Social Basis of Economic Development', in *Analytical Marxism*, edited by John Roemer, Cambridge: Cambridge University Press.

Brenner, Robert 1998, 'The Economics of Global Turbulence', *New Left Review*, I, 229: 1–265.

Brenner, Robert 2002, *The Boom and the Bubble*, London: Verso.

Brenner, Robert 2003, 'Towards the Precipice', *London Review of Books*, 25, 3: 12–18.

Brett, Edward 1983, *International Money and Capitalist Crisis*, London: Heinemann.

Bromley, Simon 1999, 'The Space of Flows and Timeless Time: Manuel Castells' "The Information Age"', *Radical Philosophy*, 97: 4–12.

Bromley, Simon 2003, 'Reflections on *Empire*, Imperialism and United States Hegemony', *Historical Materialism*, 11, 3: 17–68.

Bronfenbrenner, Kate 2001, *Uneasy Terrain: The Impact of Capital mobility on Workers, Wages and Union Organizing*, Washington: Report to US Trade Deficit Review Commission.

Brown, Will 2003, 'The World Bank, Africa and Politics: A Comment on Paul Cammack's Analysis', *Historical Materialism*, 11, 2: 61–74.

Brundtland, Harlem 1987, *Our Common Future*, London: Earthscan.

Buchanan, Pat 1998, *The Great Betrayal*, Boston: Little Brown.

Buiter, Willem and Thirukodikaval Srinivasan 1987, 'Rewarding the Profligate and Punishing the Prudent: Some Recent Proposals for Debt Relief', *World Development*, 15: 411–17.

Bukharin, Nikolai 1972 [1914], *Imperialism and World Economy*, London: Merlin.

Burawoy, Michael 1983, 'Factory Regimes under Advanced Capitalism', *American Sociological Review*, 48, 5: 587–605.

Burbach, Roger 2001, *Globalization and Postmodern Politics*, London: Pluto.

Burbach, Roger and Bill Robinson 2001, 'The Epochal Shift', in *Globalization and Postmodern Politics*, authored by Roger Burbach, London: Pluto.

Burkett, Paul 2003, 'Capitalism, Nature and the Class Struggle', in *Anti-Capitalism: A Marxist Introduction*, edited by Alfredo Saad-Filho, London: Pluto.

Burkett, Paul and Martin Hart-Landsberg 2001, 'Crisis and Recovery in East Asia: The Limits of Capitalist Development', *Historical Materialism*, 8: 3–47.

Burnham, Peter 1997, 'Globalisation: States, Markets and Class Relations', *Historical Materialism*, 1: 150–60.

Burnham, Peter 1999, 'The Politics of Economic Management in the 1990s', *New Political Economy*, 4, 1: 37–54.

Caffentzis, George 2001, 'An Essay on the Events of September 11th, 2001, Addressed to the Antiglobalization Movement': <www.commoner.org.uk>.

Callinicos, Alex 2001a, *Against the Third Way*, Cambridge: Polity.

Callinicos, Alex 2001b, 'Where Now?', in *Anti-Capitalism: A Guide to the Movement*, edited by Emma Bircham and John Charlton, London: Bookmarks.

Callinicos, Alex 2002, 'Marxism and Global Governance', in *Governing Globalization*, edited by David Held and Tony McGrew, Cambridge: Polity.

Callinicos, Alex 2003a, *An Anti-Capitalist Manifesto*, Cambridge: Polity.

Callinicos, Alex 2003b, 'War under Attack, *Socialist Review*, 273: 12–13.
Callinicos, Alex 2003c, 'The Grand Strategy of the American Empire', *International Socialism*, 97: 3–38.
Callinicos, Alex, Mike Gonzales, Chris Harman and John Rees 1994, *Marxism and the New Imperialism*, London: Bookmarks.
Caney, Simon 2001, 'International Distributive Justice', *Political Studies*, 49, 5: 974–97.
Carmen, Raff 1996, *Autonomous Development*, London: Zed.
Carson, Rachel 1962, *Silent Spring*, Harmondsworth: Penguin.
Castells, Manuel 1993, *The Informational City*, Oxford: Blackwell.
Castells, Manuel 1996, *The Rise of the Network Society*, Oxford: Blackwell.
Castells, Manuel 1998, *End of Millennium*, Oxford: Blackwell.
Castells, Manuel 2000, *The Rise of the Network Society*, Second Edition, Oxford: Blackwell.
Cavanagh, John 1997, 'The Global Resistance to Sweatshops', in *No Sweat*, edited by Andrew Ross, London: Verso.
Centre for Economic Policy and Research 2001, 'The Emperor Has No Growth': <www.cepr.net>.
Chandler, David 2001, 'International Justice', *New Left Review*, II, 6: 55–66.
Chang, Ha-Joon 2000, 'The Hazard of Moral Hazard', *World Development*, 28: 980–98.
Chang, Ha-Joon 2002, *Kicking Away the Ladder*, London: Anthem.
Chang, Ha-Joon 2003, *Globalisation, Economic Development and the Role of the State*, London: Zed.
Chang, Ha-Joon, Park, Hong-Jae And Chul Yoo 1998, 'Interpreting the Korean Crisis', *Cambridge Journal of Economics*, 22, 6: 735–46.
Chitty, Andrew 2002, 'Moralism, Terrorism and War – Response to Shaw', *Radical Philosophy*, 111: 16–19.
Clarke, Simon 1988, *Keynesianism, Monetarism and the Crisis of the State*, London: Edward Elgar.
Clarke, Simon 1992, 'The Global Accumulation of Capital and the Periodisation of the Capitalist State Form', in *Open Marxism*, Volume 1, edited by Werner Bonefeld, London: Pluto.
Clarke, Simon 1994, *Marx's Theory of Crisis*, London: Macmillan.
Cleaver, Harry 1979, *Reading 'Capital' Politically*, Austin: University of Texas Press.
Cliff, Tony 1974, *State Capitalism in Russia*, London: Pluto.
Cline, William 1982, 'Can the East Asian Model of Development Be Generalized?', *World Development*, 10, 2: 41–50.
Coates, Barry 2001, 'GATS', in *Anti-Capitalism: A Guide to the Movement*, edited by Emma Bircham and John Charlton, London: Bookmarks.
Coates, David 2000, *Models of Capitalism*, Cambridge: Polity.
Cohen, Gerry 1978, *Karl Marx's Theory of History: A Defence*, Cambridge: Cambridge University Press.
Colas, Alejandro 2002, *International Civil Society*, Cambridge: Polity.
Colas, Alejandro 2004, 'The Power of Representation: Democratic Politics and Global Governance', *Review of International Studies*, forthcoming.
Collins, Carole, Zie Gariyo and Tony Burdon 2001, 'Jubilee 2000: Citizen Action Across the North-South Divide', in *Global Citizen Action*, edited by Michael Edwards and John Gaventa, London: Earthscan.
Corbridge, Stuart 1993, *Debt and Development*, Oxford: Blackwell.
Corrigan, Phil, Harvey Ramsay and Derek Sayer 1978, *Socialist Construction and Marxist Theory*, London: Macmillan.
Corrigan, Phil and Derek Sayer 1978, 'Hindess and Hirst: A Critical Review', *Socialist Register 1978*, edited by Ralph Miliban and John Saville, London: Merlin.
Corrigan, Phil and Derek Sayer 1985, *The Great Arch*, Oxford: Blackwell.
Cowen, Mike and Robert Shenton 1996, *Doctrines of Development*, London: Routledge.
Cox, Kevin (ed.) 1997, *Spaces of Globalization*, London: Guilford.
Crotty, Jim 2003, 'The Neoliberal Paradox: The Impact of Destructive Product Market Competition and Impatient Finance on Nonfinancial Corporations in the Neoliberal Era', *Review of Radical Political Economics*, 35, 3: 271–79.

Crotty, Jim and Kang-Kook Lee 2002, 'A Political Economy Analysis of the Failure of Neo-Liberal Restructuring in Post-Crisis Korea', *Cambridge Journal of Economics*, 26, 5: 667–78.

Crotty, Jim, Gerry Epstein and Patricia Kelly 1998, 'Multinational Corporations in the Neo-Liberal Regime', in *Globalization and Progressive Economic Policy*, edited by Dean Baker, Gerry Epstein and Robert Pollin, Cambridge: Cambridge University Press.

Cypher, James and James Dietz 1997, *The Process of Economic Development*, London: Routledge.

Danaher, Kevin (ed.) 1996, *Corporations are Gonna Get Your Mama*, Monroe: Common Courage Press.

Danaher, Kevin and Roger Burbach (eds.) 2000, *Globalize This!*, Monroe: Common Courage Press.

Davis, Mike 1985, 'Reaganomics Magical Mystery Tour', *New Left Review*, I, 149: 45–65.

De Angelis, Massimo 2001, 'From Movement to Society', in *On Fire*, Anon., London: One Off Press.

Deaton, Angus 2001, 'Counting the World's Poor: Problems and Possible Solutions', *World Bank Research Observer*: 125–47.

Debord, Guy 1994, *The Society of the Spectacle*, New York: Zone Books.

Deleuze, Gilles and Felix Guattari 1998, *Anti-Oedipus*, Minneapolis: University of Minnesota Press.

Desai, Meghnad 2000, 'Seattle: A Tragi-Comedy', in *After Seattle*, edited by Barbara Gunnell and David Timms, London: Catalyst.

Desai, Meghnad 2002, *Marx's Revenge*, London: Verso.

Devine, Pat 1988, *Democracy and Economic Planning*, Cambridge: Cambridge University Press.

Dfid 2000, *Eliminating World Poverty: Making Globalisation Work for the Poor*, London: Dfid.

Dicken, Peter 2003, *Global Shift*, London: Sage.

DLC 1996, 'The New Progressive Declaration, Democratic Leadership Council': <www.ndol.org>.

Dobson, Andrew 2000, *Green Political Thought*, London: Routledge.

Dollar, David and Aart Kraay 2001 'Trade, Growth and Poverty', *World Bank Development Research Group*: <www.worldbank.org/research>.

Dorfman, Ariel and Armand Mattelart 1975, *How to Read Donald Duck*, New York: International General.

Dreze, Jean and Amartya Sen 1989, *Hunger and Public Action*, Oxford: Clarendon.

Dunkley, Graham 2000, *The Free Trade Adventure*, London: Zed.

Durkheim, Emile 1957, *Professional Ethics and Civil Morals*, London: Routledge.

Edwards, Mike 2001, 'Introduction', in *Global Citizen Action*, edited by Mike Edwards and John Gaventa, London: Earthscan.

Elson, Diane 1979, 'The Value Theory of Labour', in *Value: The Representation of Labour in Capitalism*, edited by Diane Elson, London: CSE Books.

Elson, Diane 1988, 'Market Socialism or Socialization of the Market', *New Left Review*, I, 172: 3–44.

Elson, Diane 1999, 'Socialized Markets, Not Market Socialism', *Socialist Register 2000*, edited by Leo Panitch and Colin Leys, London: Merlin.

Emmanuel, Arghiri 1974, 'Myths of Development versus Myths of Underdevelopment', *New Left Review*, I, 85: 61–82.

Emmanuel, Arghiri 1982, *Appropriate or Underdeveloped Technology?*, Chichester: Wiley.

Engberg-Pedersen, Poul, Peter Gibbon, Phil Raikes and Lars Udsholt (eds) 1996, *Limits of Adjustment in Africa*, London: James Currey.

Escobar, Arturo 1995, *Encountering Development*, Princeton: Princeton University Press.

Esteva, Gustavo 1992, 'Development', in *The Development Dictionary*, edited by Wolfgang Sachs, London: Zed.

Esteva, Gustavo and Madhi Prakash 1997, 'From Global Thinking to Local Thinking', in *The Post-Development Reader*, edited by M. Rahnema and V. Bawtree, London: Zed.

Etzioni, Amtai 1988, *The Spirit of Community*, New York: Crown.

Fairclough, Norman 2000, *New Labour, New Language?*, London: Routledge.

Falk, Richard 2000a, 'Global Civil Society and the Democratic Prospect', in *Global Democracy*, edited by Barry Holden, London: Routledge.

Falk, Richard 2000b, 'Resisting "Globalization from Above" through "Globalization from Below"', in *Globalization and the Politics of Resistance*, edited by Barry Gills, London: Macmillan.

Featherstone, Liz 2002, *Students Against Sweatshops*, London: Verso.

Feinstein, Charles 1999, 'Structural Change in the Developed Countries in the Twentieth Century', *Oxford Review of Economic Policy*, 15, 4: 35–55.

Fine, Ben 2001, *Social Capital versus Social Theory*, London: Routledge.

Fine, Ben, Costas Lapavitsas and Jonathan Pincus (eds.) 2001, *Development Policy into the Twenty First Century*, London: Routledge.

Fine, Ben and Alfredo Saad-Filho 2004, *Marx's 'Capital'*, London: Pluto.

Fisher, William and Thomas Ponniah (eds.) 2003, *Another World Is Possible*, London: Zed.

Frank, Andre Gunder 1969, *Capitalism and Underdevelopment in Latin America*, New York: Monthly Review Press.

Fröbel, Folker, Jürgen Heinrichs and Otto Kreye 1980, *The New International Division of Labour*, Cambridge: Cambridge University Press.

Furedi, Frank 1987, *The Soviet Union Demystified*, London: Junius.

Furedi, Frank 2004, 'Foreword', in *Democracy and Participation*, edited by Malcolm Todd and Gary Taylor, London: Merlin.

Garrett, Geoff 1998, *Partisan Politics in the Global Economy*, Cambridge: Cambridge University Press.

George, Susan 1989, *A Fate Worse than Debt*, Harmondsworth: Penguin.

George, Susan 2000, 'A Short History of Neoliberalism', in *Global Finance*, edited by Walden Bello, Nicola Bullard and Kamal Malhotra, London: Zed.

George, Susan 2001, 'Corporate Globalisation', in *Anti-Capitalism: A Guide to the Movement*, edited by Emma Bircham and John Charlton, London: Bookmarks.

Gereffi, Gary and Linda Hempel 1996, 'Latin America in the Global Economy', *NACLA*, 29, 4: 18–27.

Gibson-Graham, Judith-Kathleen 1996, *The End of Capitalism (As We Knew It)*, Oxford: Blackwell.

Giddens, Anthony 1985, *A Contemporary Critique of Historical Materialism*, Volume 2, Cambridge: Polity.

Giddens, Anthony 1987, *Social Theory and Modern Sociology*, Cambridge: Polity.

Giddens, Anthony 1990, *The Consequences of Modernity*, Cambridge: Polity.

Giddens, Anthony 1991, *The Transformation of Intimacy*, Cambridge: Polity.

Giddens, Anthony 1994, *Beyond Left and Right*, Cambridge: Polity.

Giddens, Anthony 1997, 'Interview with John Lloyd', *New Statesman*, 10 January.

Giddens, Anthony 1999, *Runaway World*, Cambridge: Polity.

Giddens, Anthony 2000, *The Third Way and Its Critics*, Cambridge: Polity.

Giddens, Anthony (ed) 2001, *The Global Third Way*, Cambridge: Polity.

Giddens, Anthony 2002, *Which Way for New Labour*, Cambridge: Polity.

Giddens, Anthony and Will Hutton 2001, 'In Conversation', in *On the Edge*, edited by Anthony Giddens and Will Hutton, London: Vintage.

Glasius, Marlies 2001, 'Global Civil Society Comes of Age': <www.opendemocracy.net>.

Glyn, Andrew, Arnold Hughes, Alain Lipietz and Ajit Singh 1990 'The Rise and Fall of the Golden Age', in *The Golden Age of Capitalism*, edited by Stephen Marglin and Juliet Schor, Oxford: Clarendon.

Golding, Peter 2000, 'Forthcoming Features: Information and Communications Technologies and the Sociology of the Future', *Sociology*, 34, 1: 165–84.

Goldsmith, Edward 1972, *A Blueprint for Survival*, London: Tom Stacey.

Goldsmith, Edward 1988, *The Great U-Turn: Deindustrializing Society*, Bideford: Green Books.

Goldsmith, Edward and Jerry Mander (eds.) 2001, *The Case Against the Global Economy*, London: Earthscan.

Gordon, Robert 1999, 'Has the New Economy Rendered the Economic Slowdown Obsolete': <www.econ.northwestern.edu>.

Gordon, David 1996, *Fat and Mean*, New York: Free Press.

Gore, Al 1999, 'Remarks by Vice-President Al Gore': <www.govinfo.library.unt.edu>.

Gowan, Peter 1999, *The Global Gamble*, London: Verso.

Gowan, Peter 2001a, 'Neo-Liberal Cosmopolitanism', *New Left Review*, II, 11: 79–93.

Gowan, Peter 2001b, 'Explaining the American Boom: The Roles of "Globalisation" and US Global Power', *New Political Economy*, 6, 3: 359–74.

Grabel, Ilene 1996, 'Marketing the Third World: The Contradictions of Portfolio Investment in the Global Economy', *World Development*, 24, 11: 1761–76.

Grabel, Ilene 2003, 'International Private Capital Flows and Developing Countries', in *Rethinking Development Economics*, edited by Ha-Joon Chang, London: Anthem.

Graeber, David 2002, 'The New Anarchists', *New Left Review*, II, 13: 61–73.

Grahl, John 2001, 'Globalized Finance', *New Left Review*, II, 8: 23–46.

Gramsci, Antonio 1971, *Selections from the Prison Notebooks*, London: Lawrence and Wishart.

Gray, John 2001, 'The Era of Globalisation Is Over', *New Statesman*, September 24th.

Green, Francis and Bob Sutcliffe 1987, *The Profit System*, Harmondsworth: Penguin.

Green, Peter 2002, '"The Passage from Imperialism to Empire": A Commentary on *Empire* by Michael Hardt and Antonio Negri', *Historical Materialism*, 10, 1: 29–77.

Greenspan, Alan 1999, 'Remarks at Millennium Lecture Series': <www.federalreserve.gov/BoardDocs/speeches/1999>.

Grenier, Paola 2003, 'Jubilee 2000: Laying the Foundations for a Social Movement', in *Globalizing Civic Engagement*, edited by John Clarke, London: Earthscan.

Grooteart, Christian 1997, 'Social Capital: "The Missing Link"', in *Expanding the Measue of Wealth*, World Bank: Washington: World Bank.

Guha, Ranajit 1989, *The Unquiet Woods*, New Delhi: Oxford University Press.

Habermas, Jurgen 1981, 'New Social Movements', *Telos*, 49: 33–7.

Habermas, Jurgen 1987, *The Theory of Communicative Action: System and Lifeworld*, Cambridge: Polity.

Hain, Peter 2002, 'Embrace Global Action': <www.guardian.co.uk/Archive/Article>.

Hain, Peter and Dick Benschop 2001, 'The Right Questions but the Wrong Answers', *New Statesman*, Nov 12.

Halliday, Fred 1983, *The Making of the Second Cold War*, London: Verso.

Halliday, Fred 2000, 'Getting Real about Seattle', *Millennium*, 29, 1: 123–9.

Halliday, Fred 2001, *The World in 2000*, London: Macmillan.

Halliday, Fred 2002a, 'The Pertinence of Imperialism', in *Historical Materialism and Globalisation*, edited by Mark Rupert and Hazel Smith, London: Routledge.

Halliday, Fred 2002b, *Two Hours that Shook the World*, London: Saqi.

Hamelink, Cees 1983, *Cultural Autonomy in Global Communications*, New York: Longman.

Hamilton, Clive 2004, *Growth Fetish*, London: Pluto.

Hanlon, Joe 2000, 'How Much Debt Must Be Cancelled?', *Journal of International Development*, 12, 6: 877–901.

Hanmer, Lucia, John Healey and Felix Naschold 2000, 'Will Growth Halve Global Poverty by 2015?', *ODI Poverty Briefing*, London: ODI.

Hardt, Michael 2002, 'Today's Bandung', *New Left Review*, II, 14: 112–18.

Hardt, Michael and Antonio Negri 2000, *Empire*, Cambridge, MA.: Harvard University Press.

Hardt, Michael and Antonio Negri 2001, 'What the Protestors in Genoa Want', in *On Fire*, Anon., London: One Off Press.

Harman, Chris 2000, 'Anti-Capitalism: Theory and Practice', *International Socialism*, 88: 3–59.

Harman, Chris 2002, 'The Workers of the World', *International Socialism*, 96: 3–52.

Harman, Chris 2003, 'National Liberation', in *Anti-Imperialism: A Guide for the Movement*, London: Bookmarks.

Harris, Jerry 2003, 'Transnational Competition and the End of US Economic Hegemony', *Science and Society*, 67, 1: 68–80.

Harris, Nigel 1994, 'Nationalism and Development', in *Market Forces and World Development*, edited by Renee Prendergast and Frances Stewart, London: Macmillan.

Harris, Nigel 2003, *The Return of Cosmopolitan Capital*, London: I.B. Tauris.

Harriss, John 2000, 'The Second "Great Transformation"? Capitalism at the End of the Twentieth Century', in *Poverty and Development into the Twenty First Century*, edited by Tim Allen and Alan Thomas, Oxford: Oxford University Press.

Harriss, John 2001, *Depoliticizing Development*, London: Anthem.

Harvey, David 1989, *The Condition of Postmodernity*, Oxford: Blackwell.

Harvey, David 1996, *Justice, Nature and the Geography of Difference*, Oxford: Blackwell.

Harvey, David 1999, *The Limits to Capital*, London: Verso.

Hay, Colin 2001, 'What Place for Ideas in the Structure-Agency Debate? Globalisation as a Process without a Subject': <www.theglobalsite.ac.uk>.

Hay, Colin 2003, 'What's Globalisation Got to Do with It? Inaugural Professorial Lecture', University of Birmingham: <www.bham.ac.uk/POLSIS>.

Hay, Colin and Matthew Watson 1999, 'Globalisation: "Sceptical" Notes on the 1999 Reith Lectures', *Political Quarterly*, 70, 4: 418–25.

Heartfield, James 2003, 'Postmodern Desertions: Capitalism and Anti-Capitalism', *Interventions: International Journal of Postcolonial Studies*, 5, 2: 271–89.

Held, David 1995, *Democracy and the Global Order*, Cambridge: Polity.

Held, David 1998, 'Globalization: The Timid Tendency', *Marxism Today*, Nov/Dec: 24–7.

Held, David 2001, 'Globalization after September 11th': <www.polity.co.uk/global>.

Held, David 2003, 'Violence, Law and Justice in a Global Age', in *Debating Cosmopolitics*, edited by Daniele Archibugi, London: Verso.

Held, David and Tony McGrew 2002, *Globalization/Anti-Globalization*, Cambridge: Polity.

Held, David and Tony McGrew (eds.) 2003, *The Global Transformations Reader*, Second Edition, Cambridge: Polity.

Held, David, Tony McGrew, Jonathan Perraton and David Goldblatt 1999, *Global Transformations*, Cambridge: Polity.

Helleiner, Eric 1994a, *States and the Re-Emergence of Global Finance*, Ithaca: Cornell University Press.

Helleiner, Eric 1994b, 'From Bretton Woods to Global Finance: A World Turned Upside Down', in *Political Economy and the Changing Global Order*, edited by Richard Stubbs and Geoffrey Underhill, London: Macmillan.

Helleiner, Eric 2000, 'Think Globally, Transact Locally: Green Political Economy and the Local Currency Movement', *Global Society*, 14: 35–51.

Heller, Patrick 2001, 'Moving the State: The Politics of Democratic Decentralization in Kerala, South Africa and Porto Alegre', *Politics and Society*, 29, 1: 131–63.

Henderson, Caspar 2003, 'Cancunblog: from Mexico to the World': <www.open Democracy.net>.

Hensman, Rohini 2001, 'World Trade and Workers' Rights: In Search of an Internationalist Position', in *Space, Place and the New Labour Internationalisms*, edited by P. Waterman and J. Wills, Oxford: Blackwell.

Henwood, Doug 1996, 'The Free Flow of Money', *NACLA*, 29, 4: 10–16.

Henwood, Doug 1997, 'Talking about Work', in *Rising from the Ashes?*, edited by Ellen Meiksins Wood, Peter Meiksins and Michael Yates, New York: Monthly Review Press.

Henwood, Doug 1999, 'The United States', *Monthly Review*, 51, 3: 120–32.

Henwood, Doug 2003, *After the New Economy*, New York: New Press.

Hettne, Bjorn 1995, 'Introduction: The International Political Economy of Transformation', in *International Political Economy*, edited by Bjorn Hettne, London: Zed.

Hill, Christopher 1975, *The World Turned Upside Down*, Harmondsworth: Penguin.

Hindess, Barry and Paul Hirst 1975, *Pre-Capitalist Modes of Production*, London: Routledge.

Hindess, Barry and Paul Hirst 1977, *Mode of Production and Social Transformation*, London: Macmillan.

Hines, Colin 2000, *Localization: A Global Manifesto*, London: Zed.

Hines, Colin and Tim Lang 2001 'The New Protectionism of "Localization"', in *The*

Case Against the Global Economy, edited by Edward Goldsmith and Jerry Mander, London: Earthscan.

Hirst, Paul and Graham Thompson 1996, *Globalization in Question*, Cambridge: Polity.

Hirst, Paul and Graham Thompson 1999, *Globalization in Question*, Second Edition, Cambridge: Polity.

Hobbes, Thomas 1968 [1660], *Leviathan*, Harmondsworth: Penguin.

Hobsbawm, Eric 1962, *Age of Revolution*, London: Weidenfeld and Nicholson.

Hobsbawm, Eric 1968, *Industry and Empire*, Harmondsworth: Penguin.

Hodkinson, Stuart 2001, 'Problems@Labour: Towards a Net Internationalism?', paper to Global Studies Association annual conference, Manchester: Manchester Metropolitan University.

Holloway, John 2002, *Change the World without Taking Power*, London: Pluto.

Hoogvelt, Ankie 2001, *Globalization and the Postcolonial World*, Second Edition, London: Palgrave.

Houtart, Francois 2001, 'Alternatives to the Neoliberal Model', in *The Other Davos*, edited by Francios Houtart and Francois Polet, London: Zed.

Huntington, Samuel 1996, *The Clash of Civilizations and the Remaking of World Order*, New York: Simon and Schuster.

Hurrell, Andrew and Ngaire Woods (eds.) 1999, *Inequality, Globalization and World Politics*, Oxford: Oxford University Press.

Hutton, Will 1995, *The State We're In*, London: Vintage.

Hutton, Will 2002, *The World We're In*, London: Little Browne.

Huws, Ursula 2003, *The Making of a Cybertariat*, London: Merlin.

IFG 2002, *Alternatives to Economic Globalization*, San Francisco: Berrett Kohler.

IMF 1997, *World Economic Outlook, May 1997 – Globalization: Opportunities and Challenges*, Washington: IMF.

Isaac, Thomas and Richard Franke 2002, *Local Democracy and Development: The Kerala Peoples Campaign for Decentralized Planning*, New York: Rowman and Littlefield.

Islam, Faisal 2003, 'When Two Tribes Go to War', *The Observer*, June 22.

Itoh, Makoto 1990, *The World Economic Crisis and Japanese Capitalism*, London: Macmillan.

Jameson, Fredric 1991, *Postmodernism*, London: Verso.

Jeffreys, Steven 2001, 'Western European Trade Unionism at 2000', in *The Socialist Register 2001*, edited by Leo Panitch and Colin Leys, London: Merlin.

Jessop, Bob 2002, *The Future of the Capitalist State*, Cambridge: Polity.

Jordan, John 1998, 'The Art of Necessity: The Subversive Imagination of Anti-Road Protest and Reclaim the Streets', in *DIY Culture*, edited by George McKay, London: Verso.

Kabeer, Naila 2000, *The Power to Choose*, London: Verso.

Kaldor, Mary 2003a, 'Regime Change without War', *Red Pepper*, April.

Kaldor, Mary 2003b, 'Iraq: A War Like no Other': <www.openDemocracy.net>.

Kaldor, Mary 2003c, *Global Civil Society*, Cambridge: Polity.

Kaldor, Mary, Helmut Anheier and Marlies Glasius 2003, 'Global Civil Society in an Age of Regressive Globalisation', in *Global Civil Society Yearbook 2003*, edited by Mary Kaldor, Helmut Anheier and Marlies Glasius, Oxford: Oxford University Press.

Kaplan, Lawrence and William Kristol 2003, *The Wars over Iraq*, London: Politicos.

Kauffman, Linda 2002, 'A Short History of Radical Renewal', in *From Act Up to the WTO*, edited by Benjamin Shepard and Ronald Hayduk, London: Verso.

Kay, Geoff 1975, *Development and Underdevelopment*, London: Macmillan.

Kellner, Doug 1999, 'Theorizing McDonaldization: A Multiperspectivist Approach', in *Resisting McDonaldization*, edited by Barry Smart, London: Sage.

Kessi, Alain 2001, 'Millennium Round of the WTO under Fire from Both the Left and Right', in *The Battle of Seattle*, edited by Eddie Yuen, George Katsiaficas and David Rose, New York: Soft Skull Press.

Khan, Mushtaq 2002, 'Corruption and Governance in Early Capitalism: World Bank Strategies and their Limitations', in *Reinventing the World Bank*, edited by Jonathan Pincus and Jeffery Winters, Ithaca: Cornell University Press.

Kiely, Ray 1995, *Sociology and Development: The Impasse and Beyond*, London: UCL Press.

Kiely, Ray 1996, *The Politics of Labour and Development in Trinidad*, Mona: The Press – University of West Indies.

Kiely, Ray 1998, *Industrialization and Development: A Comparative Analysis*, London: UCL Press.

Kiely, Ray 1999, 'The Last Refuge of the Noble Savage? A Critical Account of Post-Development', *European Journal of Development Research*, 11, 1: 30–55.

Kiely, Ray 2000, 'Feature Review – Globalisation: From Domination to Resistance', *Third World Quarterly*, 21, 6: 1059–070.

Kiely, Ray 2002a 'Neoliberalism Revised? A Critical Account of World Bank Conceptions of Good Governance and Market Friendly Intervention', in *The Political Economy of Social Inequalities*, edited by Vincente Navarro, New York: Baywood.

Kiely, Ray 2002b, 'The Global Third Way versus Progressive Globalism?', *Contemporary Politics*, 8, 3: 167–84.

Kiely, Ray 2002c, 'Actually Existing Globalisation, Deglobalisation and the Political Economy of Anti-Capitalist Protest', *Historical Materialism*, 10, 1: 93–121.

Kiely, Ray 2005, *The Ends of Globalisation*, London: Pluto.

Killick, Tony 1995, *IMF Programmes in Developing Countries*, London: Routledge.

Kindleberger, Charles 2000, *Manias, Panics and Crashes*, Fourth Edition, New York: John Wiley.

Kitching, Gavin 1982, *Development and Underdevelopment in Historical Perspective*, London: Methuen.

Kitching, Gavin 2001, *Seeking Social Justice through Globalization*, Pennsylvania: Penn State University Press.

Kitson, Mike and Jonathan Michie 2000, *The Political Economy of Competitiveness*, London: Routledge.

Klein, Naomi 2000, *No Logo*, London: Flamingo.

Klein, Naomi 2001a, 'The Vision Thing: Are the Protests Unfocused or are Critics Missing the Point?', in *Democratizing the Global Economy*, edited by Kevin Danaher, Monroe: Common Courage Press.

Klein, Naomi 2001b, 'A Fete for the End of the End of History': <www.nologo.org>.

Klein, Naomi 2001c, 'Reclaiming the Commons', *New Left Review*, II, 9: 81–9.

Klein, Naomi 2002, *Fences and Windows*, London: Flamingo.

Korten, David 1995, *When Corporations Rule the World*, London: Earthscan.

Korzeniewicz, Roberto and Tim Moran 1997, 'World Economic Trends in the Distribution of Income, 1965–1992', *American Journal of Sociology*, 102: 1000–39.

Korzeniewicz, Roberto and Tim Moran 2000, 'Measuring World Income Inequalities', *American Journal of Sociology*, 106: 209–14.

Krebbers, Eric and Merijn Schoenmaker 2001, 'Seattle 1999: Wedding Party of the Left and Right?', in *The Battle of Seattle*, edited by Eddie Yuen, George Katsiaficas and David Rose, New York: Soft Skull Press.

Krugman, Paul 1998, 'Saving Asia: Its Time to Get RADICAL', *Fortune*, September 7th.

Kuczynski, Pedro 1988, *Latin American Debt*, Baltimore: Johns Hopkins University Press.

Lacher, Hannes 1999, '"Embedded Liberalism", Disembedded Markets: Conceptualising the *Pax Americana*', *New Political Economy*, 4, 3: 343–60.

Lacher, Hannes 2000, *Historicising the Global: Capitalism, Territoriality and the International Relations of Modernity*, London: LSE PhD Thesis.

Lacher, Hannes 2002, 'Making Sense of the International System: The Promises and Pitfalls of Contemporary Marxist Theories of International Relations', in *Historical Materialism and Globalization*, edited by Mark Rupert and Hazel Smith, London: Routledge.

Lacher, Hannes 2003, 'Putting the State in its Place?', *Review of International Studies*, 29, 4: 521–41.

Larrain, Jorge 1989, *Theories of Development*, Cambridge: Polity.

Laxer, Gordon and Sandra Halperin (eds.) 2003, *Global Civil Society and Its Limits*, London: Palgrave.

Leadbeater, Charles 1999, *Living on Thin Air*, London: Viking.

Lee, Eric 1997, *The Labour Movement and the Internet*, London: Pluto.

LeGrain, Phillip 2002, *Open World: The Truth about Globalisation*, London: Abacus.

Lenin, Vladimir 1957 [1899], *The Development of Capitalism in Russia*, Moscow: Progress.

Lenin, Vladimir 1975 [1916], *Imperialism: The Highest Stage of Capitalism*, Moscow: Progress.

Lenin, Vladimir 1977 [1917], 'State and Revolution', in *Selected Works*, Moscow: Progress.

Lewin, Moshe 1974, *Lenin's Last Struggle*, London: Pluto.

LEWRG 2000, *In and Against the State*, London: Pluto.

Leys, Colin 1996, *The Rise and Fall of Development Theory*, London: James Currey.

Leys, Colin 2003, *Market Driven Politics*, London: Verso.

Little, Ian, Tibor Scitovsky and Maurice Scott 1970, *Industry and Trade in Some Developing Countries*, Oxford: Oxford University Press.

Lloyd, John 2001, *The Protest Ethic*, London: Demos.

Lobe, Jim 2003, 'George Bush, Anti-Globalist': <www.lewrockwell.com>.

Locke, John 1994 [1690], *The Second Treatise on Civil Government*, New York: Amherst.

Lomberg, Bjorn 2001, *The Skeptical Environmentalist*, Cambridge: Cambridge University Press.

Löwy, Michael 1981, *The Politics of Combined and Uneven Development*, London: Verso.

Löwy, Michael 1987, 'Lukács and Romantic Anti-Capitalism', *New German Critique*, 42: 17–31.

Mamdani, Mahmood 1996, *Citizen and Subject: Contemporary Africa and the Legacy of Late Colonialism*, Princeton: Princeton University Press.

Mandelson, Peter and Roger Liddle 1996, *The Blair Revolution*, London: Faber and Faber.

Mann, Michael 2003, *Incoherent Empire*, London: Verso.

Marcuse, Herbert 1964, *One-Dimensional Man*, London: Routledge.

Marquand, David 2004, *Decline of the Public*, Cambridge: Polity.

Marx, Karl 1976 [1867], *Capital*, Volume I, London: Penguin.

Marx, Karl 1977, *Selected Writings*, London: Oxford University Press.

Marx, Karl 1984 [1881], 'The Reply to Zasulich', in *Late Marx and the Russian Road*, edited by Teodor Shanin, London: Routledge.

Marx, Karl and Frederick Engels 1974, *On Colonialism*, Moscow: Progress.

Marx, Karl and Frederick Engels 1977 [1848], *Manifesto of the Communist Party*, Peking: Foreign Languages Press.

Massey, Doreen 2000, 'The Geography of Power', in *After Seattle*, edited by Barbara Gunnell and David Timms, London: Catalyst.

Mauro, Paolo 1998, 'Corruption: Causes, Consequences and Agenda for Further Research', *Finance and Development*, May: 11–14.

Mawdsley, Emma 1998, 'After Chipko: From Environment to Region in Uttaranchal', *Journal of Peasant Studies*, 25, 4: 36–54.

May, Chris 2001, *The Information Society: A Sceptical View*, Cambridge: Polity.

McKay, George (ed.) 1998, *DIY Culture*, London: Verso.

McKinnon, Ronald 1973, *Money and Capital in Economic Development*, Washington: Brookings Institute.

McMichael, Phil 2001, 'Revisiting the Question of the Transnational State: A Comment on William Robinson's "Social Theory and Globalization"', *Theory and Society*, 30: 201–10.

Meadows, Donella, Dennis Meadows, Jorgen Randers and William Behrens 1972, *The Limits to Growth*, London: Pan.

Melucci, Alberto 1980, 'The New Social Movements: A Theoretical Approach', *Social Science Information*, 19, 2: 199–226.

Melucci, Alberto 1989, *Nomads of the Present: Social Movements and Individual Needs in Contemporary Society*, Philadelphia: Temple University Press.

Mertes, Tom 2002, 'Grass-Roots Globalism', *New Left Review*, II, 17: 101–10.

Mies, Maria and Vandana Shiva 1989, *Ecofeminism*, London: Zed.

Milanovic, Branko 2002, 'True World Income Distribution, 1988 and 1993: First Calculations Based on Household Surveys Alone', *Economic Journal*, 112: 51–92.

Monbiot, George 2002, 'Black Shirts in Green Trousers': <www.monbiot.com>.
Monbiot, George 2003, *The Age of Consent*, London: Flamingo.
Monthly Review 2003, 'Editorial: What Recovery?', *Monthly Review*, 54, 11: 1–14.
Moody, Kim 1997, *Workers in a Lean World*, London: Verso.
Mosley, Paul, Jane Harrigan and John Toye 1991, *Aid and Power*, London: Routledge.
Mosley, Paul, Turan Subasat and John Weeks 1995, 'Assessing Adjustment in Africa', *World Development* 23: 1459–473.
Mueller, Suzanne 1980, 'Retarded Capitalism in Tanzania', *Socialist Register 1980*, edited by Ralph Miliband and John Saville, London: Merlin.
Munck, Ronaldo 1988, *The New International Labour Studies*, London: Zed.
Munck, Ronaldo 2002, *Globalisation and Labour*, London: Zed.
Naidoo, Kumi and Rajesh Tandon 1999 *Civil Society at the Millennium*, West Hartford: Civicus.
Narayan, Deepa and Lant Pritchett 1997, 'Cents and Sociability: Household Income and Social Capital in Rural Tanzania', Washington: World Bank.
National Security Strategy 2002, *The National Security Strategy of the United States of America*, <www.whitehouse.gov>.
Negri, Toni 1998, *The Social Factory*, New York: Semiotext(e).
Nolan, Peter 2004, *China at the Crossroads*, Cambridge: Polity.
Norberg-Hodge, Helena 2001, 'Shifting Direction: from Global Dependence to Local Interdependence', in *The Case Against the Global Economy*, edited by Edward Goldsmith and Jerry Mander, London: Earthscan.
O'Brien, Robert 2000, 'Workers and World Order: The Tentative Transformation of the International Union Movement', *Review of International Studies*, 26, 3: 533–55.
Ohlin, Bertil 1933, *Inter-regional and International Trade*, Cambridge MA.: Harvard University Press.
Ohmae, Kenichi 1995, *Borderless World*, London: Fontana.
Overbeek, Henk 1999, 'Globalization and Britain's Decline', in *Rethinking Britain's Decline*, edited by Richard English and Michael Kenny London: Palgrave.
Oxfam 2002, *Stop the Dumping: How EU Agricultural Subsidies Are Damaging Livelihoods in the Developing World*, Oxford: Oxfam.
Palma, Gabriel 2003, 'The Three Routes to Financial Crisis', in *Rethinking Development Economics*, edited by Ha-Joon Chang, London: Anthem.
Panitch, Leo 1981, 'Trade Unions and the Capitalist State', *New Left Review, I*, 125: 21–43.
Panitch, Leo 1994, 'Globalisation and the State', in *The Socialist Register 1994*, edited by Leo Panitch, London: Merlin.
Panitch, Leo and Colin Leys 2001, *The End of Parliamentary Socialism*, London: Verso.
Panitch, Leo and Sam Gindin 2003, 'Global Capitalism and American Empire', in *The Socialist Register 2004*, edited by Leo Panitch and Colin Leys, London: Merlin.
Panos Briefing 1999, *More Power to the World Trade Organization?* No. 37, <www.oneworld.org./panos/briefing>.
Parayil, Govindan (ed.) 2000, *Kerala: The Development Experience*, London: Zed.
Parfitt, Trevor 2002, *The End of Development*, London: Pluto.
Pastor, Manuel 1989, *Capital Flight and the Latin American Debt Crisis*, Washington: Economic Policy Institute.
Pepper, David 1996, *Modern Environmentalisms: An Introduction*, London: Routledge.
Perelman, Michael 2002, *The Pathology of the US Economy Revisited*, New York: Palgrave.
Perelman, Michael 2003, 'The History of Capitalism', in *Anti-Capitalism: A Marxist Introduction*, edited by Alfredo Saad-Filho, London: Pluto.
Petras, James and Henry Veltmeyer 2001, *Globalization Unmasked*, London: Zed.
Phillips, Ann 1987, *The Enigma of Colonialism*, London: James Currey.
Pianta, Mario 2001, 'Parallel Summits of Global Civil Society', in *Global Civil Society*, edited by Helmut Anheier, Marlies Glasius and Mary Kaldor, Oxford: Oxford University Press.
Pieterse, Jan Nederveen 2000, 'Globalization and Emancipation: From Local Em-

powerment to Global Reform', in *Globalization and the Politics of Resistance*, edited by Barry Gills, London: Macmillan.

Pieterse, Jan Nederveen 2002, 'Global Inequality: Bringing Politics Back In', *Third World Quarterly* 23, 6: 1023–46.

Pillay, Vella 1983, 'The International Economic Order and Economic Crisis', in *Third World Studies*, Block 4, Milton Keynes: Open University Press.

Pogge, Thomas 2002, *World Poverty and Human Rights*, Cambridge: Polity.

Pogge, Thomas and Sanjay Reddy 2002, 'Unknown: The Extent, Distribution and Trend of Global Income Poverty': <www.socialanalysis.org>.

Polanyi, Karl 1957, *The Great Transformation*, New York: Beacon.

Pollin, Robert 2000, 'Anatomy of Clintonomics', *New Left Review*, II, 3: 17–46.

Pollin, Robert 2003, *Contours of Descent*, London: Verso.

Pollock, Allyson, Jean Shaoul, David Rowland and Stewart Player 2001, *A Response to the IPPR Commission on Public Private Partnerships*, London: Catalyst.

Prins, Nomi 2002, 'The Telecoms Disaster', *Left Business Observer*, 101: 7–8.

Project for the New American Century 1997, *Statement of Principles*: <www.newamericancentury.org>.

Project for the New American Century 1998, *Letter to President Clinton on Iraq*: <www.newamericancentury.org>.

Putnam, Robert 1993, *Making Democracy Work: Civic Traditions in Modern Italy*, Princeton: Princeton University Press.

Putnam, Robert 2000, *Bowling Alone*, New York: Simon and Schuster.

Rahnema, Majid 1997, 'Towards Post-Development: Searching for Signposts, A New Language and New Paradigms', in *The Post-Development Reader*, edited by Majid Rahnema and Victoria Bawtree, London: Zed.

Ramanathaiyer, Sundat and Stewart MacPherson 2000, *Social Development in Kerala: Illusion or Reality?*, Aldershot: Ashgate.

Rangan, Haripiya 1996, 'From Chipko to Uttaranchal', in *Liberation Ecologies*, edited by Richard Peet and Michael Watts, London: Routledge.

RAWA 2001a, 'RAWA Statement on the Terrorist Attacks in the US': <www.rawa.false.net>.

RAWA 2001b, 'RAWA Statement on the US Strikes in Afghanistan': <www.rawa.false.net>.

Reddy, Sanjay and Thomas Pogge 2002, 'How Not to Count the Poor': <www.socialanalysis.org>.

Rees, John 2001, 'Imperialism: Globalisation, the State and War', *International Socialism*, 93: 3–30.

Reich, Robert 1983, *The Next American Frontier*, Harmondsworth: Penguin.

Reza, Farah (ed.) 2003, *Anti-Imperialism: A guide for the Movement*, London: Bookmarks.

Ricardo, David 1981 [1819], *Principles of Political Economy*, Cambridge: Cambridge University Press.

Rice, Condoleezza 2000, 'Campaign 2000 – Promoting the National Interest': <www.foreignpolicy2000.org>.

Rinehart, James 1996, 'The Ideology of Competitiveness: Pitting Worker Against Worker', in *Corporations are Gonna Get Your Mama*, edited by Kevin Danaher, Maine: Common Courage Press.

Ritzer, George 1993, *The McDonaldization of Society*, London: Sage.

Robertson, Pat 1999, *The New World Order*, New York: STL.

Robertson, Roland 1992, *Globalization: Social Theory and Global Culture*, London: Sage.

Robinson, Bill 2001a, 'Social Theory and Globalization: The Rise of the Transnational State', *Theory and Society*, 30: 157–200.

Robinson, Bill 2001b, 'Responses to McMichael, Block and Goldfrank', *Theory and Society*, 30: 223–36.

Robinson, Bill 2001/2, 'Global Capitalism and Nation-State-Centric Thinking – What We Don't See When We Do See Nation-States: Response to Critics', *Science and Society*, 65, 4: 500–8.

Robinson, Bill 2002, 'Capitalist Globalization and the Transnationalisation of the State', in *Historical Materialism and Globalization*, edited by Mark Rupert and Hazel Smith, London: Routledge.

Robinson, Bill and Jerry Harris 2000, 'Towards a Global Ruling Class? Globalization and the Transnational Capitalist Class', *Science and Society*, 64, 1: 11–54.

Rocha, Geisa 2002, 'Neo-Dependency in Brazil, *New Left Review*, II, 16: 5–33.

Roddick, Jackie 1988, *The Dance of the Millions*, London: Latin America Bureau.

Rodrik, Dani 2000, 'Comments on "Trade, Growth and Poverty" by D. Dollar and A. Kraay': <www.ksghome.harvard.edu>.

Rodrik, Dani 2001, *The Global Governance of Trade as if Development Really Mattered*, New York: UNDP.

Rosenberg, Justin 2000, *The Follies of Globalization Theory*, London: Verso.

Ross, Andrew (ed.) 1997, *No Sweat!*, London: Verso.

Ross, Stephanie 2002, 'Is This What Democracy Looks Like: The Anti-Globalization Movement in North America', *Socialist Register 2003*, edited by Leo Panitch and Colin Leys, London: Merlin.

Rowthorn, Bob 2001, 'Replicating the Experience of the NIEs on a Large Scale', in *Globalization versus Development*, edited by Jomo K. S. and Shyamala Nagaraj, London: Palgrave.

Ruigrok, Winfried and Rob van Tulder 1995, *The Logic of International Restructuring*, London: Routledge.

Runciman, David 2003, 'The Politics of Good Intentions', *London Review of Books*, 25, 9: 3–10.

Rustin, Mike 2000, 'The New Labour Ethic and the Spirit of Capitalism', *Soundings*, 14: 11–25.

Rustin, Mike 2003, '*Empire*: A Postmodern Theory of Revolution', in *Debating Empire*, edited by Gopal Balakrishnan, London: Verso.

Sachs, Jeffrey 1998, 'The IMF and the Asian Flu', *American Prospect*, 9, 37: 8–12.

Sachs, Jeffrey and Andrew Warner 1997, 'Sources of Slow Growth in African Economies', *Journal of African Economies*, 6, 3: 335–76.

Sale, Kirkpatrick 1985, *Dwellers in the Land*, San Francisco: Sierra Club.

Schaeffer, Robert 1997, *Understanding Globalization*, New York: Rowman and Littlefield.

Schumacher, Ernst 1973, *Small is Beautiful*, London: Sphere.

Schuurman, Frans 2001, 'Globalization and Development Studies: Introducing the Challenges', in *Globalization and Development Studies*, edited by Frans Schurman, London: Sage.

Schwartz, Herman 2000, *States against Markets*, London: Macmillan.

Scott, Alan 1997, 'Introduction: Globalization – Social Process or Political Rhetoric?', in *The Limits of Globalization*, edited by Alan Scott, London: Routledge.

Scott, Alan and John Street 2001, 'From Media Politics to E-Protest? The Use of Popular Culture and New Media in Parties and Social Movements', in *Culture and Politics in the Information Age*, edited by Frank Webster, London: Routledge.

Sellers, John 2001, 'Raising a Ruckus', *New Left Review*, II, 10: 71–85.

Sen, Amartya 1992, *Inequality Re-Examined*, New York: Russell Sage.

Sen, Amartya 1999, *Development and Freedom*, Oxford: Oxford University Press.

Sender, John 1999, 'Africa's Economic Performance: Limitations of the Current Consensus', *Journal of Economic Perspectives*, 13, 3: 89–114.

Sender, John 2002, 'Re-Assessing the Current Role of the World Bank in Sub-Saharan Africa', in *Reinventing the World Bank*, edited by Jonathan Pincus and Jeffery Winters, Ithaca: Cornell University Press.

Sender, John and Sheila Smith 1986, 'What's Right with the Berg Report and What's Left of its Critics', *Capital and Class*, 24: 125–46.

Sender, John and Sheila Smith 1990, *Poverty, Class and Gender in Rural Africa*, London: Routledge.

Shaikh, Anwar 1979, 'Foreign Trade and the Law of Value – Part One', *Science and Society*, 43: 281–302.

Shaikh, Anwar 1979/80, 'Foreign Trade and the Law of Value – Part Two', *Science and Society*, 44: 27–57.

Shaikh, Anwar 1996, 'Free Trade, Unemployment and Economic Policy', in *Global Unemployment*, edited by John Eatwell, Armonk: M.E. Sharpe.

Shaw, Edward 1973, *Financial Deepening in Economic Development*, New York: Oxford University Press.

Shaw, Martin 2002, '10 Challenges to Anti-War Politics', *Radical Philosophy*, 111: 11–19.

Shiva, Vandana 1989, *Staying Alive*, London: Zed.

Shiva, Vandana 2003, 'The Living Democracy Movement', in *Another World is Possible*, edited by William Fisher and Thomas Ponniah, London: Zed.

Shorthose, Jim 2000, 'Micro-Experiments in Alternatives', *Capital and Class* 72: 191–207.

Shukla, Shrirang 2002, 'From the GATT to the WTO and Beyond', in *Governing Globalization*, edited by Deepak Nayar, Oxford: Oxford University Press.

Silver, Beverly 2003, *Forces of Labour*, Cambridge: Cambridge University Press.

Silver, Beverly and Eric Slater 1999, 'The Social Origins of World Hegemonies', in *Chaos and Governance in the Modern World System*, authored by Giovanni Arrighi and Beverly Silver (and others), Minneapolis: University of Minnesota Press.

Silver, B. and G. Arrighi 2001, 'Workers North and South', in *The Socialist Register 2001*, edited by Leo Panitch and Colin Leys, London: Merlin.

Singer, Hans 1988, 'The World Development Report 1987 on the blessings of outward orientation: a necessary correction', *Journal of Development Studies* 24: 232–36.

Singer, Peter 2004, *The President of Good and Evil*, London: Granta Books.

Singh, Kavaljit 2000, *Taming Global Financial Flows*, London: Zed.

Sinha, Subir, Shubhra Gururani and Brain Greenberg 1997, 'The "New Traditionalist" Discourse of Indian Environmentalism', *Journal of Peasant Studies* 24, 3: 65–99.

Sklair, Leslie 1991, *Sociology of the Global System*, London: Prentice Hall.

Sklair, Leslie 2001, *The Transnational Capitalist Class*, Oxford: Blackwell.

Sklair, Leslie 2002, *Globalization: Capitalism and its Alternatives*, Oxford: Oxford University Press.

Slater, Don 1997, *Consumer Culture and Modernity*, Cambridge: Polity.

Smith, Peter and Elizabeth Smythe 2001, 'Globalisation, citizenship and technology: the Multilateral Agreement on Investment meets the Internet', in *Culture and Politics in the Information Age*, edited by Frank Webster, London: Routledge.

Smith, Tony 2003, 'Globalisation and Capitalist Property Relations: A Critical Assessment of David Held's Cosmopolitan Theory', *Historical Materialism* 11, 2: 3–36.

Social Movements' Manifesto 2003, 'Resistance to Neoliberalism, War and Militarism: For Peace and Social Justice', in *Another World is Possible*, edited by William Fisher and Thomas Ponniah, London: Zed.

Spielberg, Elinor 1997, 'The Myth of Nimble Fingers', in *No Sweat*, edited by Andrew Ross, London: Verso.

Stedile, Joao 2002, 'Landless Battalions', *New Left Review* 15 (second series): 77–104.

Stewart, Francis and Albert Berry 1999, 'Globalization, Liberalization and Inequality: Expectations and Experience', in *Inequality, Globalization and World Politics*, edited by Andrew Hurrell and Ngaire Woods, Oxford: Oxford University Press.

Stiglitz, Joseph 2002, *Globalization and its Discontents*, Harmondsworth: Penguin.

Strinati, Dominic 1992, *An Introduction to Theories of Popular Culture*, London: Routledge.

Sutcliffe, Bob 1992, 'Industry and Underdevelopment Re-Examined', in *The Political Economy of Development and Underdevelopment*, edited by Colin Wilber and Kenneth Jameson, New York: McGraw-Hill.

Sutcliffe Bob 1995, 'Development after Ecology', in *The North, the South and the Environment*, edited by Vinit Bhaskar and Andrew Glyn, London: Earthscan.

Sutcliffe, Bob 1999, 'The Place of Development in Theories of Imperialism and Globalization', in *Critical Development Theory*, edited by Ronaldo Munck and Denis O'Hearn, London: Zed.

Sutcliffe, Bob 2001, *100 Ways of Seeing an Unequal World*, London: Zed.

Sutcliffe, Bob and Andrew Glyn 1999, 'Still Underwhelmed: Measures of Globalization and their Misinterpretation', *Review of Radical Political Economics* 31, 1: 95–120.

Switkes Glenn and Elias Diaz Pena 2003, 'Water: A Common Good', in *Another World is Possible*, edited by William Fisher and Thomas Ponniah, London: Zed.

Szeftel, Morris 1998, 'Misunderstanding African Politics: Corruption and the Governance Agenda', *Review of African Political Economy* 25, 76: 221–40.

Szeftel, Morris 2000, 'Between Governance and Underdevelopment: Accumulation and Africa's "catastrophic Corruption"', *Review of African Political Economy* 27, 84: 287–306.

Teivanen, Teivo 2003, 'Conference Synthesis', in *Another World is Possible*, edited by William Fisher and Thomas Ponniah, London: Zed.

Teschke, Benno 2000, *The Myth of 1648*, London: Verso.

Thomas, Alan 1992, 'NGOs: Limits and Possibilities', in *Development Policy and Public Action*, edited by Marc Wuyts, Maureen Mackintosh and Hazel Johnson, Oxford: Oxford University Press.

Thrift, Nigel 1996, 'A Hyperactive World', in *Geographies of Global Change*, edited by Richard Johnston, Peter Taylor and Michael Watts, Oxford: Blackwell.

Ticktin, Hillel 1973, 'Towards a Political Economy of the USSR', *Critique*, 1: 20–41.

Tokar, Brian 1994, *The Green Alternative*, San Pedro: Miles.

Tomlinson, John 1991, *Cultural Imperialism*, London: Pinter.

Tomlinson, John 2000, *Globalization and Culture*, Cambridge: Polity.

Tonelson, Alan 2002, *The Race to the Bottom*, Connecticut: Westview Press.

Toussaint, Eric and Arnaud Zacharie 2003, 'External Debt: Abolish the Debt in Order to Free Development', in *Another World is Possible*, edited by William Fisher and Thomas Ponniah, London: Zed.

Toye, John 1985, 'Dirigisme and Development Economics', *Cambridge Journal of Economics*, 9: 1–14.

Toye, John 2003, 'Order and Justice in the International Trade System', in *Order and Justice in International Relations*, edited by Rosemary Foot, John Lewis Gaddis and Andrew Hurrell, Oxford: Oxford University Press.

Trotsky, Leon 1973 [1938], *The Transitional Programme for Socialist Revolution*, New York: Pathfinder.

Trotsky, Leon 1975, *The Challenge of the Left Opposition, 1923–25*, New York: Pathfinder.

Trotsky, Leon 1980 [1936], *The Revolution Betrayed*, New York: Pathfinder.

Tussie, Diane and Ngaire Woods 2000, 'Trade, Regionalism and the Threat to Multilateralism', in *The Political Economy of Globalization*, edited by Ngaire Woods, London: Macmillan.

UNCTAD 1998, *World Investment Report*, New York: United Nations.

UNCTAD 1999, *World Investment Report*, New York: United Nations.

UNCTAD 2002a, *The Least Developed Countries Report*, Geneva: United Nations.

UNCTAD 2002b, *World Investment Report*, Geneva: United Nations.

UNDP 1995, *Human Development Report*, Geneva: United Nations.

UNDP 1997, *Human Development Report*, Geneva: United Nations.

UNDP 1999, *Human Development Report*, Geneva: United Nations.

UNDP 2002, *Human Development Report*, Geneva: United Nations.

Underhill, G. 1997, 'Global Markets, Macroeconomic Instability and Exchange Rate Crises', in *The New World Order in International Finance*, edited by Geoffrey Underhill, London: Macmillan.

US Dept of Labor 2001, 'Labor Force Projections, 2000–2010': <www.bls.gov/emp/home.htm>.

de Waal, Alex 1997, *Famine Crimes in Africa*, London: James Currey.

Wade, Robert 1990, *Governing the Market*, Princeton: Princeton University Press.

Wade, Robert 2002a, 'US Hegemony and the World Bank: The Fight over People and Ideas', *Review of International Political Economy*, 9, 2: 215–43.

Wade, Robert 2002b, 'Globalization, Poverty and Income Distribution: Does the Liberal Argument Hold?, *DESTIN Working Paper*, 02–33.

Wade, Robert 2003a, 'The Disturbing Rise in Poverty and Inequality: Is It All a "Big

Lie"?', in *Taming Globalization*, edited by David Held and Mathias Koening-Archibugi, Cambridge: Polity.

Wade, Robert 2003b, 'What Strategies are Viable for Developing Countries Today? The World Trade Organization and the Shrinking of "Development Space"', *Review of International Political Economy*, 10, 4: 621–44.

Wade, Robert and Frank Veneroso 1998, 'The Gathering World Slump and the Battle over Capital Controls', *New Left Review*, I, 231: 13–42.

Wade, Robert and Martin Wolf 2002, 'Are Global Poverty and Inequality Getting Worse?', *Prospect*, March: 16–21.

Wainwright, Hilary 2003, *Reclaim the State*, London: Verso.

Wainwright, Hilary 2004, 'From Mumbai with Hope': <www.redpepper.org.uk>.

Walton, John and David Seddon 1994, *Free Markets and Food Riots*, Oxford: Blackwell.

Waltz, Kenneth 1979, *Theory of International Politics*, New York: Random House.

Warren, Bill 1973, 'Imperialism and Capitalist Industrialisation', *New Left Review*, I, 81: 9–44.

Warren, Bill 1980, *Imperialism: Pioneer of Capitalism*, London: Verso.

Waterman, Peter 2002, *Globalization, Social Movements and the New Internationalism*, London: Mansell.

Waterman, Peter and Jane Wills (eds.) 2001, *Place, Space and the New Labour Internationalisms*, Oxford: Blackwell.

Watkins, Kevin 2001, 'Pharmaceutical Patents', in *Anti-Capitalism: A Guide to the Movement*, edited by Emma Bircham and John Charlton, London: Bookmarks.

Watson, Matthew 1999, 'Rethinking Capital Mobility, Re-Regulating Financial Markets', *New Political Economy*, 4, 1: 55–75.

Webster, Frank 2001, 'A New Politics', in *Culture and Politics in the Information Age*, edited by Frank Webster, London: Routledge.

Weeks, John 1981, *Capital and Exploitation*, London: Edward Arnold.

Weeks, John 1997, 'The Law of Value and the Analysis of Underdevelopment', *Historical Materialism*, 1: 91–112.

Weeks, John 2001, 'The Expansion of Capital and Uneven Development on a World Scale', *Capital and Class*, 74: 9–30.

Weeks, John 2003, 'Developing Country Debt and Globalisation', in *Anti-Capitalism: A Marxist Introduction*, edited by Alfredo Saad-Filho, London: Pluto.

Weisbrot, Mark, Dean Baker, Robert Naiman and Gila Neta 2002, 'Growth May Be Good for the Poor – But Are IMF and World Bank Policies Good for Growth?': <www.cepr.net>.

Weisbrot, Mark, Dean Baker, Egor Kraev and Judy Chen 2002, 'The Scorecard on Globalization, 1980–2000': <www.cepr.net>.

Weisbrot, Mark and David Rosnick 2003, 'Another Lost Decade? Latin America's Growth Failure Continues into the Twenty First Century': <www.cepr.net>.

Weiss, Linda 1998, *The Myth of the Powerless State*, Cambridge: Polity.

Welton, Neva and Linda Wolf (eds.) 2001, *Global Uprising*, Gabriola Island: New Society.

Wheen, Francis 2004, *How Mumbo-Jumbo Conquered the World*, London: Fourth Estate.

White, Ben 1996, *Globalization and the Child Labour Problem*, Working Paper no. 221, The Hague: Institute of Social Studies.

White, Howard 2002, 'The Measurement of Poverty', in *The Companion to Development Studies*, edited by Vandana Desai and Rob Potter, London: Arnold.

Williamson, John 1989, 'What Washington Means by Policy Reform', in *Latin American Readjustment: How Much has Happened*, edited by John Williamson, Washington: Institute for International Economics.

Wolf, Martin 2001, 'A Stepping Stone from Poverty', *Financial Times*, December 19.

Wolf, Martin 2002, 'Doing More Harm than Good', *Financial Times*, May 8.

Wood, Ellen Meiksins 1986, *The Retreat from Class*, London: Verso.

Wood, Ellen Meiksins 1991, *The Pristine Culture of Capitalism*, London: Verso.

Wood, Ellen Meiksins 2001, 'Contradiction: Only in Capitalism?', *Socialist Register 2002*, edited by Leo Panitch and Colin Leys, London: Merlin.

Wood, Ellen Meiksins 2002, *The Origins of Capitalism: A Longer View*, London: Verso.

Wood, Ellen Meiksins 2003, *Empire of Capital*, London: Verso.

Woods, Ngaire 1999 'Order, Globalization and Inequality in World Politics', in *Inequality, Globalization and World Politics*, edited by Andrew Hurrell and Ngaire Woods, Oxford: Oxford University Press.

World Bank 1983, *World Development Report*, Oxford: Oxford University Press.

World Bank 1987, *World Development Report*, Oxford: Oxford University Press.

World Bank 1989, *Sub-Saharan Africa: From Crisis to Sustainable Growth*, Washington: World Bank.

World Bank 1990, *World Development Report*, Oxford: Oxford University Press.

World Bank 1991, *World Development Report*, Oxford: Oxford University Press.

World Bank 1992, *Governance and Development*, Washington: World Bank.

World Bank 1993, *The East Asian Miracle*, Oxford: Oxford University Press.

World Bank 1994, *Adjustment in Africa*, Oxford: Oxford University Press.

World Bank 1995, *World Development Report*, Oxford: Oxford University Press.

World Bank 1997, *World Development Report*, Oxford: Oxford University Press.

World Bank 1999, *Global Economic Prospects and the Developing Countries*, Washington: World Bank.

World Bank 2001a, *World Development Report 2000/01*, Oxford: Oxford University Press

World Bank 2001b, *Global Economic Prospects and Developing Countries*, Washington: World Bank.

World Bank 2002a, *Global Economic Prospects and Developing Countries – Making Trade Work for the Poor*, Washington: World Bank.

World Bank 2002b, *Globalization, Growth and Poverty*, Oxford: Oxford University Press.

World Development Movement 2001, *States of Unrest*: <www.wdm.org.uk>.

World Development Movement 2002, *States of Unrest*: <www.wdm.org.uk>.

World Social Forum 2002 Call of Social Movements: <www.forumsocialmundial.org/br/eng/portoalegrefinalenglis.asp>.

Wright, Steve 2002, *Storming Heaven*, London: Pluto.

Wright Mills, Charles 1970, *The Sociological Imagination*, New York: Oxford University Press.

WTO 1998, *Trading into the Future*, Second Edition, Geneva: WTO.

WTO 2000, 'Seven Common Misunderstandings about the WTO', in *The Globalization Reader*, edited by Frank Lechner and John Boli, Oxford: Blackwell.

Wuyts, Marc 1992, 'Conclusion: Development Policy as Process', in *Development Policy and Public Action*, edited by Marc Wuyts, Maureen Mackintosh and Tom Hewitt, Oxford: Oxford University Press.

Yuen, Eddie 2001, 'Introduction', in *The Battle of Seattle*, edited by Eddie Yuen, George Katsiaficas and David Rose, New York: Soft Skull Press.

Zolberg, Aristide 1995, 'Response: Working Class Dissolution', *International Labor and Working Class History*, 47: 28–38.

Index

HISTORICAL MATERIALISM BOOK SERIES

ISSN 1570–1522

1. ARTHUR, C.J. The New Dialectic and Marx's *Capital*.
   ISBN 90 04 12798 4 (2002, hardcover), 90 04 13643 6 (2004, paperback)
2. LÖWY, M. The Theory of Revolution in the Young Marx. 2003.
   ISBN 90 04 12901 4
3. CALLINICOS, A. Making History. Agency, Structure, and Change in Social Theory. 2004. ISBN 90 04 13627 4
4. DAY, R.B. Pavel V. Maksakovsky: The Capitalist Cycle. An Essay on the Marxist Theory of the Cycle. Translated with Introduction and Commentary. 2004. ISBN 90 04 13824 2
5. BROUÉ, P. The German Revolution, 1917-1923. 2005.
   ISBN 90 04 13940 0
6. MIÉVILLE, C. Between Equal Rights. A Marxist Theory of International Law. 2005. ISBN 90 04 13134 5
7. BEAUMONT, M. Utopia Ltd. Ideologies of Social Dreaming in England 1870-1900. 2005. ISBN 90 04 14296 7
8. KIELY, R. The Clash of Globalisations. Neo-Liberalism, the Third Way and Anti-Globalisation. 2005. ISBN 90 04 14318 1